Vernacular Christia[n] and Civil Discourse

Vernacular Christian Rhetoric and Civil Discourse seeks to address the current gap in American public discourse between secular liberals and religiously committed citizens by focusing on the academic and public writing of millennial evangelical Christian students. Analysis of such writing reveals that the evangelical Christian faith of contemporary college students—and the rhetorical practice motivated by such faith—is marked by an openness to social context and pluralism that offers possibilities for civil discourse. Based on case studies of evangelical Christian student writers, contextualized within nationally-representative trends as reported by the National Study of Youth and Religion, and grounded in scholarship from rhetorical theory, composition studies, folklore studies, and sociology of religion, this book offers rhetorical educators a new terministic screen that reveals the complex processes at work within our students' vernacular constructions of religious faith.

Jeffrey M. Ringer is an Assistant Professor of English at the University of Tennessee, Knoxville. He is the author of several articles and book chapters. With Michael-John DePalma, he edited *Mapping Christian Rhetorics: Connecting Conversations, Charting New Territories*, which won the Religious Communication Association's 2015 Book of the Year award.

Routledge Studies in Rhetoric and Communication

1 **Rhetorics, Literacies, and Narratives of Sustainability**
Edited by Peter Goggin

2 **Queer Temporalities in Gay Male Representation**
Tragedy, Normativity, and Futurity
Dustin Bradley Goltz

3 **The Rhetoric of Intellectual Property**
Copyright Law and the Regulation of Digital Culture
Jessica Reyman

4 **Media Representations of Gender and Torture Post-9/11**
Marita Gronnvoll

5 **Rhetoric, Remembrance, and Visual Form**
Sighting Memory
Edited by Anne Teresa Demo and Bradford Vivian

6 **Reading, Writing, and the Rhetorics of Whiteness**
Wendy Ryden and Ian Marshall

7 **Radical Pedagogies of Socrates and Freire**
Ancient Rhetoric/Radical Praxis
S.G. Brown

8 **Ecology, Writing Theory, and New Media**
Writing Ecology
Edited by Sidney I. Dobrin

9 **The Rhetoric of Food**
Discourse, Materiality, and Power
Edited by Joshua J. Frye and Michael S. Bruner

10 **The Multimediated Rhetoric of the Internet Digital Fusion**
Carolyn Handa

11 **Communicating Marginalized Masculinities**
Identity Politics in TV, Film, and New Media
Edited by Ronald L. Jackson II and Jamie E. Moshin

12 **Perspectives on Human-Animal Communication**
Internatural Communication
Edited by Emily Plec

13 **Rhetoric and Discourse in Supreme Court Oral Arguments**
Sensemaking in Judicial Decisions
Ryan A. Malphurs

14 **Rhetoric, History, and Women's Oratorical Education**
American Women Learn to Speak
Edited by David Gold and Catherine L. Hobbs

15 **Cultivating Cosmopolitanism for Intercultural Communication**
Communicating as Global Citizens
Miriam Sobré-Denton and Nilanjana Bardhan

16 **Environmental Rhetoric and Ecologies of Place**
Edited by Peter N. Goggin

17 **Rhetoric and Ethics in the Cybernetic Age**
The Transhuman Condition
Jeff Pruchnic

18 **Communication, Public Opinion, and Globalization in Urban China**
Francis L.F. Lee, Chin-Chuan Lee, Mike Z. Yao, Tsan-Kuo Chang, Fen Jennifer Lin, and Chris Fei Shen

19 **Adaptive Rhetoric**
Evolution, Culture, and the Art of Persuasion
Alex C. Parrish

20 **Communication, Public Discourse, and Road Safety Campaigns**
Persuading People to Be Safer
Nurit Guttman

21 **Mapping Christian Rhetorics**
Connecting Conversations, Charting New Territories
Edited by Michael-John DePalma and Jeffrey M. Ringer

22 **Identity and Power in Narratives of Displacement**
Katrina M. Powell

23 **Pedagogies of Public Memory**
Teaching Writing and Rhetoric at Museums, Archives, and Memorials
Edited by Jane Greer and Laurie Grobman

24 **Authorship Contested**
Cultural Challenges to the Authentic, Autonomous Author
Edited by Amy E. Robillard and Ron Fortune

25 **Software Evangelism and the Rhetoric of Morality**
Coding Justice in a Digital Democracy
Jennifer Helene Maher

26 **Sexual Rhetorics**
Methods, Identities, Publics
Edited by Jonathan Alexander and Jacqueline Rhodes

27 **Rhetorical Delivery and Digital Technologies**
Networks, Affect, Electracy
Sean Morey

28 **Rhetorics of Names and Naming**
Edited by Star Medzerian Vanguri

29 **Vernacular Christian Rhetoric and Civil Discourse**
The Religious Creativity of Evangelical Student Writers
Jeffrey M. Ringer

Vernacular Christian Rhetoric and Civil Discourse

The Religious Creativity of Evangelical Student Writers

Jeffrey M. Ringer

NEW YORK AND LONDON

First published 2016
by Routledge
711 Third Avenue, New York, NY 10017

and by Routledge
2 Park Square, Milton Park, Abingdon, Oxon OX14 4RN

First issued in paperback 2017

Routledge is an imprint of the Taylor & Francis Group, an informa business

Library of Congress Cataloging-in-Publication Data

Names: Ringer, Jeffrey M., 1976– author.
Title: Vernacular Christian rhetoric and civil discourse: the religious creativity of evangelical student writers / by Jeffrey M. Ringer. Description: 1 [edition]. | New York: Routledge, 2016. | Series: Routledge Studies in Rhetoric and Communication; 29 | Includes bibliographical references and index.
Identifiers: LCCN 2015039795
Subjects: LCSH: Religious literature—Authorship. | Evangelicalism—Miscellanea.
Classification: LCC BR44 .R56 2016 | DDC 277.3/0830883718—dc23 LC record available at http://lccn.loc.gov/2015039795

ISBN 13: 978-0-8153-8656-8 (pbk)
ISBN 13: 978-1-138-95168-6 (hbk)

Typeset in Sabon
by codeMantra

For Sarah, Zoe, and Ben

Contents

Acknowledgments

Three folks right off the bat deserve special thanks for reading early versions of this manuscript and helping make this book possible: Mike DePalma, Tom Newkirk, and Elizabeth Vander Lei all read or heard me talk incessantly about various versions of this manuscript in various states of incompletion over the last several years. Thanks to each of you for talking through this stuff with me, for being excited about it, and for helping me see it was worthwhile even when I felt otherwise.

I'd also like to thank various folks who heard my ideas at some point in the process of writing this book and offered feedback or words of encouragement or both: Emily Cope, Abby Knoblauch, Jim Webber, Mike Garcia, Steve Simpson, Meagan Rogers, Joleen Hanson, Pat Bizzell, Victor Villanueva, Mary Juzwik, Scott Richard Lyons, David Gold, Catherine Pavia, Lisa King, Tanita Saenkhum, Kirsten Benson, Russ Hirst, and Melody Pugh, among others, all responded to my ideas in some form or fashion at some point along the way. Even if you don't remember doing so, I do, and I'm grateful. Chances are, I needed to hear exactly what you said at the moment you said it. I would also like to thank all the wonderful members of the Rhetoric and Religious Traditions Standing Group at 4Cs for helping make the growing conversation about religious rhetorics in composition studies such an exciting place to be. And, of course, apologies for anyone I've left off this list.

No small amount of thanks also goes to all the mentors who have helped me along the way: Larry Prelli, for teaching me Burke and fundamentally changing my understanding of what rhetoric can do; Jess Enoch, for taking me more seriously as a scholar than I ever took myself; Paul Matsuda, for modeling what it means to be a teacher-scholar; Sarah Sherman, for helping me parse out the historical strains of American Christianity; and Toby Fulwiler, for introducing me to composition studies in the first place. I wouldn't be here were it not for you.

I also owe gratitude to the fantastic folks at Routledge who have helped make this project possible—Felisa Salvago-Keyes, Andrew Weckenmann, and Allie Simmons are as professional and capable as they come. I also owe thanks to the anonymous reviewers who gave wonderfully helpful and encouraging feedback on my proposal and manuscript.

I also have to give a special shout-out to my Spring 2015 Religious Rhetorics class at the University of Tennessee. You guys put up with my crazy, half-baked ideas for a whole semester—and you did it with grace and enthusiasm. More importantly, you read my manuscript in draft form and, in so doing, helped me understand two things: that I think I'm on to something, and that these ideas might even be accessible to undergrads. So, thanks to Katie Clabough, Elizabeth Cope, Gian Coppola, Shon Daniels, Kaley Disabatino, Jessica Hingtgen, Chase Hughes, Kyndal Hughes, Kaitlyn Moriarty, Jesse Murphy, Nathan Murray, Andrew Parker, Cici Petersen, Phil Redmon, Jessica Schue, Caleb Vibbert, Julianne Watters, Tammye Williams, Mary Wilson, and Julia Woods. I hope you guys had as much fun in class as I did.

Three more students deserve particular praise: Austin, Kimberly, and Eloise trusted me enough to share their experiences of faith and writing with me, and they did so while leading busy academic and social lives. Thanks for your grace, your humility, and your example. We have a lot to learn from you, and please believe me when I say that this book would not have been possible were it not for your willingness to talk with me. I also owe thanks to all the wonderful folks affiliated with InterVarsity Christian Fellowship who talked with me and helped me get in touch with Austin, Kimberly, and Eloise.

My colleagues at the University of Tennessee and at Lee University helped provide wonderful places to work while this project was in process. There are far too many of you to mention here, but thanks to all the folks in the Department of English at UTK (especially RWL!) and in the Department of Language and Literature at Lee. Your help and encouragement along the way has been invaluable.

Finally, to my family: to Mom and Dad, thanks for teaching me to be faithful and creative. To my in-laws, Will and Prudence and the rest of the Barker clan: thanks for continuing to be so interested in what I do. To Jen and Billy and Jonathan and Breanna: thanks for modeling how faith, family, and the academic life can coincide. And to Sarah, Zoe, and Ben: thanks for putting up with me while I was working on this thing, and for doing so with love, grace, patience, and understanding; thanks for giving me such a wonderful reason to take a break; thanks for making me laugh when I felt like crying; thanks for being such a wonderful reminder that some things are indeed more important than others. I love you all very much.

Permissions

Portions of Chapter 4 originally appeared in Jeffrey M. Ringer's "The Consequences of Integrating Faith into Academic Writing: Casuistic Stretching and Biblical Citation." *College English* 75.3 (January 2013): 272–99. Copyright 2013 by the National Council of Teachers of English. Reprinted with permission.

All excerpts from interviews with and writing by Austin, Kimberly, and Eloise are used with permission from the students. All IRB protocols for ethical treatment of human subjects were followed.

The excerpt from Katie's interview in Chapter 2 is used with permission. All IRB protocols for ethical treatment of human subjects were followed.

1 From Problem to Possibility

Evangelical Christian Students, Composition Studies, and Civil Discourse

> I end with the hope that my readers will find, or open, many more paths of invention than I have been able to name here.
>
> —Sharon Crowley, *Toward a Civil Discourse*

I remember the sense of surprise I experienced when I first read the final line of Sharon Crowley's award-winning book, *Toward a Civil Discourse: Rhetoric and Fundamentalism*. It was such an impressive analysis in so many respects that the tone of defeat and frustration in Crowley's last line took me by surprise. Sure, as an American Christian with deep evangelical roots, I had often found myself at odds with Crowley's narrow construction of fundamentalism, evangelicalism, and Christianity. I agree with Beth Daniell, for instance, when she argues that *Toward a Civil Discourse* excludes the vast Christian middle to which many of us—myself included—belong (see Daniell, "More," "Whetstones"). With Mike DePalma and Jim Webber, I thus began to work out a response to Crowley's book, an argument that we presented at the 2008 Annual Convention of the Conference on College Composition and Communication in New Orleans and later published in *Rhetoric Society Quarterly* (DePalma, Ringer, and Webber).

Crowley graciously attended our presentation and approached us afterwards in the spirit of dialogue. I distinctly remember the first words she said to the three of us: "Okay. So what do we do?" It was an honest question, one borne, I'm convinced, out of a sincere desire to do what she set out to achieve in her book: find paths of invention for addressing the political impasses that plague American public discourse in the early twenty-first century. I didn't get to talk much with her myself—others approached me to discuss the panel. But her words and the sincerity with which she spoke them remain emblazoned in my mind and attest to the sincerity of her desire for civil discourse.

In a way, this book comprises my response to Crowley's question. It does so from a vantage many readers might not anticipate: by focusing on the writing of evangelical Christian students. As I hope to show in this book, at least some evangelical Christian students—those who align with what sociologist D. Michael Lindsay calls "cosmopolitan" evangelicalism (221; see also Juzwik and McKenzie)—already appeal to and even enact a set of values that align with the civic goals of rhetorical education, values that include respect for and a sincere desire to engage with diverse views in order to open up new avenues of communication across difference. Such students do so—not all the time, not always eloquently—in ways that highlight two realities of evangelicalism: it can't be reduced to fundamentalism or right-wing conservatism, and it is undergoing significant changes in the early twenty-first century (Balmer; Bielo; Cope and Ringer; Webber). Contrary to entrenched conceptions of evangelical Christians that persist in the academy in general and rhetoric and composition in particular, the evangelical students I discuss in this book go to great lengths to (1) accommodate perspectives and beliefs that differ from their own; (2) participate as equals within deliberative discourse and even seek to constitute conditions that make such discourse possible; and (3) demonstrate a commitment to visions of the common good that address both spiritual and material concerns.

The attitudes, beliefs, and perspectives evidenced by my participants align with larger trends among what researchers have variously referred to as millennials ("Religion Among"; "Barna Millennials"), "younger evangelicals" (Webber), or "emerging adults" (Smith and Snell). Findings from the National Study of Youth and Religion (NSYR), a nationally representative survey of emerging adults, point to the fact that millennial evangelicals—the term I'll use throughout this book—honor diverse perspectives and identities to a far greater extent than previous generations of evangelicals. Drawing on the NSYR data, sociologists Christian Smith and Patricia Snell explain that millennials have been taught their entire lives "to celebrate diversity, to be inclusive of difference, to overcome racial divides, to embrace multiculturalism, to avoid being narrowly judgmental toward others who are out of the ordinary" (80). To be sure, such attitudes can lead to a dangerous erasure of diversity that can itself short circuit meaningful dialogue across differences of religion, race, ethnicity, class, sexuality, ability, and gender. But the proclivity to accept others in spite of differences constitutes an important first step when it comes to achieving civil discourse. As Crowley puts it, "rhetoric requires willingness to be addressed by an other" (29).

Back to Crowley's question: what do we do to bridge the significant gap that exists between liberal politics and certain forms of Christianity that militate against deliberative democracy? As a writing instructor who envisions the composition classroom as a public-in-training, I believe we can work toward alleviating the problem by attending to the vernacular faith of millennial evangelicals. Doing so means more than paying sincere, thoughtful attention to such students' particular constructions of faith, though this is central to my argument. It also means more than considering the inventive possibilities they might offer for civic engagement, though again I certainly make that argument and believe firmly doing so can yield beneficial results (see Shannon Carter; DePalma; Geiger; Kirsch; Ringer, "Consequences," "Dogma"; Vander Lei, "Ain't"). Attending to the vernacular faith of millennial evangelicals means teaching such students how to draw on their faith-based values, beliefs, assumptions, and identities in meaningful, creative ways toward deliberative ends. While this statement might seem evident—of course it's our job as rhetorical educators and composition instructors to teach students how to be productive citizens—it challenges the persistent assumption that faith-based topics or perspectives are best avoided in writing classrooms because they're too subjective or too difficult to manage, more hindrance than help to the work we do as socially conscious teachers of writing and rhetoric (Dively, "Censoring"; Geiger; Gilyard; Goodburn; Kirsch; Neulieb; Smitherman-Trapp; Vander Lei, "'Where'").

Numerous compositionists have argued for the inclusion of faith-based perspectives in the writing classroom. Michael-John DePalma, for instance, argues that religious discourses can serve as resources for academic writing, while Ronda Leathers Dively ("Censoring") and Kristine Hansen each make compelling cases for why valuing religious faith in the writing classroom corresponds to the democratic aims of rhetorical education. Such compositionists echo C. Jan Swearingen's frank conclusion that ignoring the "self-understandings, convictions, and … intellect" of religiously committed students comes "at very great peril to us all" ("Hermeneutics" 150). And many compositionists would agree with Elizabeth Vander Lei's hope for our religiously committed students—not that they "alter what they believe," but rather that they "use tension between faith … and academic inquiry as a way of learning more and learning better" ("Coming" 8). I agree with these scholars but also forward an argument that extends their thinking. If we pay attention to how our millennial evangelical Christian students live and negotiate their faith in pluralistic contexts—if we look at the subtle ways whereby they already alter their faiths or ways of talking about their faith in order to coexist and communicate effectively with others across difference—then we're likely to perceive a kind of creativity that offers possibilities for civic engagement.

I call such creativity vernacular religious creativity, a term I borrow from folklorist Leonard Primiano and define more fully in Chapter 2. Briefly stated, vernacular religious creativity is the conscious or unconscious process of negotiating religious beliefs in order to make sense of and potentially adjust one's faith commitments in relation to social, political, cultural, discursive, and institutional contexts. Vernacular religious creativity is an ongoing process that foregrounds interpretation: religious believers are always in the process of interpreting their beliefs in relation to their sociocultural contexts. And as their contexts change, individuals attempt to reconcile their religious beliefs accordingly—rarely in radical or wholesale ways, but often by enacting subtle adjustments in order to achieve some degree of identification with people who think and believe differently from them. My purpose in this book is to show that millennial evangelical Christian students enact vernacular religious creativity in ways that could foster deliberative discourse or the social conditions necessary for such discourse. In particular, I show how my case study participants:

- casuistically stretch beliefs to establish common ground with individuals who share a radically different set of beliefs (Burke, *Attitudes* 229–32; Ringer, "Consequences");
- articulate or connect beliefs in flexible values hierarchies in order to argue on behalf of the common good (Crowley 59–61; Perelman and Olbrechts-Tyteca 80–83); and
- translate ways of talking about faith in order to achieve the legitimacy necessary for deliberating effectively with others (Habermas 25; Hauser, *Vernacular* 67–70; Roberts-Miller 197).

As I'll argue throughout this book, these rhetorical strategies, which are grounded in the vernacular religious creativity of millennial evangelical Christian students, can help achieve a more civil civic discourse in two ways. First, each of these strategies can constitute social conditions that allow for deliberative exchange (Charland; Hauser, *Vernacular*; Roberts-Miller). Following Gerard A. Hauser, I define such conditions in terms of intersubjectivity, a state of affairs wherein interlocutors share a common reference world and perceive each other as legitimate, equal parties to discourse, even if they hold different values, beliefs, and assumptions and don't agree on issues of public concern (Hauser, *Vernacular* 66–72). Stretching beliefs to accommodate the perspectives of others, rearticulating beliefs in flexible hierarchies depending on the rhetorical situation, and translating one's faith-based discourse into terms that resonate with non-Christian audiences can constitute the very social reality that is necessary for deliberative discourse. Second, these strategies can help rhetors initiate deliberative discourse with people who already share their religious beliefs, a possibility I take up in Chapter 5. Arguing explicitly as religious citizens who embrace visions of the common good and who value diverse perspectives, millennial evangelical students might work toward rearticulating the beliefs of other evangelical Christian citizens. And given that they can argue from within their ethos as evangelical Christians, they might meet with more success than Crowley was able to achieve (see Bizzell, "Faith-Based"; Lessl; Steiner; Swearingen, "Rhetoric").

My emphasis in this book is thus on values, beliefs, and assumptions, the basic building blocks that rest at the heart of rhetorical action and education.[1] Such a focus is particularly germane to evangelical Christian students because religious commitment of any stripe brings to the fore questions of belief. By attending carefully to the beliefs (statements concerning what reality is), values (statements that name what ought to be), and assumptions (warrants that allow rhetors to connect data to claims) that millennial evangelical students enact and even reshape in their writing, I hope to prompt discussion about how the vernacular religious creativity of twenty-first century evangelical Christian students might help invigorate a more robust and inclusive civil discourse. I say "might," because as I hope to make clear, this book deals both with what millennial evangelical students are already doing and with what they could do with the right rhetorical training ("see Fleming, *City*, "The Very";

"Mt. Oread"). As writing instructors, we can help establish a more civil discourse by valuing the religious creativity of our evangelical Christian student writers and by using our status as rhetorical educators to teach them how to stretch, articulate, or translate those beliefs meaningfully for deliberative ends.

Vernacular Evangelical Faith

I make this argument by focusing on the vernacular evangelical faith of the millennials who populate our writing classes. Two key terms, vernacular and evangelical, demand further definition. By vernacular, I refer to the ways of speaking, writing, and thinking of ordinary evangelicals. Compositionists (Banks; Elbow), communication scholars (Hauser, *Vernacular*; Ono and Sloop), folklorists (Howard, *Digital*; Primiano), and sociologists of religion (Ammerman, *Everyday*, *Sacred*; Bartkowski; Wolfe, *Transformation*) have all shown that paying attention to vernacular rhetorical action or religion—or both—can be highly productive. In the case of the millennial evangelicals in our writing classes, it means assuming that their faith cannot be reduced to that of elites who speak for it and make headlines—people like Pat Robertson, the late Jerry Falwell, Tim and Beverly LaHaye, Billy Graham, and James Dobson—many of whom Crowley cites as representatives of the Christian Right and proponents of apocalyptism (102; see also M. Williams 339–41). Or to borrow a term Mark Alan Williams recently has used, it means paying attention to the "friction" that often marks our students' conflicted relationships with "dominant religious representations" (341). As I argue more fully in Chapters 2 and 3, attending to the vernacular constructions of our evangelical students' faith can open up significant possibilities for deliberative exchange.

The second term, evangelical, is harder to define, a difficulty that Emily Murphy Cope and I explore in "Coming to (Troubled) Terms: Methodology, Positionality, and the Problem of Defining 'Evangelical Christian.'" In particular, we discuss how various scholars have "wrangled over defining evangelicalism" to the point where some don't find the term fruitful anymore (106). We advocate using the term, though, largely because no better term exists. In our definition, which I use in this book, we rely heavily on historian David Bebbington's construction of evangelicalism that identifies four priorities featured within evangelicalism: conversionism, the emphasis on the importance of individual conversion to Christianity; biblicism, the view that the Bible is central to Christian faith;[2] activism, the desire to share faith and work towards social change; and crucicentrism, the belief in Christ's substitutionary atonement (Bebbington 3; Cope and Ringer 107). Contemporary evangelicalism tends to emphasize the first three because crucicentrism doesn't reflect the theology of all evangelicals (Lindsay 3–4). Evangelicals also tend to identify in various ways with the evangelical subculture, which sociologist Christian Smith defines as "a distinct, publicly recognizable collective identity" (*American* 15). That collective identity, though, is far more varied today than it was in the 1990s when

Smith initiated his research on American evangelicalism (see Balmer; Bielo; Lindsay; Webber). For instance, millennial evangelicals tend to distance themselves from traditional notions of evangelicalism and from the narrow set of political affiliations still associated with the term (Cope and Ringer 110–11; Pally; Pavia 352; Webber). In short, I use the term evangelical to describe students who evidence attitudes of conversionism, biblicism, and activism and who identify with the evangelical subculture. In the case of my participants, this subculture consisted largely of their university's chapter of InterVarsity Christian Fellowship (IVCF) and a local evangelical church they all attended (see Appendix A).

To explore the vernacular faith of millennial evangelicals, I engage with the growing scholarly discussion about religiously committed students in rhetoric and composition (DePalma and Ringer, *Mapping*; Vander Lei, et al.; Vander Lei and kyburz). I also draw on three related fields that have much to offer compositionists who seek to understand and value the vernacular religious beliefs that motivate many of our students: communication studies, folklore studies, and the sociology of religion. The first of these, communication studies—our institutional next-door neighbor—has a rich tradition of scholarship exploring the intersections of rhetoric and religion. Rhetoricians such as Thomas Lessl and Mark Allan Steiner contributed to a special issue of the *Journal of Communication and Religion* called "Civic Engagement from Religious Grounds" that is salient to my concerns. In particular, Steiner's faithful witness model of evangelical Christian civic engagement, which I define more fully in Chapter 3, is particularly germane and is thus a concept I return to throughout this book. Additionally, rhetorical scholars in communication studies who theorize concepts that haven't received much attention in composition studies can help us understand the interconnections among religion, rhetoric, and civic engagement. Hauser, whom I have already mentioned, defines vernacular rhetoric itself, while the work of Maurice Charland highlights how students might constitute social conditions that make deliberative rhetoric possible.

The other two fields, folklore studies and the sociology of religion, might not be as familiar to compositionists as communication studies but still have much to offer when it comes to understanding vernacular evangelical faith. Indeed, scholarship from these two fields helps to flesh out concepts of lived religion (Ammerman, *Everyday*, *Sacred*; Bartkowski; Hall; Wolfe, *Transformation*) and vernacular faith itself (Howard, *Digital*; Primiano). As I discuss in Chapter 2, turning our attention toward the lived or vernacular religious faith of our millennial evangelical students can help compositionists perceive and appreciate the highly creative, innovative ways whereby such students reshape or adapt their faith to accommodate audiences who hold beliefs different from their own. Highlighting such vernacular religious creativity can help rhetoricians and compositionists complicate their assumptions about religiously committed students in general and millennial evangelical Christian students in particular. Emphasizing vernacular religious creativity can also reveal the ways whereby such students bring their faith to bear on writing that deals with public problems. In Chapter 3, I extend that argument to name how millennial evangelicals might enact religious creativity strategically for rhetorical ends. By highlighting the rhetorical possibilities of vernacular religious creativity, I hope to prompt compositionists to conceive of pedagogical approaches whereby they could help students channel the energy from such creativity toward civil discourse.

The Problem of Evangelicals in Composition Studies

Before making that argument, though, it's worth acknowledging the fact that more often than not in rhetoric and composition, we tend to associate evangelical Christian students with problem rather than possibility. Indeed, while evangelical Christian students are not new to scholarship in composition studies, some readers might register surprise at the argument that attending directly to their faith might promote civil discourse. After all, many of the scholarly depictions of evangelical Christianity construct such faith and the students who espouse it as antithetical to the democratic values of tolerance, openness, and inquiry that many scholars and teachers of rhetoric and writing locate at the heart of civil discourse. We have, for instance, examples of evangelical Christian students who are dualistic (Anson; Dively, "Religious"), unaware of the situatedness of their testimonial language (Anderson), self-righteous and overly certain about their beliefs (Hunt; Perkins, "'Attentive'"), resistant to multicultural or critical pedagogies (Goodburn; Perkins, "Radical"), and dismissive of perspectives that conflict with their own (Montesano and Roen; Smart). While numerous examples exist that complicate this narrow portrayal of evangelical Christians in the writing classroom, the prevalence of these stereotypical cases reifies the status of evangelicals as "problem students" (Cope and Ringer 106) or "troublesome character[s]" (Vander Lei, "'Where'" 77). And because such stereotypes resonate with larger cultural narratives that assume evangelicals only care about "parrot[ing] narrow-minded bigotry" and championing "hyper-conservative political and theological views" (Cope and Ringer 106)—not to mention saving souls—it makes it hard to imagine how evangelical Christian faith and the students who espouse it could do anything other than perpetuate the political divide to which Crowley draws our attention. This is especially the case if we assume that evangelical Christian students perceive difference as "a threat to be overcome" (Shannon Carter 373).

Such constructions of evangelical Christian students are, of course, sometimes true: there are students like Doug Hunt's "Rob Campbell" who dig in their heels against perspectives other than their own because they're convinced they already have all of their "views and beliefs intact" prior to arriving at college (10). As Elizabeth Vander Lei has argued recently, our tendency is to construct students who espouse such faith as "outside the borders of composition" ("'Where'" 66). This is so because, given our negative associations with descriptors like evangelical or religious, we perceive such students as challenging the liberal values of tolerance and openness we hope to promote (see Smart; Vander Lei, "'Where'"). Phillip Marzluf's research bears this out: even though he found evidence complicating the "conflict narrative" that pits conservative Christian students against secular liberal academics, he also concludes that such a narrative "still plays a role" when it come to "argumentative or academic research genres" (286)—those genres wherein we most hope students would demonstrate the ability or willingness to engage meaningfully with positions other than their own.

In *Toward a Civil Discourse*, Crowley assumes that politically, socially, and theologically conservative versions of Christian faith shut down deliberative possibilities rather than open them up. Because Crowley constructs the political divide between fundamentalist Christianity and liberal politics using contrasting terminologies, she ultimately reifies the divide she hopes to bridge (DePalma, Ringer, and Webber 319–22; see also Steiner). Moreover, while Crowley recognizes early in her book that not all American Christians ascribe to apocalyptism—the belief that Jesus will return to earth, that his followers will then be raptured into heaven, and that all of this will take place against a backdrop of "worldwide devastation and suffering" (Crowley 7)—by her concluding chapter such distinctions have largely disappeared. As Beth Daniell has pointed out, this is a noteworthy conflation in and of itself ("Whetstones"), but the larger significance is that at no point in Crowley's conclusion does it seem within the realm of possibility that evangelical Christian rhetors might play a role in bridging the political divide that continues to plague American public discourse. Evangelical Christians—including purportedly those we teach in our writing classes—are part of the problem, and it's up to secular rhetoricians to invent the solution.

Crowley, of course, is not talking specifically about evangelical Christian students in writing classrooms, and yet other compositionists do construct such religious commitment as barriers to effective civic engagement. One example comes from Gesa Kirsch, who argues in "From Introspection to Action: Connecting Spirituality and Civic Engagement" that religion impedes civic engagement, while spirituality fosters it (W3). According to Kirsch, spirituality "reflect[s] our search for meaning in life and our hope for making a difference" (W12). Because it features practices like reflection and contemplation, spirituality can foster "deep commitment to civic and social issues" (W12). On the other hand, because religion has "often been oppressive and discriminatory" (W3), it tends to shut down such civic possibilities. Kirsch stresses this point in her conclusion where she makes it clear that she's not recommending that composition classes feature religious discourse, because doing so "could seriously stymie discussion, intellectual inquiry, and the advancement of knowledge" (W11).

Interestingly enough, one "conservative Christian" student in Kirsch's creative nonfiction class is able to reflect effectively on her own spiritual journey (W10). Kirsch admits to "cringing" when this student drew on "the discourse of her church and family" to write her spiritual autobiography, but the student, much to Kirsch's surprise, did so in order to explore "her changing beliefs, values, and commitments" (W10). Kirsch writes, "It turned out this student was very insightful about her religious beliefs and able to stand back, asking questions about the values she had taken for granted" (W10). What Kirsch discovers is what many other compositionists have come to realize: that evangelical Christian students can and do engage their beliefs in highly reflective, creative, intelligent ways (Shannon Carter; DePalma; Perkins, "'Attentive'"; Ringer, "Consequences," "Dogma"). Indeed, Kirsch's discovery prompts us to question killer dichotomies like that of spiritual versus religious and to rethink assumptions that religion shuts down civic engagement while spirituality makes it possible (see Ammerman, *Sacred* 23–25).

Like Kirsch, Keith Gilyard acknowledges that he is uneasy when it comes to the presence of religious perspectives in the composition classroom, admitting in *Composition and Cornel West* that he is a "rationalist" who tends to be suspicious about religion (52). Gilyard's purpose in his book, though, is to explore how Cornel West's philosophy might inform composition studies, and Gilyard knows that it is impossible to understand West apart from his Christian faith. Consequently, Gilyard investigates West's prophetic Christianity, which is explicitly democratic in its aims of social justice (Gilyard 52). Gilyard observes that West's goals align with those of critical composition studies and proceeds to explore arguments for the inclusion of faith within rhetorical education. He begins with bell hooks's argument that spirituality and academia should coexist and then addresses Ann Berthoff's remark at the 1988 convention of the Conference on College Composition and Communication about the lack of attention to Paulo Freire's Catholicism. From there, he highlights subsequent contributions—Russell Durst's observation that religiously committed students write about religion instead of issues such as race or class; Anne Ruggles Gere's observation that no language exists to articulate the spiritual in academic contexts; Amy Goodburn's analysis of fundamentalist Christian discourses from the vantage of critical pedagogy; and Lizabeth Rand's critique of how composition studies tends to trivialize the faith of evangelical Christian students (Gilyard 53–57).

Gilyard lingers on Rand due to her focus on evangelicals. Rand, Gilyard observes, calls for compositionists to create assignments wherein evangelical Christian students can conduct research into the "various religious subcultures" that encompass their faith and then "place their research within the context of wider public discourses" (qtd. in Gilyard 57). This suggestion, Gilyard continues, comes with a caution that compositionists should resist their own tendencies to interpret such discourses as "rhetorically unsophisticated or naïve" because "religion embodies a subversive character … and makes for expansive possibilities" (57). Gilyard's response, which I quote at length, reads as follows:

> While Rand's criticism is powerful, I doubt that high-volume creativity is going to flow from fundamentalist or evangelical students. Their religiosity tends not to be of the prophetic, socially ameliorative type

> but the conservative, George W. Bush type. I have several friends in the profession trying to save my soul so they can deliver it to the Republican Party. I don't see how my soul could make it to heaven from there. While Rand pressures composition to examine the faultiness inherent in some of its prevailing constructs, she does not historicize the contrast between the fundamentalist and the prophetic and includes way too little assessment of the practical link between conservative Christianity and conservative political actions. (58)

Gilyard's point is similar to Crowley's: not only is it unlikely that evangelical Christian students would be able to help achieve the democratic ends he and Cornel West both seek, but such students, because their faith is of "the conservative, George W. Bush type," would probably make it worse.

His point is well taken—Rand does not linger much on the political connections between American evangelical Christianity and American politics, a history that certainly has troubling characteristics (see Balmer; Carter, *God's Name*; Hunter; Smith, *American*). At the same time, a number of problems emerge from Gilyard's reasoning. One is that, like Crowley, he ultimately conflates evangelicalism and fundamentalism, a move that assumes and promotes a reductive view of evangelical Christian students (Canagarajah; Cope and Ringer; Daniell, "More," "Whetstones"; Lindsay 217). The second problem involves what I have come to think of as a definitional hangover: Gilyard's emphasis on the connection between "conservative Christianity and conservative political actions" assumes a construction of evangelicalism that, even in 2008 when Gilyard published his book, was splintering rapidly, particularly among millennials who sought to distance themselves from the traditional social concerns of the Republican Party (Balmer; Bielo; Cope and Ringer 109–110; Pally; Webber). Third, while Gilyard "doubt[s] that high-volume creativity is going to flow from fundamentalist or evangelical students," he offers no evidence to support his claim. This is a troubling omission given the ramifications of his assertion: if evangelical Christian students lack such creativity, then they are unable to foster democracy. This is because, for Gilyard, creativity amounts to the ability to dialogue across difference in order to promote justice and alleviate "social suffering" (5).[3] Gilyard's uncertainty as to whether evangelical Christian students are capable of such creativity parallels West's concerns that fundamentalism, which Gilyard associates with evangelicalism, poses "a threat to the tolerance and openness necessary for sustaining any democracy" (qtd. in Gilyard 59–60). In short, Gilyard perceives evangelical Christian students as intolerant and close-minded, unable (or unwilling) to think outside of their narrow frame of reference. And because of that, their rhetorical action is likely to hinder rather than facilitate deliberative discourse.

My goal in this book is to argue the opposite: millennial evangelical Christian students enact a form of creativity in their academic writing and in their social interactions in writing and rhetoric classrooms that holds potential for fostering civic civil discourse. As I noted earlier, I call such creativity vernacular religious creativity, and I argue that it represents an as-of-yet untapped resource that can help compositionists and rhetoricians foster the deliberative democracy that arguably represents the goal of rhetorical education ("Mt. Oread"). Tapping into the potential of vernacular religious creativity, however, demands that rhetoricians and compositionists rethink assumptions about millennial evangelical Christian faith and the students who espouse it. Instead of seeing such students as twenty-first century incarnations of the Religious Right or Moral Majority, we must be willing to perceive them as individuals who adapt, adjust, and interpret their religious beliefs in order to communicate effectively across difference and convey themselves as legitimate members of the pluralistic contexts in which they find themselves.

Toward Creative Possibilities

When millennial evangelical Christian students encounter situations wherein they must dialogue across difference or write for diverse audiences, they often stretch, rearticulate, or translate their beliefs in order to accommodate the perspectives of those who do not think and believe the way they do. Millennial evangelical Christian students enact such negotiations in order to constitute social conditions that might allow for deliberative exchange, conditions that, as I'll explore in Chapter 3, require interlocutors to perceive each other as equal, legitimate members of the same community who share a common reference world. Because such vernacular religious creativity features strategies of negotiating one's faith commitments in relation to pluralist social contexts, it holds significant possibilities for achieving the civic, civil discourse that Crowley, Gilyard, and many other compositionists rightly desire. But how do we as rhetorical educators and writing instructors go about recognizing this creativity? How does it show up in their academic writing, and how do we find ways to leverage its potential for deliberative ends? I take up these questions in this book because, like Crowley, I see bridging the divides in our current political climate as essential to the future of American democracy. But I also see religion, evangelical Christian faith included, as a necessary part of the solution (DePalma and Ringer, "Charting" 277–82). I agree with communication scholar Mark Allan Steiner when he notes that evangelical Christians are "uniquely positioned to show the way to public discourses that are more edifying, more productive and more humane" (291). My goal in this book is to offer examples of what that might look like.

To do so, I draw on case studies I conducted with three evangelical Christian students—"Austin," "Kimberly," and "Eloise"—all of whom were enrolled in various writing courses at "Northeast State University" (NESU), a pseudonym for a midsized public university in the Northeast.[4] Austin is a white, male, traditional first-year student who spent his childhood in the Southeast but moved to the Northeast prior to attending middle school and high school. I interviewed him during his first semester of college, the fall of 2008, when he was enrolled in English 101, NESU's traditional first-year writing (FYW) course. Kimberly, a Jamaican American who spent her early years with her devout Christian grandparents in Jamaica, moved to the Northeast at age nine to live with her single mother. Like Austin, she was enrolled in English 101, though she took it as a second-semester freshman during the spring of 2009. Also like Austin, she was a member of the Greek community at NESU. Finally, Eloise grew up in the Northeast and was of partial Iranian heritage. Early in her life, Eloise espoused the Bahá'i faith of her mother and grandmother but converted to evangelical Christianity while in high school. Eloise was an athlete who participated on the varsity track team. Because she earned AP credit for English 101, she took a writing-intensive, first-year experience course during her first semester of college (Fall 2008). This course was themed around questions of community and civic engagement.

While each student took a different writing course, all three participated in a remarkably similar set of church and parachurch activities. All three regularly attended what I will refer to as "Greenville Evangelical Church" (GEC), a nearby evangelical Christian church that was popular among students and is loosely affiliated with a national evangelical denomination. All three students also participated in NESU's chapter of InterVarsity Christian Fellowship (IVCF), one of the largest, most prominent evangelical campus ministries. Austin and Kimberly involved themselves in Greek InterVarsity, a division of IVCF that ministered to NESU's fraternities and sororities. Eloise participated in Athletes InterVarsity, the subgroup of IVCF devoted to varsity athletes. In part because of their active participation within IVCF, Austin, Kimberly, and Eloise shared a diverse and active community of millennial evangelical Christian college students. Each of them at various points talked about the importance of this network for their faith, their education, and their social lives. I noted earlier that part of the definition of evangelical involves identification with the subculture; IVCF constituted much of that subculture at NESU for Austin, Kimberly, and Eloise.

As I discuss more fully in Appendix A, I identified my participants through their affiliation with NESU's chapter of IVCF (see also Cope and Ringer). Each case study consisted of five interviews, a structure I modified from education researcher Irving Seidman's three-part interview series for phenomenological interviewing (20–23). Prior to or at the beginning of each interview, I asked students to write in response to a prompt I provided; each prompt asked them to think about their faith in relation to their academic writing or current academic context. I also collected relevant course documents, such as syllabi and assignment sheets. The second and third interviews were text-based interviews wherein students and I discussed writing they completed for their respective writing courses. For interviews after the first, I brought in excerpts from my prior interviews with the student, a strategy that helped develop continuity across interviews and allowed participants to reflect on what they had already said or written. This strategy, along with the five-part interview structure, allowed for greater "internal consistency" in what each student said (Seidman 29).

I positioned myself as an insider to evangelicalism in my interviews with students (see Cope and Ringer; Pavia). My participants knew from the outset that I identified as a Christian, came from an evangelical background, and attended an Episcopal Church near campus. When the occasion called for it, I enacted evangelical discourse during interviews, often by alluding to a biblical passage or using language common within evangelical circles. My goal in enacting such discourse was to foster trust with my participants; I wanted them to know that I understood and could enact the evangelical Christian discourse that shaped their lives (Cope and Ringer 112–14). Readers should note, then, that in some of the interview transcripts I include in later chapters, I sound as much like an evangelical Christian as I do a composition researcher.

In terms of "external consistency" (Seidman 29), I contextualize my case studies within scholarship from composition studies, rhetorical studies, sociology of religion studies, and folklore studies. Perhaps most significantly, my case studies coincide with research from the National Study of Youth and Religion (NSYR), a national-scale, multi-stage research project funded by the Lily Endowment and spearheaded by sociologist Christian Smith, one of the foremost experts on American religious practice (Smith, *American*, *Bible*; Smith and Denton; Smith and Snell). I discuss how my participants fit within the NSYR data more fully in Appendix B, but let me briefly note here that Austin, Kimberly, and Eloise match up with Smith and Snell's category of the "Devoted," the top five percent of emerging adults in the NSYR data in terms of religious devotion, commitment, and practice (259). My participants attended religious services multiple times per week, engaged frequently in devotional practices such as prayer and Bible reading, and talked at length about the centrality of faith to their lives (Smith and Snell 259). They align with Bebbington's definition of evangelicalism, at least the first three points of it. In terms of conversionism, they all talked about their own conversions or stressed the need for others to convert to Christ; regarding biblicism, they all viewed the Bible as central to their lives as Christians; and as activists, they all sought to share their faith and better the communities and worlds in which they lived.

At the same time, Austin, Kimberly, and Eloise also evidenced appreciation of diverse perspectives, an attitude that the NSYR found to be prevalent among millennials. Smith and Snell note, for instance, that emerging adults are far more likely than prior generations to recognize cultural differences (48–8); maintain an open-minded stance by "dropping old prejudices" (50); assume that the "sociocultural world" is "contingent, changeable, and particular" (50); believe "people have mutual responsibilities to [help] each other" (68); and honor diversity by refusing to "hold anything against anyone simply because they are of a different religion" (81). While such perspectives do not constitute the attitudes and behaviors of every emerging adult, the NSYR findings suggest they are pervasive. In fact, they're so deeply rooted within the millennial consciousness that they influence even the religious faith of devoted evangelicals like Austin, Kimberly, and Eloise. As I argue in the rest of this book, the significance of such attitudes for civic engagement can be profound: they serve as the motives that prompt millennial evangelicals to adapt their faith and ways of speaking about that faith to people who do not share their beliefs.

A Necessary Corollary

Of course, the willingness of millennial evangelical Christians to adapt their faith to fit their social and cultural contexts may not always be beneficial, either for students themselves or for the democratic society to which they belong. The risk for individual believers like the millennial evangelical Christian students who populate our classes is that adapting faith to fit better within a pluralistic culture waters down that faith to the point where it is rendered meaningless. And while loss or adaptation of faith in that regard might not represent a concern for every scholar and teacher of rhetoric and writing, what should concern rhetorical educators is the reality that student faith tends to get coopted by the worst that American individualism has to offer. As Princeton professor and youth minister Kenda Creasy Dean puts it, "After two and a half centuries of shacking up with 'the American dream,' churches have perfected a dicey codependence between consumer-driven therapeutic individualism and religious pragmatism" (5). In Dean's estimation, this has led to millennials exchanging their Christian commitments (if they ever had them) for "the American gospel of self-fulfillment and self-actualization" (5). What results in an insipid worldview that Christian Smith and Melinda Denton call "moralistic therapeutic deism," a perspective that bears faint resemblance to Christianity but emphasizes being happy and feeling good about oneself (162–70; see also Dean 14). Where traditional commitment to a faith such as Christianity demands sacrifice and devotion, moralistic therapeutic deism amounts to shallow relativism and "niceness," which is why Dean associates it with what she refers to derogatorily as "the Church of Benign Whatever-ism" (38–39).

The NSYR data feature multiple examples of how millennial evangelical Christian faith gets co-opted by culture in troubling ways. Vander Lei points compositionists to one example of a "young evangelical woman" who participates in missions work but who offers the following qualification regarding her belief that premarital cohabitation is wrong: "I don't know, I think everyone is different so. I know it wouldn't work for me, but it could work for someone else" (qtd. in "'Where'" 79; Smith and Snell 52). While few compositionists would advocate in favor of a student of any faith or persuasion imposing her moral beliefs on someone else, this quick shift from a moral stance grounded in faith to a cultural commonplace indicative of benign whatever-ism should concern any socially conscious rhetorical educator. Instead of commitment, this student evidences easy capitulation to a form of inclusivism that undercuts rather than celebrates difference." Much cleaner, IMHO. Our goal as rhetorical educators is to help students argue from and on behalf of their commitments in humble, thoughtful ways, not succumb to shallow relativism or cynical skepticism (Bizzell, "Beyond"; Booth, *Rhetoric* 46–47; Ringer, "Dogma").

Beyond the legitimate concerns for our students' personal faith and commitments, adapting faith to fit better in a pluralistic context can have disastrous consequences for American democracy. Stephen Carter argues persuasively in *God's Name in Vain* that religion tends to sell its soul when it gets too close to politics. In doing so, religion relinquishes its distinctive role, which is "to stand apart from politics, apart even from culture, to call us to righteousness without regard to political advantage" (*God's Name* 20). And while a call to righteousness may be unsettling for many compositionists (isn't that what folks like James Dobson and Pat Robertson want?), it's important to remember the role that such prophetic voices have played historically in American public life. For example, Carter reminds us that the abolitionist movement in the nineteenth century and the civil rights movement in the twentieth would have failed or not even entered into the realm of public imagination were it not for the insistence of Christian voices calling out for justice (*God's Name* 4). I think, too, of the many devout millennial evangelicals I've taught who have a deep, faith-based passion for addressing contemporary injustices like human trafficking, a passion that drives them to take action through advocacy, volunteering, or even seeking careers with international nonprofit organizations. The danger, then, is that if religious citizens capitulate too far—if they trade their birthright for a pottage of what Hugh Heclo calls our "democratic faith," which worships solely at the altar of personal choice (96)—then we may lose distinctive voices that could motivate meaningful, large-scale social action. In the name of tolerance, we would find our public discourse less diverse, less pluralistic, and less just.

As a committed Christian and a rhetorical educator, I take these concerns seriously. I long for a civic civil discourse wherein religiously committed citizens like evangelical Christians can speak their minds (and their faith) openly, but do so in ways that are not intentionally insulting, unnecessarily alienating, or arrogantly dogmatic (Ringer, "Dogma"). Thus I side with Heclo when he writes, "Christians can be committed to the larger democratic goal of talking through things with citizens unlike themselves, and they should be able to demonstrate that their religious opinions are not simply self-referential and beyond reasonable democratic compromises about common goods" (134–35). But I also side with Alan Wolfe when he tells "people of faith" in *The Transformation of American Religion* to "take pride in [their] flexibility and adaptability" because, "[l]ike everyone else in the United States," religious citizens "innovate and originate" their beliefs and perspectives in novel ways (4). The challenge that faces the millennial evangelical Christian students who populate our writing classes, then, is not unlike that which faces all religious citizens in the United States: how should they negotiate their faith commitments in relation to the realities of living and communicating in publics that invariably are politically, culturally, socially, and religiously diverse? As I hope to show in this book, there are possibilities, but to achieve them requires a careful balancing act on behalf of religiously committed student rhetors. That balancing act is one wherein millennial evangelicals must be willing to adapt their faith to accommodate the perspectives of others, but not to the point where they undercut their commitments; to recognize their partiality and limitations as human agents, but not devolve into crass relativism; to participate fully in civic and political discussions, but not become corrupted by self-interest, power, and fear mongering. In short, this balancing act echoes the biblical adage to be in the world but not of it.[5] Achieving such a balance is a tall order, to be sure, but it arguably parallels the work to which rhetorical educators commit themselves on a regular basis: helping students develop and maintain commitments to their own perspectives while also being open to the perspectives of those who disagree with them.

Organizing the Book

I organize the book around my case studies with Austin, Kimberly, and Eloise. The case study structure helps tell the story of each student's experience, and as sociologist of religion Nancy Ammerman suggests, it is through stories that we can best come to know and understand the lived religion of ordinary evangelicals like the students who populate our writing classes (see Ammerman, *Sacred*). Two caveats about the case study structure are worth mentioning. The first has to do with the drawbacks of such an organization, namely that it is not as efficient as a thematic approach and that each case study is prone to repetition of key concepts. However, given that I am concerned with vernacular religious creativity—a process that often takes place over time—it makes sense to tell my participants' stories as stories in order to reveal that process. My hope is that the benefits of doing so outweigh the legitimate concern of inefficiency. The second caveat has to do with the fact that I don't arrive at my case studies until Chapter 4, prompting some readers to ask whether the case studies drive the theory or vice versa. In response, I would say that the case studies largely drive the theory. I began my research with a question about how evangelical Christian students negotiate their faith in their academic writing. The evidence I gathered from my case studies led me to explore theories of lived religion and vernacular religious creativity, which led me to reanalyze the data I had collected, which led me to think about how the creativity I saw in the case studies might offer possibilities for civic engagement. Thus while I organize the book deductively—I begin by outlining the theory I use and then apply it to my case studies—I arrived at the theory of vernacular religious creativity inductively.

In Chapter 2, "Vernacular Religious Creativity: Lived Religion and Evangelical Christianity," I explore more fully the notions of lived religion and vernacular religious creativity that mark the faith of many religious Americans, including millennial evangelical Christian students. Then in Chapter 3, "Creating Deliberative Conversation: The Rhetorical Possibilities of Vernacular Religious Creativity," I discuss how vernacular religious creativity can function rhetorically. I define three specific strategies my participants used to engage civically and civilly with diverse audiences: casuistic stretching, values articulation, and translation. All three strategies function rhetorically because they aim to constitute social conditions necessary for deliberative discourse. Chapter 4 comprises my first case study. In "Effective Witness, Faithful Witness: Austin, Casuistic Stretching, and the Desire for Legitimacy," I explore how Austin wrestles with conveying evangelical beliefs and attitudes for a non-Christian audience. In doing so, Austin bumps up against the challenges of translation and discovers that identification with a non-Christian audience entails much more than changing one's language; rather, it involves a complex negotiation of values and beliefs themselves. To negotiate this problem, Austin casuistically stretches values that rest at the center of his evangelical identity. While Austin's experience raises questions about how far student rhetors should go to accommodate their audience's values, his rhetorical action ultimately opens up deliberative possibilities.

Chapter 5, "The Problem and Possibility of Ethos: Articulating Faith in Kimberly's Academic Writing," demonstrates the flexibility of values articulation as a rhetorical strategy grounded in vernacular religious creativity. It does so by considering the academic writing of a millennial evangelical Christian student writer named Kimberly. While Kimberly's writing bears no trace of her evangelical identity on the surface, analysis of the beliefs, values, and motives undergirding her persuasive essay about the human papillomavirus (HPV) vaccine reveals a powerful form of vernacular religious creativity that offers possibility for deliberative discourse. Specifically, Kimberly is able to articulate her values in situation-specific hierarchies that allow her to make an argument on behalf of the common good that departs from but does not undermine her personal morality. Kimberly's strategy of values articulation does bring her ethos into question, though, and so this chapter considers both the deliberative ends Kimberly's essay fulfilled and the ones she could have fulfilled had she been encouraged to articulate her faith in relation to her argument about a controversial vaccine.

In my final case study, I discuss how Eloise negotiates her newfound evangelical Christian faith in the context of a writing-intensive, first-year experience (FYE) honors course. While Eloise's experience resonates with Austin's—she similarly struggles to negotiate her evangelical faith in a pluralistic context—it also highlights the extent to which millennial evangelicals who are new to their faith might seek legitimacy among peers who differ from them. Chapter 6, "Changing the Way She Speaks: Eloise's Translative and Constitutive Rhetoric," thus extends concerns raised in both Austin's and Kimberly's case studies by exploring how Eloise develops a way of speaking—an ethos—that might allow her to be heard and respected by non-Christian peers. These motives emerge in the public writing she completes for her FYE course, an essay wherein she seeks to constitute her public university readers as accepting of her evangelical Christian faith as legitimate within the protopublic of her writing-intensive classroom and the wider NESU community. Finally, in Chapter 7, "The Implications of Vernacular Religious Creativity for Rhetoric and Composition," I explore the implications of vernacular religious creativity for teachers and scholars of rhetoric and writing. In particular, I discuss how the findings and concepts from this book can shape scholarship, rhetorical education, and public discourse. I also consider the implications of these findings for students themselves.

My hope is that this book, by attending to the lived, vernacular faith of millennial evangelical Christian students and the forms of creativity they likely engage in on a regular basis, can help lead to a civic discourse that is more civil and more robust than what we have experienced in recent years. In doing so, I hope we as writing instructors can feel more empowered to help our religiously committed students work towards a better, fairer, more inclusive world.

Notes

1. While I often use value, belief, and assumption interchangeably as premises for arguments or as the substance underlying Burkean identification (*Grammar*), I also recognize distinctions among them when necessary. In his discussion of enthymemes, one of the basic structures of argument, Hauser links together values, beliefs, and goals by noting that all three can function as premises on which rhetors can appeal in order to achieve common ground with audiences. However, the examples he offers of beliefs (e.g., "drug traffic threatens social welfare") and values (e.g., "we should be generous to each other") suggest distinctions: while beliefs name what reality is, values highlight what reality ought to be (Hauser, *Introduction* 125). Roberts-Miller suggests something similar when she defines *values* as "the good" (98). By assumption I mean something similar to Toulmin's notion of "warrant," which he defines as a general rule or principle that "bridges" or connects data to the claim or conclusion (125). Warrants, Toulmin suggests, can be written as if/then statements such as "Given Data D, one may take it that C" (125).
2. Biblicism as Bebbington uses it and as I use it here is not synonymous with biblical literalism, the view among some evangelical and fundamentalist Christians that all of the Bible should be taken literally. As scholars like sociologist Christian Smith (*Bible*) and literacy specialist Mary Juzwik have argued recently, American evangelical forms of biblicism are much broader in scope than literalist interpretations alone.
3. Creativity is a term that West himself frequently uses. In *The American Evasion of Philosophy*, West writes that prophetic pragmatism "invites all people of good will both here and abroad to fight for an Emersonian culture of creative

democracy in which the plight of the wretched of the earth is alleviated" (235). Earlier in the same book, West defines "creative democracy" as "a society and culture where politically adjudicated forms of knowledge are produced in which human participation is encouraged and for which human personalities are enhanced" (213). West speaks of such a democracy in populist terms, describing it as "the citizenry in action, with its civil consciousness molded by participation in public-interest-centered and individual-rights-regarding democracy" (213). Elsewhere, West notes the importance of empathy and imagination to the success of dialogue across belief systems "between secular brothers and sisters—atheistic, agnostic—and religious brothers and sisters" ("Prophetic" 95). Such attitudes derive from love: "how do you then allow [love] to spill over so that there's a robust kind of poetic orientation, so that your empathy is so broad and your imagination is so open-ended that you're willing to be open to different discourses, arguments, pushing you against the wall" (West, "Prophetic" 98).

4. I use pseudonyms for my participants and for anyone associated with their writing courses (e.g., instructors, other students in the class). The names I use for the university ("Northeast State University") and church ("Greenville Evangelical Church") that Austin, Kimberly, and Eloise attended are also pseudonyms.
5. See, for instance, John 17:14, Romans 12:2, and Philippians 3:20.

2 Vernacular Religious Creativity

Lived Religion and Evangelical Christianity

> Vernacular religion is, by definition, religion as it is lived: as human beings encounter, understand, interpret, and practice it.
>
> —Leonard Primiano, "Vernacular Religion and the Search for Method in Religious Folklife"

Early in *Souls in Transition*, a book that draws on data from the National Study of Youth and Religion (NSYR), Christian Smith and Patricia Snell tell us about an evangelical Christian college student named Amanda. By any measure, Amanda is highly committed to her faith. She attends a conservative evangelical church, goes to a Christian college affiliated with her denomination, has traveled abroad on missions trips, believes firmly in abstinence before marriage, studies the Bible regularly, prays on a daily basis, and teaches English to multilingual learners "for religious reasons" (26–27). According to Smith and Snell, Amanda "has experienced God's providence guiding her life, and in some instances has heard God speaking to her" (27). As she puts it, "I live by my faith" (qtd. in Smith and Snell 28). It should come as little surprise, then, that Smith and Snell label Amanda a "Committed Traditionalist," someone who can articulate her faith fairly well and is "committed to practicing it consistently and faithfully" (169).

At the same time, Amanda's faith does not follow lockstep with the beliefs of her church or the "extremely strict outlook" shared by other members of the same denomination (27). As Amanda puts it, "I tweak religious values my own special way," a point she exemplifies in a comment that will be discussed later in this chapter:

> My denomination tends to have a "we're right and everyone else is wrong" attitude. I don't think that's necessarily true, because, just from history, tons of different religious … people have had that attitude, and it's turned out they've been wrong. They've done terrible things. I think everyone probably has a piece of the truth and we're trying to make God a lot smaller than he is, trying to dictate every aspect of everything as either right or wrong. It's harder than that. If you take a commandment too hard, it becomes an idol.
>
> (qtd. in Smith and Snell 27, 29)

Here, Amanda clearly distances herself from an attitude of self-righteousness that, as communication scholar Mark Allan Steiner has argued, undercuts the effectiveness of American evangelical civic engagement. American evangelicals traditionally have been more concerned with "being right" than with "doing the hard work of engaging outsiders in rhetorically sensitive ways that acknowledge their humanity and dignity and that work to earn their respect and their hearing" (Steiner 311). There's no direct evidence here to suggest that Amanda attempts to communicate across difference in "rhetorically sensitive ways," but she's certainly dissociating herself from her denomination's attitude of "being right."

She's not doing so out of pure whim, though. Rather, she appeals to other values or beliefs in order to question attitudes of smugness or certainty. There's the historical appeal, for one—lots of people have thought they were right throughout history, and it has turned out they were terribly wrong. But then there's the more complex web of beliefs wrapped up in statements like "I think everyone probably has a piece of the truth," "we're trying to make God a lot smaller than he is," and "If you take a commandment too hard, it becomes an idol." Some of these beliefs, namely those about idolizing commandments and making God "smaller than he is," resonate with evangelical Christian discourse (I've often heard similar statements within my own evangelical circles). On the other hand, her belief that "everyone probably has a piece of the truth" sounds more like a cultural commonplace than traditional Christian doctrine (see Smith and Snell 135; Vander Lei, "'Where'" 79). Either way, Amanda's statement indicates that instead of ingesting her denomination's beliefs wholesale, she has negotiated them, interpreting some beliefs in ways that align with her experiences while resisting or rejecting others with which she disagrees. What results is a faith that, while it bears many of the same features and commitments shared by other American evangelicals, is also distinctly Amanda's.

Amanda thus evidences what I refer to in this book as vernacular religious creativity, the conscious or unconscious process of negotiating beliefs that religious believers enact in order to make sense of their faith in relation to their social, political, cultural, discursive, and institutional contexts. As the epigraph suggests, I derive this term from folklorist Leonard Primiano, whose definition of vernacular or "lived" religion emphasizes a form of creativity that results from "the human drive to interpret religious experience" (43). Primiano maintains that religious believers are always engaged in processes of interpreting beliefs in relation to what he calls our "human context" (44). Such processes can range from outright innovation or invention of beliefs to more conservative forms of adjusting or adapting beliefs to accommodate the perspectives or experiences of others. The upshot of vernacular religious creativity is that no two individuals will have the same exact beliefs, and that the lived religion of ordinary, everyday religious believers often will differ from institutional or official religious faith as it is promoted through creeds, denominations, authorities, spokespersons, or figureheads. And because our sociocultural contexts are always changing, religious believers likewise are constantly engaged in processes of interpreting and reinterpreting religious faith to accommodate those changes, often in subtle ways. Vernacular religious creativity reminds us that, as Mike DePalma says so well, religious believers—including our millennial evangelical Christian students—are always "in the process of becoming something different" (239).

I argue here that vernacular religious creativity functions as a terministic screen that can help reveal the complex processes whereby the millennial evangelical Christian students who populate our classes adapt their religious beliefs to accommodate the perspectives of others. Such creativity offers distinct possibilities for civil discourse because it tends to occur in relation to the prevalence of pluralism in American society (Ammerman, "Introduction" 6–10; Howard, *Digital* 167; Primiano 42–44). And if highly devout millennial evangelical students like Amanda enact vernacular religious creativity in order to accommodate to their pluralistic contexts, then such creativity might allow them to talk deliberatively across difference. I say "might" because I must make clear at the outset that not every millennial evangelical Christian student will evidence vernacular religious creativity in a manner that leads to civic, civil exchange. Primiano suggests as much when he observes that vernacular religious creativity can function to challenge or uphold the "social status quo" (47). But while vernacular religious creativity can promote or suppress deliberative discourse, recent scholarship suggests that religious creativity among millennial evangelicals trends toward appreciating diverse perspectives in ways that holds potential for deliberative discourse (see Howard, *Digital*; Smith and Snell; Wolfe, *Transformation*).

To tap into the democratic potential of vernacular religious creativity, scholars and teachers of rhetoric and composition need to turn their attention toward the lived religion of religious believers in general and millennial evangelical Christian students in particular. Consequently, my purpose in this chapter is to define vernacular religious creativity and to demonstrate that it is pervasive within American evangelical Christianity. I do so by drawing on scholarship in folklore studies and the sociology of religion that highlights the creativity whereby religious individuals adapt or reshape their faith in relation to their pluralistic social contexts. I also aim to show that vernacular religious creativity among millennial evangelicals often proceeds in a manner that holds democratic potential. Like Amanda, millennial evangelical Christians often tweak their faith as a result of questioning received beliefs they perceive to be narrow-minded or discriminatory, and they do so as a result of their interactions within pluralism. In Chapter 3, I then take up the question of how such vernacular religious creativity can function rhetorically.

Folklore Studies and Sociology of Religion

First, though, let me offer a rationale for why I turn to folklore and sociology of religion and explain how scholarship from such fields can help compositionists better understand the writing and deliberative potential of our millennial evangelical Christian students. The first reason I turn to such scholarship is because folklore and sociology of religion offer powerful theories that can help compositionists appreciate the diverse ways whereby individuals or groups enact, adapt, and create religious beliefs. The concepts of lived religion and vernacular religious creativity emerge from a rich body of scholarship within folklore and sociology that focuses directly on how religious believers live their faith. While scholars like DePalma, Elizabeth Vander Lei ("'Where'"), and Mark Alan Williams have begun to explore the vernacular, creative ways whereby our students live and negotiate their faith, scholarship from folklore studies and sociology of religion offers a fuller, broader, more nuanced picture of the vernacular religious creativity that often marks our students' religious faith than is currently available in rhetoric and composition scholarship. Such nuance is important because, as I pointed out in Chapter 1, current portrayals of religiously committed students in general and evangelical students in particular still tend to be rather narrow and reductive in rhetoric and composition (Cope and Ringer; Pavia; Thomson-Bunn; Vander Lei, "'Where'"). This scholarly representation has begun to change in recent years, but scholarship in folklore studies and sociology of religion offers ways to recognize and appreciate the complex, subtle negotiations our religiously committed students make on a regular basis.

Additionally, folklore studies and sociology of religion tend to be concerned with ordinary or everyday people, a category to which the majority of our religiously committed students belong. The voices we hear in studies such as Ammerman's *Sacred Stories, Spiritual Tribes*, Wolfe's *The Transformation of American Religion*, Howard's *Digital Jesus*, and Hall's *Lived Religion in America*, among others, tend not to be those of theologians, pastors, church officials, spokespersons, or figureheads. Rather, they are the voices of ordinary citizens who talk about their attempts to make sense of their faith in relation to their various sociocultural contexts. The modes of thinking revealed in such studies apply to our religiously committed students, who more often than not are "nonexperts" when it comes to religious faith or theology (Ammerman, *Sacred* 5). As I'll discuss below, one of the premises shared by folklore studies and sociology of religion is that ordinary believers enact and even fashion their faith in novel ways, enactments of religious faith that can differ significantly, if subtly, from the denomination or institutional religious culture to which they belong. Regardless of their degree of devotion, religiously committed students inflect their faith in nuanced ways; they are not parrots for Mormon doctrine, Pope Francis, the evangelical church to which they belong, or even George W. Bush. Scholarship in folklore studies and sociology of religion prompts scholars and teachers of rhetoric and writing to perceive religiously committed students with greater nuance and sensitivity than we currently do.

It does so, though, in ways that resonate with some of the core assumptions of composition studies. Folklore studies and sociology of religion are thoroughly social disciplines that concern themselves with how individuals interact within their sociocultural contexts. While scholars in both fields assume each individual is unique, they also emphasize that people are shaped in large part by their situatedness within particular historical and sociocultural contexts. Lived religion is no different. As I noted earlier, Primiano highlights the importance of the "human context" on vernacular religious creativity (44), while sociologist of religion Nancy Ammerman observes that "[w]e live inside a range of socially constructed stories that are not always of our own making or even fully conscious to us" (*Sacred* 8). The assumptions, methodologies, and findings from folklore studies and sociology of religion thus translate well into rhetoric and composition due to common assumptions about how individuals are shaped by social factors.

Finally, the concerns of folklorists and sociologists of religion tend to resonate with the rhetorical concerns of rhetoricians and compositionists. Even though folklore and sociology do not concern themselves with rhetoric formally, lived religion and vernacular religious creativity can be understood as fundamentally rhetorical concepts—they assume that individuals adapt or transform their beliefs in relation to their particular social situations. Like Aristotle's definition of rhetoric, theories of lived religion underscore how religious believers continually observe their given situations and adjust their faith accordingly. This does not mean that believers radically alter their faith as soon as they encounter a new audience or situation, but it does mean that believers are often attempting to adjust their faith to their cultural or social contexts (Heclo; Wolfe, *Transformation*, "Whose"). In her introduction to *Sacred Stories, Spiritual Tribes*, for instance, Nancy Ammerman explains that studying lived religion entails paying attention to how religious beliefs are "improvised in new circumstances" (8). Ammerman's point is that ordinary religious believers improvise their faith because the particular and ever-changing social circumstances in which they find themselves prompt them to do so. Consequently, Ammerman's attention to circumstances emphasizes the rhetoricality of vernacular religious creativity. Lived religion assumes something akin to rhetorical conceptions of kairos: ordinary religious believers are engaged in continuous processes of sizing up circumstances and adjusting their beliefs and the ways of communicating those beliefs accordingly. As I show in later chapters, such improvisation amounts to a form of creativity that offers possibilities for deliberative discourse.

The Process of Vernacular Religious Creativity

With that rationale in mind, I draw on scholarship from folklore studies and sociology of religion in order to expand the definition of vernacular religious creativity I mentioned earlier. I do so by discussing how vernacular religious creativity is an active, ongoing process whereby religious believers adapt or adjust their beliefs in relation to their sociocultural contexts—contexts that, in the United States of the early twenty-first century, tend to feature pluralism. Before I proceed, I should offer one note about terminology: to the extent possible, I use the term vernacular religious creativity to denote the active, continuous processes religious believers enact, while I use lived religion or vernacular religion interchangeably to signify the faith or set of religious beliefs produced by those processes. Lived or vernacular religion results from vernacular religious creativity.

In his article "Vernacular Religion and the Search for Method in Religious Folklife," folklorist Leonard Primiano defines vernacular religious creativity as a process whereby individual religious believers interpret their faith in relation to a variety of factors that fit within our human context, a concept I'll discuss more fully below (44). For Primiano, interpretation is a key act associated with the process of vernacular religious creativity. He writes, "The omnipresent action of personal religious interpretation involves various negotiations of belief and practice including, but not limited to, original invention, unintentional innovation, and intentional adaptation" (43). According to Primiano, religious believers don't just espouse or hold religious beliefs. They interpret, create, invent, adapt, negotiate, integrate, shape, and reshape religious beliefs. Such acts foreground reflection on or questioning of existing beliefs; like Amanda, an individual believer can actively disagree with beliefs even if such beliefs align with the religious tradition to which he or she ascribes. This is why Primiano calls for "special attention to the process of religious belief," a process he describes in terms of "human artistry," on par with "the creation, performance, and communication of any number of folklore genres which have interested … scholars for generations" (43–44). Without getting into a primer on the various kinds of artifacts that folklorists tend to study, the point that Primiano makes here is a significant one. He's saying that vernacular religious creativity results in a product—lived or vernacular religion—that is as unique and worthy of study as the verbal, material, or customary lore that folklorists concern themselves with and assume to be expressive of traditions, cultures, and societies (see Wilson).

Primiano is not the only scholar who sees vernacular religion as arising from ongoing, creative processes. Religion historian David D. Hall, writing in his introduction to *Lived Religion in America*, describes "lay men and women" as "actors in their own right, fashioning (or refashioning) religious practices in accordance with local circumstances" (viii). Like Primiano, Hall's notion of lived religion centers on the fact that people continuously engage in creative practices of interpreting their faith in relation to their sociocultural contexts. Similarly, in his contribution to Hall's collection, religion scholar Robert Orsi stresses the creative impulses that mark lived religion. Orsi notes, for instance, that his concern in studying lived religion is with "how particular people, in particular places and times, live in, with, through, and against the religious idioms available to them in culture—*all* the idioms, including (often enough) those not explicitly their 'own'" (7, original emphasis). Vernacular religious creativity is an action: religious believers "live in, with, through, and against" expressions of religion available to them. There is, then, the possibility of active selection or deselection of beliefs in processes of vernacular religious creativity. And in fact, lived religion for Orsi arises from "cultural bricolage"—it is "assembled" from available cultural and religious resources (7). To Primiano's list of actions associated with vernacular religious creativity, then, we can add assemblage and bricolage: religious believers make use of the cultural materials at hand to fashion their faiths. As Orsi puts it, "People appropriate religious idioms as they need them, in response to particular circumstances. All religious ideas and impulses are of the moment, invented, taken, borrowed, and improvised at the intersections of life" (Orsi 8).

By this point, readers might have picked up on the parallels that exist between vernacular religious creativity and contemporary thinking about rhetorical invention. Since the social turn, scholars in rhetoric and composition have conceived of invention as a social act, a phrase that Karen Burke LeFevre helped make part of our disciplinary lexicon via publication of her 1987 book of the same title. The argument is that invention is not a solitary but rather a social process. Invention involves other people as readers, interlocutors, or collaborators; it is mediated by symbol systems and genres that are necessarily socially constructed; and it is always inflected by "social collectives" like institutions or governments (LeFevre 1–2). More recent theories preserve the idea of invention as a social act but also extend its definition to include processes like assemblage, remix, reproduction, and recontextualization (Banks; Johnson-Eilola and Selber; Palmeri; Simonson). For example, when rhetorician Peter Simonson states that "remix is invention, too" (318), what he means is that invention does not entail creating something new out of nothing. Rather, invention entails drawing on the cultural, social, discursive, embodied, generic, linguistic, experiential, and technological materials at hand to fashion something appropriate to the situation. Frank Farmer refers to such forms of invention as bricolage, which entails "using only those materials and tools readily available" in order to make "new objects out of worn ones" (31). The basic idea, then, is that rhetorical invention makes use of a variety of resources and processes, from collaborating with other people to remixing or assembling together ideas, tropes, sayings, discursive features, forms, or genres in order to create something novel and useful for the rhetorical situation at hand.

Vernacular religious creativity parallels these definitions of rhetorical invention in two ways. First, as I have been arguing, vernacular religious creativity amounts to a form of bricolage, a term that both Orsi and Ammerman use explicitly to define lived religion (Orsi 7; Ammerman, "Introduction" 8). Religious believers make use of the religious and cultural beliefs and practices at hand in order to fashion faiths that fit their given situations. Second, as I have also suggested, vernacular religious creativity is a fundamentally social process that is prompted by interactions within what Primiano calls the "human context" (44). By human context, Primiano means a range of factors that shape religious believers, including "physical and psychological predispositions, the natural environment, family, community affiliations, religious institutions, the socialization process, tradition, education and literacy, communication media, as well as political and economic conditions" (44). Other scholars who comment on lived religion say something similar: Hall points to the influence of "local circumstances" on lived religion (viii), while Orsi stresses "particular places and times" as well as "culture" (7). Similarly, Ammerman underscores "the power of the social context" ("Introduction" 6). Like rhetorical invention, we might say that vernacular religious creativity is a social act.

And like any social act, vernacular religious creativity is not unidirectional but rather moves in two ways: from the wider society or culture toward the individual, and then from the individual outward. Primiano says as much when he recognizes the "influences of environments upon individuals and of individuals upon environments in the process of believing" (44). Believers are shaped by their contexts and, in turn, shape the contexts in which they find themselves. As a result, vernacular religious creativity highlights how individual believers create their own vernacular forms of faith, but it also underscores how vernacular iterations of faith in turn influence those believers' social, cultural, and political contexts. I take up the latter concern more fully in the next chapter when I discuss the rhetorical possibilities of vernacular religious creativity.

Two more points about vernacular religious creativity demand further consideration before moving on. The first has to do with the nature of the social contexts that shape religious creativity in the United States of the early twenty-first century, namely that they are decidedly pluralistic. Nancy Ammerman comments on the relationship between pluralism and lived religion in her introduction to *Everyday Religion* when she writes that pluralism represents "part of the cultural and structural world in which people are living their lives" and fashioning their religious beliefs ("Introduction" 8). By pluralism, Ammerman refers primarily to religious pluralism—she notes that there are "literally hundreds of different religious denomination and traditions" in existence in the United States in the early twenty-first century (7). But she also acknowledges the importance of ideological, cultural, and social pluralism, underscoring the influence of secularism in the twentieth century along with trends related to immigration and globalization (6–10; see also Lövheim). While these forms of pluralism certainly shape the religious lives of individual believers, that fact for Ammerman "is neither a plus nor a minus, neither a guarantor of vitality nor a harbinger of doom" when it comes to religious faith (8). Pluralism for Ammerman is simply a reality that shapes the lives and faiths of individuals (6). Of course, not every scholar would agree that pluralism does not pose a challenge to traditional religious faith (Carter, *God's Name*; Heclo), and even Ammerman is careful to stress that pluralism does not "*necessarily* weaken the overall presence and influence" of religion for "individual lives or in society as a whole"

(8, original emphasis). What pluralism does do is offer religious believers in the United States of the twenty-first century a wealth of cultural, religious, social, and institutional resources from which to assemble or fashion or reshape religious beliefs.

But just because religious believers have that choice does not mean they devise their own religions that have no relation to traditional faiths such as Catholicism or evangelical Christianity. Several scholars I have cited here underscore the influence of institutions such as formal religious traditions on individuals' lived religions (Ammerman, "Introduction" 10; Orsi 20). And that constitutes the final point I wish to make about vernacular religious creativity—a point about what it tends not to be. Some of the verbs associated with lived religion (e.g., innovate, invent, create, fashion) might lead readers to believe that vernacular religious creativity amounts to individuals making up their own idiosyncratic religions along the lines of what Robert Bellah and his researchers call "Sheilaism." As they explain in *Habits of the Heart*, "Sheilaism" comes from a woman named Sheila Larson who developed her own personal religion but affiliated herself with no formal religious tradition (Bellah, et al. 221). While vernacular constructions of religion could come to resemble Sheilaism, such a case likely would be the exception rather than the rule.[1] Religious believers in the United States engage in vernacular religious creativity in ways that more often than not retain connections to recognizable religious traditions. For example, of the ninety-five people Ammerman and her researchers studied for *Sacred Stories, Spiritual Tribes*, the majority of them aligned with a formal tradition such as mainline or conservative Protestantism, Catholicism, or Judaism (306). The lived religions each individual discusses in that study are certainly vernacular, but none is so idiosyncratic as to be completely devoid of any connection to a recognizable faith. Rather, they evidence continuity with a tradition and share beliefs in common with other members of the same tradition (Carter, *God's Name* 173–74). In fact, as I'll discuss later in this chapter, processes of vernacular religious creativity can be authorized by other members of the same faith tradition. When I use the term vernacular religious creativity in this book, then, I do not mean Sheilaism. Instead, I mean something closer to what Amanda exemplifies. Amanda shares many beliefs and practices in common with other evangelical Christians—she attends church, reads the Bible, prays regularly—but she also evidences a willingness to question some of her denomination's beliefs. If her vernacular religious creativity entails bricolage, it does so in ways that involves taking many of the beliefs and practices available to her through her evangelical Christian tradition while also grafting in certain cultural beliefs about pluralism (e.g., "everyone probably has a piece of the truth").

In short, vernacular religious creativity is a process whereby religious believers adapt or adjust their beliefs to fit their social context. While it can lead to radical revisions to one's belief system, vernacular religious creativity is often more conservative in nature, representing not a break with tradition or continuity but rather a series of adjustments. Such adjustments are prompted by individuals' interactions within their human contexts, both the "local circumstances" that Hall names and the larger, pluralistic society of twenty-first century America discussed by Ammerman. Like rhetorical invention, vernacular religious creativity is a social act, but it also often functions as bricolage or assemblage, the act of fashioning something new or slightly different out of the cultural, social, religious, material, and institutional resources at hand. Finally, the upshot of vernacular religious creativity is that no two religious believers—even if they participate in the same denomination, church, or small group—will share the same beliefs in the same way. Vernacular religious creativity reminds us that religious believers—including our millennial evangelical Christian students—are always negotiating their faith in relation to their sociocultural contexts. They are always "in the process of becoming something different" (DePalma 239).

Examples of Vernacular Religious Creativity

As the previous section suggests, vernacular religious creativity is not an isolated phenomenon; rather, it is pervasive. Primiano, for instance, argues that because "religion inherently involves interpretation, it is impossible for the religion of an individual not to be vernacular" (44). If we take Primiano at his word, then that means that anyone who professes any kind of religious belief whatsoever has engaged in some form of vernacular religious creativity. Of course, it's impossible to prove or disprove such a broad claim. It is possible, though, to point to numerous examples of vernacular religious creativity in scholarship about evangelical Christians. In order to demonstrate how pervasive vernacular religious creativity is, I provide a number of brief examples below. The first few come from sociology and folklore studies:

- Sociologist John P. Bartkowski describes how twenty evangelical Christian men "integrated traditional ideas about gender difference, popular in evangelical family discourse, with notions of masculine sensitivity rooted in the New Man ideal that has pervaded secular American society in recent decades" (156). Even though these men were involved with Promise Keepers, the evangelical Christian movement popular in the late 90s that stressed patriarchal male roles in the family, they generally rejected the role of male "headship" and embraced more progressive ideals and practices (155–56). They assembled their family roles from secular and religious discourses (156).
- Sociologist D. Michael Lindsay identified key trends among 150 evangelical leaders he interviewed. Lindsay defines one trend, elastic orthodoxy, as "the ability to maintain a core set of convictions without being so rigid that it cannot cooperate with others who do not share them" (216). Such elasticity constitutes a means whereby evangelicals engage with pluralism and "allows evangelicals to undertake certain projects

that might seem hypocritical to others" (217). Lindsay offers as examples the global AIDS crisis and legislation such as the Victims of Trafficking and Violence Protection Act.

- Folklorist and communication scholar Robert Glenn Howard found evidence of tolerance within an online forum hosted by *RelevantMagazine.com*, a website that reaches a largely millennial audience. Howard writes, "Among the new generation of Christians growing up with network communication technologies fully integrated into their daily lives, there seems to be a greater awareness of the diverse beliefs of others" (*Digital* 167). Such awareness means that millennials might be "in a better position to recognize" the importance of "engaging in discourse and that the expression of intolerance silences participants" (*Digital* 167).

While these examples come from outside of rhetoric and composition, there are multiple examples that come from within the field:

- Gesa Kirsch's representation of her "conservative Christian" student suggests that the latter evidences mild disagreement with received beliefs (Kirsch W10; see also Chapter 1, this volume). The student draws on "the discourse of her church and family" when writing her spiritual autobiography, but does so in order to explore "her changing beliefs, values, and commitments" (W10). As Kirsch puts it, "this student was very insightful about her religious beliefs and able to stand back, asking questions about the values she had taken for granted" (W10).
- Emily Murphy Cope notes that "Ember" evidences a kind of "pluralistic evangelicalism" (Cope and Ringer 117; see also Cope). As Ember puts it, "I think that people can get to God through Jesus without knowing it," later adding, "I would hope that everyone could have the opportunity to know Him, but in their own way, not in the way that someone prescribes to them" (qtd. in Cope and Ringer 117). Based on a desire to distance herself from the church she grew up in, Ember "critiques traditional evangelical models of conversion that specify one narrow route to God" (Cope and Ringer 116–17).
- Priscilla Perkins's "Sara" wrestles with the implications of how to read John 3.16. "Taken literally," Sara writes, "this statement means that all those who do not believe that God is the ultimate truth *will* perish. In my daily life, however, I encounter great numbers of people who do not believe" (qtd. in Perkins, "'Attentive'" 82, original emphasis). When asking herself if this means that she will go to heaven while nonbelievers will perish, Sara's "carefully considered answer is no" (qtd. in Perkins, "'Attentive'" 82).
- Mark Alan Williams's discussion of the OneWheaton campaign from Wheaton College emphasizes how a religion like evangelical Christianity "can be transformed through deliberate acts of public rhetoric and the critical deployment of personal experience" (353). The creative move

featured in the OneWheaton media campaign is the fusion of its members' LGBTQ and religious identities.

- My own "Chris" evidences vernacular religious creativity when writing about Yann Martel's *Life of Pi*. In my article, "The Dogma of Inquiry", I discuss how Chris rethinks a belief common among evangelical Christians—that one should have "no other gods" and serve only Christ—in response to Pi's sincere acceptance of Christianity, Islam, and Hinduism. Chris's inquiry leads him to a "new way of thinking" that is slightly different from his "previous understanding of salvation" (Ringer, "Dogma" 362).

Moreover, in a recent religious rhetorics course I taught at a large public university in the Southeast, I asked students, many of whom espoused some form of evangelical Christianity, to write brief responses to a class discussion about vernacular religious creativity. Two key examples underscore the presence of vernacular religious creativity among millennials. The first excerpt comes from "Esther," while the second is from "Rachel." Both students are white female undergraduates who come from an evangelical background.

> I regularly attend a Baptist church and the church's stance against abortion is very strong. My political opinion supports allowing abortion to remain a choice for women, but I have had to justify my decision to support keeping something legal when I also feel it is wrong. The higher abstraction I lean toward in this scenario is one of child welfare, influence of poverty on children, etc. Basically me reconciling my politics with my faith.
>
> —"Esther"

> I identify as Christian—not really sure about a denomination. A popular belief (& hot topic) in Christianity is that gay marriages or relationships are wrong. Well, I just disagree. Because I take my personal experience and belief in an accepting and loving God, and I 'stretch' it to come to the reality that I don't believe in a discriminatory or exclusive God.
>
> —"Rachel"

As these examples suggest, evangelical Christians across generations and income brackets negotiate their beliefs in response to their diverse social contexts. What these examples do not show, though, is the extent to which vernacular religious creativity is a process enacted by religious believers in order to make sense of their faith in relation to their pluralistic social contexts. In the remainder of this chapter, I comment on two examples that offer insight into vernacular religious creativity as a process. These examples also reveal how vernacular religious creativity can amount to adjusting one's faith within the context of a religious tradition, such that accommodating religious faith does not necessarily entail "the surrender of sacred truths" (Carter, *God's Name* 174). Equally important, the examples I discuss below point to the possibilities that vernacular religious creativity can have for civic engagement.

For the first example, I return to Amanda. As I discussed earlier, Amanda saw herself as adjusting her religious beliefs such that they don't square completely with her theologically- and socially-conservative denomination (Smith and Snell 28–9). Because she is a devout evangelical Christian who is relatively articulate about her faith, Amanda illustrates the fact that "vernacular religion can highlight the creative interpretations present in even the most ardent, devout, and accepting religious life" (Primiano 47). She also is clearly sensitive to the fact that she lives in a pluralistic society wherein people hold a variety of religious or nonreligious beliefs. Smith and Snell tell us that Amanda appreciates "human diversity" as part of her faith and that she aims "to build" such an appreciation of diversity "into her outlook" (29). As Amanda puts it, "There are different people, everything's different, and we all have different personalities and ways of worshipping" (29). When responding to a question about if and how this proclivity toward appreciating difference applies to her interactions with people who do not share her faith, Amanda responds as follows:

> The best answer to that question is in C. S . Lewis's *The Last Battle*. Even if people do not have the gospel explained to them in words, there are still choices they make. How do you live your life? Are you going to live for yourself or others? Other religions, they don't necessarily have to call it God, but they can worship the Christian God. It's hard for me because I know the Bible says you have to worship Jesus. But if you don't know who Jesus is, how are you supposed to make that choice? Maybe God embraces everyone who really lives for him, whether they know it or not.
>
> (qtd. in Smith and Snell 29)

In this excerpt, Amanda refers to a scene near the end of the final book of C. S. Lewis's Chronicles of Narnia series wherein a follower of Tash (an evil god) is admitted into the heavenly Narnia because Aslan (the good god) valued the purity and sincerity of the follower's devotion. The plot of the book as a whole serves as a kind of analog to Christian beliefs about the second coming of Christ: matters in Narnia grow progressively worse until Aslan returns; those who followed him make their way through a door into the heavenly Narnia, while those who didn't follow Aslan descend into oblivion. The old Narnia then passes away, and the depiction of life in the new Narnia is one of bliss, joy, and new creation (Lewis 171–84). While the book's apocalyptist overtones and binary of good versus evil would assuredly strike some readers as divisive, those who have been taught traditional Christian views of heaven and hell—and who, like Amanda, have grappled with the implications of such views in relation to her pluralistic human context—would likely take some solace in the possibility that people could make it to heaven without expressly confessing faith in Christ. This is especially true given the fact that the thinking comes from C. S. Lewis, a highly respected writer and thinker within evangelical circles.

Amanda's reference to Lewis's *Last Battle* is not uncommon for an evangelical. In fact, my second example deals with the same book. In an interview I conducted for a related study during the summer of 2006, a white, female, evangelical Christian graduate student in English studies cited Lewis's book for similar reasons. She did so because she said reading it helped her negotiate an identity in graduate school that allowed her to retain her faith commitments while not feeling the need to cast judgment on her non-Christian peers. I quote an excerpt of my interview with "Katie" at length. I had just asked her what she understood to be negotiable and non-negotiable in terms of her faith:

Katie: I think it's a big deal to think that Christ is the Son of God. But I also [laughs]—this is going to get kind of hairy—but I also think that there's a way that people who don't know or accept Jesus—primarily people of other faiths or other cultures—might still be pursuing Jesus in a way that is okay with God without really naming or understanding that.

Jeff: Where did that come from?

Katie: I know exactly where it came from. … Book 7 of *The Chronicles of Narnia.* … I really agree with that. So there's the two sides, and one guy's obviously the bad guy, and there's, like, Aslan and he's god and he's the good god. And there's one person who's been following the bad god—I forget what his name was—but even though he had been following him and trying to help this other guy who was actually the bad guy, it was like his motives and his heart were directed toward the good and toward following what was good and what was right, and he ended up in the eternal Narnia or whatever it was with Aslan. And I think that made a lot of sense to me. And I know it's—like, it's not a very good argument, because it's really hard to defend to the nil—like, every little thing—because in a way, it's hard to set that out in words. In another way, it really made sense to me. [.… I]f you're in a culture that's completely anti-Jesus, to the point where you don't really even know about him or give him a chance, but you're pursuing good and truth and righteousness, then maybe you're one of those people who is pursuing God or Jesus without really [knowing it.] It's, like, terminology at some point? I don't know. It's really confusing in my mind. (Katie)

While Katie remains uncertain about her thought process, it's clear that Lewis's *Last Battle* authorizes a form of vernacular religious creativity whereby she attempts to reconcile exclusivist Christian doctrine with her pluralistic context. Note, though, that she's not abandoning her faith. Primiano might say that Amanda and Katie both are attempting to "accommodate not only their sub-culture, but their religious roots and sacramental sensibilities as well" (51).

These examples from Amanda and Katie help demonstrate how vernacular religious creativity functions as a process. At the risk of oversimplification, that process seems to go something like this: at some point in their lives as evangelical Christians, both Amanda and Katie arrived at the realization that they lived in pluralistic contexts where not everyone ascribes to the same faith that they hold to be true. In fact, Amanda and Katie arrive at this realization in strikingly similar ways: they both allude to the fact that there are people who don't even know who Jesus is, a reality that poses a problem for their Christian belief that, as Amanda puts, "you have to worship Jesus" in order to be saved. One answer to this problem arises from reading a book by C. S. Lewis, a respected voice within evangelical Christianity. When they are presented with the fictional possibility that people might make it to heaven even if they don't expressly believe in Christianity, they are able to reinterpret their received belief in Christian exclusivism (i.e., that salvation comes only through expressed faith in Christ). Thus while their vernacular religious creativity emerges as a response to pluralism, it is also authorized by a respected voice in Christian tradition. Their creativity involves encountering a religious resource in the form of a belief about the possibility of Christian inclusivism (i.e., that explicit knowledge of Christ is not necessary for salvation through Christ) and fusing it onto their belief systems. Such bricolage prompts them to question the Christian exclusivism they received through their faith traditions. And through that adjustment to their faith, they are able to readjust themselves to their pluralistic contexts.

My point in lingering on these examples is not to suggest that all instances of vernacular religious creativity will proceed similarly—vernacular religious creativity isn't always prompted by religious authorities like C. S. Lewis. Rather, my point is to underscore the nature of vernacular religious creativity as a process. It is also to emphasize the fact that religious creativity can be prompted by interactions within pluralism and authorized by perspectives that come from within a faith tradition. And the possibilities for civil discourse that arise from such negotiations are significant. Adjusting one's faith toward Christian inclusivism makes it possible for millennial evangelicals like Amanda and Katie to sidestep a way of thinking that often gets evangelicals in trouble when it comes to public discourse. Steiner calls this the mentality of "being right," and he explains that it tends to coalesce around concerns of "who is in the kingdom of God and who is not" (311). Through adopting a more inclusive faith via vernacular religious creativity, Amanda and Katie would be better positioned to deliberate with others who do not expressly share their faith.

Of course, such accommodations also raise concerns about millennial evangelicals' commitment to Christian faith. As I noted in Chapter 1, there's a risk in adjusting one's religious beliefs to the wider culture, and that risk entails undercutting one's religious faith to the point where it resembles the culture far more than it does any recognizable faith tradition. The examples of Amanda and Katie, though, suggest that millennial evangelicals can engage in vernacular religious creativity and still maintain continuity with a religious tradition. Amanda and Katie demonstrate what Lindsay calls elastic orthodoxy: they hold on to "core convictions" while finding ways to interact meaningfully "with a variety of different groups, some of other faiths and some of no faith at all" (216–17). Or to borrow Stephen Carter's terms, Amanda and Katie seem to be accommodating their faiths "to the world" without giving up "sacred truths" (*God's Name* 174). Of course, if one sees a claim to Christian exclusivism as a sacred truth or a core conviction, then what Amanda and Katie have done amounts to a potential undercutting of their faith. But as the example from C. S. Lewis indicates, Christian inclusivism is not that extreme of a position within Christian tradition. Equally important, it enables Amanda and Katie to articulate their faith in ways that could allow them to find some degree of identification with non-Christian peers when communicating across differences of belief.

Chapter Conclusion

I have argued in this chapter that a form of creativity marks the lived religion of evangelical Christians, and that such vernacular religious creativity is pervasive and tends to be motivated by believers' attempts to reconcile their faith with pluralism. Many of the examples I discussed here thus underscore how the vernacular religious creativity of even highly devout millennial evangelical Christians emphasizes tolerance and inclusion, both of which are central to democratic practice. However, vernacular religious creativity primarily shapes religious belief itself; as a concept, it is not aimed directly at the rhetorical concerns regarding civic engagement and deliberative discourse. Thus the question remains: how can the vernacular religious creativity of millennial evangelical Christian students function rhetorically to foster deliberative discourse or help bring about the conditions that make such discourse possible? That is the question I take up in the next chapter.

Note

1. However, as Bellah et al. point out, the individualism that corresponds with a "faith" like Sheilaism is rampant in contemporary American society.

3 Creating Deliberative Conversation

The Rhetorical Possibilities of Vernacular Religious Creativity

> Deliberative democracy makes high demands of citizens. We must treat one another with empathy, attentiveness, and trust; we must take the time to invent and continually reinvent our ideas in the light of informed disagreement; we must care enough about our own views to try to persuade others of them, but not so much that we are unwilling to change them; we must listen with care to people who tell us we are wrong; we must behave with grace when other views prevail; we must argue with passion but without rancor, with commitment but without intransigence.
>
> —Patricia Roberts-Miller, *Deliberate Conflict*

> ... the beliefs of individuals themselves radiate and influence the surrounding environments.
>
> —Leonard Primiano, "Vernacular Religion and the Search for Method in Religious Folklife"

Patricia Roberts-Miller's description of deliberative democracy in the first epigraph above underscores just how elusive such democracy can be. Reading that description, one gets the idea that achieving deliberative democracy—or enacting deliberative rhetoric, the type of rhetoric that concerns itself with how to define and achieve the common good and that arguably constitutes the lifeblood of a democracy—amounts to balancing on a tightrope. Lean too far to one side, and interlocutors find themselves clinging arrogantly (and loudly) to viewpoints they're unwilling to negotiate; lean too far to the other, and commitments give way to acquiescence or opportunistic horse-trading. Given the careful balancing act required by deliberative discourse, it should come as little surprise that Roberts-Miller understands the possibilities for achieving such discourse as tenuous at best. As she puts it, "The question is not whether or not it will go wrong, but whether or not it will go at all" (187). It should also come as little surprise, then, that Roberts-Miller frames her description of deliberative discourse by naming the attitudes or dispositions rhetors need to have in order to achieve it. Without a mutual sense of "empathy, attentiveness, and trust" among interlocutors, it's hard to imagine why anyone would want to get on the tightrope, much less stay on it.

Part of Roberts-Miller's point, then, is that deliberative rhetoric rarely if ever happens by accident. On the contrary, rhetors must work to make deliberative discourse possible. They can do so by adopting the attitudinal stances she names and by making rhetorical choices that foster the social conditions necessary for deliberative exchange. Communication scholar Gerard A. Hauser suggests as much when he argues in *Vernacular Voices* that public or deliberative conversation "requires at least two individuals who are able to open a space of intersubjectivity from which a shared world may emerge in the course of their dialogue" (66). The phrase "open a space" is key: Hauser grants to rhetors agency to bring about the conditions that would foster the deliberative conversation he sees as essential to public life. In Roberts-Miller's terms, if you treat interlocutors with "empathy, attentiveness, and trust," there's a chance that everyone involved will exert the effort it takes to get on the tightrope. Conversely, if rhetors speak in ways that evidence arrogance, unresponsiveness, and suspicion, they can create social conditions that shut down deliberative possibilities. The upshot here is that rhetors play an active role in creating the social realities that militate against deliberative conversation or make it possible, and my purpose in this chapter is to explore how vernacular religious creativity can function rhetorically to facilitate it.

In the previous chapter, I explored scholarship in folklore studies and sociology of religion to make a case for the possibility that religiously committed individuals in general and millennial evangelical Christian students in particular engage in vernacular religious creativity. Vernacular religious creativity, however, primarily directs our attention toward how individual believers shape their faith itself. It does not theorize how such believers engage in deliberative discourse or establish conditions that could encourage such discourse. In the second epigraph, though, Leonard Primiano acknowledges the possibility that lived religion can influence the "surrounding environments" of individuals, by which he means their social or human contexts (44). This point of Primiano's relates to his contention that vernacular religious creativity operates bidirectionally. As I noted in Chapter 2, Primiano recognizes the "influences of environments upon individuals and of individuals upon environments in the process of believing" (44). If Primiano is right, then some form of rhetorical action can arise from religious beliefs negotiated via vernacular religious creativity, and it's possible that such rhetorical action could play a role in fostering the intersubjectivity necessary for deliberative conversation.

My purpose in this chapter, then, is to theorize this outward-looking emphasis of vernacular religious creativity. The rhetorical possibilities of vernacular religious creativity feature strategies that religiously committed individuals use to speak about their faith or from a faith-based perspective in order to enact deliberative rhetoric across difference or constitute the intersubjectivity that makes deliberative conversation possible. As I discussed in the previous chapter, vernacular religious creativity tends to occur in response to the pluralistic contexts individual believers such as millennial evangelical Christian students encounter on a regular basis, especially in the context of public universities. My concern here is thus with situations wherein such students adapt, adjust, or reinterpret their religious beliefs in order to communicate effectively with people who do not share their beliefs or do not espouse them in the same way. Understanding the rhetorical possibilities of vernacular religious creativity that millennial evangelical Christian students might enact in their writing and classroom practice can help compositionists and rhetoricians leverage such creativity for deliberative ends. In what follows, I first define deliberative rhetoric and discuss how the conditions for its existence are constituted by discourse that assumes the legitimacy of other voices. I then define the three rhetorical strategies of vernacular religious creativity that I identified in my case studies—casuistic stretching, values articulation, and translation.

Before doing so, I need to stress the fact that facilitating deliberative conversation is a possible but by no means necessary outcome of these strategies. As I pointed out in Chapter 2, vernacular religious creativity can function to perpetuate the status quo, in which case the vernacular religion of individuals could influence their human contexts in ways that constrain deliberative exchange. As I also suggested in Chapter 2, though, findings from large-scale studies like the National Study of Youth and Religion, along with numerous examples of lived religion from sociology of religion, folklore studies, and rhetoric and composition, indicate that it is not uncommon for millennial evangelical Christians to enact vernacular religious creativity in ways that lead to greater appreciation of diversity. The case studies I explore in the next three chapters also underscore the possibilities of vernacular religious creativity. While achieving deliberative discourse or constituting the social conditions necessary for it will never be easy, the rhetorical possibilities of vernacular religious creativity should offer scholars and teachers of rhetoric and composition a measure of hope. The religious motives and creativity of millennial evangelical Christian students *can* foster civil civic discourse.

Creating Deliberative Conversation

Deliberative rhetoric is policy-oriented rhetoric. In general, it addresses questions regarding the best course of action for a community or society. Aristotle, for instance, defines deliberative rhetoric in terms of "utility" and explains that "deliberation seeks to determine not ends but the means to ends, i.e., what is most useful to do" (I.6.17–20). Consequently, deliberative rhetoric tends to concern itself with what could or should happen rather than what happened in the past (forensic rhetoric) or what is happening in the present (epideictic rhetoric). As Wayne Booth puts it, deliberative rhetoric "attempts to make the future," offering the example of politicians who "debate about how to act or vote" (*Rhetoric* 17). And while it's possible for deliberative rhetoric to involve only one person (each of us at some point has weighed the pros and cons of a decision in our own minds), theories of deliberative rhetoric tend to assume it takes place in communities or societies. Thus when Booth writes that deliberative rhetoric makes the future, he also could have said that it makes society itself. He suggests as much when he explores the various ways whereby rhetoric creates our social realities regarding politics, war, interpersonal relations, and even the laws and mores that constitute society itself (Booth, *Rhetoric* 14–15).

Consequently, deliberative rhetoric assumes the existence and importance of a common or public good. Rhetors engaged in deliberative rhetoric tend to argue on behalf of what they believe to be in the best interest of the community as a whole. While deciding on a best course of action is rarely an easy task when multiple people are involved, doing so is arguably more difficult when the society or community in question is a pluralistic democracy like the United States in the early twenty-first century. Separated as we are by religion, region, race, class, gender, ethnicity, education, language, sexuality, ability, political persuasion, and so on, what looks like the common good to one constituency might amount to oppression or irrationality for another. While definitions of deliberative rhetoric assume the presence (or at least the possibility) of a common or public good, determining a good that is fittingly common or public is no small task. Indeed, Hauser maintains that one of the goals of deliberative rhetoric is to arrive at public understandings of what a populace considers to be "preferable," and people accomplish this "by knowing how to resolve a problem in line with the views of those being addressed" (*Vernacular* 98). Roberts-Miller says something similar when she stresses the importance of talking outside of "enclaves," those communities wherein "people speak only to people who share their values" (41). While recognizing that sharing ideas with like-minded individuals is important, Roberts-Miller makes it clear that "people *must* engage in critical discourse outside of enclaves as well" (41, original emphasis). Otherwise, arriving at notions of the good that are sufficiently common will remain elusive in diverse societies.

Accordingly, another overarching feature of deliberative rhetoric is that it is rhetoric aimed at negotiating one's perspectives and beliefs with people who think and believe differently. Roberts-Miller says as much when she defines deliberative rhetoric as "listening for difference," the title of the chapter she devotes to the subject. For Roberts-Miller, deliberative rhetoric prioritizes "reaching across one's own differences in order to understand another's" (183). Such listening involves more than simply hearing what someone else says. In Roberts-Miller's estimation, it demands that rhetors recognize others as "real people with compelling commitments that are different from one's own" (183). If rhetors can do this, then they might be better prepared to engage in the kind of translative work Roberts-Miller locates at the center of deliberative exchange. According to Roberts-Miller, deliberative democracy "requires that people try to present their own arguments in ways that people who are very different might understand" (197). Booth similarly emphasizes the reciprocal relationship between listening and talking. In discussing his version of deliberative rhetoric, Booth argues that "listening-rhetoric," or LR, ideally involves interlocutors participating in "a trusting dispute, determined to listen to the opponent's arguments, while persuading the opponent to listen in exchange" (*Rhetoric* 47). Like Roberts-Miller's description of deliberative rhetoric in the epigraph, Booth's LR necessitates a balance between commitment to one's own perspectives and openness to the beliefs of others. Rhetors always need to accommodate their audiences by making their messages accessible across difference, but not to the extent that they relinquish their own commitments. Deliberative rhetoric necessitates as much respect for one's own perspectives as it does for the perspectives of others (see Crowley 28–31).

A final feature of deliberative rhetoric worth acknowledging is that it places argument at the center of decision-making processes, though theories of deliberative rhetoric tend to promote broader, more capacious definitions of argument than do liberal theories of discourse. While liberal public spheres tend to reject arguments not based in reason or on universal conceptions of the common good, deliberative rhetoric embraces argumentation that features "narrative, attention to the particular, sensibility, and appeals to emotion" (Roberts-Miller 5). Given this understanding of argument, it is clear that Crowley advocates for a version of deliberative rhetoric in *Toward a Civil Discourse* when she calls for readers to move away from rational forms of argument and invent arguments that feature emotion and narrative (197–201). It's worth noting, though, that deliberative discourse does not see argument as the ultimate goal of deliberative rhetoric, a point Roberts-Miller underscores when she distinguishes between deliberative and agonistic theories of argument (132). The goal of argument in deliberative rhetoric is to forward perspectives in order to make decisions that are in the best interests of the society or community. Toward that end, Roberts-Miller and Booth agree that parties to a debate should make up their minds based on whose argument is best, not on who has the higher socioeconomic standing or the most power (Booth, *Rhetoric* 47; Roberts-Miller 5).

At a minimum, then, deliberative rhetoric is policy-oriented rhetoric aimed at arriving at a best course of action for a given society or community. It presupposes talking across difference, respecting the viability of other positions, and potentially changing one's mind. And while it shares some features in common with liberal forms of argumentation (by, for instance, assuming the existence of a common good), it also welcomes arguments based on narrative, emotion, and personal experience. But if that's what deliberative rhetoric is, how do rhetors go about achieving it? As I acknowledged at the beginning of this chapter, deliberative rhetoric doesn't just happen; it requires a certain set of social conditions in order for it to "go at all" (Roberts-Miller 187). Thus it requires more than the ability to make a strong case for one's perspective or listen to the perspectives of others—it also requires that interlocutors share what Gerard Hauser, following Charles Taylor ("Language"), refers to as intersubjectivity.

Hauser defines intersubjectivity as "a partnership in which topic, language, and meanings are shared in some significant way" (*Vernacular* 66). It is a social phenomenon wherein parties to discourse perceive themselves and each other as sharing what Hauser calls a common reference world. While sharing a common reference world does not mean that all parties to discourse must always agree with each other, it does mean that the perspectives they share must exist within a "common projection of possibilities for human relations and actions" (Hauser, *Vernacular* 70). For example, two citizens of the United States do not need to espouse the same political leanings or ideology in order to experience intersubjectivity. Theoretically, a Republican and a Democrat who disagree on which candidate would make the best president could talk in ways that evidence intersubjectivity. To do so, they would need to understand that they both share the same reference world as U.S. citizens who believe in the efficacy of democratic election processes, who consider the presidency important to the future of our country, and who agree that the act of talking about the merits of one candidate over another is itself meaningful. In this regard, even when accounting for the polarized nature of our current political scene, it would be far more likely for a Democrat and Republican to constitute intersubjectivity with each other than for either of them to do so with a citizen of, say, an isolationist communist country such as North Korea. This is because members of a democracy like the United States, even if they disagree significantly about the role of government in public life, still share a common reference world that they may not share with members of a radically different sociopolitical system.

Intersubjectivity also requires that parties to discourse perceive the perspectives held by each other as legitimate. Such legitimacy follows from the sharing of a common reference world. Interlocutors can achieve intersubjectivity if they communicate in ways that evidence shared social meanings and if they perceive each other as sharing those meanings. As Hauser contends, intersubjectivity demands that communication volunteered by a participant in a conversation must be treated not as "an object of discussion" but as "a dialogizing intersection" that is "interacted *with*" (Hauser, *Vernacular* 70, original emphasis). Intersubjectivity can thus be derailed if one party to discourse offers an argument that amounts to what Hauser calls "alien communication," a perspective that "emanates from a reference world beyond [a society's] horizon of comprehension" (*Vernacular* 70). Returning to the preceding example, Democrats and Republicans can achieve and sustain intersubjectivity so long as they voice perspectives that assume the importance of the presidency and the democratic process. If, however, one member of the conversation sincerely argues a perspective that falls outside of the realm of possibility (e.g., that the president of the United States should be given unlimited executive powers along the lines of a totalitarian dictator, or that our country is illegitimate in the first place and that we should still be answering to the British monarchy), then intersubjectivity might dissolve, along with the chances of engaging in deliberative discourse. The conversation has ceased to assume a common range of possibilities.

Finally, intersubjectivity can exist to the extent that parties to discourse perceive each other as relatively equal participants who can make legitimate contributions to the discussion at hand. Philosopher Charles Taylor talks about this stance in terms of what he calls the "complementarity of 'I' and 'We'" ("Language" 27). Such complementarity assumes the legitimacy of others because it values the participation of individuals in the formation of a mutual relationship. As Hauser puts it, conversation marked by intersubjectivity "can be sustained only if that [conversational] space accommodates the appearance of the individual's *I* as a source of contribution" (66, original emphasis). If a community or group excludes certain individuals for whatever reason, then that individual is unable to participate in the conversations that would allow for a sense of mutuality or togetherness to emerge. Habermas says something similar when he notes that the "collective identity" of a democratic society should reflect the contributions made by religious citizens, but that those citizens must be treated "as equal members of the same democratic society" (24). His point is that religious citizens do not need to set their religious perspectives aside when participating in public discourse. In Taylor's terms, they don't need to forsake their "I" for the sake of the "We." In fact, Hauser makes the point that each party to discourse "must not be subsumed by the relationship or the relationship itself is lost" (66). Intersubjectivity assumes the formation of mutuality—a sense of We-ness—but it also respects the individuality of each participant. Intersubjectivity in this regard is a state of affairs wherein parties to discourse are valued for their individual contributions to the conversation, and where the combination of multiple, legitimate perspectives come to constitute new social meanings or strengthen existing ones (Hauser, *Vernacular* 68–69).

I linger on the notion of intersubjectivity because I see it as a necessary precondition for deliberative rhetoric: unless parties to discourse share a common reference world, deem each others' perspectives as legitimate, and perceive each other to be relatively equal members of a shared community, achieving deliberative discourse will remain elusive. Lacking intersubjectivity, parties to discourse would find it much harder to arrive at or deliberate about shared notions of the common good. They would also find it much harder to listen with the attentiveness, trust, and empathy that Roberts-Miller names and that Booth *(Rhetoric)* and Crowley echo. I also linger on intersubjectivity because while vernacular religious creativity can lead directly to deliberative discourse, what is often more apparent in my case studies is how such creativity functions to constitute intersubjectivity. As I'll show in subsequent chapters, my participants enacted rhetorical strategies grounded in vernacular religious creativity that functioned to constitute intersubjectivity across differences of belief, often with peers who do not share their faith.

Before defining what those particular strategies entail, it's worth reiterating a point I made in Chapter 2, namely, that engaging in vernacular religious creativity does not necessarily entail distancing oneself from a faith tradition. In fact, evangelical Christian discourse itself contains resources that can motivate processes of vernacular religious creativity that can lead to intersubjectivity and deliberative discourse. In his article "Reconceptualizing Christian Public Engagement: 'Faithful Witness' and the American Evangelical Tradition," communication scholar Mark Allan Steiner discusses how values, assumptions, and beliefs drawn from Christian tradition can help evangelical rhetors communicate civically and civilly from their faith-based perspectives. Steiner acknowledges that American evangelicalism's "inordinate concern" for drawing harsh boundaries between people who share their beliefs and those who do not has hindered their attempts to engage in deliberative discourse (311). Nevertheless, Steiner contends that evangelical Christians are "uniquely positioned" to foster civil discourse if they appeal to their "own best values" (291–92). Such values include the beliefs that humanity is fallen and finite, that human epistemology is always limited, that humans have freewill and can reject arguments, and that talking across difference necessitates "building trust" with and respecting the humanity of others (310–11). Adopting these beliefs and speaking as faithful witnesses affords evangelical Christians a means by which to participate in civic discussions without alienating others and without reneging on their own deepest convictions. Thus while deliberative discourse is not the first thing that comes to mind when thinking about evangelical Christianity, the two can and do coexist. Steiner's faithful witness model offers a way to think about how values and beliefs from the evangelical tradition can align with the goals of deliberative discourse and motivate forms of vernacular religious creativity that might foster intersubjectivity. Accordingly, I return to his model frequently throughout this book.

Rhetorical Strategies of Religious Creativity

With these notions of deliberative discourse, intersubjectivity, and faithful witness in mind, I now turn to a discussion of specific rhetorical strategies grounded in vernacular religious creativity that might allow for deliberative exchange. Based on my case study data, I identified three strategies whereby my participants enacted vernacular religious creativity in order to constitute intersubjectivity with differently-minded audiences. By "constitute," I refer to constitutive rhetoric, which communication theorist Maurice Charland defines as rhetoric that seeks to position or interpellate audiences into certain subjectivities rather than persuade them outright. Because constitutive rhetoric functions to "insert 'narratized' subjects-as-agents into the world," such rhetorical action can shape how individuals and groups see themselves in relation to others (Charland 143). This point of Charland's resonates with Booth's and Hauser's contentions that social realities are constituted by discourse. What we say to each other and how we say it can open up space for deliberative conversation or shut it down. The rhetorical possibilities of vernacular religious creativity are thus constitutive: language choices create social realities that shape how people talk to each other (Booth, *Rhetoric* 14–16; Hauser, *Vernacular* 62–63). Casuistic stretching, values articulation, and translation all hold the potential to constitute the social conditions necessary for deliberative rhetoric.

Casuistic Stretching

One strategy grounded in religious creativity that emerged from my case study data corresponds to what Kenneth Burke calls casuistic stretching, which he defines in *Attitudes toward History* as a process whereby an individual "introduces new principles while theoretically remaining faithful to old principles" (229). Through casuistic stretching, individuals are able to reconcile or "unite" opposing values by appealing to a third value, which Burke calls a "'higher' abstraction" (231). According to Burke, a value that functions as a higher abstraction "contains opposites" to the point where it can reveal how "everything is its other"—the concepts of bad and good are both contained in the notion of morality, for instance (231). By way of example, imagine that two college roommates meet for the first time. One is a lifelong Boston Red Sox fan, the other a diehard fan of the New York Yankees. While no love tends to be lost between fans of these bitter archrivals, the roommates might achieve some common ground by appealing to the fact that they're both fans of the game. The Boston fan would be able to stretch the value "I'm a Red Sox fan and thus despise the Yankees" to the point where it can encompass respect for a fan of the team that Bostonians refer to as the Evil Empire. The stretched value might look like this: "While I'm a Boston fan and thus hate the Yankees, I'm also a fan of the game and thus respect other people who are fans of the game, even if they cheer for the Yankees." This doesn't mean the Boston fan loves the Yankees or vice versa. It does mean, though, that the roommates have found a way to modify their core values to achieve some degree of identification across significant disagreement, and they do this by appealing to the higher value that it's good to be a fan of the game. If the two roommates hit it off and continue to talk and think in terms of the higher abstraction and not the original binary between Boston and New York, then they might over time reshape their values more permanently. They might think primarily in terms of whether or not someone is a fan of the game, a new opposite that could in turn be reconciled by another higher abstraction if the need arises.

This example points to two realities of casuistic stretching: it is a common feature of everyday life, and it is also a process whereby diametrically opposed positions can be merged to the point where they no longer seem diametrically opposed. Thus Burke advocates on behalf of casuistic stretching because he sees it as a way to stave off what he calls "dissociative trends" (*Attitudes* 232). By that phrase, he refers to the human tendency to divide and categorize people and beliefs into groups with distinct boundaries, a tendency he refers to colloquially as "adherence to a 'party line'" (232). Contrary to such boundary making, Burke sees casuistic stretching as promoting "integrative thought," which allows for the possibility that seemingly rigid boundaries between categories like good versus bad or Red Sox versus Yankees are fluid (232). Such integrative thinking holds potential for constituting the intersubjectivity necessary for deliberative discourse. In the previous section, I noted Steiner's point that evangelical Christians often constrain deliberative possibilities by thinking in terms of who is right and who is wrong. As Steiner puts it, evangelicals tend "to draw hard and unhelpful moral boundaries between groups of people"—conservative Christians are good while "secular humanists" are bad (297). Casuistic stretching offers a means whereby evangelical Christians seeking to engage in public discourse could bridge even these divides. Appealing to one of the higher abstractions Steiner offers, namely that of human fallenness and finitude, could allow evangelical Christians to think in terms of how all people, Christian or otherwise, are finite in their knowledge and capable of both good and evil. Casuistic stretching could thus provide a starting place from which to initiate rhetorical action that might allow for a degree of intersubjectivity between those who ascribe to Christian beliefs and those who do not.

To illustrate in more detail how this might work, let me return to the anecdotes I discussed in Chapter 2 about Amanda and Katie and their references to C. S. Lewis's *The Last Battle*. Both anecdotes evidence casuistic stretching in that Amanda and Katie invoke "new principles while theoretically remaining faithful to old principles" (Burke, *Attitudes* 229). The old principle to which they theoretically remain faithful is that of Christian exclusivism, the belief that expressed faith in Christ is the only way to salvation. As Amanda puts it, "the Bible says you have to worship Jesus" (qtd. in Smith and Snell 29). Arguably, this principle has played a leading role in fostering exclusionary perspectives and rigid us versus them thinking that often constitutes "hard and unhelpful moral boundaries between groups of people" (Steiner 297). Such boundaries tend to name those who have professed faith in Christ as good while designating all those who haven't as bad. Given Amanda and Katie's human context of pluralism, though, they seek a means to negotiate this boundary in order to achieve some degree of identification with people who ascribe at least nominally to different belief systems.

Reading *The Last Battle* supplied Amanda and Katie with a general principle that allowed them to stretch their original belief (one must profess Christ to achieve salvation) to encompass a new one (non-Christians have a means other than professing Christ whereby they can likewise achieve salvation). The higher abstraction that might unite these opposites is that of mystery (Downs 43; Ringer, "Dogma" 357, 363; Steiner 308–10). The keyword Amanda and Katie both use that points to mystery as the higher abstraction is "maybe." Amanda puts it this way: "But if you don't know who Jesus is, how are you supposed to make that choice? Maybe God embraces everyone who really lives for him, whether they know it or not" (qtd. in Smith and Snell 29). Katie says something similar: "[I]f you're in a culture that's completely anti-Jesus, to the point where you don't really even know about him ..., but you're pursuing good and truth and righteousness, then maybe you're one of those people who is pursuing God or Jesus without really knowing it." Mystery serves as the abstraction that unites Christian and non-Christian. If salvation for those who profess Christ is itself mysterious, then mystery allows for the possibility that those who don't explicitly profess Christ might also find salvation. And if that idea is even possibly true for Amanda and Katie, then such a principle could serve as the premise for rhetorical action that fosters rather than constrains intersubjectivity. It redraws the boundaries of legitimacy to include those who profess faith in Christ and those who don't.

Burke makes clear that for casuistic stretching to achieve its fullest creative potential, which is remoralization as opposed to demoralization, its processes must be overt and explicit rather than covert or implicit. It must be "subjected continually to *conscious* attention" (Burke, *Attitudes* 232, original emphasis). For Amanda and Katie to maintain their Christian conviction and not descend into some form of syncretism or relativism that undercuts their commitments as evangelicals, they must be aware of the fact that they have stretched their values and work to maintain balance between the new principle and the old. Burke suggests that this can't occur via the elimination of casuistry—we're always stretching terms and values as we encounter new and different situations. The goal, then, is to make casuistic stretching "apparent" by clarifying it as a methodology rather than using it only as a method (Burke, *Attitudes* 230). If rhetorical educators can help religiously committed students arrive at a methodological awareness of how they can and do stretch values, they might be able to help such students invent strategies for communicating effectively with people who hold beliefs different from their own (Burke, *Attitudes* 230). As I'll argue in Chapter 4, this is precisely the guidance that Austin needed. Austin casuistically stretched values related to his evangelical beliefs in order to accommodate the perspectives of a non-Christian audience, a powerful rhetorical move that can constitute intersubjectivity across differences of belief. However, Austin was not fully aware of what he was doing, and it is that lack of awareness that can lead to demoralization. Austin needed help understanding both the identity consequences and the deliberative possibilities of casuistic stretching.

Values Articulation

The second strategy grounded in religious creativity that emerged in my case studies is values articulation, which I derive from Crowley's discussion of belief in *Toward a Civil Discourse*. At the core of Crowley's analytical and inventional methodologies is a notion of articulation that she develops by drawing on the work of Stuart Hall, Ernst Laclau, and Chantal Mouffe.

Crowley defines articulations as "formulations of moments" and "connections made among" such moments, with "moment" referring to a "belief that is more or less firmly situated by a history of its use within one or more discursive contexts" (60). Citing Hall, Crowley sees articulation as bearing a "double sense": it "means to utter, to speak forth, to be articulate," but it also means an assemblage where "two parts are connected to each other, but through a specific linkage, which can be broken" (qtd. in Crowley 60). The beliefs or values that comprise an articulation can thus be disarticulated or disconnected and then rearticulated in different ways. Equally important, different articulations of belief give rise to different arguments. As Crowley puts it, "Rearticulation and disarticulation of common elements occur all the time within a given community, and these processes constitute rhetorical lines of force" (61).

Values articulation as a rhetorical strategy grounded in vernacular religious creativity emphasizes the rhetorical possibilities—the lines of force—that result from strategic rearticulations or reprioritizations of belief. One of the key features of values articulation is flexibility: rhetors are able to rearticulate beliefs and values in different ways depending on the rhetorical situation. By doing so, however, rhetors do not necessarily give up one or more of the values in play; rather, they connect those values in different ways, often by subordinating one belief to another. Crowley, in fact, uses the phrase "hierarchy of values" to name how beliefs can be superordinated or subordinated to each other (65). In this way, Crowley's notion of belief articulation echoes Chaïm Perelman and Lucie Olbrecht-Tyteca's discussion about values hierarchies in *The New Rhetoric*, where they explain that understanding how arguments work necessitates understanding that values exist in hierarchies (80). According to Perelman and Olbrechts-Tyteca, values are "interconnected," and it is that "very connection" that serves as "the basis of their subordination" (81). Perelman and Olbrechts-Tyteca even go so far as to contend that value hierarchies are "more important to the structure of an argument than the actual values" (81). This is due to the fact that just because an audience holds a belief does not mean they will hold it as intensely as another. Parents of a prospective college student might believe in the importance of prestige, but if they value frugality more intensely, then their daughter's argument that her parents should pay for her to attend an expensive private college over a less expensive public university might fail. The parents still believe prestige is important, but they also believe it is more important to be frugal.

Crowley offers another example of belief articulation that demonstrates Perelman and Olbrechts-Tyteca's point about values hierarchies. In *Toward a Civil Discourse*, Crowley discusses the relationship between the values of patriotism and free speech, pointing out that virtually everyone in the United States would agree that both are good (77–78). In the context of events like 9/11, though, free speech in the form of dissent against military involvement in Afghanistan or Iraq takes a back seat to another value, namely patriotism (or "super-patriotism," as Crowley calls it). The hierarchy that exists between free speech and patriotism in the wake of events like 9/11 often subordinates the former to the latter. Perelman and Olbrechts-Tyteca likely would argue that appealing to the value of free speech in such instances would be less persuasive than it might be at other times because the audience's allegiances would lie more with patriotism. This doesn't mean the value of free speech has somehow disappeared. Rather, it has been subordinated to patriotism in that context. As such, the merit and influence of values, far from being universal, shift in relation to circumstances and contexts, such that the appeal of values is highly kairotic and contingent. In terms of Crowley's analysis, it also stands to reason that values hierarchies can be structured and restructured in the same way that beliefs can be disarticulated and rearticulated. And as a rhetor or community rearticulates or reprioritizes values and beliefs, different arguments emerge or are deemed persuasive.

As a rhetorical strategy grounded in religious creativity, values articulation highlights instances when students structure or restructure belief hierarchies for rhetorical ends. This can happen in two ways. First, values articulation can help religiously committed student rhetors reprioritize beliefs to fit a given rhetorical situation, a strategic move that demonstrates accommodation to an audience but does not negate other beliefs the rhetor might hold. In this way, the flexibility that marks values articulation represents a means by which millennial evangelical Christian rhetors can constitute conditions that can lead to deliberative exchange. This is because they're able to prioritize values in ways that appeal to the situation and audience at hand, a move that can underscore the extent to which rhetor and audience share a common reference world and perceive each others' perspectives as legitimate. And they can do this without reneging on their commitments. As I'll show in Chapter 5, Kimberly enacts this type of creativity when she argues for why parents of young girls should vaccinate their daughters against the human papillomavirus, or HPV. Kimberly makes this argument even though it departs from her own personal morality, which emphasizes abstinence. Kimberly is able to shift between two different values hierarchies depending on the situation: abstinence outweighs vaccination when it comes to her own personal morality, but when it comes to larger questions of public health, vaccination trumps abstinence because Kimberly believes it is more important to save lives. Kimberly's ability to rearticulate her beliefs allows her to make an argument about a public issue premised on the common good as opposed to her own personal morality.

The second way values rearticulation can function as a rhetorical strategy grounded in religious creativity is by introducing a novel or unexpected values hierarchy into a given rhetorical situation, especially by a rhetor who has a degree of situated ethos with the audience or community in question. Here again, Kimberly serves as an example. Part of my argument in Chapter 5 is that Kimberly had an opportunity to argue from her ethos as an evangelical Christian on behalf of the HPV vaccine. As an evangelical Christian who values life over abstinence when it comes to the public good, Kimberly could have argued for an articulation of values that would have challenged the values hierarchies espoused by other evangelical Christians who prioritize abstinence over vaccination (see Pollit; "Safe Sex"; Schwyzer). Arguing from her ethos as an evangelical Christian that valuing life is more important than abstinence could challenge other members of her evangelical Christian enclaves to rethink their own assumptions about the common good. Such rethinking could prompt them to reprioritize or at least question their own values hierarchies and entertain the possibility that personal morality and the public good might represent values that can be rearticulated in different ways without giving up either one. Such flexibility offers a range of premises that could be useful for evangelical Christian rhetors who seek to engage in deliberative exchange across differences of belief.

Translation

The third rhetorical strategy grounded in religious creativity that emerged from my case studies is translation. All three of my participants recognized at some point during our interviews that the evangelical discourse they employ in their religious enclaves (e.g., InterVarsity Christian Fellowship, Greenville Evangelical Church) might not work in non-Christian contexts such as their writing classrooms. Because of their desire to be perceived as legitimate among their peers at NESU, they thus recognized the need to speak in a manner that would communicate their beliefs to an audience who does not share them. In many ways, this recognition of the need to speak in accessible terms rests at the heart of evangelicalism itself. The goal of many evangelical Christians is, after all, to share their faith with others, an act that necessitates communicating effectively with people who don't espouse their beliefs. Certainly, there are examples of arhetorical evangelism that feature "Christianese" and fail to connect with nonbelievers. I think here of the street preachers who frequent my campus and rattle off Bible verses and platitudes in ways that simultaneously alienate and fascinate public university students but do not promote meaningful dialogue or foster intersubjectivity. Rather than perceiving the street preachers as legitimate parties to dialogue, public university students often see such evangelists as operating in a reference world radically different from own.[1]

Street preachers aside, American evangelicalism historically has sought to remain culturally relevant, which at the current moment means speaking in ways that resonate with a twenty-first century audience (Balmer; Bielo; Hunter; Magolda and Eben-Gross; Webber). As such, evangelicalism tends to emphasize the need for translation, which I define here as the strategic act of selecting, negotiating, or interpreting values in order to communicate ideas effectively outside of enclaves and with an audience that holds a substantively different worldview. Jürgen Habermas speaks to the need for such translation in his contribution to *The Power of Religion in the Public Sphere*. Continuing his about face from his early work that excluded religion from the public sphere, Habermas acknowledges and even calls for the influence of religious voices in public discourse. Echoing John Rawls, Habermas recognizes that the "liberal constitution itself must not ignore the contributions that religious groups can well make to the democratic process *within civil society*" (24, original emphasis). This is so, Habermas contends, because "as long as religious communities play a vital role in civil society and the public sphere, deliberative politics is as much a product of the public use of reason on the part of *religious* citizens as on that of *nonreligious* citizens" (24, original emphasis). Habermas goes so far as to say that "vital and nonfundamentalist religious communities can become a transformative force in the center of a democratic civil society—all the more so when frictions between religious and secular voices provoke inspiring controversies on normative issues and thereby stimulate an awareness of their relevance" (25). Thus there are preconditions: in Habermas's view, certain kinds of religious voices (e.g., nonfundamentalist) should be welcome in public discourse. Moreover, religious and nonreligious citizens must "recognize each other as equal members of the same democratic community" (24).

This last point resonates with many of the assumptions I noted above as foundational for deliberative rhetoric. It particularly resonates with Hauser's notion that intersubjectivity is a necessary precondition for effective public dialogue because it assumes a common reference world. Though Habermas does not speak of intersubjectivity, he recognizes the importance of sharing a common reference world. According to Habermas's "translation proviso," citizens "should be free to decide whether they want to use religious language in the public sphere" (25). If they choose to do so—and if they hope such perspectives "find their way onto the agendas of parliaments, courts, or administrative bodies and influence their decisions"—then Habermas maintains that citizens must translate the "truth contents of religious utterances ... into a generally accessible language" (25–26).[2] Otherwise, religious citizens might find what they say "fall[ing] on deaf ears" (Habermas 26). Speaking across differences of religious belief, whether publicly or privately, entails some degree of translation if the desired outcome is deliberative discourse or even the intersubjectivity that can lead to such discourse. Anyone who has ever attempted to engage in such translation, though, likely has firsthand experience with the problems posed by Habermas's translation proviso. Craig Calhoun notes that "not all that religious citizens have to say is 'translatable'" (128), Charles Taylor argues that translation ultimately leaves "something ... behind" (qtd. in Butler, et al. 116), and Stephen Carter goes so far as to say that such provisos are "undemocratic and unrealistic" (*God's Name* 55). Finding a way to speak from or about religious faith in a way that makes sense to nonreligious interlocutors amounts to a challenging and controversial task.

Habermas defends his proviso by highlighting his hope that translations would occur solely at the level of language and not of value or belief. And yet, as rhetoricians and compositionists have been arguing for decades, language is never value neutral but is epistemic (Anderson; Berlin) and even constitutive (Charland; Hauser, *Vernacular*). As Chris Anderson says so well, "if we change the *way* students write, change their language, we also change *what* they think, what it is possible for them to think" (15, original emphasis). Thus acts of translation can't be solely linguistic; they necessarily implicate values, beliefs, and assumptions. Despite these very real consequences, translation does hold creative potential. As Taylor puts it, "when these insights jump over these boundaries and inspire people, and then they find, maybe, another language for it ... very often the original spark is still burning there. [I]t is some kind of real creative, inspiring move, which I think can very often bring everybody farther ahead" (qtd. in Butler, et al. 116). Taylor thus underscores both the problem and the possibility of translation: while religious citizens might not be able to say everything they want to say in universally accessible terms, they can find ways to talk across difference without sacrificing the "original spark," what Stephen Carter might call "sacred truths" (*God's Name* 174).

The upshot of all this is that while religious citizens can bring their values and beliefs across boundaries into the public sphere, in doing so they often must make some effort to translate those values and beliefs into terms that can be understood. And while I certainly recognize the shortcomings of Habermas's translation proviso, it resonates with characteristics of deliberative rhetoric I discussed earlier. Roberts-Miller, for instance, recognizes that deliberative democracy demands that citizens to "try to present their own arguments in ways that people who are very different might understand" (197). For Roberts-Miller, there's a kind of translation that must take place in order for people to speak and be heard and understood outside of their enclaves. As she puts it later in her book, deliberative rhetoric requires that individuals make their "argument[s] understood in the words *others* use" (213, original emphasis). Similarly, Hauser reasons that for "discourse to be mutually intelligible and sensible as a conversation," interlocutors "must enter a partnership in which topic, language, and meanings are shared in some significant way" (*Vernacular* 66). He later adds that individuals "must acquire" a community's "*vernacular language* in order to share rhetorically salient meanings" (67, original emphasis).

Finally, while Steiner doesn't talk directly in terms of translation, he implies that something akin to it must take place. When he talks, for instance, about the difference between "proclamation" and "persuasion," he notes that the faithful witness model presupposes that "a concern with truth and with God's glory means a passion for *sharing* them" (308, original emphasis). Steiner recognizes this work as "difficult" because it entails communicating with people who hold a different mindset: "It is much easier to dwell among and interact exclusively with people who already share the same values and commitments" (308). Thus the hard work of communicating perspectives based on one's religious beliefs to people who don't share them requires a high level of "commitment" to achieving persuasion, which by definition necessitates some degree of tailoring one's message to the audience in question (308). Elsewhere in his article, Steiner refers to this work as a "rhetorical struggle" (304). The overarching point here is that engaging in deliberative rhetoric often entails acts of translation: to speak outside of one's religious or political enclaves and be heard, rhetors must find ways of speaking with audiences who don't share their beliefs.

Multiple examples emerge from my case studies that feature translation as a rhetorical strategy grounded in religious creativity. In Chapter 4, I discuss how Austin seeks to argue on behalf of Christian education for an audience that actively disavows the existence of the Christian god. Such a rhetorical situation prompts Austin to translate what would be a distinctly Christian argument into terms and values that might appeal to his non-Christian audience. Similarly, Eloise in Chapter 6 seeks to change the way she speaks in her first-year experience course: instead of proclaiming truth, a rhetorical stance that alienated her from her peers, she realizes she needs to speak in more personal terms about her faith. Austin's and Eloise's experiences demonstrate that translation represents a rhetorical struggle that can constitute the intersubjectivity necessary for deliberative discourse but can also give rise to questions of identity and commitment. Translating values changes a rhetor's relationship to those values.

Chapter Conclusion

These three processes, casuistic stretching, values articulation, and translation, are rhetorical strategies grounded in religious creativity that constitute methods by which millennial evangelical Christian students attempt to engage in deliberative conversation or establish the intersubjectivity that might allow for such discourse. And while each strategy poses its own set of risks—especially when engaged in unconsciously—their enactment within the writing of millennial evangelical first-year writing students highlights distinct possibilities for civic engagement. To echo Craig Calhoun, the presence of such strategies suggests that these students understand that "[c]onstructing a democratic life together" involves engaging in creative acts that "give shared form" to diverse citizens' lives (129). Through analysis of the writings of Austin, Kimberly, and Eloise and through discussion of my multiple interviews with each, I hope to show that millennial evangelical Christian students employ a form of creativity necessary for deliberative conversation, and that they can indeed contribute to a more civil discourse. I begin with Austin, whose experience underscores the difficult rhetorical work that comes with communicating deeply held beliefs outside of one's enclaves.

Notes

1. Hauser might say that the street preachers' manner of talking constitutes them as "object[s] of discussion" who are "interacted *about*," which differs from exchanges marked by intersubjectivity wherein interlocutors interact with each other and thus engage in "a dialogizing intersection" (Hauser, *Vernacular* 70, original emphasis).
2. It's important to point out that Habermas here isn't concerned so much with vernacular talk within publics as he is with the "formal deliberations of political bodies that yield to collectively binding decisions" (26). Habermas offers his translation proviso in regards to the latter, not the former. When it comes to everyday exchange, Habermas maintains that religious citizens should be able to speak in their religious language without having to translate. While the motives behind Habermas's distinction between official and everyday deliberations are good—he's making a good faith effort to honor what he calls the "polyphonic diversity of public voices" (26)—in reality his distinction might not amount to much. This is because, whether engaged in formal deliberations or not, religious citizens who want to constitute themselves as "equal members" of the same community must make an effort to demonstrate that they share a common reference world with their interlocutors (Habermas 24).

4 Effective Witness, Faithful Witness

Austin, Casuistic Stretching, and the Desire for Legitimacy[1]

> I walked out of class feeling very—almost down—because I didn't say anything. 'Cuz, well, one thing I was—I said I wasn't very offended. I was actually, like, I wanted to flip out, to be honest. But ... the way I was thinking, I was like, there's no way I can step out right now and be an effective witness if I am to act out aggressively. ... Like, I was—I get very defensive. Because, um, and I didn't want to do that. And I was praying, like, "God, if there is a chance that I can jump into this conversation, please, just give me the words to speak ..." It just, it never came. Or the opportunity came and I didn't see it.
>
> —Austin, on Chris's comment about religion

> It's been a real struggle the past week to write it. ... I thought about, why don't I just change this topic? It would be a lot easier. Like, this is really frustrating. But I felt God saying, "No, just keep plugging away at this." And I just couldn't, like—I was just like, "God, how—I just can't write this right now. Why did you tell me to write this? I don't know what to say."
>
> —Austin, on writing "Christian Schools vs. Public Schools"

Austin's sense of frustration in the two epigraphs above derive from a rhetorical challenge he faced, namely that of how to communicate his faith-based perspective to an audience that did not share his beliefs and even evidenced hostility toward them. In the first passage, which comes from our second interview, Austin recounts his initial response to the in-class exigency that eventually prompted the direction he took for his final assignment of the semester in his first-year writing (FYW) course. As Austin recalled it, that exigency involved a class discussion about "how religious schools have affected our society" and how students from such schools "are going out blind and they're not being taught the theory of evolution and things like that." During the course of that conversation, one of Austin's classmates voiced a disparaging comment about religion that Austin took personally. As Austin recalls it, his classmate "Chris" exclaimed, "Agh! There is no God! It's just fake!" As the first epigraph makes clear, Austin didn't respond initially, though he had much to say. Austin's fear, though, was that in the moment he would respond in an aggressive, defensive manner that would not reflect his desire to be what he calls an "effective witness."

The second epigraph centers on Austin's frustration writing one of the major assignments for his FYW course, a persuasive research essay that also functioned as a response to Chris. Austin chose to research and write an argument about the effectiveness of Christian schools, since he attended one in middle school. Austin takes the opportunity to do what he didn't do in class: respond to Chris in order to defend religious schools and his evangelical Christian faith in a manner that might foster intersubjectivity. As Austin discovers in the process of writing "Christian Schools vs. Public Schools," conveying a perspective that rests on values, beliefs, and assumptions not shared by one's audience poses a significant challenge, a rhetorical problem akin to what Mark Allan Steiner calls "the considerable burden of working to find and to build upon common ground in the face of significant and even profound moral differences" (310–11). To accomplish this, Austin attempts to translate an argument deeply grounded in his evangelical Christian faith into terms that might resonate with his audience's values while still reflecting his faith commitments.

Unlike many of the other white, male, evangelical Christian FYW students profiled in composition scholarship, Austin thus proves rather adept at thinking rhetorically. He devotes significant time and energy to considering the beliefs he assumes his audience will hold, and he goes to great lengths to accommodate his audience's values in his essay. Indeed, as I'll show in this chapter, Austin's goal in his writing has as much to do with making a case for the viability of religious education as it does with legitimizing himself and his evangelical Christianity within the human context of his FYW classroom. To achieve such legitimacy, Austin enacts key elements of Steiner's faithful witness model. Specifically, Austin enacts the kind of ethos Steiner advocates, both in terms of establishing trust and seeking common ground with an audience that holds views quite different from his own.

Austin's desire to achieve common ground is both problematized and made possible by his use of biblical citation in his essay. Citing the Bible helps Austin achieve common ground, because the passage he cites and the manner in which he cites it allows him to appeal to a value he believes his audience espouses, namely the freedom of choice. By appealing to a biblical text in terms of his audience's values, Austin works toward establishing a set of conditions that might allow for intersubjectivity between an evangelical Christian rhetor and non-Christian audience in a way that could make deliberative conversation possible. As the first epigraph suggests, such conditions did not appear to exist in his FYW course; part of Austin's rhetorical purpose, then, was to call those conditions into being (Hauser, *Vernacular*; Charland). At the same time, Austin's attempt to achieve common ground via biblical citation is risky, because his non-Christian audience could be alienated by the fact that Austin cites the

Bible at all. Moreover, because Austin is unaware of the extent to which he modifies his view of choice to accommodate his audience, his casuistic stretching could lead to demoralization rather than a greater appreciation of pluralism (Burke, *Attitudes* 229).

Accordingly, this chapter highlights how one millennial evangelical Christian FYW student attempts to do "the hard work" of communicating a faith-based perspective outside of his evangelical Christian enclaves (Steiner 311). Austin's experience provides insight into both the possibilities and consequences of speaking from a faith-based perspective in a FYW classroom at a public university in the Northeast. I proceed by first exploring Austin's faith and the context of his FYW course. I then discuss in more detail the exigency that ultimately prompted Austin to write his Christian schools essay. From there, I analyze Austin's writing, paying particular attention to his assumptions regarding how writing about his faith might allow him to communicate in ways that reflect his evangelical identity. The final third of the chapter explores Austin's casuistic stretching in depth and does so by underscoring its identity consequences and deliberative possibilities.

Austin's Faith

Like many evangelicals who grew up in church, Austin couldn't quite pinpoint the exact moment of his conversion. "It was a really gradual process," he told me in our first interview. "I knew there was a time … that I accepted Jesus. But to be honest, I really don't remember the exact time I did. It just kinda—happened." He also recalled that faith wasn't particularly important to him "until about fifth grade" when he began to have significant religious experiences: "This one night I was just praying and the presence of God was so there," Austin said. "That was a very defining moment in God saying, 'I'm real. I want to be with you. You're my child.'" Austin also pointed to a Christian summer camp he attended that impacted his faith: "I was so on fire for God coming out of that camp. I was like, 'We're going to church, right?' I was all pumped up about it." Austin's biblical literacy, a central component of his faith, also developed at an early age. As a child attending a Bible church in the South, Austin remembered owning a "little green Bible" that "had all these different Bible stories in it." In our first interview, he recalled reading one story in particular:

> One thing I vividly remember was they had the story of Jesus dying on the cross. They had Jesus hanging on the cross. One thing that I remember is Jesus turning to the guy next to him and saying, "Your …"—I can't remember the exact words—but it talks about how "Your faith has earned you a place in heaven," and the other guy's saying, "Oh, you're a fool." That just—I don't know why—but that just kinda always stuck out to me.

Though Austin admits he didn't completely understand the story at age eight, he took the opportunity in our interview to reflect on what it meant to him as a college student:

> I just see, like, the love Jesus had when he was dying for everyone. He was pleading for the forgiveness of the Roman soldiers who were persecuting him, just saying, "Father, forgive them. They don't know what they're doing." I look at that now and it's just so piercing. And just how, no matter what you do, Jesus is up there praying for you, saying, "God, please, just forgive these people. Save them." I feel Jesus gives that to us as Christians to be praying for those who don't know Him, and just knowing that if they aren't saved, they are going to the worst place imaginable. It breaks my heart. I don't want to see that happen to anybody.

After moving to the Northeast, Austin enrolled in a Christian middle school for grades five through eight. He described the school as nondenominational and named two particularly influential teachers, one of whom was Catholic, the other Protestant. Both were "phenomenal Christians," Austin told me, adding that when one "would have Bible time with us, he just—he just knew how to connect with us. He just knew what to do." Attending a Christian middle school for Austin served as "a defining moment of [his] walk with Christ." As he put it, "I became a Christian at that school" (first interview). That's not to say Austin's faith looked the same in college as it did in middle school. Indeed, Austin went through periods of what evangelical Christians often call backsliding, which basically entails growing less committed to one's faith over a period of time.

Such an experience corresponds with trends identified in the National Study of Youth and Religion (NSYR). Christian Smith and Patricia Snell, for instance, note that "the transition from the teenage to the emerging adult years reflects a great deal of religious continuity and stability, but also a significant amount of religious change, most of which works in the direction of religious decline" (212). For Austin, the decline occurred during his high school years when he was involved in sports and social life in such a way that his faith took a backseat. "I started to fall away from God," Austin said in our first interview. "I started to drink." However, after he knew he was going to attend Northeast State University (NESU) for college, he looked into InterVarsity Christian Fellowship (IVCF) and was invited to attend a pre-semester retreat, an event that affected him profoundly: "The whole summer I was very stagnant and then the week before I came here I went to Summit—a retreat with InterVarsity. Oh, my goodness. God was so present there. All of us were in the same place. I was very adamant on getting my relationship back with God." Thus Austin's experience involved both kinds of change noted by Smith and Snell—away from his faith during his high school years, and then dramatically back toward it upon arriving at NESU.

Several times over the course of our interviews, Austin noted the significance of attending that conference with IVCF. In our first interview, for instance, he said that "God gave" everyone who attended it "such missional hearts while we were there. Like, we just came back to campus just so on fire to go and just tell everyone on campus. Like, being bold about Jesus." Like many evangelicals, Austin senses a call from God to share his faith. As he put it, "God has really put on my heart, like, just wanting to reach campus and reach those around me." But the missional characteristic of his faith, which emphasizes connection and engagement with his community, influenced what he felt evangelism should entail (McLaren 115–25; Newbigin 222–33; Webber). He told me that he wanted to help "break down the stereotype of what people perceive to be Christianity," a stereotype that he describes in terms of "the crazy evangelical Christian" who comes across as "holier than thou" and seeks out any occasion to tell people they're "sinner(s)" who "need to have Jesus." His view of this type of evangelism is not positive: "Like, that's not gonna get people—that just puts people on a guilt trip." As such, it's a mode of evangelism that does more harm than good, primarily because it hinders what D. Michael Lindsay might call the cosmopolitan goal of legitimizing evangelical Christianity in public spheres (221).

Austin's model of evangelism, which he adopted from the IVCF conference, thus took a different approach: "You know, like, we need to look at how Jesus approached the woman at the well." While Austin mentioned some of the details of the biblical story about Jesus and the Samaritan woman in our first interview, here I explore them more fully in order to develop the point he sought to make. The story of the woman at the well was featured in a sermon Austin heard at the IVCF retreat and came to shape not only Austin's notion of evangelicalism, but also how he went about writing his Christian schools essay. The story, which is often cited as evidence for the radical nature of Jesus' message, appears in John's gospel and involves Jesus talking to a Samaritan woman drawing water from a well. According to the gospel writer, Jesus was on his way to Galilee from Judea and decided to go through Samaria. For an orthodox Jew like Jesus, traveling through Samaria was significant in and of itself because "bitter and widespread" hostility existed between the Jews and Samaritans (Morris 227). Nonetheless, Jesus stopped to rest around midday while his disciples entered a nearby town in search of food. A woman approaches the well where Jesus was resting to draw water. Jesus asks her for a drink and the Samaritan woman replies, "How is it that you, a Jew, ask a drink of me, a woman of Samaria?" (*HarperCollins Study Bible*, Jn 4.9a). The question is appropriate for the Samaritan woman to ask of a Jewish male because she knew there were "three strikes against" her: she was a woman from Samaria who, because she had been married five times, was also a "sexual sinner" (Morris 225). Jewish males weren't supposed to commune with anyone who fit one of those characteristics, much less someone who met all three. But

Jesus does talk with the Samaritan woman, and her life is changed. Her testimony then leads to a revival in Samaria.

This story is significant for Austin because it demonstrates how Jesus, in Austin's words, "broke down the stereotypes" between Jews and Samaritans. Such dismantling of traditional stereotypes—the traditional ways of doing things, including evangelism—becomes Austin's example for living in a university community where his faith was not widely held. Most pertinent to my purposes here, it comprises the example he follows when it comes to enacting vernacular religious creativity and communicating his beliefs for an audience he knows does not share them. Austin himself connects learning about this mode of evangelism with writing his Christian schools essay. The following excerpt comes from our fifth interview:

> [W]hat helped me write this paper was when I went to Summit with IV. I was in the evangelism track. And what I was really frustrated with at that point ... was like, "Why can't I just go and tell somebody about Jesus and they'll just be like, 'Okay, I'm on board'?" I've found it's not like that. Like, what Jesus did was he came down onto people's radars, into people's levels of understanding. It's kinda like when Jesus went to the woman at the well. Like, he really, he moved down onto her level. He spoke to her, like, not [as] this high and mighty rabbi. ... And that's what I was trying to do in an academic setting. I really wanted to portray my faith in an academic way but it didn't take away from—it's, like, I didn't wanna say like, "You read the Bible and you'll be okay." ... But I tried to portray my faith in an academic way, and that's difficult because I've never really done that before.

Because Austin longs to be heard in such a way that both he and his evangelical Christian faith can earn a degree of legitimacy with those who don't share it, he realizes that he must make his "argument understood in the words *others* use" (Roberts-Miller 213, original emphasis). He must find ways to communicate with his non-Christian peers by "mov[ing] down onto [their] level" and yet "not taking away from his faith"—that is to say, while remaining true to his convictions. As Austin discovers, translating his faith in such a manner is no easy task.

Austin's FYW Course

When I interviewed Austin in the Fall of 2008, he was a traditional first-semester student enrolled in NESU's required FYW course. Like many FYW courses, his class numbered about twenty students and was taught by a graduate teaching assistant. "Meghan" was a white female doctoral student in literature who had Catholic roots and who told me at one point during the semester that Austin was one of her favorite students. Indeed, the two of them seemed to get along well: Austin reported on numerous occasions during our interviews that he felt Meghan respected his beliefs. He also found her feedback encouraging and helpful. The mandatory conferences that Meghan held with each student ("at least once for each of the three major assignments," the syllabus stresses) seemed especially helpful for Austin. He noted in our fourth interview—the same interview wherein he talked at length about how stressed he was trying to finish his Christian schools essay—that he had just met with Meghan who gave him "all these really good ideas" about where to take his argument.

Meghan's course emphasized several standard practices from NESU's FYW program. The course syllabus indicates that in addition to conferencing regularly with her students, Meghan required weekly reading responses, structured each assignment such that students would write "at least two drafts," offered students the option of revising graded assignments, used textbooks recommended by the program, and required students to complete three major assignments: "a critical analysis with an annotated bibliography, a researched persuasive essay, and a personal narrative." One difference between Meghan's approach and that of other instructors was that, as the order of the previous list suggests, Meghan assigned the personal narrative last. Thus the assignment that tended to be the most challenging for many students—the persuasive essay I focus on in this chapter—occupied the middle of the course. Like many other instructors who had taught NESU's FYW course, Meghan encouraged students to choose their own topics. In our second interview, when Austin described the persuasive research assignment, he admitted that he initially could not "quite think of something that [he] would research and persuade someone on."

While much of Meghan's syllabus consists of standard material for a FYW course, including NESU's policy on plagiarism, the composition program's attendance policy, and information regarding the writing center and disability services, it also features elements that point to a civic undercurrent in the course. The course overview reads as follows:

> The ability to articulate ideas, communicate thoughts, and share concerns is vital to participation in communal, academic, and civic discussions. Whenever a person engages in such discussions, he or she *must* possess the skills of reading, writing, and thinking critically that enable him or her to share observations and ideas, voice questions and concerns, and articulate positions and arguments. In our class this semester, you will practice and hone these skills so that you are able to effectively communicate your ideas to a variety of audiences. (original emphasis)

Later in the syllabus, Meghan includes a statement on "Respect and Courtesy" that seems aimed at helping students achieve such participation:

> One of our goals as a class is to become a community of writers. Discussions, debates, and group work require excellent communication

> and openness. Being respectful to others at all times will ensure meaningful and efficient interactions. This course gives us a unique opportunity to engage in an open and inter-disciplinary atmosphere—let's take advantage of it.

As I'll discuss, Austin's interactions in his FYW class certainly were meaningful, though it's questionable just how open the class atmosphere was for certain perspectives. Indeed, as I've already indicated, some of Austin's classmates were outspoken about the fact that they held no religious beliefs and seemed to assume such beliefs were worthy of ridicule. Of primary importance for Austin was Chris, who made the comment in class that God and religion amounted to a joke. Austin also mentioned another male student, "Ian," who was similarly outspoken. The following exchange comes from our first interview; Austin was talking about what it was like to be a Christian at NESU:

Austin: And being in a place where God is so—like, people laugh at God here. It's like, it's, um, being in a place like this, it almost strengthens my faith to show people, like, you may laugh, but you're laughing at something that should—you shouldn't be laughing at.

Jeff: I mean, have you—have you really heard that?

Austin: Well, it's, um, like, there's definitely people who are just like—there's a kid in my English class who's very opinionated and ..., like, spoke about religion one day.

Jeff: Do you remember what he said?

Austin: He was just like, "Oh, I've never been to church in my life and I'm never going to. I don't need it." And it's like that. It's like, oh—he's just very opinionated on the statement. And, it was in the middle of class so I wasn't about to be like, "Well!"

Despite the presence of students like Ian and Chris, not everyone in Austin's FYW course held an agenda against religion. In our second interview, when we were first beginning to talk about Chris's comment that God doesn't exist, Austin noted that he knew of one other student in the class who identified as Christian: "We've gotten together and played some worship songs together," Austin said. "He's on his worship team back home."

To an extent, Meghan seemed to share Austin's frustration with Chris's and Ian's outspokenness. In our fourth interview, after Austin had conferenced with Meghan about his "Christian Schools vs. Public Schools" essay, Austin said, "'Cuz it's, 'cuz there are a lot of kids in my class, who—like, I told you Ian, and I actually mentioned Ian with [Meghan] upstairs and she's like, 'Oh, yeah.'" While it's difficult to capture Austin's tone in writing, the audio recording makes it clear that he's trying to convey Meghan's exasperation with Ian. One gets the sense listening to Austin that Meghan would have rolled her eyes when saying "Oh, yeah." That's not to say that Meghan dismisses outspoken students like Chris or Ian, but this exchange underscores the fact that Austin perceived Meghan to be supportive of his position—and, ultimately, of his attempts to craft an argument that would respond civilly to their positions.

Exigency and Effective Witness

Because my interviews with Austin started in early October and ran through the end of the semester, they largely coincided with Austin's writing of the persuasive research assignment. I first became aware of the exigency that prompted Austin's writing of "Christian Schools vs. Public Schools" in the letter he wrote for our second interview. The prompt invited Austin to describe his experience as an evangelical Christian in his FYW course. Austin decided to write to Chris, the same student who had voiced the disparaging comment about religion. He opens the letter as follows:

> In class the other day I remember we were talking about possible topics for our next paper and the idea of religious schools came up. You went on to say how you thought everything was just a big joke and there was no God. I'm not offended by your comment but would like to tell you about how being Christian affects my class work. When I'm given an assignment or have discussions in class, the morals and values I hold to be true do not waver because it is schoolwork. If anything I bring my faith into every situation I am in. My relationship with God is something I can never be separated from, no matter the circumstance.

When I asked Austin in our interview if he had said any of this in class, he responded by saying, "I didn't." The rest of his response comprises the first epigraph above, but I include it again here for sake of reference:

> I walked out of class feeling very—almost down—because I didn't say anything. 'Cuz, well, one thing I was—I said I wasn't very offended there. I was actually, like, I wanted to flip out, like, to be honest. But—'cuz I just, like—but the way I was thinking, I was like, there's no way I can step out right now and be an effective witness if I am to act out aggressively right now. … I get very defensive. Because, um, and I didn't want to do that. And I was praying, like, "God, if there is a chance that I can jump into this conversation, please, just give me the words to speak, and …" It just, it never came. Or the opportunity came and I didn't see it.

I discuss Austin's letter to Chris more fully below. For now, though, it's worth noting the extent to which the tone of the letter differs from the way Austin wanted to respond in the moment. Lines like, "I'm not offended by your comment but would like to tell you about how being Christian affects my class work" are a far cry from the defensiveness and desire to "flip out" Austin sensed in the moment.

As his response indicates, part of the reason why Austin remained silent in class has to do with the fact that he feared he might not come across as an "effective witness." For Austin, "act[ing] out aggressively" and speaking in a defensive manner could undercut his ability to achieve his sense of mission as an evangelical Christian. In our fourth interview, for instance, Austin explained that God "wants us to be effective witnesses. He wants us to be effective Christians. He wants us to go out and bring people to him. He's like, 'These are my children and they're lost. I'm giving you this mission to go and help these people.'" As I discussed previously, though, being an effective witness entails a certain type of evangelism, one wherein Christians, modeling themselves after Jesus' meeting with the Samaritan woman at the well, attempt to speak across difference in a manner that's accessible. Again, part of Austin's goal as an evangelical Christian involves breaking down stereotypes: "Like, there's so many stereotypes built up about Christians," he said in our first interview. "Like, the guy who stands on the corner on a soap box saying, 'The world's gonna end in so many years! You need to have Jesus!' Like, that's not gonna get people to be Christians" (see also Cope and Ringer 110). If Austin spoke out aggressively and defensively when responding to Chris, he fears he would have enacted such a stereotype in ways that would have prevented him from gaining a hearing. Not unlike the street preachers I mentioned in Chapter 3, Austin might have hindered the possibility of establishing intersubjectivity.

In a number of ways, Austin's invocation of "effective witness" resonates with Steiner's faithful witness model of evangelical Christian civic engagement. Steiner argues that the faithful witness model "reflects Christ's approach to public and cultural engagement" and functions as "an inventional resource for speaking and living conviction in a pluralistic and even hostile cultural context" (294). Acting as faithful witnesses would allow evangelical Christians to "engage in civic discourse that is true to the values of their own faith traditions" while "increas[ing] the likelihood that their ideas and values will earn a greater hearing" (295). Austin clearly perceives his FYW context as one that was "pluralistic and even hostile" toward his beliefs; he also evidences a desire to "earn a greater hearing" with his classmates, a desire underscored by his recognition that responding aggressively would impede his ability to be an effective witness. Austin thus senses that speaking out in anger would threaten his ability to be heard and contribute to healthy discourse. To an extent, Austin implicitly identifies with a core value Steiner attributes to faithful witnesses, namely the Christian recognition of human fallenness, the belief that humans are imperfect and thus in need of redemption. Austin's awareness that he can "get very defensive" taps into this sense of fallenness. It also seemed to prompt in Austin the kind of "profound and sober self-questioning of one's own assumptions and motives" that Steiner identifies as central to the enactment of faithful witness (297).

Indeed, Austin's process of responding to Chris—a process that consisted of writing his "Christian Schools vs. Public Schools" essay—seemed to involve a significant degree of "self-reflection" (Steiner 297; see also Kirsch; Ringer, "Dogma").

Before moving on to discuss Austin's essay itself, it's worth lingering on the letter he wrote to Chris for our second interview. The prompt asked Austin to describe what it's like to be a Christian in his FYW course, and to do so in a letter written to someone in his class. Austin's letter thus bears many of the characteristics of what Roberts-Miller would call expressive discourse (12–13). At the same time, Austin's letter also functions as an attempt to achieve intersubjectivity. Austin expresses himself in such a way as to achieve mutual recognition of a shared reference world with Chris, a necessary condition for deliberative conversation to take place. Since I quoted only a portion of it above, I include the letter in its entirety here, with surface errors emended for ease of reading:

> Dear Chris,
>
> In class the other day I remember we were talking about possible topics for our next paper and the idea of religious schools came up. You went on to say how you thought everything was just a big joke and there was no God. I'm not offended by your comment but would like to tell you about how being Christian affects my class work. When I'm given an assignment or have discussions in class, the morals and values I hold to be true do not waver because it is schoolwork. If anything I bring my faith into every situation I am in. My relationship with God is something I can never be separated from, no matter the circumstance.
>
> Since I have been at school, there have been a lot of things that have challenged me in my faith. Not necessarily school-related but things outside of class. Since I am in the process of becoming a brother in [a fraternity at NESU], I have been faced with things that directly oppose my faith. On bids night, I left my brothers because there was a stripper who was going be there. It was a difficult decision for me because I wanted to hang out with my new brothers but I couldn't go against what I knew was right.
>
> When I look at how my faith has made my life better or worse, I can't see myself moving without God. I honestly feel paralyzed. There are times like when I left my brothers that I felt very challenged in my faith but if anything that strengthened me in my walk with God.
>
> In my everyday life, apart from school, my faith is what guides me in every aspect of my life. My God is who wakes me up in the morning and gives me the strength to go out and do his will everyday. I pray that God will give me the words to speak and he does, whether I know what I'm saying is working or not. In the Bible it also gives us the way on how to talk to other people. The most important being, Treat

> others in the way you would like to be treated. Also the rules that God has given us, like not having sex before marriage, show us that there are things like sex jokes that should not be said.
>
> I don't know if anything I've said has changed your idea on whether God exists or not but I hope that this has shown you how my faith affects my life. If you have any questions I'd be more than happy to sit down and talk with you. Let me know.
>
> —Austin

I should note at the outset here that a number of points Austin makes would likely strike a non-Christian audience like Chris as odd or confusing—the idea, for instance, that Austin "can't see [himself] moving without God" or that "God is who wakes [him] up in the morning." Moreover, a reader such as Chris might be alienated by the sentence, "Also the rules that God has given us, like not having sex before marriage, show us that there are things like sex jokes that should not be said." The emphasis on "rules" here, coupled with the inclusive pronoun "us," may send the signal to Chris that he should be following these rules, and that if he isn't, he's a rule-breaker and thus potentially illegitimate in Austin's (not to mention God's) eyes. And those are significant concerns. It's worth pointing out, though, that Austin's goal is not to sidestep or ignore his faith but rather to communicate it to Chris. Austin wants to be perceived as legitimate in Chris's eyes, but he also wants to be known as an evangelical Christian. In Stephen Carter's terms, Austin is attempting to reveal rather than conceal some of the "sacred truths" that inform his faith (*God's Name* 174).

It's also worth recognizing how different this letter sounds from Austin's initial reaction. Instead of sounding caustic or defensive—qualities that the tone of Chris's comment certainly could have evoked—Austin comes across as someone who is reasonable, thoughtful, level-headed. Toward that end, he's not so much defending Christian schools as he is attempting to inform his audience about how his faith shapes his everyday life. The assumption underlying his letter seems to be something like this: If I can reason with my audience about the importance of faith, maybe I can position him as someone who sees faith-based identities as legitimate. In other words, Austin seems more interested in establishing the conditions necessary for deliberative exchange than he is in actually engaging in that exchange. That's not to say he doesn't want to discuss public versus religious education—as I'll argue, the essay he writes attests to the fact that he does. But in this particular instance, he's attempting to act like the effective witness he knew he wouldn't be able to pull off in the moments following Chris's in-class comment.

Moreover, Austin's construction of ethos in this letter resonates with Steiner's recommendations regarding how evangelical Christians should respect ethos when engaging in public discourse. For Steiner, respecting ethos leads to trust, the development of which "is an obligation shared by all participants in public discourse and public life" (310). As such, respecting ethos "entails the considerable burden of earning the right to be heard by others who see things differently" (310). By constructing his ethos as someone who is reasonable, thoughtful, and committed to his faith, Austin attempts to earn "the right to be heard" by Chris, who certainly "sees things differently" from Austin. There's less evidence here that Austin is fulfilling Steiner's point that respect for ethos entails finding "common ground in the face of significant and even profound moral differences" (311). And yet Austin does not seem to fall into what Steiner might call the trap of "being right" (311). Rather, his letter evidences Steiner's contention that "public argument and public persuasion" occurs "within and between *human beings*" (311, original emphasis). Toward that end, Austin not only cites the Golden Rule—in his words, "Treat others in the way you would like to be treated"—but also attempts to enact it discursively through the tone of his letter.

To be sure, Austin alone cannot achieve intersubjectivity—Chris would have to be part of that process in order for such conditions to arise (Booth, *Rhetoric* 47). But the tone of the letter, along with Austin's expressed desire at the end to "sit down and talk with" Chris, evidences a rhetor who attempts to fulfill his end of the bargain in terms of constituting intersubjectivity. Austin seems to recognize that if he and Chris are to share a common reference world, then he has to invite Chris into his world. And while I don't know if Austin ever actually gave his letter to Chris in an effort to dialogue with him, my hunch is to assume that Austin's letter is sincere, especially since the type of writing he produces in his letter to Chris aligns with the essay he ultimately writes about Christian schools. Indeed, Austin uses his persuasive research essay assignment to respond to Chris in a manner appropriate for his audience yet reflective of his evangelical identity. In "Christian Schools vs. Public Schools," Austin attempts to translate his faith for an audience that does not share his beliefs in order to constitute the intersubjectivity necessary for deliberative conversation.

Speaking Loudly, But Not Too Loudly

Prior to writing "Christian Schools," Austin began coming to terms with the extent to which he would have to balance competing interests: his faith commitments on the one hand and his audience's dismissal of them on the other. He said the following in our third interview:

> 'Cuz the essay I'm going to write now, I know it's gonna, like, speak loudly. Because it's about, like, faith. It's about religion. And a lot of people—like, especially in my class, I told you there are a couple of people in my class that are just like, they're just like, "It's not real." … And I don't want them to think I am this hardcore, like, evangelist standing on the street corners going, "The end of the world's coming!

> You need Jesus! The devil's gonna getcha!" Like, I don't wanna do that. I want something that's—they're gonna be able to relate to, and they're gonna be able to see and say, "Oh, now I see, like, why Christian schools ... actually are good."

Given the makeup of his audience—non-Christian peers, some of whom evidenced hostility toward his beliefs—and his desire to write something "they're gonna be able to relate to," the challenge Austin faces is akin to threading a needle. Even though he wants his essay to be about faith and religion, he wants to write in a way that won't alienate them but will rather foster intersubjectivity. He wants to speak loudly, but not too loudly.

Austin's concern for ethos along the lines of Steiner's faithful witness model is accompanied by the recognition that he would have to translate his beliefs into terms that his differently-minded audience would understand. As I discussed earlier, those beliefs are thoroughly evangelical. Two brief examples, however, demonstrate what those beliefs look like in writing. Prior to our first interview, Austin wrote a poem he was eager to share with me. It's called "Break the Silence," and Austin wrote it purely for devotional purposes. It begins as follows:

> I'm dying to stand in this silence
> And proclaim the love that is [flowing] through me
> My heart beats for You
> Lord shine Your light so all can see
> That You are the Alpha and Omega
> The beginning and the end

Later Austin observes, "Lord You're the only one that can save them / For it was your love that saved me from death." He then goes on to insert himself in the Christian narrative of guilt and redemption. "I was the leader," Austin writes:

> I was the one you looked at and said be gone Satan
> And you still died for me
> I was the one that denied You
> I was the one that betrayed You
> Yet you still hung from that cross
> Pleading for me

He concludes with a prayer that highlights his evangelicalism: "Abba, my Father, forever use my voice for those around me / Let it ring with the beauty of Your love." In writing from the "I," placing himself within Christ's passion story, and praying that his voice would "ring with the beauty of [God's] love," Austin clearly "liv[es] inside the Bible" (Shannon Carter 576).

Austin shared this poem with me because he felt it expressed his true self. It represents the kind of writing he feels flows out of him spontaneously, demonstrates his "true colors," and doesn't need to be forced. A second example—the personal essay he wrote for the final assignment of his FYW course—enacts a similar subjectivity. In it, he narrates the moment he told his coach that he would be leaving the crew team to focus more on his studies and relationship with Christ. The essay is remarkable in that Austin frequently interjects brief prayers rendered in italics. Here, for instance, is the moment right before Austin talks to his coach:

> I stood over my erg knowing it would be the last time and smiled at how I had conquered my final workout in first place. The team dispersed slowly from the practice room as I racked my mind for words to say to my coach. *Lord Jesus, I ask you for words. I am ready to fulfill Your will. Give me strength. Amen.* My stomach turned as I walked up to my coach. Our eyes locked and I said, "Hey Coach, can I talk to you for a minute?"

Austin then tells his coach he needs to leave the team. When his coach asks why, Austin replies, "God is calling away crew right now." The narrative ends on a sense of relief—and on another prayer:

> It felt as if a weight had been lifted off my shoulders and a peace filled my heart. I ... stuck my hands in my pockets for the long walk back to my dorm, watching the sunrise. *Thank you Father God for giving [me] the courage and strength [to] fulfill your plan for me. I know leaving crew is what you planned for me. I put my faith and trust in you and walk blindly in your shadow, led only by your mercy. Amen.*

Both the poem Austin wrote and his personal essay "speak loudly" about his faith, which is clearly grounded in the assumption that God, in the person of Jesus Christ, is close at hand and intimately interested in the daily affairs of his followers.

Austin anticipated that writing "Christian Schools vs. Public Schools" would parallel his devotional or personal writing. When Austin told me in our third interview that he was going to pursue writing "Christian Schools" for his FYW course, he said, "this will be the first paper that I've ever written that's really gonna show, like, what I think and what I believe." Indeed, Austin seemed to believe that because he'd be writing about "God and Jesus" via an argument in favor of Christian schools, he'd be able to tap into his evangelical identity and show his "real self" in his academic writing. To an extent, he does. But the problem he faces as he begins writing is that of how to render his faith in ways that would earn him a "serious hearing with diverse audiences" (DePalma 237). Early in his drafting process, for instance, Austin confessed that the writing had been "a lot different" from what he anticipated: "I thought it would be kinda like what I had written on my own, like, the poems that I had written. ... Trying to write this has been much more difficult than I thought" (fourth interview). And at the end of our fourth interview, which took place a few days before the assignment was due, Austin highlighted the conflict he sensed: "I almost feel everything I said in that last interview I've totally contradicted with this right now. I said, 'Oh, yes I think it'll be easy, really good to write about this paper.' And now I'm here saying, 'It's so hard! I can barely write this!'"

Austin's difficulties with invention—in his words, "finding coherent points to say why Christian schools are better" than public schools—stemmed from the dilemma that lay at the heart of communicating religious beliefs across difference, a dilemma that pits Austin's evangelical identity and motives against the needs and expectations of his audience. Austin put it this way:

> It's really hard because right now I feel like the things I'm saying in my paper are really watered down, and I don't want to do that. ... I want to put, like, me in this paper .... I want you guys to see, like, the love of Christ in me. I really, I love Christian schools because they teach this, but because you don't believe it, it's really hard to get that across to people. You know? [T]hat's just the hardest part about it, is writing it for non-Christians. I was telling this to Meghan, saying, I want, I could go into really deep spiritual, theological things here, but I feel that that would really detract from my argument. Because ... people would automatically say, "That's not true." (fourth interview)

One senses the frustration Austin experienced in communicating with an audience that does not share his beliefs and values. And, in many ways, his frustration illustrates Charles Taylor's concern that translation can never be complete because inevitably "something is left behind" (qtd. in Butler, et al. 116). Austin acutely senses the reality that he might be leaving something behind. Indeed, much of his frustration stems from the tension between his desire to convey "the love of Christ in me" and his fear that "go[ing] into really deep spiritual, theological things" might hinder his ability to achieve intersubjectivity with his audience. What is available to him given the circumstances is an argument that he senses is "watered down." Analysis of his essay suggests that most of his arguments center on concerns his audience might care about, such as economics and quality of education. Largely absent are any arguments that tap deeply into Austin's evangelical Christian faith.

"Christian Schools vs. Public Schools"

From the outset of "Christian Schools vs. Public Schools," it's apparent that Austin has carefully considered his audience's perspectives. Much like in his letter to Chris, Austin adopts an informative tone: "Throughout the history of the United States, Christianity in schools has been a significant part of its culture. However, during the past century, it has dwindled from the public school system." He goes on to say that "privately run Christian schools" were developed in response to the diminishing influence of Christianity in public education. By the end of his first paragraph, Austin offers his thesis: "Many argue that attending a Christian school takes away from an education, but because they are private learning [institutions], they are able to provide a stronger education while also teaching morals that students are able to apply to their lives outside of the classroom." Austin's objective voice, inclusion of a thesis statement, and use of subordination and third person all signal that he's enacting academic discourse (Ivanič).

Austin mostly maintains this objective stance throughout his essay. He assiduously avoids the use of "I," and the personal experience he does incorporate comes by way of interviews he conducted with peers who had attended Christian schools. There are moments, however, when his language belies his evangelical identity. Such "Christianese" emerges as early as the second paragraph where Austin notes that homeroom at a Christian school usually includes a time of prayer where students "lift up their days to God." And prior to meals or athletic events, "teachers and students ask for God's blessing on the food" while "coaches and teams pray for God to strengthen them and for Him to receive the glory whether they win or lose." Though Austin is reporting on one of the key differences between Christian and public schools, the fact that he does not attribute this language to another source or convey it using scare quotes suggests that he identifies with it (Ivanič 190, 232).

Austin's keen attention to audience continues throughout his essay. The first argument he selects, for instance, is largely economic: Christian schools are private, have good student-to-teacher ratios, and thus prepare students for college better than public schools. Austin believes that, because his audience values academic success, they will fear that religious "brainwashing" might hinder it. If Austin can convince his readers that Christian schools help students succeed, perhaps they will be more likely to accept the faith-based perspective promoted by such schools. This argument thus bears the stamp of Austin's desire for legitimacy. By emphasizing concerns such as success and education, he's attempting to communicate the idea that, at least in his audience's eyes, there's something "normal" and "acceptable" about Christian education (Lindsay 221). Austin hopes to establish that he and his non-Christian audience share a common reference world, despite differences of religious faith.

Austin's consideration of his audience also emerges in his decision to raise and respond to criticisms that have been leveled against Christian schools. One criticism he tackles is that Christian schools fail to teach alternative perspectives. Austin writes, "Many people think that Christian schools shelter their students from outside perspectives such as the theory of evolution, the Big Bang theory, alternate religions, and secular views on Christian principles." In response, Austin argues that Christian schools do teach competing views. To support his argument, Austin cites a fellow student who had attended a Christian high school before matriculating to NESU. Austin explains "that she was not only taught alternate theories to creation, but also exposed to the philosophy of other world religions." He then goes on to add an important clarification: "Although these topics were not taught as truth, it still gave students an opportunity to understand different worldviews, thus providing the student with a well rounded education."

A few points are worth noting here, not the least of which is the fact that Austin again devotes a significant amount of time to thinking through his audience's concerns. Much of the structure of his essay follows this pattern of raising his audience's concerns and attempting to respond to them. While his response in this instance entails disagreement, the tone of the disagreement is civil rather than defensive or caustic. Through that tone, Austin evidences respect for his audience and constructs an ethos that aligns with Steiner's faithful witness model. Moreover, through his approach he attempts to construct himself and the evangelical Christianity he represents as legitimate within the context of his FYW course. As an evangelical Christian, though, he also senses the need to be true to his convictions. Toward that end, the subordinate clause "Although these topics were not taught as truth" functions to remind Austin and his audience that he espouses a worldview that locates the Christian God at the center of truth. Austin does want to accommodate his audience's values, but he doesn't want to undercut his own. Thus the subordinate structure he adopts allows him to reiterate his Christian perspective and emphasize the point that he wants his non-Christian audience to come away with, namely that Christian schools provide students "with a well rounded education" by helping them "understand different worldviews." The values hierarchy he constructs in his subordinate clause is aimed at accommodating his audience and maintaining his faith.

To be sure, many readers would not share his claim to Christianity as absolute truth. But what's worth stressing here is Austin's impetus to connect with an audience that espouses a different set of beliefs while communicating the perspective he holds. What's impressive throughout Austin's essay is his attempt—and, at times, his struggle—to balance these twin goals, goals that, as I discussed in Chapter 3, in large part comprise the tension that rests at the heart of deliberative discourse. Austin seems to have some sense of what Roberts-Miller calls the "high demands" that deliberative democracy makes of citizens: he "care[s] enough about [his] own views to try to persuade others of them," but he's also attempting to address his interlocutor "with empathy, attentiveness, and trust" while "tak[ing] the time to invent … ideas in the light of informed disagreement" (187).

Indeed, Austin even goes so far at one point as to acknowledge the drawbacks of attending a Christian school—not with the aim of refuting such criticism, but rather to concede the point. He writes, "Although there are many positive aspects in attending a Christian school, … inadequate social training is a drawback that many students are faced with when entering a secular social environment." He goes on to name specific concerns related to alcohol and sexuality, noting in relation to the latter that because "many Christian schools neglect teaching sexual education," students who attended Christian schools are "at a disadvantage when entering a secular social setting." Austin's response is to offer a policy argument regarding how Christian schools could do better: "To resolve this deficiency," he writes, "Christian schools need to incorporate secular topics into their curriculum in order to adequately educate their students for the conflicting ideas [they will encounter] when they will leave a Christian environment."

To be sure, Austin includes here a number of questionable assumptions, not the least of which is an overly simplistic binary between "secular topics" on the one hand and Christian education on the other. Again, though, what's impressive about this passage is the extent to which Austin is attempting to construct an ethos that would earn him the right to be heard by an audience that holds a fundamentally different viewpoint regarding religious education. Austin's ability to recognize the shortcomings of Christian schools constitutes a point of common ground between his vernacular perspective as a millennial evangelical Christian attending a public university and the decidedly non-religious perspective of his audience. Even if his readers don't feel strongly about sex-ed being taught in schools, whether religious or secular, there's a possibility that they can appreciate and respect his ability to point out a legitimate flaw in the type of education he promotes.

What Austin still feels is missing in his argument, though, is an element that would more fully satisfy his desire to emphasize his faith as part of his identity. Even though he's able to accommodate his audience's perspective, he doesn't feel as if he has communicated his own evangelical Christian beliefs as fully as he could. He still feels his argument is "watered down," a reality that threatens the possibility of achieving genuine intersubjectivity. That's because for intersubjectivity to exist, it has to involve not just Austin understanding his audience, but his audience understanding Austin—which necessitates that they understand key aspects of his faith. So Austin decides to cite the Bible in his essay, a risky move that offers deliberative possibilities but can also lead to identity consequences.

Joshua 24.15 and the Freedom of Choice

Austin spoke on several occasions about his desire to cite the Bible, which he felt "would bring a lot of weight to [his] paper. Because it's saying, like, this is what's in the Bible, and this is what Christian schools are doing" (fourth interview). Austin believes that citing the Bible would strengthen his paper not because it is appropriate for his audience, but because it encompasses much of the authority of the evangelical Christian tradition to which he belongs. As he put it in our second interview, "What I believe is that the

Bible is God-inspired, even though it's gone through hundreds of translations, God has facilitated all of that. God would not let his word be altered." This statement clearly indicates that Austin holds a view of the Bible that corresponds with biblicism and thus with David Bebbington's definition of evangelicalism (3; Cope and Ringer 107). Because of the Bible's importance to American evangelical Christianity in general and Austin's own faith in particular, citing the Bible would help assuage his fear that he's watering down his argument. The act of biblical citation also aligns with Habermas's belief that "all citizens should be free to decide whether they want to use religious language in the public sphere" (25)—or in the context of a FYW classroom at a public university in the Northeast.

Austin does decide to do so, and the results of his decision illustrate Judith Butler's contention that "translation is a very complex … process" (Butler, et al. 112). Indeed, even though Austin does include religious language in the form of biblical citation in his argument, the underlying assumption to which Austin appeals aligns more closely with his audience's pluralism than with his own evangelicalism. As such, while Habermas holds out hope that translation would "allow [interlocutors] to arrive at reasons that are more general than the ones in the original [religious] language" (Butler, et al. 114), the process for Austin involves more reshaping, adapting, and stretching of values than mere arrival at reasons. In Elizabeth Vander Lei's words, Austin's citation underscores his "patched-together nature, a hybridity that results from [his] membership in both religious and academic communities" ("'Where'" 78).

The verse Austin cites comes from the Old Testament book of Joshua and appears late in his paper. Austin writes,

> In the Bible, it states that it is in your own free will that you choose to believe or not believe in God's Word. In the book of Joshua in the Old Testament of the Bible, Joshua, one of the leaders of the Israelites at around 1200 BC, states, "But if serving the LORD seems undesirable to you, then choose for yourselves this day whom you will serve" (*The Holy Bible*, Josh. 24.15). As said in the Bible, God does not force people into believing in what He says. Since Christian schools are based upon the Bible they should follow the same criteria and not force these ideas on their students.

Note Austin's attention to audience. The manner in which he introduces Joshua 24.15 suggests that he understands his readers may not know that Joshua appears in the Old Testament, or even that the Old Testament is part of the Bible. Interestingly, Austin's language parallels that of the Advanced Placement test that Janice Neulieb discusses in "'Spilt Religion': Student Motivation and Values-Based Writing." According to Neulieb, that prompt begins as follows: "The first chapter of *Ecclesiastes*, a book of the Bible, concludes with these words …" (41, original emphasis). Like the AP test writers,

Austin aims to inform, perhaps even to teach. Moreover, he's attempting through such audience-focused discourse to constitute a social reality that includes himself and his interlocutors as legitimate parties to debate. While he's certainly taking a single verse out of context, the rhetoricality of his citation suggests that it amounts to much more than proof-texting.

His audience awareness is evidenced also by the principle he extracts from the verse, namely free will. The assumption underlying Austin's argument in this paragraph is that people ought to be free to choose what they believe or that it is bad to force people to believe something. The value he promotes is one he suspects will have traction with Chris, Ian, and other non-Christian readers who suspect that Christian schools brainwash their students. And, to an extent, Austin also shares this belief. In our first interview, he noted that neither God nor his parents forced him to adopt Christianity, arguing instead that free will is God-given. In a later interview, Austin said, "God doesn't force us to believe. [I]t's almost naturally, when we're told to believe something, told to do something, we don't want to do it. But because my parents were very—they let me figure out my own faith. And I found Jesus on my own. Like, my parents were very encouraging." Austin attributes a similar kind of freedom of belief to his experience attending a Christian school, where faith "was never forced on us." Even in his Bible classes, "people weren't shoving down, like, 'Oh, you, if you're not a Christian, you're not good enough.'" But Austin's emphasis on freedom of choice is held in tension by another motive, namely the desire to see all of humanity come to know Jesus Christ as savior, a desire that stems from his belief that Christianity is universally true. Austin articulated his passion for evangelical activism in our first interview when he noted that Christians need "to be praying for those who don't know Him, and just knowing that if they aren't saved, they are going to the worst place imaginable"—a fate Austin doesn't "want to see … happen to anybody."

Austin's evangelical ideal was all the more important given his public university context. During our first interview, Austin reflected on the IVCF conference he had attended recently: "we just came back to campus just so on fire to go and just tell everyone on campus. Like, being bold about Jesus." In reference to the party atmosphere on campus, he also noted "how much" he believed his "campus needs Jesus." And in our third interview, Austin said, "I want to reach the people who don't know Christ. We can't give up. We can't stop, like, reaching to the lost. … Because that's what God calls us to do—make disciples of all nations." As a result, Austin's evangelical assumption is that people need to believe in Christ in order to be saved, or Christianity is the one right way—a different assumption from the one that undergirds his citation of Joshua 24.15. In either construction, individuals have options: they can choose to believe or not believe. The difference is that while the assumption underlying his citation of Joshua 24.15 offers options that are equally legitimate, the one that undergirds his evangelical identity marks one choice as right and all others wrong.

But given that Austin's audience does not share his belief that Christianity represents absolute truth, the question arises as to what extent Austin is appealing to a common value. Does Joshua 24.15 forward the same principle that Austin purports to draw on, and how does it match up to his evangelical belief that salvation comes solely through Christ? Joshua 24.15 is part of a larger story wherein Joshua convinces the tribes of Israel to abandon the many gods they had worshipped in Egypt and turn back to Yahweh alone. Joshua tells this by recounting significant moments when God aided the Israelites—leading Abraham to the land of Canaan, sending Moses and Aaron to deliver the Israelites from Egypt, helping them defeat various enemies, and so forth. Joshua speaks for God, preceding his narration with, "This is what the Lord, the God of Israel, says" (*The NIV Study Bible*, Josh. 24.2). The recitation of significant events is wrapped in quotation marks; the "I" that speaks is Yahweh speaking through Joshua.

The entirety of Joshua's declaration, much of which Austin omits, reads as follows:

> Now fear the Lord and serve him with all faithfulness. Throw away the gods your forefathers worshipped beyond the River and in Egypt, and serve the Lord. But if serving the Lord seems undesirable to you, then choose for yourselves this day whom you will serve, whether the gods your forefathers served beyond the River, or the gods of the Amorites, in whose land you are living. But as for me and my household, we will serve the Lord.
>
> (*The NIV Study Bible*, Josh. 24.14–15)

Joshua's command to follow the Lord and abandon other gods ends with his own family's declaration that they will serve Yahweh. As the Israelite leader who had just spoken for God, Joshua had significant ethos. Declaring that he and his family will serve Yahweh indicates he wasn't as much offering a choice as telling his audience that they should choose to serve God, an imperative reflected by Joshua's commands to "fear the Lord and serve him with all faithfulness" and "[t]hrow away" other gods. By speaking as Yahweh, Joshua stacks the deck against choosing not to believe. That Joshua wasn't actually offering a choice is underscored by the fact that Joshua's audience unanimously agreed to serve and obey Yahweh, a decision later sealed by a covenant (see Josh. 24.16–27).

As a result, there's a significant difference between the kind of choice that Joshua 24.15 offers—a choice that parallels Austin's belief in Christianity as universal truth—and the choice that Austin promotes for his non-Christian audience. In Burkean terms, Austin has casuistically stretched his original principle (that Christianity is true and that all people need to accept Christ to be saved) to accommodate his audience's values (people should be free to choose to believe what they will, and it's okay for people not to choose Christianity). Though his casuistic stretching may not quite represent what

Burke would call a "perversion of casuistry" (*Rhetoric* 154), the difference between "one should choose to serve God" and "one has the freedom to choose" is significant. It's as if Austin is admitting it's okay not to choose to serve God, that maybe such a position is as legitimate as his belief that people need to choose to serve God to escape damnation. In casuistically stretching Joshua 24.15, Austin stretches one of his core evangelical beliefs to encompass his audience's pluralistic perspective, and the higher abstraction that unites the opposites of "people should choose God" and "people don't have to choose God" seems to be that of the freedom of choice itself. Choice as an abstraction encompasses the decision to choose God as well as the decision not to choose God.

To be sure, Austin was beginning to confront the implications of pluralism prior to writing his Christian schools essay. Throughout our interviews, Austin hinted at the tension he sensed between his belief that Christianity is universal and his understanding that others, including his non-Christian audience, might reject such a claim. While talking about the process of writing "Christian Schools vs. Public Schools" in his fourth interview, for instance, Austin said, "[T]his is what I believe to be true, and what is true. And that's what I'm really struggling to do right now with my paper because I don't want to sound like ... those Bible-thumping Christians who turn people away from Christianity." The shift from "what I believe to be true" to "what is true" is significant. Evangelical theologian Lesslie Newbigin explains the significance of such a shift when he ventriloquizes a postmodern perspective with which he disagrees: "Opinions about how [reality] *ought* to function can only be personal opinions, and any assertion that the purpose for which human life exists has in fact been revealed by the One whose purpose it is, is treated as unacceptable dogmatism" (18, original emphasis). This perspective, Newbigin argues, "insists that truth claims about God and about the nature and destiny of humankind must be in the form 'This is true for me,' not in the form 'This is true'" (19). Austin's statement above suggests that he intuits this distinction: as soon as he makes a personal comment ("This is true for me"), he reframes it in universal terms ("This is true"). But appealing to such universality then leads him to the question of what he calls "force" in his Joshua 24.15 paragraph. He feared that if he made an argument about Christianity as absolute truth, he would sound like a Bible-thumper "who turn[s] people away from Christianity." He would, in other words, undermine his desire to be an effective witness.

Austin is thus caught in a bind, one that emerges in the way he sets up his casuistic stretching of Joshua 24.15. He begins the paragraph wherein he cites that verse as follows: "Whether or not Evolution or Creationism is taught in a Christian school, Creationism is always taught to be true and the Bible is the Word of God. Even though these things are regarded as truth, students are never forced to believe them. In the Bible, it states that it is in your own free will that you choose to believe or not believe in God's Word." The bind in which Austin finds himself involves a dialectic between truth on the one hand and coercion or force on the other. What Austin attempts to communicate here is his belief that the Bible is true. If something is regarded as true, it should be believed. Austin, though, must make space for the reality that his audience does not share his belief. After all, no one's forcing students to believe what Christian schools teach as truth. But if someone does not believe the truth, isn't that person wrong or misguided? Of course, Austin can't make such a claim, because he knows it will alienate his audience and likely delegitimize himself in their eyes. Thus he foregrounds choice—free will—in an attempt to "[take] up the slack" between his own belief in what counts as truth and his audience's divergent perspective (Burke, *Attitudes* 229).

To find this "happy medium," as Austin described it in our fourth interview, Austin cites Joshua 24.15 in such a way that he emphasizes the freedom of choice (one can choose one way or the other) over the fact that the verse commands readers to serve God because doing so amounts to believing and following truth. Austin, though, must drop the truth part of the equation because it gets him into thorny territory. He instead summarizes his point completely in terms of choice or non-coercion: "As said in the Bible, God does not force people into believing in what He says. Since Christian schools are based upon the Bible they should follow the same criteria and not force these ideas on their students." Thus while force and truth cluster together at the beginning of this paragraph, by the end truth disappears in favor of choice. Indeed, in a remarkable twist, Austin even goes so far as to base his policy argument ("Christian schools ... should ... not force these ideas on their students") on the Bible's authority. As such, Austin's desire not to force anyone to believe anything prompts him to make an argument that brings into question his assumptions about truth. The perspective he ultimately aligns himself with and promotes has more to do with honoring his audience's proclivity to reject Christianity than with his desire to promote it.

Austin's casuistic stretching of a biblical passage represents a messy, convoluted move, one that bears significant risk. At the same time, what's remarkable is the extent to which Austin goes to accommodate his audience. His casuistic stretching functions as a form of vernacular religious creativity in that Austin modifies his evangelical Christian belief in response to his human context, namely his classmates who don't espouse his evangelical Christian faith. But his casuistic stretching also functions rhetorically because it allows him to speak across difference in a way that reflects a version of his faith while simultaneously accommodating his audience's values. Austin thus enacts a form of evangelism similar to what he learned at the IVCF conference he attended: rather than alienating his readers by sounding like a Bible-thumper, he attempts to come "down onto people's radars, into people's levels of understanding" (first interview). And, in doing so, he's hoping to dismantle stereotypes that his non-Christian audience likely has of evangelical Christianity in general and of himself in particular. Austin hopes to legitimize himself in the eyes of an audience that holds a fundamentally different worldview from his own.

Possibilities of Casuistic Stretching

Austin's casuistic stretching has significant consequences, largely because he's unaware of the extent to which he has stretched a belief that rests at the center of his evangelical identity. I explore these consequences more fully below, but I want to linger for a moment on the possibilities that Austin's casuistic stretching affords him, particularly in terms of civic engagement. Casuistically stretching Joshua 24.15 helps Austin establish a shared social reality, one wherein he and his audience share a common reference world. This is a social reality that honors Austin's belief in the Bible and his audience's belief that being coerced or brainwashed into believing anything is bad. As such, Austin's casuistic stretching works toward a two-way sense of legitimacy between rhetor and audience. That is to say, Austin's movement toward legitimizing his audience's perspective invites his audience to move toward Austin's perspective. In this way, Austin's citation of Joshua 24.15 is rhetorically savvy. By inviting his readers to see the value of free will through a biblical lens, Austin offers them space to identify with a sacred text that encompasses much of the authority of Christian tradition and his own evangelicalism. From a rhetorical perspective, his approach to citing the Bible differs from other examples in composition scholarship, one example of which comes from Doug Hunt's *Misunderstanding the Assignment*. While Rob Campbell, a fundamentalist Christian student, adopted a "testimonial" approach that involved using "the text or the world to illustrate" the truth he already knows (Hunt 127), Austin gives careful thought to his audience, considering their values in relation to his own. Austin is certainly attempting to fulfill "the function of the composition classroom," which is, in Shannon Carter's words, "to enable [students] to speak to readers who do not ... 'live inside the Book'" (578).

Indeed, Austin's stretching of Joshua 24.15 and the principle of choice should give rhetorical educators hope, as it offers evidence that FYW students are capable of going to great lengths to speak across difference, not in spite of deeply held beliefs, but rather because of them. Following the example of Jesus's communication with the Samaritan woman, Austin engages in vernacular religious creativity in order to communicate his faith in order to constitute intersubjectivity. Concerning evangelical Christian students in particular, the possibility that faith might motivate rhetorical awareness is under-acknowledged in rhetoric and composition. Rob Campbell again serves as a counterpoint. In many ways, Rob is the archetypal fundamentalist student entrenched in dualism: "I had most of my views and beliefs intact before I came [to college]," Rob tells Hunt. "In fact [*he laughs*], I had them all intact" (10, original emphasis). Rob goes on to discuss his religious background—about being raised in church, about being influenced by his brother's faith, about his belief in creationism and the Bible as Truth (10–11). But Rob is not an ideal student: he misses long stretches of class and doesn't turn in assignments. What he does turn in reflects his dualism. Hunt explains that Rob interprets one assignment as follows: "Decide which of these two television families is good and which is bad. Give evidence for your view" (78). As a result, Rob turns in a draft "filled with short sentences delivered as self-evident truths" on which he does not fare well grade-wise (79). In Hunt's estimation, Rob "didn't come to the university to see the world from a perspective other than his own," an assessment that links Rob's dualism—and resistance—to his faith (104). And when Rob is confronted with relativism, he "retreats toward Dualism" (Hunt 103; see also Perry).

Though Austin certainly has dualistic tendencies—the title of his essay, "Christian Schools vs. Public Schools," suggests as much—he very much attempts "to see the world from a perspective other than his own" (Hunt 103). In Cornel West's words, Austin demonstrates that he's "open to different discourses" and "arguments" ("Prophetic" 98). And, far from retreating toward dualism, Austin goes to significant lengths to establish a set of conditions such that he and his audience could engage in deliberative conversation—to "sit down and talk," as Austin put it at the end of his letter to Chris. Again, what prompts Austin to proceed in such a manner is the model of evangelism he took away from the IVCF conference. Because he didn't want to be pigeonholed as a "crazy evangelical Christian," Austin sought to be an effective witness in his FYW classroom and in the writing he was asked to do for that course.

As rhetorical action grounded in vernacular religious creativity, casuistic stretching can function as a means by which individuals engage with a perspective other than their own in order to foster intersubjectivity. Such an encounter will invariably alter the rhetor's beliefs, likely in ways that indicates progress toward what William G. Perry calls commitment in relativism. Writing about dualistic students, Perry explains that encounters with pluralism in college can raise questions of whether or not absolute truth exists (68). Such encounters with "otherness" eventually lead to "transformations in [the] structure" of dualistic thought (71). These transformations are not ones in which students will immediately abandon dualism. Rather, Perry explains, dualism "is first modified and loosened by a series of accommodations necessitated by its assimilation of the pluralism of both peer group and curriculum" (61). These accommodations lead individuals to acknowledge what Perry calls the "potential of legitimacy in otherness," the view that there are legitimate perspectives other than one's own (64, 71). What facilitates such recognition of legitimacy is the fact that, as Perry and his researchers found, "students appear to bring with them the expectation of identification with the college community" (65). Of course, an expectation to identify with peers and the curriculum may not come to fruition—some students, upon encountering pluralism, will retreat toward dualism. But the very encounter with pluralism, coupled with the desire for identification, is what can shift students like Austin away from binaries of us versus them or good versus bad toward what Burke calls "integrative thought" (*Attitudes* 232).

And as Steiner suggests, moving away from such thinking is essential to achieving the kind of ethos he locates at the center of his faithful witness model of civic engagement. As I pointed out in Chapter 3, Steiner blames the American evangelical propensity to think dualistically—their "inordinate concern for boundary-drawing and boundary-policing"—as leading to the poor reputation evangelicals have when it comes to public discourse (311). Such dualistic thinking fuels a polarized worldview that divides people into reductive categories of good versus bad and ultimately dehumanizes people of other belief systems (Steiner 311). Austin's rhetorical strategy of casuistic stretching, which is grounded in his vernacular religious creativity and reflects his desire to represent his faith in a way that might be understood by readers who hold beliefs different from his own, represents an initial step toward transcending such polarity. It points toward the possibility that evangelical rhetor and non-Christian audience are united by virtue of the fact that they are all human beings who are worthy of dignity and respect (Steiner 311; see also Crowley 30; Hauser, *Vernacular* 66–70). Communicating that sense of legitimacy through his writing could lead to the intersubjectivity that would allow Austin and non-Christian readers like Chris the opportunity to "sit down and talk," potentially in deliberative ways.

Consequences of Casuistic Stretching

Of course, casuistic stretching doesn't come without consequences (Burke, *Attitudes*; Carlson; Ringer, "Consequences"). As I noted in Chapter 3, Burke himself names demoralization as the eventual consequence (*Attitudes* 229). For Austin, demoralization away from his original principle could result eventually in a loss of faith, since the principle he stretched was intimately connected to his belief that Christianity represents truth and encompasses the means to salvation—beliefs that rest at the core of his evangelical Christian faith. Of course, such a loss of faith would not occur overnight, especially by virtue of a single writing assignment in his FYW course. Rhetoric is habituating, though, and if Austin continues to encounter human contexts wherein he must stretch his values to achieve intersubjectivity with people who don't share his beliefs, he could find himself demoralized from core beliefs that rest at the center of his evangelical Christian faith and identity. Austin himself would then face a choice: he could reject the trajectory of his demoralization and, like Rob Campbell, retreat toward dualism; he could reject Christianity outright as being too exclusive; or he could attempt to fuse together his faith and his stretched values in order to assemble what various compositionists might refer to as a hybrid subjectivity (Bizzell, "Rationality"; LeCourt; Vander Lei, "'Where'").

Elizabeth Vander Lei explores this possibility in "'Where the Wild Things Are': Christian Students in the Figured Worlds of Composition Research." In that essay, she comments on a related discussion of Austin that I published in *College English* (see Ringer, "Consequences"). Referring to Austin's casuistic stretching as a kind of "grafting," she notes that such acts can result in "a scarred rhetorical surface" ("'Where'" 79). By way of example, she points to an anecdote from the NSYR that I mentioned in Chapter 1. The story Vander Lei relates is the one about the "young evangelical woman" who, while "explaining that for religious reasons she does not believe in cohabitation before marriage," tells the NSYR researchers, "I don't know, I think everyone is different so. I know it wouldn't work for me, but it could work for someone else" (qtd. in Vander Lei, "'Where'" 79). Vander Lei comments on this passage as follows: "Patched together from Christian morality and cultural mores, this woman's response bears linguistic and logical scars that testify to its grafted nature" ("'Where'" 79). And while she recognizes that scholars like Bizzell and me see possibilities in such grafting, she rightly acknowledges that it can be problematic. Indeed, Vander Lei's concern with such bricolage aligns with Kenda Creasy Dean's fear that millennial Christians don't espouse Christianity so much as moralistic therapeutic deism, the feel-good sentimentality bereft of anything amounting to substance or commitment that I mentioned in Chapter 1.

Vander Lei concludes her point by observing that the kind of grafting that accompanies casuistic stretching might be more common than not. She writes that it's possible "to imagine that we are, all of us, rhetorical monsters, fascinating, complicated, and powerful" ("'Where'" 79). The potential ubiquity of the "monster discourse" that Vander Lei recognizes resonates with Burke's understanding of casuistic stretching itself as ubiquitous. Burke puts it this way: "Since language owes its very existence to casuistry, casuistic stretching is beyond all possibility of 'control by elimination.' The best that can be done is to make its workings apparent by making casuistry *absolute* and *constant*" (*Attitudes* 230, original emphasis). As I discussed in Chapter 3, for casuistic stretching to remoralize as opposed to demoralize, its processes must be "subjected continually to *conscious* attention" (Burke, *Attitudes* 232, original emphasis). For casuistic stretching to afford rhetors and audiences "clarification" as opposed to "mystification," it would have to undergo "explicit conversion of a method into a methodology" (Burke, *Attitudes* 232). In short, students like Austin and the young evangelical woman Vander Lei cites would need help understanding that they are stretching their beliefs and that such acts offer both possibilities and consequences.

Chapter Conclusion

Austin's case study offers insight into the challenges that millennial evangelical Christian students face when attempting to represent their faith in written arguments that attempt to engage with a differently-minded audience. At the same time, it points to the deliberative potential that marks the evangelical Christian faith espoused by millennials like Austin. In line with the NSYR findings, Austin appreciates and respects the differences that exist between himself and his audience (Smith and Snell 48–8, 81). As I have tried to show in this chapter, Austin's desire to foster intersubjectivity with an audience that largely disagrees with him is motivated in large part by his desire to be an effective witness, a motive that resonates with Steiner's faithful witness model of civic engagement and with Jesus's example in the story of the Samaritan woman. As such, Austin's evangelicalism is less an impediment to civil discourse than it is a set of values, beliefs, and assumptions that prompts him to engage in it. To be sure, he doesn't enact his rhetorical strategies grounded in his vernacular religious creativity with complete eloquence and effectiveness. He needed further guidance in learning how to articulate his beliefs in order to constitute intersubjectivity with his audience while also remaining "true to the values" of his faith (Steiner 295). Arguably, Austin doesn't fare as well with the latter part of the equation than with the former, a complete reversal from the all-to-common narrative of the unyielding fundamentalist Christian student in composition scholarship who, like Rob Campbell, arrives at college with a well-defined and predetermined set of beliefs.

In my next chapter, I discuss a case study that differs in key ways from Austin's. While Kimberly evidences similar rhetorical acumen as Austin—she's able to think equally impressively about her audience's beliefs and values—she largely compartmentalizes her faith from an argument about a public health issue that, as I'll show, could have benefited from explicit inclusion of her "nonfundamentalist religious perspective" (Habermas 25). Like Austin, Kimberly needed guidance to achieve the full rhetorical potential of her vernacular religious creativity. But also like Austin, the religious creativity she does evidence holds significant potential for deliberative discourse.

Note

1. A different version of this chapter appeared in *College English* in the January 2013 issue. See Ringer, "Consequences."

5 The Problem and Possibility of Ethos

Articulating Faith in Kimberly's Academic Writing

> Not when writing it. Looking back on it. But I guess it's probably just the subconscious of the value that I have as a Christian to not judge others and to approach the situation being open to whatever they have to offer.
>
> —Kimberly, on how faith influenced her writing

> I have to make sure that I'm not going against anything that I personally believe in.
>
> —Kimberly, on writing "HPV Vaccine Prevents Cancer"

Kimberly differs from Austin in a few key respects, not the least of which is race—Kimberly is a student of African descent who was born in Jamaica and raised by her grandparents before moving to the Northeastern United States at age nine to live with her single mother. For some researchers, this would disqualify her from the ranks of evangelicals, since it's widely agreed that evangelicalism is a white phenomenon that has a troubled relationship with black Protestantism due to the former's historical views on slavery and civil rights (Emerson and Smith; Steensland, et al.). Kimberly, though, fits sociologist D. Michael Lindsay's observation that African Americans who align with evangelicalism tend to affiliate with "mostly white congregations" (259, n. 27). Kimberly participated extensively in the largely white evangelical subculture at Northeast State University (NESU), where she belonged to many of the same campus ministries as Austin, including InterVarsity Christian Fellowship (IVCF), Greek InterVarsity, and Campus Crusade for Christ. She also regularly attended Greenville Evangelical Church (GEC), the mostly white evangelical church popular among NESU's evangelical Christian student population. Moreover, Kimberly enacted evangelical discourse in ways that reflect evangelicalism's emphasis on personal piety and biblicism (Bebbington 3; Juzwik; Smith, *Bible*). She also engaged regularly in evangelical activities such as reading her Bible daily, praying frequently, attending religious services more than once a week, participating in Bible studies, avoiding alcohol, seeking out accountability partners, abstaining from premarital sex, sharing her faith with her peers, leading Bible studies with her sorority sisters, emphasizing the importance of having a personal relationship with Jesus Christ, and speaking of God's will for her life.

That's not to say that race doesn't matter to Kimberly and her faith—it certainly does. When race came up in our interviews, it was often to acknowledge the fact that she was one of the few black students at NESU, a reality that shaped how she participated in her academic context. In our second interview, Kimberly said, "Sometimes I do find it awkward to, like, raise my hand and say something. And, even if I come [in to class], like, a second after the teacher begins, everyone's stared at me anyway. Or, I don't know—my pencil falls, and people are, like, looking at me." In such instances, Kimberly's awareness of race separates her from her largely white peers. Such awareness at times led her to adopt a strategy of silence, or at least to deliberate—even pray—about whether or not to speak in class:

> So I just find that I usually, I slip back into my head and I say, "Okay, God, should I be—should I volunteer my answers? Should I speak? Or maybe I should just sit here?" And then, like, sometimes I'll just see my hand just go up and my teacher is, like, shocked, and then like, "Kimberly, do you have something to say?" I'm like, "Yeah." So, yeah. Sometimes I just step into my head and say, "Okay, when is the right time for me to speak?" And allow God to just work through that, to give me that boldness, not feel stupid in front of my classmates, or feel like I'm not relating my thoughts in a way that they could understand. (second interview)

The parallels between what Kimberly says here and what Austin said about remaining silent in class in the moments following Chris's disparaging comment about religion are striking. Both Kimberly and Austin evidence a sense of kairos that informed whether or not they should speak; both see such kairos in divine and social terms. God could prompt them to speak, but how they appear socially in relation to their peers comprises a central concern.

The difference, of course, is that Kimberly's concern is motivated by racial differences while Austin's derives from the emotionally charged, negative comment that Chris made. Nothing from my case study data suggests that Austin's whiteness prompted him to remain silent. What Kimberly and Austin did share, though, is an awareness of context and the related question of whether and how to speak in their respective FYW classrooms. As I discuss in this chapter, Kimberly largely compartmentalized her faith from her academic context, a fact that aligns with Smith and Snell's finding that even highly committed religious believers "can keep their faith quite privatized in a way that does not violate American society's broader 'culture of civility' that requires tolerance and acceptance of difference" (166–67). However, when the context shifts for Kimberly from an academic one to her evangelical Christian enclave, she has little trouble speaking publicly, even in front of largely white audiences. In our fourth interview, for instance, Kimberly talked about speaking to the entire IVCF group: "they asked me to, like, do a message in the beginning of the school year. Um, InterVarsity.

Just like being on campus and freshman experience. So that came, like, naturally, just relating that to that audience and just saying how my faith played out coming to, like, this new environment." When it came to interacting with her faith community, Kimberly's relationship to her audience and her level of comfort changed dramatically. Her comments suggest that her blackness didn't serve to separate her appreciably from her largely white peers who participated in IVCF, even though she gave her testimony as a first-semester freshman. In fact, she compared her speaking engagement at NESU to a sermon she delivered as a graduating senior for "youth Sunday" at her home church, an African Methodist Episcopal (AME) church with a largely black congregation. Kimberly noted that writing her talks for both audiences, white and black, came "naturally" to her.[1]

It did so arguably because it was non-academic writing that allowed her to draw on her personal experiences and integrate her faith in ways she felt she couldn't do when writing academically. In fact, the distinction between academic and extracurricular writing and contexts was instrumental in shaping how Kimberly saw her faith in relation to her rhetorical practice. The fact that she felt equally comfortable delivering a sermon to her longtime black congregation and a testimony for her relatively new and largely white parachurch community at NESU attests to the possibility that, at least in Kimberly's view, common faith served to unite individuals, despite racial differences. What Kimberly didn't feel comfortable doing is what Austin sought to do: integrate faith explicitly into academic writing. I say "explicitly" because, as I'll discuss in this chapter, faith does play an implicit role in Kimberly's academic writing, and it does so in ways that evidence vernacular religious creativity.

Kimberly alludes to the implicit role faith plays in her writing in the first epigraph above when she observes that her "subconscious" values and beliefs "as a Christian" shape the writing she does for her FYW course. While Kimberly's academic writing bears little overt trace of her evangelical identity, it evidences an underlying foundation of values that corresponds to her faith but that is also flexible and malleable in ways that hold significant potential for deliberative discourse. Kimberly is able to achieve some of that potential through her rhetorical strategy of values articulation: she is able to prioritize her values in a manner that allows her to make an argument on behalf of the common good even though it departs from her own personal morality. At the same time, Kimberly's ability to achieve the full deliberative potential of her vernacular religious creativity remains frustrated by the fact that she has been conditioned to compartmentalize her faith from her academic practice, a conditioning that is reified by her FYW instructor's warning to avoid topics that might invite religious perspectives. Part of my argument in this chapter, then, is that such dictates limit the rhetorical education of millennial evangelical Christian students like Kimberly. If she had been encouraged to think about how her religious beliefs and values could have informed her writing, she might have been able to accomplish even more impressive deliberative goals than the ones she was able to achieve. She also might have arrived at new ways of understanding how the values she espouses as a millennial evangelical Christian can be brought to bear on public problems that feature a religious dimension.

The public issue about which Kimberly writes involves the human papillomavirus vaccine (HPV), a topic that has garnered significant controversy among evangelical Christians who espouse "family values" because of the fear that giving the vaccine to young girls might encourage sexual behavior (see Crowley 134–36). While Kimberly barely touches on this religious aspect of the debate in her writing—in her words, she couldn't "see the place for it"—she ultimately realizes that she must come to terms with how her own faith-inflected morality aligns with the argument she makes in her persuasive essay. Specifically, because Kimberly has chosen to abstain from premarital sex—a decision grounded in her faith—she decides not to take the HPV vaccine when it is offered to her in high school. This ultimately prompts her to question the ethics of making an argument that does not correspond with her own personal morality. As she puts it in the second epigraph, "I have to make sure that I'm not going against anything that I personally believe in." Kimberly made this statement while she was drafting her argument in favor of the HPV vaccine, and it's indicative of what I refer to in this chapter as her ethos problem, a problem that, as I'll show, arises from the fact that Kimberly's faith-based abstinence aligns her closely with the values of the audience she attempts to persuade. Kimberly could have avoided her ethos problem if she had been encouraged not to ignore her faith but rather to write directly from her ethos as a millennial evangelical Christian who has chosen to remain abstinent but who nonetheless values doing whatever is necessary to save the lives of young girls. Arguing from this perspective would have given her a significant degree of leverage with her invoked audience of parents who would prefer their daughters remain abstinent.

Kimberly's case study thus differs from Austin's in key ways. While Austin's experience largely centers on his concern of how to foster intersubjectivity with an audience who held views radically different from his own, Kimberly's case deals with the deliberative potential her vernacular religious creativity holds for both differently-minded and like-minded audiences. Certainly, her religious creativity would allow her to foster intersubjectivity across difference of belief and morality: values articulation as a rhetorical strategy affords her the flexibility to communicate effectively with audiences who do not see evangelical Christian morality as the basis for public health policy. But the missed opportunity I see in Kimberly's writing is one wherein she could prompt other evangelical Christians, especially those who adhere to a family values ideology, to rethink their own values hierarchies when it comes to matters of public health. In other words, Kimberly prompts us to think about the deliberative ends she might have achieved had she been encouraged to make her argument not outside of but within her evangelical Christian enclaves (Roberts-Miller 41, 206). This chapter thus forwards two interrelated arguments. I begin by acknowledging and describing the vernacular religious creativity in which Kimberly engages, namely that of values articulation. I then turn to a consideration of what Kimberly might have achieved had she been encouraged to explore her own faith in relation to the religious arguments that frame the debate about the HPV vaccine.

Kimberly's Faith

Like the majority of millennial evangelicals, Kimberly's faith background is complex. While she doesn't describe periods of backsliding like Austin does, she migrates from black Protestantism (i.e., her AME church at home) to white evangelicalism upon arriving at NESU (i.e., IVCF and GEC). According to the NSYR data, such a shift is not uncommon. Smith and Snell found that one-fifth of black Protestant emerging adults migrated to evangelicalism, explaining that "In many—if not most—of these cases, there is little religious transformation or conversion going on; rather, youth with probably mostly the same beliefs and dispositions are merely switching Protestant congregations" (110). This certainly seemed to be the case for Kimberly, since her faith practices paralleled those of Austin's, namely Bible reading, prayer, witnessing, church attendance, and campus ministry involvement. Kimberly even joined a sorority at NESU during her second semester and, like Austin, involved herself with Greek InterVarsity in order to commune with other evangelical Christians in the Greek system and witness to her sisters through prayer and Bible study. Kimberly's shift to white evangelicalism coincided with her move to NESU, where her options for religious engagement were limited to white evangelicalism or mainline Protestantism. On several occasions, she noted that she loved GEC and felt comfortable there. When I asked her to speak about how GEC compared to her home church, the only difference she noted dealt with superficial features such as the structure of each service and the type of music. The manner in which she talked about her home church—particularly in terms of its biblicist orientation and emphasis on individual believers developing their own personal relationships with Christ—resonated with the theology of GEC.

Kimberly offered insight into her faith in the letter she wrote to her instructor prior to our first interview:

> I [am] currently living my life as Christian—meaning I believe in God and his son, Jesus. I grew up in [a] household where faith in God was a given. My grandparents were fervent believers and strived to be what God wanted them to be. It was instilled in me the importance of praying, fasting, and reading the bible. I was encouraged to attend church and gain as much as I could from Sunday school teachers and pastors. ("First letter")

In the interview, I asked Kimberly to talk further about what she felt she gained from her pastors and Sunday school teachers:

> Just the whole, you know, do unto your neighbor type of thing, the Golden Rule. And then, like, as I got older and continued in Sunday School, just establishing that personal relationship between me and God, and just knowing that, you know, if I ever sin, or do something—like, drink—I have the opportunity to be forgiven. Like, now I find that that's one reason that I also go to church. I could read the Bible on my own and I could process that within myself, but going to church I get to see it from another perspective. And with my church at home, my pastor, his style of preaching, he does a story and then tie[s] the Scripture into it. So it makes me see it from a different perspective. So I'm like, "Oh, okay. That's how it applies to my life." And then I'll take it from there. So that's just, that personal connection and knowing that God is, like, my own, type of thing.

A number of key themes emerge from this passage that offer insight into Kimberly's faith. The first is that she understands her faith in terms of a personal relationship between herself and God, a key trope within evangelicalism.

A second theme involves Kimberly's biblicism, which can be summed up in terms of life application and aligns her with Bebbington's definition of evangelicalism (3; Cope and Ringer 107). The Bible doesn't exist for Kimberly as an artifact or as a set of historical documents; rather, it exists so that believers can find ways to apply its precepts to their lives (Juzwik; Smith, *Bible*). Correlative to this is the notion that these life applications emerge as a result of community involvement through the medium of preaching—but also via a form of vernacular religious creativity. When Kimberly says "I'll take it from there," she's talking about how she will apply those biblical principles to her life and thus her human context. In our fourth interview, Kimberly expounded on this possibility by talking about how she journals in conjunction with her devotional Bible reading: "[W]hen you're writing in reference to the Bible, it's like you can, you can write in a way that it relates to your life. And you can show your experience to that particular verse or chapter and how that plays out in your life." She later adds that "the Bible is, like, very personable." While I don't have examples of Kimberly's devotional writing, the way she describes her act of "writing in reference to the Bible" suggests it entails a form of casuistry. By thinking actively about how a "particular verse or chapter" applies to her life, she's recontextualizing biblical stories and principles in relation to her own experience, an act that amounts to casuistry because it involves "removing words from their 'constitutional' setting" and placing them in a new one (Burke, *Attitudes* 309). Thus a process that aligns with vernacular religious creativity, namely casuistry, rests at the core of her biblicism, which in turn represents a central component of her faith.

The Bible also serves as a form of evidence she uses when debating others about the veracity of Christianity. In the letter she wrote to one of her spiritual mentors prior to our fifth interview, Kimberly said the following: "Being in courses where the topic of religion come[s] up, I do prepare myself for what others might say. There is going to be some against Christianity. In those instances, I say what I have to say—simply because God has been so good." We had the following exchange about this passage in our fifth interview:

Kimberly: There's always an atheist or someone ready to argue or defend what they believe, and I don't like getting into religious debates the majority of the time. I just say my piece and then it's done, type of thing? Like, "This is what I believe." That's that, and it's done. And just like those other viewpoints, sometimes I have to prepare myself for people who would, like, personally come against me with something against Christianity or something. And I'm just like, "Well, I have proof." So, that type of thing.
Jeff: What's your proof?
Kimberly: Well, the Bible.

To be sure, this attitude doesn't offer much hope for deliberative discourse—Kimberly here appeals to the same absolutist assumptions that, in many ways, constitute the exigency for the discussion about religiously committed students in composition studies (Anderson; Shannon Carter; Dively, "Religious"; Goodburn; Hunt; Perkins, "'Radical'"; Rand). This attitude emerged rarely over the course of our case study, though, and didn't seem to play a significant role in shaping Kimberly's attitude toward public discourse. The debates Kimberly alludes to here center on Christianity itself. While the argument she writes about HPV implicates her faith, it doesn't focus on it, and that seems to afford her the space to proceed in a far more deliberative manner.

Kimberly also saw her faith itself in such deeply personal terms that she largely compartmentalized her faith from rhetorical practice that didn't directly involve it. As the following passage suggests, faith became more personal for Kimberly as she matured:

> [W]hen you're younger, you see it as being forced to go to church, or your parents drag you to church. And, you know, as I got older and came to know Christ on that personal level and have that personal relationship with him, church was—like, I looked forward to going to church. Um, we would have, like, meetings during the week, and I willingly went to those meetings, or willingly went to those Bible studies and practices. And just like being in church, I'm just able to say, like, "It's all about God," as opposed to when I'm out in my day, you can get consumed by so many things that you often—that often put God on the back burner until the hecticness is over.

For Kimberly, faith is deeply personal—it emphasizes a believer's decision to become a Christian as well as the ensuing decisions to develop and maintain a personal relationship with Christ. But Kimberly also points to the possibility of compartmentalization, one wherein she "put[s] God on the back burner" because "other things" take precedence in daily life. As I'll show later in this chapter, such compartmentalization was by no means absolute, but it did shape the writing Kimberly completed for her FYW course.

For the moment, though, it's worth lingering on the deeply individualistic bent to Kimberly's faith that emerged in relation to two topics we returned to frequently throughout our interviews: abstinence and evangelism. Kimberly referenced her beliefs concerning abstinence numerous times over the course of our case study. In our first interview, Kimberly spoke of "how God [was] working in [her] life": "even though I'm in college and even though I'm surrounded by drinking or, like, sex, and, um, drugs and all this stuff on a daily basis, I'm able to stay grounded." And in her second interview she referenced the fact that identifying herself as a "young Christian" often came as a shock to people who assumed that college students are "expected to live on the edge—drink or party or have sex or whatever." Kimberly's decision not to engage in these activities is thus a choice she makes that is based in her faith: for Kimberly, "young Christians" choose to lead lives that look different from the lives college students are expected to lead. Kimberly highlighted this difference when talking about sharing her faith with her sorority sisters: "But the messages that I've received [from my sisters] [are] just like, you know, 'I'm in college right now, and I just find it hard to maintain [a Christian lifestyle] and try to, like, not drink or not have premarital sex or whatever'" (first interview). Kimberly thus defines premarital sex as at odds with her faith, a belief that pervades evangelical Christian discourse, particularly among millennials (Freitas; Regnerus; Smith and Snell; Webber). She also sees abstaining from sex as a personal choice she has made that other teenagers or college students do not make.

Moreover, Kimberly locates personal choice at the center of evangelism itself. While Kimberly does share her faith with others, she's very careful about how she does so and takes great pains to respect the beliefs of others, a quality that reflects the NSYR data (Smith and Snell 81). In the following passage, notice how Kimberly's assumptions about individualism and personal choice intersect with her perspectives on evangelism:

Kimberly: I feel like … people have, um—I'm very open to people having their own way to salvation. But Christianity works for me. And I'm willing to share that with people. And, um, but I'm very open to whatever they believe. I wouldn't condemn anyone for it. So.

Jeff: A lot of Christians would say Jesus is the way, the truth, and the life. Nobody gets to the father except through him. So, I don't know, what place is there—do you see a place in there for other religions, or?

Kimberly: I feel like other religions exist, type of thing? So people are gonna, um—I feel like people explore a lot, and, um, I feel like the—some people go through that process of picking and exploring, and once they find that religion that works for them then they stick to it, type of thing. Um, but I'm pretty open—I don't feel like—like, personally I don't feel like they're going to hell because they're like Buddhist or Jewish or whatever. But, um, 'cuz I understand that people have different ways of believing. (fifth interview)

For many evangelicals, the idea of multiple ways to salvation would be anathema, since much of evangelicalism rests on the belief that, as I put it in the interview, Jesus Christ is the way, the truth, and the life; no one comes to the Father except through him.[2] What Kimberly is doing here, though, reflects her vernacular religious creativity and resonates to some degree with the creativity of Amanda and Katie, whom I discussed in Chapter 2. Amanda, profiled as part of the NSYR, and Katie, a graduate student I interviewed for an earlier study, both appealed to C. S. Lewis's *The Last Battle* as authorizing them to casuistically stretch their evangelical Christian faith to accommodate their non-Christian peers and thus relieve them of the guilt of not evangelizing everyone they know. While this particular instance of vernacular religious creativity doesn't deal directly with Kimberly's potential for civic engagement, it is motivated by a principle of respect for others' beliefs that offers possibilities for deliberative discourse.

Indeed, Kimberly's articulation of lived religion resonates with Amanda's and Katie's vernacular religious creativity on the basis that her creativity is grounded in her human context. "I'm very open to people having their own way to salvation," Kimberly states, later adding that she "understand[s] that people have different ways of believing." And it's important to recognize that Kimberly does still evangelize—in the first paragraph, she notes that she's "willing to share" her Christian faith with others, a practice she participated in frequently as a member of her sorority and that aligns her with Bebbington's priority of evangelical activism (3; Cope and Ringer).[3] Her desire to share her faith and respect the beliefs of others is founded on a premise that is both individualistic and pluralistic: "Christianity works for me," she notes, adding later that she "understand[s] that people have different ways of believing." Later in the interview, I asked Kimberly if she thinks it's "a good thing" when people convert to Christianity. Kimberly's response sheds light on how she negotiates her faith in relation to religious pluralism:

> Others see it as, like, a good thing or, like, a one-up [kind of thing]. I see it as that personal relationship. And if you're willing—'cuz you can't say, "Oh, yeah, I believe in God," but then have no substance behind it, type of thing—or believe in Jesus and have no substance behind it? It's, you know, like, doing what the Bible says. Praying. And building that faith so that in times of desperation, and in times

> of celebration—good times—um, you're able to turn to God for everything. So, um, if they're willing to take that step—'cuz I feel like just sometimes it's, "Oh, yeah, I believe in God now, so that's it." But I feel that action with words definitely works.

Partly what she's getting at here is an aversion to modes of evangelism that force or coerce others into accepting Christ, what one student in Peter Magolda and Kelsey Eben Gross's ethnographic study of a campus ministry refers to derogatorily as "guerilla tactics" (83). Kimberly seems to echo what one of the campus ministry leaders from that same study said in relation to evangelism: "We *don't* want to force it on them. Find out if they are willing to try to accept the Lord. Be respectful; don't be pushy or aggressive" (qtd. in Magolda and Eben Gross 146, original emphasis).

Kimberly espouses a similar perspective: individuals have to decide for themselves whether or not to embrace Christianity. Thus when Kimberly says she sees faith as a personal relationship, what she means is something akin to personal choice. In her view, it's this sense of choice that allows for what she calls "substance" behind belief in the Christian God. Without such a personal decision to believe, faith is hollow—words without action, to echo her terms. Accordingly, there's something distinctly orthodox in her thinking, especially in terms of American evangelicalism's historical ties to individualism. Believers must make personal choices that align with—and align themselves with—the faith they purport to espouse, a point similar to one that Amanda makes when she emphasizes the reality that Christians and non-Christians alike must make choices about how to live their lives (Smith and Snell 29). This emphasis on choice also resonates with the motives undergirding Austin's citation of Joshua 24.15. In such constructions of salvation, humans have agency to choose to follow God or not, and subsequently to choose to live their lives as Christian or not. Kimberly's soteriology thus is more Arminian than Calvinist, more Charles Finney than Jonathan Edwards (Balmer 19–20).

Kimberly's perspective also aligns with the NSYR data. After discussing the extent to which emerging adults are radically inclusive, Smith and Snell explain, "Most emerging adults do not hold anything against anyone simply because they are of a different religion. Whatever anyone else wants to believe is fine with them" (81). Among white evangelical Protestants, the NSYR found that equal numbers of emerging adults (45%) believed that "Only one religion is true" and that "Many religions may be true" (135). The numbers among black Protestants favored "Many religions may be true" (49%) over "Only one religion is true" (38%), but both populations soundly rejected the notion that "There is very little truth in any religion," with only seven percent of white conservative Protestants and eight percent of black Protestants agreeing (Smith and Snell 135). The upshot of these numbers is that Kimberly is not an anomaly. Millennial evangelicals are as likely to believe that truth exists in other religions as they are to believe it exists only in Christianity. This finding cuts both ways. On the one hand, such a belief can help diminish the kind of us versus them thinking that Steiner recognizes as contrary to the kind of ethos necessary for effective civic engagement. On the other hand, such a premise can lead to "tensions and incongruities" between culture and Christian faith that can lead to demoralization (Smith and Snell 81).

I'll return to the question of how such tensions play themselves out in Kimberly's faith and experiences. I'll also return to Kimberly's particularly individualistic take on evangelical Christianity, as it constitutes an assumption that undergirds both her faith and the persuasive essay she writes that deals with a public problem. For the moment, though, the point worth stressing is that Kimberly's vernacular evangelical Christian faith emphasizes her understanding and acceptance of the idea that people make choices, and that even if she doesn't make a similar choice, that doesn't mean she condemns them. In a way, Kimberly's perspective approaches the postmodern assumption that understanding as opposed to agreement should serve as the basis of effective communication (Hauser, *Vernacular* 53–55). Like the majority of emerging adults Smith and Snell discuss in *Souls in Transition*, Kimberly operates on the premise that her human context is pluralistic and diverse, particularly in terms of belief systems (see also Ammerman, "Introduction" 6–8). And it is that assumption of pluralism that allows Kimberly to make a public argument in her FYW course that departs from but does not contradict her own personal morality, a move that, as I'll show, opens up some rhetorical possibilities while constraining others.

Kimberly's FYW Course

Like Austin, Kimberly was enrolled in NESU's traditional FYW course. Her instructor, "Stephanie," was a graduate student in English who was pursuing an MFA in fiction. While Stephanie had limited teaching experience, she was popular among her students. In our first interview, for instance, Kimberly told me she "really like[d]" Stephanie:

> You just get all these opinions about first-year professors and, oh, blah blah blah, all this writing. And when we do, like, our individual conferences, or like conference over a paper, it's just like she understands where I'm coming from and she appreciates that. She understands, you know, why I'm writing this way as opposed to I'm not structuring my paper that way.

From this comment, it's clear that Kimberly had developed a sense of trust in Stephanie, at least in terms of her writing. My interviews with Kimberly took place during the second half of the semester and ended during finals week. By the time of our first interview, then, Kimberly had completed the first half of the semester and had had ample time to develop a relationship with Stephanie. And the respect seemed to be mutual: Kimberly reported that, at mid-semester, Stephanie praised her for being "a reliable voice in the class," because she "always" raised her hand and offered comments and responses to questions (second interview).

Like Austin's instructor Meghan, Stephanie enacted many of the practices recommended in NESU's FYW program, including one-to-one conferences with students, which, according to the course schedule, occurred four times during the semester. Further analysis of the course syllabus suggests that Stephanie followed her writing program's English 101 common syllabus quite closely. Stephanie adopted the same three-course sequence of the common syllabus—personal essay, analysis, persuasive essay—though she took a more traditional route than Meghan and assigned the persuasive essay last. Stephanie also used the default textbooks recommended by the writing program.

One aspect of Kimberly's FYW course worth noting involves the role of the personal in academic writing. The final paragraph in the overview of the course syllabus reads as follows: "I want you to think of 'you' as the thread that connects you from one unit to the next. We'll begin with reflection, move to investigation/exploration, and end with persuasion. Within all three sections, the goal will be to think about the experiences that have shaped you, and how you, in turn, can shape the world." To say this course sequence emphasizes the personal would be something of an understatement. However, despite the course's emphasis on the personal—and in spite of Kimberly's level of trust in Stephanie—Kimberly's faith remained largely unknown to others in the class. When I asked Kimberly if Stephanie knew about her faith, she responded as follows:

> I don't think so. Like, the opportunity never came up for me to, like, share my faith or something like that. And being in English 101, the class is pretty, um—it's pretty structured. It's pretty packed in. And the writing is very curtailed to, like, whatever, so. There hasn't been [much] opportunity for me to, like, put my faith into writing or share that.

Kimberly also spoke of her class as rather quiet—she was, in fact, one of the few students who participated in class discussions on a regular basis. In our second interview, Kimberly said, "I feel like we hardly talk in that class," further observing that dialogue would occur in small group settings but that whole-class discussions tended to be subdued at best.

In that same interview, Kimberly also referenced a class discussion wherein Stephanie encouraged students not to choose topics for their persuasive essay that might elicit a religious response. Kimberly told me about this comment when I asked her if religious topics ever came up in class:

> Ah, no. I don't think—no. Um, I feel like she shies away from those type of discussions. Like, her—when introducing … our [persuasive essay] she said, you know, abortion or those type of—like, picking those topics can bring in the religious aspect of it. And maybe, you know, that's

> not the route you'd want to go for that paper. It was something about, like, faith being subjective ... She was just like, "Don't really go into the religious aspect of it." So.

Many writing instructors would likely identify with Stephanie's warning against choosing topics that have a pronounced religious component—especially hot-button and seemingly unresolvable issues like abortion (see Crowley 28–29). Such a stricture was not uncommon in the FYW program at NESU. Some instructors shared informal lists of banned topics for English 101, a strategy that resonates with persistent beliefs in rhetoric and composition that religious topics or approaches should be off-limits (Anderson; Dively, "Censoring"; Gilyard; Kirsch; Neulieb; Vander Lei, "'Where'"; Vander Lei and Fitzgerald). Stephanie's stricture does not appear in the course syllabus or on the persuasive essay assignment sheet. According to Kimberly, Stephanie made the comment in class when introducing the assignment.

My point here is not to criticize Stephanie for marking such a boundary—she was, after all, a relatively inexperienced writing instructor doing the best she could to make the course as efficient and effective as possible. But I do find it necessary to acknowledge the effect this stricture had on Kimberly's mindset regarding the relationship between academic writing and religious faith. For instance, when I asked Kimberly how she felt about this proscription, she said the following:

> [M]y question is ... not necessarily would my grade be effected, but would—if I chose to go that route ..., like, what would be her reaction to that? Yeah, I feel like with the HPV topic that I chose, I went from, like, a more general standpoint. I don't know if there are any ethical-ish—not ethical, um—religious aspects that play into it. But I guess we'll see as my research goes on.

While Kimberly alludes to the possibility that she could have chosen to focus on the religious dimension of the debate, she also notes here the concerns she might have developed had she decided to go in that direction. Would writing about a religious issue negatively affect her grade? Would Stephanie respond in other ways that Kimberly might want to avoid? Coupled with the fact that Kimberly had been conditioned to compartmentalize her faith from her academic practice, Stephanie's dictate against religious perspectives or topics likely dissuaded Kimberly from exploring the many religious aspects of the HPV vaccine debate. And it likely hindered Kimberly from learning how her faith might shape her rhetorical practice in productive ways.

The HPV Debate

Kimberly's comment that she's not sure if there are any religious dimensions of the HPV vaccine debate is surprising, because the debate arguably would not exist were it not for outspoken evangelical Christian activists. To best understand Kimberly's essay on the HPV vaccine, it's thus important to contextualize it within the largely religious controversy that surrounds the vaccine in the early twenty-first century. The human papillomavirus is a sexually transmitted disease that can lead to cervical cancer in women. In 2006, the FDA approved a vaccine that can protect women against contracting HPV and recommended that it be given to young girls before they become sexually active, a recommendation that proved to be controversial. Much of the controversy came from evangelical Christian organizations that promote family values, largely because sexual purity in the form of abstinence before marriage tends to be a key moral issue for evangelicals (Crowley 134–36). Indeed, even before the HPV vaccine was approved by the FDA in June 2006, socially and politically conservative Christian organizations in the U.S. had started to oppose the vaccine. The Family Research Center (FRC), a Washington-based lobby group whose motto is "Defend Faith, Family, and Freedom," received particular media attention. An April 2005 *New Scientist* article cited Bridget Maher, a spokesperson for the FRC, as saying that "Abstinence is the best way to prevent HPV" and that "[g]iving the HPV vaccine to young women could be potentially harmful, because they may see it as a license to engage in premarital sex" (Mackenzie). This perspective generated no shortage of critique. In a May 2005 article in the *Nation*, Katha Pollit lambasted the "Christian right" because they don't "like the sound of this vaccine at all" (9). The reason has more to do with sex than with life: "With HPV potentially eliminated," Pollit writes, "the antisex brigade will lose a card it has regarded as a trump unless it can persuade parents that vaccinating their daughters will turn them into tramps, and that sex today is worse than cancer tomorrow" (9). This leads Pollit to conclude forcefully: "What is it with these right-wing Christians? Faced with a choice between sex and death, they choose death every time" (9).

The FRC later came to support the vaccine, albeit with the stipulations that it should not be touted as a failsafe against HPV (it only targets two of the four strains of HPV) and should not be mandated by the government. Peter Sprigg, the FRC's vice president for policy, writes in a July 2006 op-ed piece in the *Washington Post* that his organization "oppose[s] any effort by states to make [the vaccine] mandatory." Families should be able to make such decisions for themselves, especially since the disease is transmitted "only through sexual contact" and not "casual contact or blood." A similar argument emerged in a 2007 *Christianity Today* (*CT*) editorial, "'Safe Sex' for the Whole Nation: Why Mandating the HPV Vaccine Is Not a Good Idea." In it, the editors disagree not so much with the vaccine itself as with the possibility that the government might require it. And their concerns are decidedly more about sex itself than the vaccine. The editorial concludes, "While we must respond wisely to political policies that press upon us—like the HPV vaccine—we need to spend more time discerning how to get our own house in order, so we can bring Christ's light to a culture losing its way in sexual darkness" (27). Directly responding to *CT*, evangelical author Hugo Schwyzer adopted a "more nuanced position" on teen sex and criticized the *CT* editors for "placing our fear of pre-marital sexual activity ahead of our fear of cancer." Schwyzer writes, "I don't want my children becoming sexually active before they are fully ready to accept the emotional, physical, and spiritual consequences of sex. That's a tall order, if you think about it. But I'd have no problem consenting to my daughter receiving Gardasil." Schwyzer, an evangelical Christian, sides more with Pollit than with *CT* or the FRC.

In short, much of the public debate about the HPV vaccine revolves around the moral and political concerns of socially and politically conservative evangelical Christians. And it is a debate that continues to garner such discussion within the publics that have formed around the vaccine and its controversy. Typing the words "Christian HPV" into Google, for instance, returns about half a million hits, while the search term "evangelical HPV" turns up over two million. As I'll show, however, Kimberly largely avoids any exploration of the religious component of this debate. There are a number of reasons for this absence. Stephanie's stricture certainly is influential, but so are Kimberly's perceptions of how faith should or should not connect to academic practice such as writing a persuasive essay for a FYW course. Despite the fact that Kimberly largely ignores the religious dimensions of the HPV controversy, her faith does play an implicit role in her argument in favor of the HPV vaccine. Motives that align with her faith emerge most directly in her essay when she states at the outset that she refused the vaccine because she is not sexually active, a somewhat cloaked nod toward her faith-based decision to remain abstinent. More importantly, Kimberly's faith is implicated in her HPV essay because her argument rests on values she negotiates via vernacular religious creativity while writing her argument. Specifically, Kimberly engages in values articulation, a rhetorical strategy that allows her to make an argument that departs from her personal morality but that does not undercut it.

Values Articulation in Kimberly's Essay

As I discussed in Chapter 3, values articulation represents a rhetorical strategy grounded in vernacular religious creativity that allows rhetors to reprioritize values and beliefs depending on the rhetorical situation. I derive my definition of values articulation from Sharon Crowley, who defines articulation as an assemblage of two or more beliefs that can be disconnected and reconnected in different ways (60). Crowley also contends that belief articulations exist in hierarchical structures, a point that echoes Perelman and Olbrechts-Tyteca's contention that values hierarchies are "more important to the structure of an argument than the actual values" themselves (81). Taken together, Crowley's concept of values articulation and Perelman and Olbrechts-Tyteca's emphasis on hierarchies suggest that values and beliefs can be assembled into flexible hierarchies that can shift depending on the context. The flexibility that marks values articulation helps reveal the complex interplay of values and beliefs that undergirds Kimberly's persuasive essay.

In "HPV Vaccine Prevents Cancer," Kimberly argues that parents should vaccinate their young daughters against the human papillomavirus. When Kimberly and I met for our first interview, she was in the process of deciding what to write for the final assignment of the semester. Kimberly chose to write her persuasive essay about HPV because she had been offered the vaccine as a senior in high school. She opted against getting the vaccine because, like many evangelical Christians, she was not sexually active at the time and even wrote in her essay that she was not "plan[ning] on having sex anytime soon." As I noted earlier, Kimberly's motives for abstinence are wrapped up in her faith. She may be a college student who faces pressures to "live on the edge" by partying or having premarital sex, but she chooses not to engage in such activities because she identifies as a "young Christian" (second interview).

The logic undergirding Kimberly's personal morality can be rendered as the following enthymeme: *Major premise*: Young Christians should make choices to avoid immoral behavior; *First minor premise*: I am a young Christian; *Second minor premise*: Pre-marital sex is an immoral behavior; *Conclusion*: Therefore, I choose to abstain from pre-marital sex. Kimberly's vernacular faith thus assumes an articulation of beliefs wherein remaining abstinent is linked to her identity as a millennial evangelical Christian.

Students had the option of writing their persuasive essays as letters addressed to a specific audience. At some point in the writing process, Kimberly's instructor urged her to go this route. Kimberly thus addresses her letter to "parents of young girls," and her goal in the essay is to encourage her audience to have their daughters vaccinated against HPV. Kimberly states her purpose clearly at the outset of her essay: "I am writing to inform you about a new vaccine recommended for your daughters." Almost to a fault, Kimberly stays true to this promise and maintains an informative stance throughout the bulk of the essay. In her second paragraph, for instance, Kimberly explains what HPV is and how it causes cervical cancer: "To get a better understanding of HPV and the cervical cancer relationship, let us start from the top. The cervix is an important part of our anatomy. During menstruation, the cervix allows blood to flow from the uterus into the vagina." Kimberly goes on to explain how HPV causes cells in the cervix to grow abnormally and why the vaccine can be beneficial for young girls. By maintaining this declarative stance, Kimberly positions herself as a "presenter" of "information" who is "attempting to influence [her] interlocutors' knowledge and beliefs" (Ivanič 269).

She also wants to persuade her audience to vaccinate their young daughters against HPV. To do this, she first argues that teenage girls will often be sexually active without their parents knowing it. She cites statistics related to teen pregnancy and to the number of teenage girls who contract HPV. In doing so, she responds to one of the criticisms of the vaccine—that it will serve to promote sexual activity among teens by giving them a false sense of security. She argues that what these critics "fail to understand is that girls are already taking the initiative" to have sex. Even though Kimberly embraces abstinence for herself, she recognizes that "young people are having sexual intercourse anyway." Because "sex is so prevalent among girls," she writes, "the HPV vaccine does not impact that activity. The vaccine simply offers protection against a threat to their female bodies."

In the remainder of her essay, Kimberly provides further support for her argument. She offers statistics about how many women will develop cervical cancer each year and how many will die from it. She also includes personal testimony from a mother who had her daughters vaccinated. Like Austin, Kimberly responds to potential counterarguments, notably those that deal with the high cost of the vaccine, the concern that mandating inoculation infringes on the rights of parents, and the fears about possible side effects of the vaccine. She closes her essay by returning to some of her strongest points: we live in a society wherein "sex bombards every aspect of our lives," and because young people are going to have sex anyway, the possibility of them contracting an STD like HPV is real. Kimberly concludes with a direct appeal to her audience: "As parents it is your responsibility to be proactive in the sexual education of your children. It is your duty to protect your child the best way possible. Knowing that HPV causes cervical cancer is sufficient to taking active steps in your daughter's health. I encourage young girls to be vaccinated against HPV to prevent a common cancer among women." For an essay written by a first-year student, "HPV Vaccine Prevents Cancer" is well crafted. It includes sound research, a logical argument, and audience-based appeals.

And there's a distinctly deliberative component to Kimberly's essay, especially if we define deliberation as entailing a kind of dialogue among relatively equal parties, one in which each party recognizes the legitimacy of others, takes a stance on a debatable claim, and seeks to construct an ethos marked by humility rather than self-righteousness (Booth, *Rhetoric*; Crowley; Hauser, *Vernacular*; Roberts-Miller; Steiner). Throughout her essay, Kimberly invokes an audience that can and should engage in deliberation concerning the health of their daughters. She's partially successful at achieving these deliberative ends, largely because of the form of her argument, which, like Austin's Christian schools essay, entails raising counterarguments and responding to such concerns civilly. The counterarguments Kimberly addresses come from her research, and she makes a good faith effort to consider them. She's not setting up a strawman argument but genuinely attempting to inhabit her interlocutor's perspective.

Much of her ability to understand her interlocutor's perspective rests on the fact that she actually espouses a version of that perspective. As I noted above, Kimberly personally committed herself to abstinence, and her decision to remain abstinent arguably is one that many members of her audience would hope for their own daughters. Early in her essay, for instance, Kimberly invokes an audience of parents who would prefer their "young girls" remain abstinent. She writes, "As parents, it is difficult to monitor your child's activity, especially sexual activity. Despite efforts promoting abstinence, young people are having sexual intercourse anyway." As became clear over the course of our case study, though, Kimberly also held a belief in the importance of doing whatever is possible to save lives. In the context of an argument aimed at parents of young girls, Kimberly prioritizes her belief in the importance of saving lives over her belief in the importance of remaining abstinent. Kimberly thus enacts a values hierarchy in her HPV essay that differs from the values hierarchy on which she bases her attitude toward premarital sex. While her personal morality is such that she values abstaining from sex and thus does not need to take the HPV vaccine, her experience within her human context (e.g., her sorority and home church) prompts her to adopt a different orientation toward what she ultimately proposes as public policy—that parents should vaccinate their daughters to protect them from contracting HPV.

A closer look at a key passage early in Kimberly's essay highlights this particular values articulation as well as the fact that Kimberly is able to inhabit both of the key perspectives regarding the HPV vaccine. In her second paragraph, Kimberly writes the following:

> It is true that those who abstain from sex are not at risk for sexually transmitted diseases, but what about [the] millions of girls who are? In reality, your child could be one of them. Administering a vaccine to girls who risk exposure to a virus anytime throughout their lives benefits their personal health. According to the Center for Disease Control, 1 in 5 girls between ages 14 and 19 were infected with HPV in 2004. Obviously it's 2009, so that number is likely to have increased.

The reference in the first sentence to "those who abstain from sex" includes Kimberly, a point she hints at in her first paragraph when she notes that she is "not sexually active" and doesn't "plan on having sex anytime soon." But she's also able to inhabit the second part of that sentence ("what about [the] millions of girls who are?") because of her personal experience in her home church and sorority with teenage girls and college students who are pregnant or at least sexually active. Kimberly can identify with both the argument and the counterargument in this sentence because they reflect her experience.

In our second interview, for instance, Kimberly mentioned "drugs or sex or STDs" as key issues faced by her generation. She elaborated even further in our fourth interview:

> Well, my position is that girls are having sex anyway. The state that we're in—like, as a culture—sex is everywhere, kids are doing it. And

> I don't see any way of getting out of it. And so just having this vaccine, it just prevents, like, further self-destruction type of thing. 'Cuz they're already going down that road anyway. And they're gonna do what they want regardless. But my experience with, like, teenagers my age, they're gonna rebel regardless. Once your parents tell them not to do something, that's just a go ahead to do it anyway. So this vaccine just offers the protection—from HPV—that would possibly eventually lead to cervical cancer. So that's my perspective on it.

Kimberly's articulation of beliefs here deals with a range of concerns, but the major argument can be constructed as the following enthymeme: *Major premise*: We should take whatever steps necessary to protect young people from potentially fatal diseases; *Minor premise*: HPV is a potentially fatal disease; *Conclusion*: Therefore, we should take whatever steps necessary to protect young people from HPV.

Kimberly developed this major premise at least in part because she belonged to the Greek system at NESU, a community that she perceived to be highly sexually active. But it was also developed based on experiences at her home church. In our fourth interview, Kimberly spoke to how the local context of her home church shaped her response to this issue—and perhaps allowed her the space to make an argument for the common good that doesn't reflect her personal moral choices. After asking how the influential Christian women in her life might respond to her argument about HPV, Kimberly laughed and said the following:

> I feel like the majority would have the opinion that young people shouldn't be having sex anyway. But they understand that—like, we have girls in our church—teenage pregnancies. So they know young people are having sex. I feel like in response to the vaccine, they—I feel like they would be okay with the vaccine. They would say, you know, you're—"Young people are in a state of self-destruction. There are, you know, teen pregnancies, STDs. And, if this prevents one of them, why not?"

Of course, Kimberly is speculating here, and I have no way of knowing from my data whether her mentors in her home church would have agreed with this line of reasoning or not. Her logic for thinking they would do so, though, is plausible and can be represented by the following enthymeme: *Major premise*: When it comes to protecting young people from self-destructive behavior, it makes sense to adopt a realistic approach rather than have unrealistic expectations; *First minor premise*: There are young girls in our church putting themselves at risk of contracting STDs; *Second minor premise*: A realistic approach to protecting young girls from such self-destructive behavior would be to vaccinate them against HPV; *Conclusion*: Therefore, we should encourage young girls in our church to take the HPV vaccine. A similar logic undergirds the public argument Kimberly makes in her HPV essay.

Kimberly's "HPV Vaccine Prevents Cancer" essay thus reveals her vernacular religious creativity, namely her ability to articulate her personal and public beliefs surrounding sexuality in flexible, context-specific values hierarchies (Crowley 65; Perelman and Olbrechts-Tyteca 83). In the context of her own life and private morality, Kimberly privileges abstinence over vaccination. Similar to her views on evangelism, Kimberly assumes that abstinence is a personal choice, one that not every college student or teenager will make. Consequently, when thinking about a public context that is populated at least in part by peers who are engaging in sexual activity, she prioritizes vaccination over abstinence. Every indication suggests that Kimberly espouses both values. Before she wrote her persuasive essay and even while writing it, Kimberly reiterated her belief that, as a millennial evangelical Christian, she was personally committed to abstinence. And as the second epigraph suggests, Kimberly did engage in direct reflection on whether the argument she was making lined up with her beliefs. When she stated in our third interview, "I have to make sure that I'm not going against anything that I personally believe in," Kimberly was in the process of revising her final version of "HPV Vaccine Prevents Cancer." The fact that she reflected directly on her argument as it relates to her beliefs—coupled with the fact that she announced her abstinence in an essay that argues in favor of the vaccine—points to the reality that she espouses both beliefs. Kimberly recognizes, though, that the value of abstinence underpinning her personal morality may be unrealistic in a situation rife with sexual activity and the risk of life-threatening disease. When considering her human context and the public prospects of her argument, Kimberly agrees with Katha Pollit and Hugo Schwyzer: she values life first.

In the context of an academic argument about a public health issue, Kimberly's ability to separate her personal convictions from her public outlook is laudatory. She's able to recognize that her own personal beliefs about morality might not be appropriate for the wider public, a recognition that could go a long way toward constituting the intersubjectivity necessary for deliberating about thorny topics like morality and public health. And as I have suggested, Kimberly's vernacular religious creativity does not appear to undermine her personal belief in abstinence. She believes in the importance of abstinence and in the importance of doing what is necessary to protect life, but she's able to rearticulate them in different hierarchies depending on the context. And while she has difficulty articulating specific ways that doing what is necessary to save lives might articulate with her evangelical Christian faith (she notes in our fifth interview that while "probably there are" biblical passages that would support such a perspective, she "can't think of any"), she is able to determine that it does not undermine her personal stance on abstinence. She can simultaneously choose to remain abstinent and argue for the HPV vaccine because she espouses both values.

Kimberly's ability to articulate values in flexible, context-specific hierarchies amounts to a form of vernacular religious creativity that offers significant possibilities for engaging in deliberative discourse with people who do not share her faith. It does so because it allows her to advocate on behalf of the public good without imposing her personal morals on people who do not share them. Arguing from such a perspective would increase Kimberly's chances of fostering intersubjectivity with interlocutors across differences of belief. Even if she had positioned herself explicitly as a millennial evangelical Christian in the argument she wrote in favor of the HPV vaccine, Kimberly's flexible values hierarchies would allow her to establish the fact that she shares a common reference world with non-Christian members of her audience and perceives them as legitimate. Indeed, if Kimberly could come to articulate her motives for encouraging the vaccine even when she herself refused to take it—motives that, as I have shown, align with her faith—she could position herself to become what Habermas calls a "vital and nonfundamentalist religious" voice "in the center of a democratic civil society" (25). Given that debates in American public discourse about issues of health and morality like the HPV vaccine controversy tend to be polarized between religious voices on the one hand and secular voices on the other, the inclusion of an evangelical Christian voice arguing on behalf of a more liberal conception of the public good could be transformative.

Kimberly's Ethos Problem

I say "could" because Kimberly does not position herself explicitly as a millennial evangelical Christian in her HPV essay. The closest she comes to doing so is by stating at the outset of her essay that she refused the vaccine because she is not sexually active. But as I mentioned earlier, her religious motives remain cloaked. And while Kimberly's concern for public health is admirable, it lands her in an ethical dilemma. Because she refused the vaccine based on her own conviction to remain abstinent, she lacks a degree of credibility when arguing that parents should vaccinate their daughters. Kimberly spoke to this concern in our third interview:

> I guess me not taking the vaccine myself, I have to make sure that I'm not going against anything that I personally believe in? Because I didn't take the vaccine. So how am I gonna advocate for a vaccine I didn't take? So, just like establishing that, and who my audience is—which is parents of young girls. And, just that whole approach to it, and where to go from here. What do I present to the audience? What aspects do I focus on, versus what aspects I don't focus on?

Any rhetorical educator would applaud Kimberly's struggle here. Like Austin when writing "Christian Schools vs. Public Schools," Kimberly here is thinking in decidedly rhetorical terms, considering carefully who her audience is in order to appeal to what they value. But she's also aware of the ethical ramifications of her argument. As she puts it, "I have to … make sure that

I'm not going against anything that I personally believe in." Kimberly shares the assumption that good arguments reflect the beliefs of the rhetors who voice them. She wants to be a good woman speaking well.

More than Austin, then, Kimberly seems to be aware that there are consequences to the argument she might make. To be sure, she doesn't ever speak to the fact that arguing something that departs from her personal belief might have bearing on her sense of self as an evangelical Christian in a public university context. But she does recognize that her beliefs are wrapped up in the arguments she makes. What she's not able to do fully is reconcile her personal beliefs with her public argument. In other words, she never fully addresses the ethos problem in her written argument. This problem emerges most clearly in the first paragraph from her final draft of "HPV Vaccine Prevents Cancer" (I number the sentences for the sake of analysis):

> (1) I am writing to inform you about a new vaccine recommended for your daughters. (2) I was offered this vaccine my senior year of high school when I went to receive my required vaccines for college. (3) This vaccine is intended to prevent the strains of HPV that lead to cervical cancer in women. (4) I declined the vaccine because my risk of acquiring HPV is low. (5) I mean, I am not sexually active nor do I plan on having sex anytime soon. (6) Compared to girls my age, though, engagement in sex starts around 18 or younger. (7) The Advisory Committee on Immunization Practices recommends the vaccination for girls 11–12 years old, particularly before sexual activity. (8) With cervical cancer being a leading cause of death among women, I encourage young girls to get vaccinated against HPV.

Note the moves Kimberly makes to establish her ethos. She begins by asserting a non-aggressive stance: she seeks to inform parents about a vaccine recommended for their daughters (sentence 1). Then, in sentence 2, she observes that she was offered the vaccine, a statement that lends her argument credibility from the outset: she's writing as someone who has personal experience with this vaccine. In the next sentence (3), she returns to her informative stance, noting what the vaccine purports to do. It's in sentences 4 and 5, which are buried in the middle of the paragraph, that Kimberly discloses the information she knows is potentially threatening to her ethos: she "declined the vaccine because [her] risk of acquiring HPV is low" (sent. 4). She then offers a reason why, and does so in distinctly personal terms: "I mean, I am not sexually active nor do I plan on having sex anytime soon" (sent. 5). Recognizing that her personal admission of refusing the vaccine potentially undermines her ethos, Kimberly shifts to a more objective stance and displaces her authority onto the Advisory Committee on Immunization Practices (sent. 7). After constructing her enthymematic thesis in the last line—"With cervical cancer being a leading cause of death among women, I encourage young girls to get vaccinated against HPV" (sent. 8)—Kimberly largely adopts an objective stance throughout her essay. The pronoun "I" appears only once more in the remainder of the essay—in her concluding line where Kimberly restates her thesis.

Kimberly's inclusion of her personal stance in the first paragraph of her essay came at the behest of her instructor. In our third interview, which took place while she was drafting her HPV essay, Kimberly noted that Stephanie wanted her to make her essay "more personal," a suggestion that aligns with the course syllabus's overt emphasis on the personal as central to each of the three major assignments (e.g., "I want you to think of 'you' as the thread that connects you from one unit to the next."). Stephanie also suggests that Kimberly write her essay as a letter. In our fourth interview, which took place the week before her final persuasive essay was due, Kimberly spoke directly to the fact that she was trying to make her essay more personal:

Jeff: How about—what about your voice in terms of [your HPV essay]? Do you feel like your voice is coming across here?
Kimberly: Um, yeah, since it's like a letter format, I—yeah, I try to work my voice into it a little. Like, "Young people are having sexual intercourse, anyway." So, you know.
Jeff: So, kind of the stuff that's more conversational, more natural to say?
Kimberly: Mm-hmmm.

And it is in the first paragraph where this conversational voice emerges most directly, particularly in sentence 5 when Kimberly writes, "I mean, I am not sexually active nor do I plan on having sex anytime soon."

As a result, it's possible to understand Kimberly's ethos problem as stemming largely from the genre of the assignment (i.e., a persuasive essay that involved research) coupled with Stephanie's encouragement to write more personally. Had Stephanie not encouraged Kimberly to include her personal voice, Kimberly might not have written her first paragraph in the way she did. She also might have been able to avoid any explicit mention of the fact that she refused the vaccine. The fact remains, though, that writing her essay prompted Kimberly to confront the question of how her personal beliefs should or should not pertain to conceptions of the public good and to the argument she makes on behalf of the vaccine. That's why when she names her ethos problem—"I have to make sure that I'm not going against anything that I personally believe in"—she does so in terms of her personal belief and not in terms of, say, the requirements of the assignment itself. In other words, while she's concerned with doing well on the assignment, she's also interested in representing herself and her beliefs ethically and accurately. She'd rather avoid horse-trading.

In fact, latent within the first paragraph we see evidence of the manner in which Kimberly had come to articulate her belief in abstinence with the value she placed on saving as many lives as possible from cancer. Through her conversational tone and use of the personal pronoun in her "I mean" sentence (5), Kimberly announces her identity as someone who has chosen to remain abstinent, but she does so in terms that are overwhelmingly personal. Kimberly uses "I" only nine times throughout her essay; a third of them appear in this one sentence. And given the fact that her abstinence is tied closely to her millennial evangelical Christian faith, Kimberly's attempt to make her writing more personal ironically defies her instructor's stricture against drawing on religious perspectives. Through her "I mean" sentence, Kimberly's evangelical Christian belief as represented by her decision to remain abstinent emerges subtly—and somewhat awkwardly—in an essay that is otherwise devoid of writing in the personal mode.

Moreover, the fact that Kimberly buries this sentence in the middle of the paragraph suggests that she hopes to subordinate the idea. Indeed, where she goes in the remainder of the paragraph speaks to this hierarchical relationship. The very next sentence reads, "Compared to girls my age, though, engagement in sex starts around 18 or younger" (sent. 6). She's acknowledging the fact that she's an exception—in terms of her lived religion, she has chosen to remain abstinent, but the majority of teenage girls can't be expected to do the same. The next two sentences shift the burden of authority from her personal belief and experience to the FDA and then to the Advisory Committee on Immunization Practices. In the final sentence, we see the second half of her belief articulation: "With cervical cancer being a leading cause of death among women, I encourage young girls to get vaccinated against HPV" (sent. 8). Kimberly thus ends her paragraph on the idea she hopes to emphasize, namely that it's important to do whatever is necessary to protect women from "a leading cause of death," and that doing so should outweigh any belief in abstinence as public policy.

While Kimberly's argument is praiseworthy due to its public health focus and reasonableness—she is, after all, encouraging parents to vaccinate their young daughters and not calling for the vaccine to be mandatory—it is also deeply ironic. The irony arises from the fact that her personal morality aligns more closely with the assumptions held by her invoked audience than with the perspective she adopts in her argument. Kimberly does not define her audience as evangelical Christian parents, an audience that would overwhelmingly favor abstinence for their daughters. However, as I noted earlier, Kimberly does invoke an audience of parents who would prefer that their daughters remain abstinent. Because Kimberly has chosen to defer sexual activity until marriage, she arguably represents the ideal daughter in the eyes of such an audience. In the context of her argument, though, the fact that Kimberly refused the vaccine due to her personal commitment to remain abstinent until marriage potentially threatens her ethos. Wouldn't she be able to argue much more credibly and authoritatively if she had taken the vaccine? To an extent, yes. If she had taken the vaccine, Kimberly would have had available to her a potentially powerful line of argumentation grounded in her ethos: Even though I took the vaccine, I still remain abstinent; thus your fears that the vaccine will encourage young girls to have sex are unfounded. Of course, the problem with such a line of thinking is that not every teenage girl will choose the same course of action as Kimberly. Her personal anecdote can't outweigh the statistics she points to in her essay about the high percentage of teens who engage in sexual activity. There's another option, though, one grounded in Kimberly's ethos as an evangelical Christian college student who chose not to take the vaccine because of her personal moral stance on abstinence but who still values doing whatever is necessary to protect life.

The Possibility of (Evangelical) Ethos

Earlier, I cited Katha Pollit's polemic against "right-wing Christians" who "choose death" over sex "every time" (9). The line of articulation undergirding the thinking of such a socially-conservative stance can be constructed as follows: while the risk of contracting HPV is bad, it's worse to do anything that might promote premarital sex among teenagers. Comparing this to Kimberly's articulation of values as it emerges in her persuasive essay, it's clear that the two hierarchies are reversed: Kimberly privileges life over abstinence, while Pollit's "right-wing Christians" prioritize abstinence. As the debate about HPV among evangelicals suggests, values hierarchies that privilege protection of life over abstinence from pre-marital sex rarely exist or get short shrift if they do. While Hugo Schwyzer promoted a similar argument, he acknowledged its relative unpopularity among evangelical Christians—and even went so far as to position himself against the perspective of *Christianity Today*.

The question for commentators such as Pollit is clear: how do we change the minds of politically- and socially-conservative Christians who espouse the view that abstinence outweighs life? To put this in Crowley's terms, how do we rearticulate the beliefs of such Christians for the sake of the common good? Crowley's answer as to how to go about doing so features belief and commitment rather than liberal reason. Individuals who are passionately committed to, say, feminism or gay rights or universal healthcare or pacifism might be able to argue with conviction in ways that could counter the fervor with which fundamentalist Christians advance their positions. Crowley's means of addressing the deliberative impasse in which we as Americans find ourselves, then, is to pit democratic passion against apocalyptist zeal in the hopes that the former would find resonance with a wider populace and, in doing so, work towards disarticulating fundamentalist ideologics. What Crowley doesn't envision is a state of affairs wherein evangelical Christians are part of the solution.

As Mike DePalma, Jim Webber, and I have argued, what Crowley emphasizes in her last chapter of *Toward a Civil Discourse* is largely agency-centered and thus pragmatic, a reality underscored by the fact that she opens the final section of the book by naming "strategies and tactics that may be of use in some situations" (Crowley 197; DePalma, Ringer, and Webber 320). She's talking about the means by which rhetors might foster civil discourse. And while the strategies she names are useful, it's important to consider a question she doesn't linger on, a question that centers on ethos: who should make these arguments? As one reads the final section of *Toward a Civil Discourse*, it becomes clear that those who do the persuading are liberal, secular rhetors who have embraced the full range of rhetorical strategies promoted by ancient rhetorical theory. The interlocutors—those who need their beliefs changed—are the fundamentalist Christians who embrace apocalyptism and who are thus unpersuaded by "common sense" (Crowley 199). In other words, a binary emerges: liberals, leftists, and secularists are the rhetors attempting to do the persuading, while "Christian activists" (199), "apocalyptists" (200), and "conservative Christians" (200) are those who need to be persuaded. Crowley doesn't entertain the possibility that evangelical Christian rhetors might be best positioned to persuade other evangelical or fundamentalist Christians to adopt policies that might bolster democracy or benefit the common good. The implicit assumption is that evangelical Christians are unable to enact deliberative rhetoric.

Steiner acknowledges this same shortcoming when he writes that Crowley's "analysis prematurely discounts any edifying role for religious voices by conflating them into a 'theology-driven fundamentalism'" that militates against democratic practice (qtd. in Steiner 292). Steiner aims to provide a "corrective" to Crowley's argument in his discussion of what an evangelical Christian faithful witness might look like, arguing that "religious public voices" can "contribute to a discursive environment that empowers and nourishes conviction in public life and allows for genuine acknowledgment and healthy respect for difference" (292). I suggest that Kimberly could have functioned as an edifying religious public voice had she been encouraged not to avoid her religious faith but rather to ground her argument directly in her ethos as a millennial evangelical Christian.[4] Doing so would have alleviated her ethos problem and offered her a powerful vantage from which to make her argument.

As I have shown, Kimberly's strategy for dealing with her ethos problem is to bury her personal decision to refuse the vaccine in an essay that otherwise aims to inform via rational, de-personalized argumentation. That strategy leaves her with a lingering question as to whether what she's arguing lines up with her personal commitments regarding abstinence. It would also likely leave her intended readers—parents of young girls who favor abstinence—with a similar lingering question. "Wait a minute," they might say. "You didn't take the vaccine; why should my girls do so? Why can't I assume that they'll remain abstinent like you? Why can't I use you as an example that teenage girls can save sex for marriage?" However, the very identifying factor that threatens to undermine Kimberly's argument—her ethos as a millennial evangelical Christian student who remains abstinent and yet still supports the vaccine for public health reasons—could have served as one of her most powerful appeals for her invoked audience. Inherent in Kimberly's ethos problem is a potential solution, and that solution could have looked something like this:

Kimberly is writing for parents of young girls who are on the fence concerning the HPV vaccine, if not outright opposed to it. As such, it's possible to imagine that a significant portion of Kimberly's audience would identify with some form of Christian faith that stresses abstaining from sex until marriage as part of Christian morality. This possibility doesn't require much of an imagination: as I pointed out earlier, evidence from Kimberly's essay suggests she assumed her audience saw abstinence as the best course of action for their daughters. And while not every parent who might espouse such a question would identify with evangelical Christianity or another form of Christianity, a large segment of the population that espouses this position—especially those who are vocal about this issue in public discourse—do identify with some form of theologically conservative Christianity (see Crowley 134–43). As a millennial evangelical who made the conscious decision to remain abstinent, Kimberly could have grounded her ethos in that decision. Her argument could have gone as follows: "While I choose to remain abstinent as a result of my faith and thus opted against taking the vaccine, I argue that you should consider having your daughters vaccinated anyway. This is because while I understand the importance of abstinence, I also understand the importance of life. And in my opinion, life is more important than abstinence." Making this argument would have helped Kimberly further establish her ethos by meeting her audience's potential concerns head on. Additionally, clarifying her motives for why she did not take the vaccine but still argues in favor of it would help Kimberly fulfill her instructor's request that she make her writing more personal.

Of course, doing so would also mean that Kimberly would have to defy Stephanie's stricture against religious perspectives, a point I'll return to below. By making this argument, though, Kimberly could leverage her vernacular religious creativity in deliberative ways and add an important perspective into a debate that features evangelical Christian discourse. In Chapter 3, I cited Habermas's contention that "vital and nonfundamentalist religious communities can become a transformative force in the center of a democratic civil society—all the more so when frictions between religious and secular voices provoke inspiring controversies on normative issues and thereby stimulate an awareness of their relevance" (25). Certainly, friction exists in the debate between religious and secular citizens concerning the HPV vaccine. And while it's possible to interpret Habermas's statement about "transformative force" as meaning that religious communities can frame debates in ways that give rise to moral or religious dimensions of issues that might otherwise go unnoticed, another interpretation suggests something closer to what Kimberly might achieve. As a nonfundamentalist black evangelical Christian, Kimberly could work to transform how her local evangelical communities (e.g., IVCF, Campus Crusade, GEC, even her

AME church at home) perceive and interpret debates about sex, morality, and public health. She could do so by generating arguments from the vernacular religious creativity she enacted, namely a values hierarchy wherein she prioritizes life over abstinence in the context of public debates surrounding the HPV vaccine. Within her enclaves, she could then deliberate with other evangelical Christian citizens and argue in support of a common good that benefits everyone in a given society, not just other Christians (McLaren 115–25).

Given that an evangelical audience would value her personal stance on abstinence, she would be able to foreground her personal stance on morality as one that would establish her as an insider who understands the religious motives underpinning abstinence. But then she'd also be able to tell stories, not only about the difficulties of remaining abstinent in a public university context, but also about teenage girls she knows in her home church who are sexually active and thus at higher risk for contracting HPV (see Ammerman, *Sacred*). Somewhat ironically, then, one possible answer to Kimberly's ethos problem—at least for an evangelical, family values audience—is not to avoid the fact that she rejected the vaccine, but rather to foreground her motives for doing so and then argue on behalf of what she believes is more important than abstinence: doing whatever is possible to protect the lives of the "young girls" she invokes at the beginning of her letter.

Unlike Austin, Kimberly wouldn't be striving to achieve intersubjectivity across significant differences of belief when making such an argument; she wouldn't be writing to constitute herself as legitimate within a human context that perceives her faith as suspect. Rather, she'd be working from the start within a common reference world, one wherein interlocutors already perceive themselves as sharing significant social—even religious—meanings. Consequently, the rhetorical possibilities stemming from Kimberly's evangelical Christian ethos underscore a rhetorical application for vernacular religious creativity different from what Austin's experience suggest, namely the ability to enact deliberative discourse within one's enclaves. Despite the fact that Kimberly would be communicating with people who share much in common with her, she'd still be arguing for a perspective that her interlocutors may not hold, a possibility that Stephen Carter underscores when he writes that "Christians have sharp disagreements" (*God's Name* 61). Following from Roberts-Miller's description of deliberative democracy, Kimberly would need to approach her interlocutors with "empathy, attentiveness, and trust"; she would need to be prepared to "listen with care" if they disagree; and she still would have to "argue with passion but without rancor, with commitment but without intransigence" (187). If she could do this with civility and conviction within her enclaves and within the publics that emerge from the HPV debate, Kimberly could function as a Habermasian "transformative force" by helping to rearticulate values about an important public health issue that continues to provoke debate within various publics.

Chapter Conclusion

I recognize that I'm asking a lot from Kimberly. I recognize, too, that I'm likely taking her writing more seriously than she herself took it. After all, wasn't she doing what so many of our students do and just writing for the teacher? Wouldn't that reality undermine any hope that she could become a Habermasian transformative force? Certainly, it could, and to an extent I think Kimberly was writing for Stephanie—Kimberly's concern regarding how her grade might be affected if she incorporated her religious perspective into her persuasive essay suggests as much. At the same time, there's also evidence to suggest that Kimberly was able to imagine an audience of parents of young girls. As I pointed out earlier, one of Kimberly's primary rhetorical strategies is to raise objections that her target audience might have with her argument. To my knowledge, Stephanie was not a parent, so it seems plausible that Kimberly was thinking rhetorically as she crafted her argument. Arguably, then, Kimberly succeeds at least in part in grounding her argument in values she assumes her intended audience holds.

And that's where I see in Kimberly's experience a missed rhetorical opportunity—not so much that she would actually become a transformative force within her evangelical Christian enclaves, but rather that she would have an opportunity to see how religious beliefs, values, and identity can inform public arguments in productive, deliberative ways. Coming to an understanding of these connections, though, would require careful, intentional mentoring. Kimberly would need help knowing that she has an ethos problem, one that centers on how her faith informs her perspective about the HPV vaccine. She would need encouragement to look more deeply into the religious component of the debate in order to understand the key values and beliefs that motivate those perspectives. She would also need guidance positioning herself as an advocate for the vaccine even if she didn't take it due to her decision to remain abstinent. In short, Kimberly would need help becoming a better, more thoughtful rhetor, one who is able to draw on the range of discursive resources she has at her disposal, including those that align with her deeply held religious beliefs.

This is the kind of mentoring that rhetorically-focused FYW courses should be able to offer, but it is also the kind of help many such courses fall short of providing if they rule out religious perspectives and topics. Unfortunately, this was the very stricture Kimberly faced in her FYW course, a stricture that, as I have suggested, influenced her approach to the essay she wrote. As a result, I am left to wonder what Kimberly might have written had she been encouraged to explore the HPV debate from the perspective of a millennial evangelical college student who refused to take the HPV vaccine based on her decision to remain abstinent. How might she have interpreted and analyzed the debates surrounding the vaccine—especially those that were formed within and about evangelical communities—as a Jamaican American millennial evangelical Christian? Her essay in the end might not have looked much different from what she produced—she might have still made the same argument. But she hopefully would have begun to recognize how the faith tradition to which she belongs shapes and is shaped by public discourse. She might have been able to articulate her faith with a public issue that has been molded significantly by debates centered in the evangelical Christian community. Indeed, she might have articulated her faith in ways that could in fact "shape the world" along the lines of Stephanie's stated hope in the course syllabus.

Despite her missed rhetorical opportunity, Kimberly's writing suggests she was capable of a form of vernacular religious creativity that offers significant potential for deliberative discourse. As an evangelical Christian who has committed herself personally to abstinence, she demonstrated an ability to rearticulate her values effectively in order to argue on behalf of the public good. Thus while she did not achieve the full range of deliberative possibilities that her evangelical Christian ethos makes possible, what she did achieve is no less important: the ability to separate personal morality from her concern for the public good without sacrificing either. Given that Kimberly evidenced at least some awareness of how the argument she wrote implicated her beliefs and values, her strategy of values articulation seems to offer little long-term risk in terms of demoralization. The accommodations Kimberly made differ from those that Austin made. Kimberly does not legitimize the belief systems of people who espouse a different faith or no faith at all. Rather, she's responding to the reality she has experienced within her human context, a reality wherein numerous peers in her home church and sorority put themselves at risk for an STD that could cause cancer. Indeed, as I pointed out earlier, Kimberly already seemed to have ample room in her outlook for people who choose different ways of living and believing. She may be enacting vernacular religious creativity by rearticulating her beliefs, but such creativity seems to be grounded in a flexibility she already possesses.

In some respects, the next chapter takes up where this one leaves off. Eloise, who was new to her faith, ultimately demonstrates what is possible when a student rhetor chooses to write directly from her ethos as a millennial evangelical Christian, for academic as well as public purposes. To get there, though, she must come to terms with the limits of some forms of evangelical discourse in secular, pluralistic contexts like a public university classroom. Eloise must change the way she speaks in order to "gain a serious hearing" (DePalma 237) with peers who do not share her faith.

Notes

1. Kimberly described her process of writing that sermon as follows: "I just went through the Bible and picked verses in reference to, um—because my audience was upcoming high school seniors—so I did um you know around the points of God always being there, um, he has a will and purpose for your life, so do what you have to do. And um just don't be scared, and just have faith and trust in him and continue to go to church like you're doing now and, um, maintain those

values that you grew up with. 'Cuz most of them I was in Sunday School with. And stuff like that" (second interview).

2. This is a reference to John 14.6 (*The NIV Study Bible*).
3. Kimberly offered an example of what evangelism looks like for her in our third interview: "I feel like just being in a sorority, and my sisters see me in this light that they probably generally don't see their other sisters in that particular light. And, um, they would come to me with questions surrounding faith or come to me and say, you know, 'Kimberly, could you pray about this for me?' And, um, I'm just honored in a way, because it's just like, 'Whoa. Hmm. Okay, thank you. You see me in a way that you really don't see anyone else—for me to extend prayer for you.' It's a deep thing."
4. While ethos is a tricky subject that has garnered no shortage of critical discussion, I use it here in ways that align with Isocrates's notion of ethos rather than Aristotle's. See James Baumlin's discussion of these two threads of ethos in his introduction to *Ethos: New Essays in Rhetorical and Critical Theory*. See also Hyde; Jarratt and Reynolds; and Perkins, "'Attentive.'"

6 Changing the Way She Speaks

Eloise's Translative and Constitutive Rhetoric

> I think I have to change the way I talk about stuff. … I guess I have to be more of, like, the sort of quiet voice than like the pressuring voice. Like, I never told anyone, "This is how it is, this is why you should be a Christian," but it's more of like the, this is why *I* am. Like, these are the factors that influenced me.
>
> —Eloise on changing the way she talks about faith

Eloise is a female of Caucasian and Iranian descent from the Northeast who, along with Austin and Kimberly, was a traditional first-year student at Northeast State University (NESU). Like Austin and Kimberly, Eloise participated actively in Intervarsity Christian Fellowship (IVCF) and attended Greenville Evangelical Church (GEC). Eloise competed as a member of NESU's varsity track and field team and belonged to Athletes InterVarsity, a subgroup of IVCF. Unlike Austin and Kimberly, Eloise was new to Christianity. While in high school, Eloise converted to Christianity in part because of her relationship with an evangelical Christian boyfriend, Daniel, whom she continued to date while in college. Eloise's acceptance of Christianity occurred over the course of several months during her senior year of high school, and her conversion was thorough and powerful. "I don't know when exactly it was," Eloise told me in our first interview, adding that her actual moment of conversion may have occurred "a week before summer camp in the … mountains. I prayed to God and asked him to save me before I went to bed." Eloise's faith clearly reflects conversionism, the first priority in David Bebbington's definition of evangelicalism (3; Cope and Ringer 107).

Prior to her conversion, Eloise was raised in the Bahá'i tradition and had by no means led a profligate life. She admitted to peccadillos such as swearing, having a few drinks, and hanging out with the wrong crowd, but her Christian conversion led her to rethink even those actions. She told me that, as a result of becoming a Christian, she changed her lifestyle and developed a sense of purpose: "It's like, now there's more meaning to life. Like, there's a purpose, whereas before I was just kinda like, 'Oh, this is fun.' Like, 'We're having a good time. It's—there's no purpose in anything we're doing.'" That Eloise's conversion to evangelical Christianity provided her with a sense of meaning for her life and actions resonates with findings from the National

Study of Youth and Religion (NSYR). In *Soul Searching*, Christian Smith and Melinda Lundquist Denton note that some of the teens they interviewed "live in what we might call a 'morally significant universe'" (156). Those who perceived themselves as doing so reported having "significant direction and purpose," such that they viewed their lives as "inescapably bound up to a larger framework of consequence" (156). And according to Smith and Snell in *Souls in Transition*, this sense of purpose was more pronounced among devout millennials like Eloise than among the less religious (268–69).

Eloise's sense of purpose derives at least in part from her evangelical Christian faith. While that purpose reflects a distinct desire to share her faith with others, it also evidences her long-standing desire to serve others in a variety of ways. She actively sought out opportunities to volunteer for various community service initiatives and expressed a desire to be politically active in order to help achieve her vision of the common good. Such qualities again align with the NSYR data: Smith and Snell report that highly devout millennials were far more likely to volunteer for community service than those who evidenced lower levels of devotion (262–63). Eloise's desire to engage in community service also aligns with the belief shared among a minority of emerging adults that they can "make a difference" and "impact society for the better" (Smith and Snell 73). Additionally, Eloise's conception of evangelical Christian activism—the third priority in Bebbington's definition of evangelicalism—emphasizes both spiritual and material concerns, a trend that recalls the social Gospel movement of the early twentieth century and thus offers distinct possibilities for civic engagement (see Duffy; see also Shaver).

Indeed, Eloise's commitment to social action constituted much of her motivation for taking the writing-intensive (WI), first-year experience (FYE) course that I discuss here. While her Investigations course, as I'll call it, differs from the traditional FYW course that Austin and Kimberly took, its theme of community allows for direct consideration of the possibilities for civic engagement that exist within the vernacular faith and religious creativity of millennial evangelical students. Eloise's enactment of vernacular religious creativity follows from her realization that, as the epigraph makes clear, she needed to change the way she communicated her faith in her Investigations course and in the larger NESU community. Eloise's rhetorical action grounded in her vernacular religious creativity thus features translation—finding a way of speaking within the context of her class and university community that would allow her to foster intersubjectivity with her classmates. Like Austin, then, Eloise faces the challenge of speaking outside of evangelical Christian enclaves and walking a fine line between religious commitment and community identification at NESU.

Translation isn't Eloise's sole rhetorical strategy, though. When given the opportunity to write publicly for a university-wide audience, she directly attempts to constitute her readers as potentially accepting of her evangelical Christian faith, and she does so in order to participate civically as a legitimate member within the publics that comprise her university community. Her strategy for constituting her audience involves undertaking what Kimberly did not attempt to do, namely writing directly from her ethos as an evangelical Christian. By demonstrating how she has successfully integrated herself into various aspects of community life at NESU, Eloise attempts to rearticulate her readers' assumptions about evangelical Christians. Specifically, she attempts to show that evangelical Christians are not concerned solely with converting people and can be productive members of society. In order to do so, Eloise enacts her changed manner of speaking: she writes personally and, rather than proclaiming truth, invites her readers to experience NESU from her perspective. To put it in terms of the epigraph, she translates her "pressuring voice" into a "quiet" one. Eloise's academic writing, then, functions as one medium through which she strives to come to terms with how to interact civically and civilly as an evangelical Christian within a pluralistic context. Consequently, her experience offers scholars and teachers of rhetoric and writing insight into how one millennial evangelical Christian student attempts to gain a "serious hearing with diverse audiences" (DePalma 237) and constitute a set of conditions that might allow for deliberative conversation.

I proceed by first describing Eloise's faith and her Investigations course. I then discuss Eloise's growing awareness of what Mark Allan Steiner might call "the limits" of evangelical forms of persuasion (303–04). From there, I analyze two pieces of writing Eloise produced for her Investigations course. In the first, she attempts to rearticulate her readers' and her own perceptions of evangelical Christianity by arguing that not all forms of evangelicalism are loud, obnoxious, and forceful. This first essay functions aspirationally. Through it, Eloise attempts to construct herself as the kind of evangelical Christian she wants to be and thus anticipates the writing she produces for the second paper I analyze, the public, personal essay that features her translative and constitutive rhetoric. I should stress here that Eloise's story differs significantly from Austin's and Kimberly's because, I believe, Eloise was so new to evangelical Christianity. While Austin and Kimberly had been conditioned to keep silent about their faith in certain social situations (e.g., caustic classroom discussions about faith or even academic contexts in general), Eloise had not developed such habits. As a result, some of the perspectives Eloise offers here may strike readers as naïve, especially her expectation that she would be welcomed and accepted when speaking as an evangelical Christian in her Investigations course. That naïveté, though, renders even more significant her later realization that she should change the way she speaks. It suggests that even students who are outspoken and zealous about their faith—qualities that in rhetoric and composition scholarship tend to cluster around those evangelicals we deem to be "problem students" (Cope and Ringer 106; see also Perkins, "'Attentive'")—may be rhetorically aware and capable of enacting vernacular religious creativity in ways that could foster deliberative rhetoric. Moreover, it suggests that students who appear to be entrenched in their perspectives are capable of change, and that such changes become evident across multiple student texts over time.

Eloise's Faith

While Eloise was new to evangelical Christianity, she was not new to faith in general: she had grown up in the Bahá'i tradition of her mother and grandmother, both of whom were Iranian. Eloise admitted early in our first interview that she never felt fully committed to Bahá'i: "But for me, there were never any kids around, 'cuz we didn't live in, like, a large community. ... So that was hard because it was like, it's me and a bunch of adults. Like, I don't see any movement here, trying to better the world." Eloise went on to say that she was "becoming kind of apathetic to that point of view. Like, 'Oh, this is just something I do on Sundays,' or 'I just go somewhere every nineteen days and say some prayers.'" Shortly thereafter, Eloise met Daniel and started attending his evangelical Christian church regularly, both for youth group during the week and services on Sunday. While Eloise's mother did not approve, her father, a non-practicing Catholic, was less resistant; he would often pick up Eloise from church on Sundays. After church or youth group, Eloise would have long conversations about Christianity with Daniel; Eloise described those conversations in our first interview as "very informational" and said that Daniel "never really pushed" her to convert. During those conversations, Eloise said she "kept realizing, 'Wow, this is true.'" Her moment of conversion took place the summer before she arrived at NESU. As she put it, "That's when I just made my decision, like, I prayed to God and asked him to save me before I went to bed."

The first letter Eloise wrote for our study offers insight into her evangelical Christian faith. Eloise addresses the letter to her roommate, Michaela, who was enrolled in the same Investigations course as Eloise. Eloise and Michaela did not get along well, a point Eloise acknowledges at the beginning of her letter: "As you know, being my classmate and even more so, my roommate, we do not always see eye-to-eye on things." Much of the reason for their differences of opinion had to do with Eloise's faith, which Michaela did not share. Eloise's purpose in her letter, then, is to help Michaela "understand [her] convictions." Her purpose is also to witness or testify to her newfound faith: Eloise observes that while she "only recently became a Christian a little over a year ago," her conversion "is definitely something that has changed [her] life for the better." While Eloise doesn't spell out completely what her life consisted of prior to her conversion, she admits that it was "headed in a not so respectable direction" and that "faith saved me more than one could know." Eloise writes, "Even though I struggled with the decision to accept Jesus into my heart for quite some time, I just knew in my heart that it was the right thing to do. That unless I was saved, I would be missing out on so much more than a merely secular life could give me." Eloise ends the letter by reiterating how her conversion has changed her for the better: "I am a Christian and have given my life to God," she writes, later adding, "I just know where I am going when I am done with this world and I can honestly say that that is a comfort I can attribute to my beliefs as a Christian and knowing all that Jesus has done for us and all that he has promised us."

While Eloise in her letter never prompts Michaela outright to consider converting to Christianity, her use of the inclusive personal pronoun "us" in her last sentence suggests an evangelical motive. And as became clear throughout our case study, sharing her faith was central to Eloise's conception of Christianity. In the letter Eloise wrote prior to our second interview, Eloise references sharing "the good news" and notes that, as "a born-again Christian," she is "still new at all of this excitement and the feeling of completely wanting to share my faith." And in our second interview, she referenced attending the same evangelism conference Austin had attended, where she learned more about how to share her faith with others. However, Eloise also admitted to being fearful about sharing her faith. In our fifth interview, she said the following:

> Being a new Christian, I'm kind of uncomfortable with trying to, like, evangelize. And like, so when I think of missions trips, I think of more of, like, the projects you're doing to help people, so that they in turn can evangelize. Like, when my church went to Guatemala, they worked at a youth camp that was meant for teens to go to and do stuff. So, I dunno. I see it as the physical work rather than the actual talking.

Evangelism in Eloise's estimation doesn't necessarily entail talking about one's faith; it can also entail acts of service that constitute the "good news." Regardless of the form it takes—whether meeting people's material needs or talking to them—Eloise's faith emphasizes evangelical forms of activism (Bebbington 3; Cope and Ringer 107).

It also emphasizes relationship. In the first letter she wrote to Michaela, Eloise explains, "To me, Christianity is not just some religion but rather, it is an amazing relationship that has brought me closer to God and opened my eyes to the truth." The idea that Christianity is a relationship and not a religion is an American evangelical commonplace that underscores the belief that Christian devotion should be marked by passionate, wholehearted devotion (relationship) as opposed to shallow, unfeeling rule following (religion). Relationships are dynamic; religion is sterile. And while Austin and Kimberly alluded to this distinction at various points, Eloise stressed it more. In our first interview, Eloise said she had come to realize that Bahá'i felt like a religion to her, while Christianity emphasized relationship. She went on to observe that she prefers using the term relationship to describe her faith because other people tend to equate religion with stereotypes, an issue that, as I'll show, became a central concern for Eloise.

Arguably, Eloise attempts to foster her relationship with God via engaging in practices associated with evangelical Christianity. Like Austin and Kimberly, Eloise defines her faith in part by the activities she chooses to engage in or avoid. As she puts it in her first letter to Michaela, "I stick to my morals. In place of drinking (something I do not believe a Christian should partake in for it dampens their testimony) and being promiscuous in any way, I spend my time on the important things in life." She goes on to list those "important things": attending church on Sundays, going to IVCF three days a week, and waking up early so she can hold daily devotions. She told me in our first interview that her daily devotions consisted of reading passages from the Bible and then journaling about what the writer is saying and how the passage applies to her life. Like Kimberly, Eloise's biblicism emphasizes practical application (see Bebbington 3; Juzwik; Smith, *Bible*). Given that Eloise also attended GEC and the sermons there tended to stress life application of biblical texts, this commonality should come as little surprise. Eloise also described her church at home in biblicist terms: "It's straight from the Bible kind of teaching thing" (first interview).

Eloise's emphasis on what she chooses not to do as a Christian—drinking, having sex—aligns her morality with Austin and Kimberly as well as with findings from the NSYR. Smith and Snell report that devout millennials are far less likely to use or abuse alcohol or engage in premarital sexual activity than their peers (265, 274). Like Austin and Kimberly, Eloise's morality is intertwined with her faith. While Eloise does not write about such concerns for her Investigations course, she brought up the themes of alcohol and sex throughout our interviews. Perhaps the most important instance involves discussing the topic of sex with her roommate Michaela. Early in our first interview, I asked Eloise if she could remember when she first shared her faith with Michaela. Eloise talked about how, prior to arriving at NESU, she and Michaela chatted via Facebook to get to know each other. As Eloise recalls it, "The whole issue of, like, having sex in the dorm room came up. And I'm like, 'Well, I have a boyfriend …, but we're both virgins, 'cuz we believe in wait until marriage.' And she's like, 'Oh, so you must be a Christian?' And I was like, 'Yeah.'" This initial conversation between Eloise and Michaela likely set the stage for the tension that marked their relationship; their divergent attitudes regarding faith and morality constitute much of the reason Eloise and Michaela do not "see eye-to-eye on things." And as I'll show, similar tensions existed between Eloise and many of the other members of her Investigations course.

One final point to underscore about Eloise's faith is her ability to prioritize core beliefs as more important than others. In the fourth paper she wrote for her Investigations course, Eloise explains that "[t]he basic pillar of Christianity is acknowledgement that Jesus is our Savior." She goes on to say that "the many other topics which people bring up and associate with Christianity"—she mentions opposition to homosexuality as one—are not part of the "common faith" of Christianity. Eloise echoes this sentiment in our fifth interview when recounting part of the discussion she had with her new roommate after Michaela moved out:

> And then I brought up what I believe, the whole not judging people but not agreeing with it. And [my new roommate's] like, "That makes

> sense." Um, and then I told her, like, one big thing ... I have a problem with is people don't understand that, like, when you're a Christian, it's because you all believe in Jesus, like, not all the other little things. Like, even though the Bible says there's a right and wrong for all the other ways, that's not what connects Christians. Like, it's the fact that you believe that Jesus is your savior and because of that you're going to heaven.

Eloise's statement that "the Bible says there's a right and wrong for all the other ways" certainly is debatable and evidences questionable assumptions in line with some forms of American evangelical biblicism (see Juzwik; Smith, *Bible*). But the larger idea Eloise invokes when she distinguishes between belief in Christ and "all the other little things" evidences a potentially productive enactment of vernacular religious creativity. Namely, she articulates a values hierarchy in such a way as to prioritize core beliefs over peripheral ones, and she does so in relation to her human context. According to Eloise, belief in Jesus is "what connects Christians," and it's possible to disagree with people while not judging them for holding different beliefs.

Eloise's Investigations Course

Eloise did not have to take NESU's traditional FYW course because she earned AP credit in high school that fulfilled the university-wide requirement that all students take ENGL 101. In its place, she took an honors writing-intensive course that, in many ways, paralleled the curricula and pedagogy featured in many FYW programs. The Investigations course she took was part of the university's growing FYE program. Students in the FYE program take themed seminars that are taught by faculty across disciplines but bear many similarities to FYW courses: they're small (twenty students on average), reading and writing intensive, themed around topics such as human rights or environmentalism, and promote active learning strategies favored by many rhetorical educators and compositionists. The particular course Eloise took centered on the topic of community and civic engagement. In particular, it focused on the individual's relationship to various communities and required students to participate in at least twenty hours of community service during the semester. Half of the course grade came from six five-page papers. While I focus on two of the assignments in more detail below, all six asked students to engage with course concepts and ideas on a personal level. Consistent with the university's WI guidelines, the course featured informal writing in the form of reading responses and service-learning journals.

Course readings will strike many compositionists as familiar. Students read Geoffrey Canada's *Fist, Stick, Knife, Gun*, Lorene Cary's *Black Ice*, Barabara Ehrenreich's *Nickel and Dimed*, and Greg Mortenson and David Oliver Relin's *Three Cups of Tea*,[1] along with other articles and book chapters. The course was taught by a tenured, female faculty member in psychology who specialized in women's studies, community engagement, and service learning. As Eloise made clear in the interviews, the class did not take a discipline-specific approach. In our second interview, for instance, Eloise said, "We don't use psychological terms a lot. It's more of—it's an easy to understand basis." Thus while the disciplinary component of the course differed from that of many FYW courses, the experience Eloise had in the course paralleled that of students enrolled in FYW courses. Equally important, the course structure resonates with trends in composition studies, including Anne Beaufort's call for writing classes to adopt a "freshman seminar model" that highlights the importance of "subject matter knowledge" (148). It also parallels Roberts-Miller's suggestion that writing classes introduce students to deliberative discourse by immersing them in a topic that allows for "intensive discussions" (194). While Eloise's FYE course differs from traditional FYW courses, its pedagogical practices resonate with trends in rhetoric and composition.

As an honors student, Eloise could choose from multiple Investigations courses. When I asked Eloise why she chose the one she did, she said, "This one just stuck out to me. I do community service a lot. ... It deals a lot with how the community interacts" (second interview). The syllabus makes clear that the purpose of the course is to help students "explore how we as individuals are shaped by the communities we are a part of and how we in turn can impact our communities" ("Investigations"). It goes on to list "three key questions" the course will tackle: "(1) What is an effective community? (2) How does community impact individual development? (3) How do individuals make a difference in their community?" Students address these questions through reading and writing assignments, participation in class, and service learning. A quarter of each student's grade came from their service-learning journal; in it, students were expected to write reflectively and informally about what they learned at their service-learning sites and "how it connects with course concepts." Eloise acknowledged in our second interview that the service-learning requirement was appealing to her. She also acknowledged that the disciplinary emphasis of the class didn't factor much into her decision. As she put it, "I didn't take it because it's a psych class. I took it because it deals with issues that I'm interested in" (second interview).

While the idea of community constituted the course, it also underscored the class's living arrangement. Eloise described her FYE course as a "community living class"—students lived in the same dorm, many on the same floor. Eloise and Michaela, at least for the first half of the semester, were roommates. The "live and learn" component of the course certainly marks it as structurally different from Austin's and Kimberly's FYW courses; it also likely informed the intense social friction that Eloise described as common in the course. The friction that Eloise experienced had much to do with her faith. Eloise described the majority of students in the class as not ascribing to Christianity (or any other faith, for that matter), though there were exceptions. Eloise often referenced "Thomas," another evangelical

Christian student in the class who, according to Eloise, seemed to face less resistance than she did.[2] She also said that one of her classmates was the daughter of a local Unitarian minister, although that student tended to hold views more in line with Michaela and the other members of the class than with Eloise.

Eloise said in our second interview that it was common for class discussions to feature plenty of "heated discussion," the presence of which can be attributed to the makeup and structure of the class and to the professor's non-authoritarian stance in the classroom. In our second interview, Eloise described her professor as a "non-biased person" who "just sits back and listens." This willingness on the professor's part to allow discussion of controversial topics in class reflects the goals of Investigations courses at NESU. According to the FYE program's website, one of those goals is to help students become "independent thinkers" who consider "challenging problems from a number of viewpoints." The course syllabus likewise made this objective clear, describing the class as a "discussion seminar" wherein "the bulk of the learning will take place through interacting with one another." Eloise's reported experience—namely that of not feeling as if she had an equal voice in the Investigations course—suggests that Roberts-Miller is correct when she argues that "in the public sphere (as in the classroom), a perfectly unconstricted and unmoderated public sphere, ironically enough, inhibits participation" (191).

The Limits of Evangelical Discourse

Much of the reason Eloise's classmates did not listen to her was because, as became clear over the course of our case study, she initially spoke in ways that alienated her from the class. Eloise admitted that she was rather up-front about sharing her faith early on in the course. Perhaps the clearest description of how Eloise spoke about her faith emerged early in our first interview:

> I don't find it hard to really tell people where I come from. Like, say someone's using foul language. I'm like, "Hey, can you stop that? I don't really appreciate the swearing." And they're like, "Oh, why?" And then I explain. And everyone knows I go to InterVarsity three nights a week. Everyone knows I go to church on Sundays. So.

This passage echoes what Eloise wrote in the opening paragraph of the letter she wrote to Michaela for our first interview: "Obviously you know that I am a Christian for there is no way I would hide my faith ..." And in the letter she wrote to Michaela for our second interview, Eloise alluded to the boldness with which she shared her faith in class early in the semester: "I put myself out there, explaining what my faith meant to me almost on a daily basis, not even stopping to consider what others thought of me." Eloise goes on to lament how frustrating it is for her when "no one wants to hear the good news" she was trying to communicate in class.

As could be imagined, Eloise's boldness about sharing her faith did not go over well in a northeastern public university classroom where few students identified with any religion, much less evangelical Christianity. Clear parallels can be drawn here between Eloise and "Tina," the eccentric, outspoken evangelical Christian student enrolled in one of Priscilla Perkins's upper-level writing classes. Like Tina, Eloise "regularly offered unsolicited religious advice" and found herself alienated from her classmates ("'Attentive'" 79–80). Also like Tina, Eloise was not afraid to speak up for what she believed to be true—the "good news" that Eloise assumed her peers would want to hear. Perkins points out that one of Tina's problems in attempting to communicate with her classmates derives from her "flattened" sense of ethos: writers like Tina (a "biblical literalist," according to Perkins) assume that their "credibility comes entirely from [their] reliance on biblical authority" (84). Because of this assumption of unmediated authority, writers like Tina feel no compulsion to do the "hard work" that Steiner suggests is necessary for successful evangelical rhetorical action across difference, namely the work of "engaging outsiders in rhetorically sensitive ways that acknowledge their humanity and dignity and that work to earn their respect and their hearing" (311). Perkins says something similar when she argues that evangelical forms of ethos like the one Tina evidences lack "humanness" (84).

Early on in the semester, Eloise evidenced a similar notion of ethos: she assumed she needed no credibility outside of the truth she was proclaiming, and so her communication with her classmates tended to lack the human quality that Perkins and Steiner emphasize. And that led to a significant problem for Eloise: her peers came to see her through the lens of a stereotype for evangelical Christians in American culture. That stereotype, as Eloise understood it, depicts evangelicals as narrow-minded rule-followers who are outspoken, intolerant, moralistic, and staunchly conservative. In our first interview, for instance, Eloise said, "[P]eople make so many stereotypes about a religion. And, like, even between the roommates and the people in my class, it's like, 'Oh, religion is bad. It's something that puts rules on you and it forces you to do stuff.'" Then in our fifth interview, Eloise said, "And it's really hard, because I live with these people [from my Investigations course], so you [would] think they'd see me as just me more or less. But a lot of the time, it's like, 'Oh, she's going to InterVarsity. She's a Christian, and so she believes this.'" Eloise's emphasis on "this" in the spoken interview suggests she meant it to function metonymically: her identification as an evangelical Christian reduces her to a set of narrow, predictable beliefs. And because Eloise suspected that her peers viewed her as one-dimensional, she often reiterated some form of the following idea: "I want [my classmates] to see me as me, rather than as a Christian. 'Cuz they have a lot of stereotypes about Christians" (second interview).

Eloise thus faces a dilemma not unlike Austin's: she wants to speak in class in a way that reflects her faith commitments, but she also wants to belong and be heard. She wants her peers to see her as a human and fellow college student who is also an evangelical Christian. Eloise speaks to this dilemma in the letter she wrote for our second interview. She again addresses the letter to her roommate Michaela and begins by noting that the IVCF conference she recently attended "opened [her] eyes to a lot of things that have been happening"—in Eloise's personal life, in her relationship to others in the Investigations course, and, of course, in relation to her faith. Eloise writes that the conference impressed upon her the need to "really ... be a disciple" of Jesus Christ, rather than just thinking him to be "cool." For Eloise, this meant seeing Christ in all of his complexity, rather than selecting "bits and pieces that interest" her. But the real implication comes in the form of her relationships with others: "I need to put myself out there," Eloise writes, "feel more vulnerable, but also more confident and tell those who I care about who [Jesus] really is." The reason for doing so is evangelical to the core: "God wants someone from every community"—including her Investigations course—"to come to him."

In the next paragraph, Eloise introduces the other side of the dilemma. She explains why, prior to attending the IVCF conference, she had grown increasingly silent in class:

> I guess I am just fed up with the fact that it never seems as if people are listening to what I have to say. It truly does hurt when you are being shut down class after class because no one wants to hear the good news that you are telling them. In a way, I am more nervous and almost embarrassed to share my faith because just as any other person, I long to have platonic relationships with others. The environment in which our discussions take place has turned rather unwelcoming recently and I feel as if I should almost give up.

Eloise is aware that she has alienated herself from the other members of her Investigations course—her immediate human context—and that doing so threatens her ability to befriend her peers. Later in the letter, though, Eloise returns to the other pole of the dilemma and expresses her desire to resume sharing her faith in class, regardless of outcome: "From this point out, though, that is going to change. I know now not to be embarrassed about my faith because it makes me who I am. Rather than hiding it, I am going to fully embrace it and if that means becoming a lot more vulnerable, well, then that is just how it is going to have to be."

Eloise's statement evidences her assumption that the problem exists within her own reservations and not in the class's attitudes toward her faith—that if she can just get over her own fears and inhibitions, then she'll feel heard. In our second interview, I raised the question of whether Eloise thought her classmates would listen to her, especially given that her prior attempts had been unsuccessful. She responded in a way that suggests she had arrived at a rhetorical strategy grounded in vernacular religious creativity that might allow her to mitigate the dilemma she faced:

Eloise: I think I have to change the way I talk about stuff. Because, I guess like, I'm not judgmental, but I may seem that I'm judgmental when I put something out there because of the whole idea that on this campus you have to be unbiased and tolerant of everything. Um, so Christianity kind of doesn't fit into that the way the public views it, even though in reality it's open to everyone and we don't judge because it's not our job to judge ... I guess I have to be more of, like, the sort of quiet voice than like the pressuring voice. Like, I never told anyone this is how it is, this is why you should be a Christian, but it's more of like the, this is why *I* am. Like, these are the factors that influenced me.

Jeff: Hmm. And you think that, so talking about it more from ...

Eloise: A personal ...

Jeff: ... this is my experience—from a personal experience—will have more ...?

Eloise: I think so.

Eloise's realization that the problem rests not necessarily in what she says about her faith but in how she says it suggests that she has begun to recognize the limits of evangelical discourse. Rather than speaking from a flattened notion of ethos like Tina, Eloise is coming to realize that she needs to speak from an ethos that assumes "the limitations of the human subject *as a knower*" (Steiner 302, original emphasis). And as I'll discuss, it is this realization that leads Eloise to adopt the rhetorical strategy of translation in her public writing.

Before she attempts that strategy, though, she tackles a different but related problem, namely her peers' lingering perceptions of her. This problem, as Eloise conceived of it, was definitional and associational. Eloise's manner of speaking at the beginning of the semester—as an evangelical proclaiming truth—fit all too neatly within her peers' views of evangelical Christianity. They already associated evangelical Christians with descriptors like outspoken and moralistic, and Eloise's approach to the class early on in the semester only served to reify those stereotypes. As Eloise puts it in the excerpt above, "Christianity kind of doesn't fit into that the way the public views it," and what she means is that evangelical Christianity as it is actually lived doesn't align with popular conceptions of it, especially those promulgated by the media (see M. Williams 338–41). Consequently, Eloise comes to the realization that she needs to redefine evangelical Christianity itself so her peers might come to perceive it as legitimate. When Eloise and her peers are asked to define activism for one of the major writing assignments in the Investigations course, Eloise takes the opportunity to describe the vernacular, lived form of evangelicalism that she aspires to enact and with which she seeks to be associated. By rearticulating evangelicalism for her peers, Eloise simultaneously rearticulates it for herself and anticipates the translative, constitutive rhetoric she ultimately enacts in her public writing.

Rearticulating Vernacular Evangelicalism

Like Austin, Eloise uses her academic writing as a means of responding to exigencies in her Investigations course. For their fourth paper, which the course instructor called a "Definitions of Activism" paper, students were asked to profile someone they deemed to be an activist in order to construct a definition of activism. "The definition of activist is left up to you," the prompt reads, "although in your paper you should make clear why you have chosen this person and how they fit your definition of an activist." Eloise chose to write about her boyfriend, Daniel, who was instrumental in her conversion to Christianity. As she explains in her essay, Daniel functions as an activist because he promotes evangelical Christianity on his campus, a public university in a nearby northeastern state.

Eloise begins "All Shapes and Sizes" by admitting that she associates activism with radicalism. Eloise explains that this association reflects the media: "This is due to the fact that usually the people who are filmed, written about, and remembered … are radicals who go to the extremes." But then Eloise suggests that such a notion of activism is not necessarily true; activists do not need to be "vigorous and forceful." Her thesis, which she includes at the end of her first paragraph, reads as follows: "There are a great deal of 'normal' people out there who follow the rules and still manage to get the word out there in terms of the cause they are advocating for." In her second paragraph, Eloise continues to disarticulate activism from radicalism by linking the former to the "common good," which she defined in our third interview as "what's best for everyone" in a society. Her formal definition of activism appears at the end of the second paragraph: "an activist is someone who focuses their energy on something other than themselves so that they might promote said something which in the end can be seen as for the greater good." When we talked about this definition in our third interview, Eloise observed that her professor "really liked" her conception of activism, largely because of how it connected to topics then under discussion in the course.

By the third paragraph, we learn who Eloise's exemplary activist is: her "best friend," Daniel. Eloise emphasizes Daniel's soft-spokenness ("he is rather shy") and then tells us the cause to which he is committed, namely evangelism. In the next few paragraphs, we learn more about Daniel's particular brand of evangelical activism: "he does not impose his beliefs on others," though "he does uphold certain moral standards on a personal basis"; he "does not claim to be anything close to perfect," but "he does hope that others might [see] him as a good example"; he "continues to advocate his ideals and set standards for others to strive for"; he "work[s] to promote social change" by going on missions trips, "volunteering" with non-profits like Heifer International, and "taking part in fundraising activities for his high school environmental club." This last point is significant, because through it Eloise underscores the fact that not all of the social change for which Daniel works is "focused on Christianity"—neither Heifer International nor the environmental club he participated in while in high school prioritizes evangelism. By drawing attention to Daniel's diverse forms of activism, Eloise attempts to rearticulate her readers' assumptions regarding evangelical Christians. Millennial evangelicals may want to spread their faith, but they also want to feed the hungry and save the environment.

In our third interview, Eloise talked about the audience she had in mind while writing "All Shapes and Sizes." She explained that her choice of Daniel did not sit well with Michaela, who ended up factoring prominently into Eloise's conception of audience. When I asked Eloise to talk about the audience she envisioned while writing, she said, "I guess I was kinda thinking about my roommate, because right before I started writing [the activism paper], Michaela was like, 'How are you writing about your boyfriend? Like, he's not an activist. No way is he an activist.' And so I was kinda mad when I went about writing my paper." Eloise's anger emerges at the end of her paper:

> While many may see Evangelism as a waste of time that is not the case. It is unfortunate, but it is the radicals who I first mentioned that give a bad name to Christianity. It is the small but quite loud and obnoxious group of far right Christians who take things to the extremes and create an even larger dilemma for the rest of us as they twist what the bible teaches. In place of proclaiming that homosexuals are terrorists and that anyone who is friends with one is going to Hell (which is nowhere stated in the bible) they should get their facts straight.

At the outset of this passage, Eloise directs her ire toward her roommate and other classmates who silenced her or demonstrated intolerance toward her faith. Halfway through, though, she redirects her criticism toward "loud and obnoxious" evangelical Christians who "take things to the extremes." She attempts to distance herself from such extremists by pointing out their error, namely that of appealing to biblical authority to marshal radically intolerant perspectives. Eloise then provides an example of the most egregious of these unbiblical perspectives by constructing a symbolic mash-up worthy of restatement: these "far right" Christians consider homosexuals to be terrorists and even go so far as to damn anyone who befriends one to hell.

The hoped-for effect of what she says here is to distance herself and Daniel from the type of right-wing Christian she suspects her peers perceive her to be. She makes this point clear in her penultimate paragraph when she writes, "People like Daniel (myself included) should not be lumped in this group," later adding, "as a Christian I am sick and tired of being associated with those who go to the extremes and distort God's message to his people." Because Eloise's purpose is to help her peers rearticulate their assumptions about evangelical Christians in general, the conclusion Eloise hopes her readers will reach goes something like this: *if* it's true that the "loud and obnoxious" Christians constitute only a small group of evangelicals, then perhaps the rest of the evangelical Christian population isn't so bad. To borrow terms Eloise uses throughout her essay, perhaps "normal," "quiet," "humble," even "shy" evangelical Christian activists are different from the radicals who make the news.

Of course, there's an obvious irony here: even if Eloise doesn't "twist what the Bible teaches" and "distort God's message" in the way she sees radical evangelicals as doing, her approach to sharing her faith in the Investigations course arguably aligns her more closely with the forceful style of the radicals than with Daniel's quiet, humble, and even shy approach. Eloise admitted in our second interview, for instance, that she had been more of the "pressuring voice" than the "quiet voice," and that even if she didn't consider herself to be judgmental, she came across as such in the way she spoke to her classmates. By her own admission, Eloise knows that she was perceived as loud and obnoxious in her Investigations course. Thus, if we match up Eloise against the definition of vernacular evangelical activism she constructs in "All Shapes and Sizes," it's possible to conclude that she's not quite the kind of evangelical she praises. It's also possible to speculate that if other students in the Investigations course had read "All Shapes and Sizes," they might have rejected its claims based on its apparent two-facedness. Instead of practicing what she preaches, Eloise comes across as lacking self-awareness.

There's another way to read "All Shapes and Sizes," though, and that is as part of her process of vernacular religious creativity, a process whereby religious believers adjust and even remake themselves and their faith to fit better within their particular human contexts. Certainly, Eloise in her activism essay aims to define a version of evangelical Christianity that could be described as vernacular. Eloise is arguing that there's a difference between the lived religion of ordinary evangelical Christians and the radical Christians frequently portrayed in the media. Consequently, her argument parallels key assumptions about lived or vernacular religion, one of which is the idea that non-elite religious believers will live their faith in ways that differ from institutional, official, or highly visible iterations of it (see Ammerman, "Introduction," *Sacred*; Howard; Orsi; M. Williams 341; Primiano; Wolfe, *Transformation*). As I stressed in Chapter 2, though, vernacular religious creativity is less a thing that exists in the world than it is a process. Leonard Primiano emphasizes this notion of process when he writes, "The omnipresent action of personal religious interpretation involves various negotiations of belief and practice including … original invention, unintentional innovation, and intentional adaptation" (43). Or as Robert Orsi puts it, vernacular religion describes "how particular people, in particular places and times, live in, with, through, and against religious idioms available to them in culture" (7). For Primiano and Orsi, religious believers engage in processes of vernacular religious creativity in order to refashion, reshape, adapt, or negotiate their beliefs in relation to their human contexts.

"All Shapes and Sizes" can be read as part of Eloise's process of vernacular religious creativity. More specifically, it can be read as a form of aspirational rhetoric—as an attempt on Eloise's part to adjust her faith to her human context and rewrite herself in order to become the kind of evangelical Christian she desired to be. While Eloise and I did not talk directly about how she saw her activism essay fitting into the development of her faith, she wrote it at a time when she was wrestling with how to "gain a serious hearing" with her peers (DePalma 237). My second interview with Eloise—the one where she said she needed to change the way she talks about her faith—took place a few days after she submitted her final version of "All Shapes and Sizes," and Eloise referenced her essay in our interview. Shortly after making her comment about needing to change the ways she speaks, Eloise said, "When we wrote the activism paper, I wrote it about a small person, because I hate the idea that Christians are always looked down upon because of the radicals who get put in the paper." The interview goes on to highlight a number of related concerns, including the fact that Eloise felt stereotyped by her peers and that she wanted to be more open or vulnerable when talking about her faith. Worth noting here is the fact that Eloise began to develop these ideas after attending the IVCF conference, which she references both in her activism paper and in the letter she wrote to Michaela prior to our second interview. In that letter, Eloise observes how the conference shaped her thinking about how to share her faith in class. She writes, "I need to put myself out there, feel more vulnerable, but also more confident and tell those who I care about who [Jesus] really is." But the ending of her second letter speaks most clearly to the fact that Eloise at this point in the semester envisioned herself as engaged in a process of figuring out how best to communicate her faith in her Investigations course: "While I am a born-again Christian, I am still new at all of this excitement and the feeling of completely wanting to share my faith. In time though, I will definitely become more open and unabashed about relating my faith more wholeheartedly to the class."

My point here is that Eloise wrote this second letter, gave her second interview, and wrote "All Shapes and Sizes" within the span of a few days. All three thus reflect the same set of concerns, and one of the most important concerns for Eloise was the question of how best to go about speaking as an evangelical Christian in class. Eloise's approach to answering that question at this point in the semester involved looking to other ordinary millennial evangelicals who successfully connected with people who don't share their faith. She talked in our second interview, for instance, about Thomas, the other student in her Investigations course who identified as an evangelical and participated in IVCF. Eloise observed how Thomas was better able to communicate his faith in class without alienating his classmates. As she put it, Thomas was "taken better" because he can "relate [his faith] more to other people rather than just say what you believe." Eloise then mused on what she could do to be equally successful: "I feel like I always have to explain myself, why I think one way or not. Because they think a different way, I feel like I have to explain it. So, I guess I have to give them more credit and realize that I don't have to explain, 'I think this way because I'm a Christian.' Like, I should just be able to say, 'Well, I think this.'" After a pause she added, "I feel like I've been coming off as close-minded to [my classmates]. Even though, like, I always said, 'I don't drink, but I don't care if you drink,' I think they focus on the first part rather than the last part." What's noteworthy here is that, more than simply recognizing she had to change the way she communicated her faith, Eloise is musing on how to go about doing so. And part of her method for thinking through how she might adapt her approach to talking about her faith entails looking to other successful millennial evangelicals as models—in this case, her classmate Thomas.

"All Shapes and Sizes" evidences a similar thought process, though with Daniel as the exemplar. Eloise praises Daniel for having a voice that is "quiet" rather than "vigorous and forceful"—Daniel "does not impose … beliefs on others." Those words come from "All Shapes and Sizes," but they resonate with Eloise's realization in our second interview that she needed to become "more of, like, the sort of quiet voice than like the pressuring voice." And if we read "All Shapes and Sizes" as exemplifying part of Eloise's process of vernacular religious creativity—not only her realization that she aspired to a different form of evangelicalism than what she had enacted, but also her initial attempts to assemble a new version of faith by drawing on resources provided by other successful millennial evangelical students—passages that might have led readers to conclude that Eloise lacks self-awareness take on a much different meaning. Namely, they underscore what she hopes to become rather than what she has failed to be. For example, immediately after noting that she does not want to be "lumped" together with radical evangelicals, Eloise writes, "Nowhere in their work do [ordinary evangelicals like Daniel] alienate or put out another person. Despite the fact that there are definitely lines within the Bible … which are not to be crossed, it is not our place to judge." If we link this idea to what Eloise said in our second interview—that Christianity is "open to everyone and we don't judge because it's not our job to judge," a point she made immediately after recognizing that she needed to transform her manner of speaking—it's possible to read her statement in her activism essay as part of her attempt to constitute herself as a quiet, non-pressuring evangelical like Daniel. It's almost as if Eloise is acknowledging that she herself needs to stop alienating her classmates, and that she herself needs to talk in nonjudgmental ways. Eloise is not just praising "small" evangelicals like Daniel and Thomas in "All Shapes and Sizes." She's trying to write herself as one.

Even though Eloise does not yet enact her rhetorical strategy of translation in “All Shapes and Sizes,” writing her definition of activism essay functions as a meaningful, aspirational step in her process of enacting vernacular religious creativity. By attempting to rearticulate her readers’ conceptions of evangelical Christianity as not always “loud and obnoxious,” Eloise begins to rearticulate her own relationship to evangelism. In the process—and with the help of models like Thomas and Daniel—she begins to work out what a quiet, non-pressuring approach to enacting her faith might look like. Despite its significance, though, Eloise faces two limitations with “All Shapes and Sizes.” The first is that it reaches no reader outside of herself and her professor. Short of handing her classmates the essay and asking them to read it, Eloise has no mechanism for reaching the audience she told me she had in mind while writing her essay: her roommate and, by extension, the other members of her course who perceived her as a stereotypical evangelical Christian. Of course, given the essay’s aspirational qualities, it’s also possible that Eloise wrote her essay as much for herself as she did for the class. “All Shapes and Sizes” certainly bears the stamp of self-exploration: in light of her failed attempts to interact legitimately in her human context, she’s trying to sort out who she is and who she can be as an evangelical Christian in her Investigations course. To put this in terms of James Kinneavy’s basic aims of discourse, “All Shapes and Sizes” appears to be as private and expressive as it is transactional and persuasive, and there’s even reason to believe that the primary audience she attempts to persuade is herself.

Moreover, while Eloise argues on behalf of vernacular evangelicalism, she still does so in a manner that reflects the way she initially spoke in class: her tone is forthright (“While many may see Evangelism as a waste of time that is not the case”), blunt (“I am sick and tired of being associated with those who go to the extremes”), and moralistic (“they should get their facts straight”). Even if she did have a venue through which to share this essay with Michaela and her classmates, she might have found herself reifying rather than redressing her status as a stereotypical evangelical Christian in the eyes of her peers. Eloise thus jumps at the chance to write a public essay that would allow her to enact her vernacular religious creativity in writing. In “In My Own Words,” Eloise begins to realize the aspirational possibilities she began to articulate in her activism essay. She translates her faith into terms that are less moralistic, more personal, and arguably more successful at fostering intersubjectivity with her peers.

“In My Own Words”

For their fifth essay, students in the Investigations course were asked to write an assignment the professor called a “Diversity Analysis” wherein students were to discuss and reflect on particularly meaningful qualities of their social identities. Eloise’s professor also invited the class to consider submitting their essays for a public writing feature at NESU called "Write Your Life," an initiative aimed at highlighting successful students who have made the most of their college experience. Eloise brought up this assignment during our third interview when I asked her what she was writing next:

Eloise: It's—have you heard the, NESU's thing called Write Your Life?
Jeff: I have—I've heard of that, yeah.
Eloise: Yeah, so we just have to make ours. So, like, you have to talk about why you came to NESU, and your time here. … Our teacher had us read a couple at the beginning of the year, and now she just wants us to write our own.
Jeff: Yeah. Did you read them on—oh, I guess they get published online?
Eloise: They print them out, too, like, and put them on posterboards around campus.

This public nature of the Write Your Life initiative powerfully shaped how Eloise approached the assignment. Later in our third interview, Eloise spoke to her conception of audience: "I was writing it for everyone because I saw the posters all around—like …, they had pictures of someone and then their story. And so it wasn't, like, specifically for the teacher. It was more for anyone to be able to read and be like, 'Oh, yeah, that's me.' Like, 'I can do that, too.'" From the outset, Eloise conceived of writing for an audience of real readers and not just for herself or her professor—a marked difference from the partially personal, expressive focus of "All Shapes and Sizes."

Because she envisioned her audience as consisting primarily of readers from across the NESU community, Eloise approached the assignment as an opportunity to name herself publicly as a successful NESU student with diverse interests and commitments, evangelical Christianity among them. And while Eloise's professor did not require students to submit their essays to the Write Your Life feature, Eloise indicated her intentions of doing so:

Eloise: It was kind of fun to write. Like, just to be able to know that you could submit it and put it out there.
Jeff: Fun—you mean, submit it to …?
Eloise: The Write Your Life site.
Jeff: So, it was fun in the sense of, it would have a larger audience?
Eloise: Yeah. And fun in the sense that it'd be easier for people to understand me through this, because it's a personal experience rather than just having to tell them and try to explain to them. (third interview)

It's clear, then, that Eloise conceived of the diversity analysis assignment as public writing that had the potential to reach an audience made up of the larger NESU community, and that reaching a wider audience significantly informed Eloise's motives for writing her essay.

What's also clear is that Eloise directly connects her writing of "In My Own Words" to her vernacular religious creativity. This connection emerges in the excerpt above when she said it was "fun" to write "because it's a personal experience" through which Eloise's audience might come to "understand" her better. Our discussion from the third interview continues:

Jeff: So—personal experience. I mean, do you mean, like, what we were talking about ...?

Eloise: Yeah, like, how I should talk to my class in personal terms rather than this is right and this is wrong.

Jeff: Huh. Okay.

Eloise: I think it's 'cuz I always relate to personal experiences better than someone just telling me how it is. 'Cuz, it's kinda like, "Ok, well, that's how it is for you. How do I know it's going to work for me?" Like, I wanna hear exactly how it is.

Eloise speaks directly to the fact that she conceived of writing "In My Own Words" as a next step in her process of adapting her faith to fit her human context. If "All Shapes and Sizes" afforded Eloise an opportunity to articulate a successful approach to speaking as an evangelical by looking to a model like Daniel, then "In My Own Words" allows Eloise to try out her new way of speaking about her faith. To put this in Eloise's own terms, if the activism essay provided Eloise with the opportunity to critique the pressuring voice that she herself had enacted, the writing she produces for the Write Your Life feature allows her to adopt the quiet voice she thinks might resonate better with her peers and with the wider NESU community. Eloise thus aims to translate her faith into terms she believes her non-Christian readers will appreciate, but in the process of doing so she also hopes to constitute her readers as potentially accepting of evangelical Christianity. If she can do both, Eloise stands a chance of fostering the kind of intersubjectivity that might allow her to participate as an equal, legitimate member in her Investigations course and in NESU as a whole. In what follows, I briefly summarize the essay and then discuss its translative and constitutive moves.

"In My Own Words" is a personal essay—Eloise uses "I" and weaves aspects of her recent past into a coherent reconstruction of experience. She opens on a somewhat confessional tone: "In high school, I was never the most popular girl." She goes on to say that while she had plenty of friends, most fulfilled the role of acquaintance rather than confidant. Indeed, she admits that she has "never had a best (female) friend." By the end of the first paragraph, she increases the tension by noting changes among her closest friends while in high school: "Rather than hanging out and doing the goofy things we normally did, they were becoming interested in 'adult' things like drinking and partying." While Eloise doesn't mention her conversion specifically in this essay, she does describe her senior year as one of "self-realization," a "transition time" she needed to determine that she "didn't need to change who [she] was just to fit in." She then adds, "With this new understanding, I was ready to head off to college." In her third paragraph, Eloise discusses her college selection process, the main criterion of which entailed finding a place that wasn't too "far away from home" where she "felt most comfortable" and could "start off fresh." Eloise again alludes to her Christian conversion: "Knowing who I was and the kind of person I wanted to be was something new to me and, in a sense, I wanted to take this feeling for a test run."

Eloise identifies herself with evangelical Christianity in her fourth paragraph, which begins on page 3, the center of her five-page essay. She leads into this topic by naming various ways whereby she has "continued to create more bridges" to others within the larger NESU community: she's an "active member" on her hall and a student in the honors program. Then she admits that while she's "not a shy person in any manner," she does experience "fears in terms of not being accepted." This leads into the first instance where she explicitly names herself as a Christian. While Eloise does recognize that "there are often stereotypes made against" her due to her religious identity, she ultimately de-emphasizes this point in favor of a much more positive outlook: her peers see past reductive labels and recognize her as a human with diverse interests. Eloise goes on to explain that the acceptance and respect she has experienced allows her "to be an effective Floor Representative" for her dorm's "Hall Council." She constructs herself as inhabiting a position that might best be described as an intermediary between students and the residential staff: "I am able to give back to the people on my floor in terms of letting them [know] what is going on around campus and in the dorm or bringing up issues that they may be having in front of our Hall President and Hall Director." Because other residents are willing to share their problems with Eloise, she reasons that she has been effective in her role as floor representative. She states, "While I am definitely giving back to [my peers] in this sense, I feel like they have given me so much more in terms of feeling comfortable."

Eloise then discusses how she is a member of the varsity track and field team at NESU and admits that while she has "not quite figured out what [her] role is in this community as of yet," she nevertheless "look[s] forward to competing for the next four years." From there, she introduces the "mini-community" that "has probably made the most significant impact on [her] time" at NESU: InterVarsity Christian Fellowship. Noteworthy here is Eloise's decision to describe IVCF by paraphrasing its mission statement: "We are a movement of students who follow Jesus as Savior and Lord: growing in love for God, God's Word, God's people of every ethnicity and culture, and God's purposes in the world." Following that, Eloise begins to conclude. She writes, "I truly believe that being involved within this college community is what keeps me going," and she strives to make it clear that what she means by "college community" transcends a single organization or social identity:

> By connecting with others who have similar interests as myself, as well as those who are my complete opposites, I continue to build upon not only my human capital (in terms of my education) but more importantly, my social capital. In this sense, the greater my social capital, the more effective and productive citizen I will be. In other words, the bigger difference I will be able to make on campus throughout the up and coming years.

After mentioning that she hopes to become a resident assistant, Eloise ends by reiterating her desire "to help others and show them what they too can make of their college experience as long as they stay involved and meet new people who appreciate who they are without any facades."

Translation

How does "In My Own Words" enact Eloise's rhetorical strategy of translation? First, it's evident that she's writing personally: the pronoun "I" appears almost ninety times in her essay, while it only appears thirteen times in "All Shapes and Sizes" and nine times in Kimberly's essay about the HPV vaccine. And while Austin includes "I" approximately twenty times in "Christian Schools vs. Public Schools," none of them refer to him; every instance occurs in a quotation from someone else. Of course, genre is a consideration here: "In My Own Words" is a personal essay, while "All Shapes and Sizes" is a definitional argument; Kimberly and Austin both wrote persuasive essays. Eloise told me in our fourth interview, though, that some of the Write Your Life essays were written in the third person, and that she consciously decided to write hers from the first person. Thus while genre certainly influenced how Eloise approached "In My Own Words," she also made the intentional decision to use "I" instead of "she." As she explained it, "I was telling someone a story, rather than I was telling someone about someone else. Like, I think this is the sort of paper it would have been more awkward to write in the third person."

This was no small decision for Eloise, because as she made clear in our third interview, writing personally was "awkward" for her. In high school, she had been asked to "use the third person" almost exclusively, so writing from that perspective came to feel "automatic." Eloise even commented on how she might have written about her faith at that point: "Even if I wrote about the fact that I was a Christian in high school, it would have been in the sense that this is right and what you think is wrong." And, as I discussed earlier, it is such moralizing that got Eloise in trouble early on in the semester. What's noteworthy about her public writing, though, is its absence of moralistic discourse: at no point does she talk in terms of right or wrong or make arguments about how things ought to be. Rather, she describes some of her core beliefs as an evangelical Christian and allows her readers to make of them what they will. To put it in her terms, Eloise translates statements that declare "This is how it is" into writing that expresses "This is how *I* am."

To illustrate what this translative move looks like in her writing, it's worth comparing passages from "All Shapes and Sizes" and "In My Own Words" that deal with the potentially divisive topic of evangelism. Near the end of "All Shapes and Sizes," Eloise adopts a tone that might best be described as preachy:

> While it may seem a great feat to keep a good standing by [living according to] God's standards, this is not enough, for it is said that we should "Be joyful in hope, patient in affliction, faithful in prayer. *Share with God's people who are in need*" (Romans 12.12–13). To simply live a life pleasing to God does not begin to amount for everything that is asked of us. … As Christians, we too must walk on water. (original emphasis)

While she's using inclusive pronouns like "we" and "us" here, she's doing so in a way that assumes her readers believe the same thing she does. Equally important, she's writing in the imperative: here's what "we should" be doing, here's what "is asked of us," here's what "we too must" do. She's not translating her manner of speaking in order to foster intersubjectivity with an audience who might not share her beliefs. Rather, she's trying to command them, and she's doing so from a clear sense of what she perceives to be right. Contrast this passage with how she talks about evangelism in "In My Own Words":

> Although simply hanging out with each other is something we [IVCF members] love to do, we do indeed serve a greater purpose, which is to reach out to the darkest edges of campus just as Jesus reached out to the poor, the sick, the orphans, and the prostitutes … [W]e really believe in reaching out to those who need us most, those who are in the most need to hear God's word.

Eloise still uses personal pronouns here, but she's no longer writing in the imperative. She's describing some of IVCF's core beliefs for an audience who does not share them, and she's doing so without moralizing. Moreover, her use of "really" gives this passage a conversational tone, such that we could imagine her sitting around with a group of peers and talking about her beliefs rather than, say, standing behind a podium and proclaiming them. In this contrast, we see evidence of how Eloise has come to translate her way of talking about her faith: rather than employing the pressuring voice she had used in class and that is still evident in "All Shapes and Sizes," she adopts a quiet, less-pressuring voice like Daniel's. Through her rhetorical strategy of translation, Eloise speaks in a manner that increases her chances of fostering intersubjectivity with her non-Christian peers at NESU.

Eloise's decision to include the IVCF mission statement in her essay also factors into her translative strategy. That mission statement as she quoted it reads as follows: "We are a movement of students who follow Jesus as Savior and Lord: growing in love for God, God's Word, God's people of every ethnicity and culture, and God's purposes in the world." When I asked Eloise in our fourth interview why she chose to include the mission statement, she said, "Because I think a lot of times when kids think of InterVarsity ..., they think, 'Wow, this is a bunch of Jesus Freaks.' Like, 'They have no purpose. They're trying to convert us all and, like, be a big cult.' Where, like, I found this mission statement was a little bit more toned down." Eloise goes on to say that the mission statement is "more accepting than a lot of what people think" because it references "people of every ethnicity and culture." Of course, Eloise included the phrase at least partly out of an evangelical motive: she wants readers to consider joining IVCF and becoming Christians. But she's attempting to do so in ways that might resonate with rather than alienate her peers. She's not telling her audience what they should think, do, or believe. Instead, she's describing for them some of IVCF's core beliefs, and she's doing so in ways that she hopes will find purchase with her audience. If translation amounts to making ideas "understood in the words *others* use" (Roberts-Miller 213, original emphasis), then Eloise sees the mission statement as a resource that amounts to a kind of found translation: citing it allows her to name her faith in ways that might correspond with assumptions and values held by her non-Christian audience.

Finally, Eloise's public essay also features another, more subtle form of translation, one that differs from the forms of translation I described above because it omits explicit references to her faith. For example, Eloise alludes to her Christian conversion early in her essay without referring to it directly. She describes her senior year in high school as a "transition time" of "self-realization" that results in her arriving at a new understanding of "the kind of person" she wanted to be. As I described earlier, Eloise's major transition during high school was her conversion to evangelical Christianity. Rather than talking about her new-found faith in explicitly Christian terms in her public writing, though, Eloise employs what Habermas might call more "generally accessible language" (25). Whereas in talking about IVCF Eloise still used Christian language (e.g., "Jesus," "God's word"), here she conceals her faith in ways that Shari Stenberg might call "cloaking" (279) or historian George Marsden might call "self-censorship" (*Outrageous* 13). Eloise's faith, though, is still present early in her essay, even in the sections where she avoids naming it directly. In a manner not unlike Kimberly's writing, Eloise's faith ripples just below the surface. She might not be using religious terminology, but her religious motives are still present, motives that bubble up closest to the surface when Eloise announces at the end of her first paragraph that the "drinking and partying" her high school friends had become interested in "just wasn't [her] scene." Like Kimberly's line, "I mean, I am not sexually active nor do I plan on having sex anytime soon," Eloise in colloquial terms announces moral choices that align with her faith. But by avoiding distinctly religious terminology regarding her conversion early in her essay, Eloise reduces the likelihood that readers would pigeonhole her as "The Christian" and instead identify with the fact that she was experiencing a time of transition. While not every high school student can relate to a conversion to evangelical Christianity, the vast majority can sympathize with the idea that senior year of high school represents a significant period of transformation and change.

Before moving on to discuss how Eloise attempts to constitute her readers, it's important to address the consequences of her translative rhetoric. One consequence is that Eloise arguably devalues her faith by translating it. Stephen Carter would likely say that because she sees announcing her faith directly in her public writing as a liability, she is forced to trivialize it (*Culture*). Based on her interactions with her human context at NESU, Eloise realizes that her faith must be cloaked or shrouded—at least to some degree, and at least in some circumstances. While Eloise's motives for cloaking her faith at least initially in her public writing are good—she wants to foster intersubjectivity with the wider NESU public so that they might come to see her faith as legitimate—such a move does raise questions about just how inclusive writing classrooms in particular and public universities in general can be (Roberts-Miller 188–89). A second consequence of Eloise's translative rhetoric is that she must leave behind any explicit claim to the universality of her faith (Butler, et al. 116). By shifting from making claims about how things are in general to how they are for her, she cannot assume authority solely based on the fact that she's sharing absolute truth (see Perkins, "'Attentive'" 84). Rather, she must couch it in personal terms—what is true for her. In this regard, Eloise's translation and Austin's casuistic stretching share similar implications. In Chapter 4, I discussed Lesslie Newbigin's argument that shifting from statements of "This is true" to "This is true for me" presupposes the postmodern belief that truth claims cannot be universal, a perspective that would conflict with modernist articulations of evangelical Christianity and could serve to undercut the foundation of such a faith (19). Like Austin, then, Eloise's vernacular religious creativity could result in demoralization.

Also like Austin, though, Eloise shifts from the declarative to the personal because she recognizes that her classmates do not share her assumptions; she already encountered firsthand the extent to which using moralistic discourse (e.g., "This is true") served to alienate her from her classmates in the Investigations course. Equally important, Eloise's translation aligns with Steiner's faithful witness model of effective evangelical civic engagement, a model that "acknowledge[s] the limitations of the human subject *as a knower*" (302, original emphasis). Steiner argues that, in order to communicate effectively across difference, evangelical Christians need to "speak from their own context and experiences" (302), and this is precisely what Eloise does in "In My Own Words." Steiner also argues that doing so does not necessarily "deny transcendent and intersubjectively binding truth" (302). While I have no direct evidence that Eloise maintained her belief that Christianity represents transcendent truth, my sense is that she did: her public writing still bears witness to the centrality of faith and Christian community to her life. Indeed, translating her faith into more personal terms (e.g., "this is why *I* am") allows Eloise to enact a form of evangelical testimony. Because she speaks personally as an evangelical Christian, Eloise is able to testify in her public essay to her belief that Jesus is "Savior and Lord" and to her belief that the Christian God cares about "people of every ethnicity and culture." She's also able to testify to her sense of belonging at NESU, especially in communities like IVCF, her dorm, and the track team, among others.

As a result, Eloise does what neither Austin nor Kimberly was able to do: she foregrounds her own evangelical Christian ethos as a central feature of her writing. Again, genre plays a role here. It's arguably easier to write from one's ethos in a personal essay that invites such a first-person perspective rather than a persuasive essay that demands explicit integration of research. As I noted earlier, though, Eloise did not have to write from her first-person perspective. Moreover, as her ability to cloak her religious conversion in more general terms indicates, she also didn't need to draw as much attention to her faith as she ultimately did. By translating her faith into personal terms, Eloise foregrounds her evangelical Christian ethos in "In My Own Words," and she does so in order to foster the intersubjectivity with her peers that so eluded her earlier in the semester. She wants to participate fully in the civic life of her Investigations course and of NESU generally, but she knows that achieving such a goal necessitates communicating with her peers in terms that they will understand.

Constitutive Rhetoric

By definition, intersubjectivity cannot be achieved by one person alone. For intersubjectivity to exist, all parties to discourse must agree that they share a common reference world. It is possible that Eloise's act of translating her faith into personal terms could result in her peers changing their perceptions of her, but Eloise does not stop at translation. She also attempts to constitute her peers themselves as inhabiting a subjectivity that welcomes her evangelical Christian faith as legitimate within the context of a public university. As I discussed in Chapter 3, Maurice Charland defines constitutive rhetoric as rhetoric that does not persuade audiences so much as it positions or interpellates them. Constitutive rhetoric functions to "insert 'narratized' subjects-as-agents into the world," and so rhetorical action that constitutes audiences can powerfully shape how individuals and groups perceive themselves in relation to others (Charland 143). As Wayne Booth explains, such forms of rhetoric create the very social realities in which we exist (*Rhetoric* 14–16).

Eloise's constitutive move emerges most clearly in the passage where she first introduces her faith:

> As a Christian, there are often stereotypes made against me. I was lucky enough to meet a few other Christians on my floor as well as a bunch of other great people who have wanted to get to know me for me. While being a Christian is not something I try to hide (because it is part of my identity and something that influences my actions), I am glad that people don't see me as "The Christian" but rather as just Eloise.

What's curious about this passage is that in many ways it doesn't reflect the reality Eloise experienced. As I have discussed throughout this chapter, Eloise found herself increasingly alienated from the class over the first two months of the semester. In our second interview, Eloise admitted that she felt stereotyped by her peers in a manner that directly contradicts the vision of acceptance she constructs in "In My Own Words":

Eloise: I want them to see me as me, rather than as a Christian.
Jeff: Okay.
Eloise: 'Cuz they have a lot of stereotypes about Christians?
Jeff: And you think that's—maybe they're seeing the stereotype and they're not seeing Eloise?
Eloise: Yeah.

Contrary to Eloise's hopes, she has been stereotyped as "The Christian." Thus the world that Eloise experiences in reality directly contradicts the one she constructs in her public writing.

Arguably, Eloise constructs this image of acceptance in her writing because she knows she wouldn't gain anything, especially intersubjectivity, by castigating her peers for excluding her. And from a genre perspective, Eloise seems to recognize that typified responses in the kinds of situations wherein she finds herself (i.e., writing her success story for a university-wide audience) should stress positivity over negativity. Thus Eloise rightly reads the rhetorical situation as one that would not tolerate complaining or criticizing. Similar to "All Shapes and Sizes," then, there's a deeply ironic component to "In My Own Words." Even though Eloise hasn't experienced fully the acceptance she names, she writes her essay as if she has. But that's the constitutive move: readers of Eloise's essay—her classmates and members of the wider NESU community who might encounter her essay on the web or on a poster around campus—would find themselves inhabiting a subjectivity that privileges acceptance of Eloise's evangelical Christian identity. Eloise attempts to position her readers as subjects who accept her as more than "The Christian." She is "just Eloise," a multifaceted college student who involves herself in various roles within the NESU community: athlete, honors student, community service activist, friend and listener, dorm floor representative, role model, and potential resident assistant, among others. The overwhelming image Eloise provides for her readers is that of a social reality marked by significant intersubjectivity: she may be an evangelical Christian, but she shares a common reference world with her peers and is thus able to communicate effectively with them (and with dorm leaders) about issues of shared concern.

The ideology into which Eloise attempts to constitute her readers is a more inclusive form of liberalism than that which they already espouse. Eloise perceived her peers as embracing liberal attitudes like tolerance, though she pointed out in our fifth interview that such tolerance didn't seem to extend to evangelical Christians like her. As she put it, "it's kinda weird, because at the same time, I don't feel like those people have to accept, like, what being Christian means." She later added that tolerance "doesn't seem like it's a full circle. It seems like it stops" (fifth interview). What Eloise unearths here is a commonplace in liberal politics, namely that there's no tolerance for those who are perceived as intolerant. But that is why Eloise attempts to construct herself as tolerant and accepting of others in her public essay: she "connect[s] with others who have similar interests" and with "those who are [her] complete opposites." If she can demonstrate that her vernacular form of evangelical Christianity does not bar her from accepting others, then perhaps she can position her readers as embracing a broader, more inclusive form of tolerance, one wherein evangelical Christianity can find a seat at the democratic table. Eloise rewrites the narratives of existence her peers inhabit—narratives that make it possible to extend tolerance to some groups and not others—so as to write herself into their scope of inclusivity (see Roberts-Miller 188–89).

Eloise's public writing is savvy in the way it positions readers. But doesn't such positioning raise concerns? Couldn't we interpret such a move as manipulative? Charland himself recognizes such a possibility when he uses the term "trickery" to describe constitutive rhetoric (137). Katja Thieme similarly recognizes that the kind of "political positioning" Charland ascribes to constitutive rhetoric "tends to presuppose, rather than lay open, how it has been historically formed and on what values it is founded" (42). Not unlike Burke's concern with impure forms of casuistic stretching, constitutive rhetoric could work to conceal rather than reveal motives. Legitimate questions arise: is Eloise tricking her audience? If so, wouldn't such trickery conflict with the aims of deliberative discourse? These concerns are all the more appropriate for evangelical Christianity because of its tendency toward an all-too-familiar sleight of hand: I'll befriend you on neutral terms at first, but eventually I'll try to convert you. The argument could be made that Eloise's constitutive move forestalls rather than makes possible deliberative rhetoric. She might want to be considered an equal party to discourse and achieve intersubjectivity, but parity remains frustrated if she attempts to achieve it through manipulation.

While constitutive rhetoric certainly could conceal motives rather than reveal them, it's significant that Eloise interpellates her readers into the very ideology she ascribes to them, namely a brand of liberalism that embraces a more capacious notion of tolerance. Moreover, it's worth considering Eloise's use of constitutive rhetoric pragmatically. What are her ultimate motives in effecting such a rhetorical move? While Charland does note that the effect of constitutive rhetoric is that of "conversion" (142), he means it in a more general sense than religious conversion. Constitutive rhetoric interpellates an audience "into a new subject position" by causing it to recognize "the 'rightness' of a discourse and of one's identity with its reconfigured subject position" (142). For Eloise, such "rightness" has much less to do with Christianity than with legitimacy (see Lindsay 221). Her goal in "In My Own Words" is not so much to convert her peers to Christianity as it is to convert them to a conception of liberal tolerance that welcomes her at the deliberative table. She's attempting to convert her peers to a mindset wherein she might be perceived as an equal (Habermas).

One of the possible outcomes of constitutive rhetoric involves the formation of what Charland calls a "collectivized subject position" that transcends "individuality" and allows people "to participate in a collective political project" (142). In considering Eloise's essay, it's possible to identify the collective project she attempts to promote. For Eloise, that collective project is one wherein she longs to participate fully as a member of the communities in which she finds herself—her Investigations course, her dorm, and NESU as a whole. Consonant with Hauser's notion of intersubjectivity, Eloise seeks to be recognized as a legitimate, equal member of these communities, someone who shares a common reference world with her non-Christian peers. Through writing "In My Own Words," Eloise also hopes to constitute her readers—other members of those same communities—as participants within the collective project she invokes. She wants her peers to see beyond the stereotypical cultural images toward shared iterations of the common good, a common good wherein citizens—including those who ascribe to some form of evangelical Christianity—have a voice in democratic processes. As she puts it, "the greater my social capital, the more effective and productive [a] citizen I will be" ("In My Own Words"). Eloise thus enacts her constitutive move so she can be part of the deliberative processes she sees as central to life as a productive citizen-student at NESU. Eloise is not trying to break the rules. She's trying to locate herself within them.

Chapter Conclusion

Eloise's experiences in her Investigations course point scholars and teachers of rhetoric and writing toward a number of possibilities and questions. First and foremost, her experiences suggest that outspoken, moralistic evangelical

Christian students are capable of change, and that seemingly inappropriate rhetorical action in the form of proclaiming absolute truth might eventually lead to revised or transformed versions of student faith that fit better within pluralistic contexts. Indeed, Eloise's experiences suggest that it is because she initially enacts her faith in overly-zealous ways that she comes to realize the need to translate it into terms that might earn her a degree of legitimacy within her academic contexts. Given that many other religiously committed students profiled in rhetoric and composition are represented as students who, like Hunt's Rob Campbell, already have their "views and beliefs intact" (10), Eloise's transformation over the course of a single semester is significant. It prompts scholars and teachers of rhetoric and writing to think about how the outspokenness of other students might indicate not the refusal to change but rather engagement that leads to change.

Related to this, Eloise's writing suggests that vernacular religious creativity might emerge in rhetorical action that functions aspirationally. Students might use writing assignments to rewrite their faith or ways of communicating their faith in a manner that reflects the values and assumptions of the communities in which they find themselves or in relation to discourses they find unfamiliar. Consequently, Eloise's experience offers rhetoricians and compositionists an example of how first-year students can use multiple assignments to rewrite their social identities over the course of a semester. It also offers insight into how students might rewrite the very social contexts in which they finds themselves. Eloise's writing of "In My Own Words" suggests that first-year students are capable of enacting constitutive rhetoric in impressive ways. To date, little scholarship in rhetoric and composition takes up the question of how or even if students employ constitutive rhetoric, though Brian Gogan recently has discussed the constitutive potential of student-written letters to the editor. Eloise's writing prompts scholars to devote more attention to how students might draw on that particularly powerful rhetorical strategy. Like Eloise, they might attempt to redraw the boundaries of legitimacy so that they can participate as fully fledged members of the publics or communities in which they find themselves.

In short, Eloise's case study offers scholars and teachers of writing and rhetoric a glimpse into how students can develop socially, rhetorically, and religiously over the course of a semester. In Eloise's case, these threads of development seem to be intimately related, to the point where it might be safe to say that her social experiences within her human context, which are marked by no shortage of friction and tension, result in both her religious and rhetorical development. When we consider William Perry's point that dualistic perspectives are dislodged as much by peer groups as they are by curricula, this interconnectedness seems all the more feasible (61). Indeed, it resonates with Primiano's point that interactions within one's human context lead believers to adjust, adapt, or negotiate their faith accordingly. Social change begets religious change. But Eloise's experience also underscores a point I have been making throughout this book: that religious faith, far from inhibiting rhetorical development, can function as a primary motivation for students to find new ways to communicate their beliefs civically and civilly across difference.

Notes

1. The veracity of the book had not yet been questioned. The course took place in the fall of 2008, and the episode of *60 Minutes* that challenged Mortenson's claims didn't air until 2011.
2. Incidentally, I invited Thomas to participate in this study, but he was unable to do so.

7 The Implications of Vernacular Religious Creativity for Rhetoric and Composition

> ... individuals' belief systems are never simply a mirror of the institutions—religious or otherwise—with which they align themselves. Instead, they are always a complex web of viewpoints in the process of becoming something different.
>
> —Michael-John DePalma, "Re-envisioning Religious Discourses as Rhetorical Resources in Composition Teaching"

The epigraph comes from Mike DePalma's 2011 *College Composition and Communication* article, and I find it fitting to include at the beginning of my final chapter because in many ways it sums up the argument I have been making throughout this book, namely that our religiously committed students, including millennial evangelical Christians, are neither static in their religious beliefs nor in their rhetorical awareness. On the contrary, they are always in the process of developing or changing—of becoming something different—by virtue of the fact that they are adapting or adjusting their religious beliefs and finding new ways to communicate those beliefs across difference. And they engage in such processes of vernacular religious creativity as a result of interactions within their diverse, pluralistic human contexts. Millennial evangelical Christian students are indeed creative, and they are creative in ways that can foster deliberative discourse or constitute the social conditions that would allow for such discourse.

In this concluding chapter, I take up more fully the implications of vernacular religious creativity for scholars and teachers of rhetoric and composition. I do so by first suggesting that the presence of vernacular religious creativity in the rhetorical action of students like Austin, Kimberly, and Eloise prompts rhetoricians and compositionists to rethink assumptions about religiously committed students like millennial evangelical Christians. I also discuss how vernacular religious creativity invites religiously committed students to rethink themselves. I then consider how vernacular religious creativity might have bearing on composition scholarship, public discourse, and rhetorical education. My hope in doing so is to highlight ways whereby we as scholars and teachers of rhetoric and writing can encourage students to enact vernacular religious creativity responsibly and draw on its resources for deliberative ends. If we can do so, then we might just be able to help transform our public discourse itself into something different—a public discourse that is more civil and more democratic than it currently is.

Rethinking Religiously Committed Students

The presence of vernacular religious creativity in the rhetorical action of millennial evangelical Christian students like Austin, Kimberly, and Eloise prompts rhetoricians and compositionists to interrogate their assumptions regarding millennial evangelical students as well as students who ascribe to other faiths. Specifically, the presence of vernacular religious creativity prompts us to envision our students not as passive recipients of ideologies such as religious traditions but as interpreters, innovators, and negotiators of belief systems. In Mark Alan Williams's terms, such students are "active participants, makers of discourses," and among the discourses they make are those that we would call the religious (339). In saying this, I should reiterate a point I made in Chapter 2, namely, that I do not mean to suggest that each of our students creates her own idiosyncratic religion—I'm not talking about Sheilaism (Bellah, et al. 221). Lived religion as it emerged in my case studies with Austin, Kimberly, and Eloise does not evidence a break from Christian tradition in general or American evangelicalism in particular. Rather, lived religion emphasizes the fact that individual believers will put their own "accent" on the religious traditions to which they ascribe (Ammerman, *Sacred* 89, 94). And such accents, as I have attempted to show in this book, often trend toward greater appreciation of diverse perspectives that offer hope for civic engagement.

If our religiously committed students are makers and interpreters of discourses, then teachers and scholars of rhetoric and writing must question not only the labels they use to describe such students but also the ideological and cultural associations that cluster around such labels. While rhetoric and composition has made significant gains in recent years regarding how to think more sensitively about religiously committed students, negative cultural associations that coalesce around labels like religious, Christian, evangelical, fundamentalist, and Mormon, among others, persist in the academy and in popular representations (Cope and Ringer; Pavia; Tobin and Weinberg; M. Williams). As I pointed out in my discussion of Eloise in Chapter 6, such labels tend to function metonymically: as soon as we associate one with an individual or group, it's all too easy to reduce that individual or group to the cultural images we link to that label. While accounting for vernacular religious creativity does not necessitate that we stop using labels altogether, it does mean recognizing that those labels are always partial. To echo Smith and Snell's Amanda, our millennial evangelical Christian students are always tweaking their faith in ways that render them at least somewhat different from popular conceptions of evangelical Christianity. The possibility of vernacular religious creativity invites scholars and teachers of rhetoric and writing to seek out such differences, differences that

Mark Alan William describes in terms of the "friction" that exists between our students' lived religion and the faith traditions with which they align themselves (338–39).

As a terministic screen, vernacular religious creativity directs our attention toward the individual negotiations religiously committed students make as they encounter new social contexts, discourses, or assignments that might pose a challenge to their faith. It also offers rhetoricians and compositionists a lens through which to recognize and name how students might be negotiating or even enacting religious faith in ways that differ from popular cultural associations. For example, because Austin integrated his faith explicitly into his writing via the discursive feature of biblical citation, an instructor encountering his Christian schools essay might conclude that what Austin produced is little more than a "born again" paper that belongs outside of the boundaries of the composition classroom (Anderson 12; Vander Lei, "'Where'"). Viewing such texts through a lens of vernacular religious creativity, however, can reveal how discursive features like biblical citation may amount to more than a student parroting religious discourse. Such features might highlight how a writer like Austin is attempting to negotiate his faith commitments with perspectives and beliefs that differ from his own. Accordingly, vernacular religious creativity as a terministic screen helps reveal the complex ways whereby our religiously committed students might be meeting goals we hope they will achieve through rhetorical education: the ability to engage meaningfully with interlocutors who think differently while also clarifying their own commitments—goals that, as I discussed in Chapter 3, align with the demands of deliberative democracy (Shannon Carter; Roberts-Miller 187).

The prevalence of vernacular religious creativity also prompts scholars and teachers of rhetoric and composition to perceive religiously committed students as always in process. Given that we only see many of our students for a single semester or quarter, the reality that students are constantly engaged in processes of development can be difficult to perceive. But the example of a student like Eloise serves as a reminder of just how much a student can change, even over the course of a single semester. For a good part of the semester, Eloise was moralizing and proclaiming her faith in class, enactments of faith that would align her with other "problem students" in rhetoric and composition scholarship (Cope and Ringer 106; see also Perkins, "'Attentive'"). But she also came to realize that her manner of speaking was part of the reason she found herself alienated from her peers, and so she enacted vernacular religious creativity by translating her faith into terms her peers might accept. I can only guess here, but my hunch is that this change was far less visible to her peers and her professor than were her initial, moralistic enactments of evangelical Christian faith. Unless they read her public writing, they might not know that she had undergone any change at all, except that she talked less at the end of the semester than she did at the beginning. My case study with Eloise suggests that even outspoken, moralistic evangelical Christian students can transform their faith as a result of the frictions that arise from interactions within social contexts like a writing-intensive classroom.

I know that Eloise's experience is not necessarily representative of other zealous millennial evangelical Christian students, especially given the fact that she lived with the peers from her Investigations course, a living situation that doubtlessly shaped her rhetorical action and prompted her vernacular religious creativity. And yet I wonder: if Eloise can change over the course of two or three months, then what about other students like her? If we encounter students like Eloise—or Hunt's Rob Campbell, Goodburn's Luke, Perkins's Tina, Downs's Keith, or Smart's Frankenstein writer, among others—and we assume that they, like Rob Campbell put it, already have all their beliefs intact, might we be missing the subtle, imperceptible ways whereby they're changing even while they're in our classes? The prevalence of vernacular religious creativity within the rhetorical action of religiously committed students invites scholars and teachers of rhetoric and writing to perceive even the seeming inflexibility of religiously committed students as evidence of the possibility that they are not only more complex than we imagine but also engaged in the difficult process of becoming something different. Such students may be grappling with different discourses or perspectives in ways that are leading to (or ultimately can lead to) productive change—change that, as I hope I have made clear throughout this book, might allow students to maintain their faith commitments while finding ways to negotiate them rhetorically in relation to others.

Implications for Student Faith and Identity

In the same way that vernacular religious creativity prompts rhetoricians and compositionists to rethink religiously committed student writers, it also prompts students to rethink themselves. If religious believers are always engaged in processes of negotiating their faith in relation to their social contexts, then religiously committed students must also see themselves as works in process. They are not arbiters of unmediated truth or unbiased representatives of a faith tradition, but rather are shapers and interpreters of that faith. This realization can be jarring for devout religious believers because it may fly in the face of what they have been taught by their parents, pastors, or other spiritual mentors. Such a realization, though, aligns with Mark Allan Steiner's point that the faithful witness model of civic engagement emphasizes "the limitations of the human subject *as a knower*" (302, original emphasis). When working with religiously committed students who fear that negotiating their faith might undercut it, rhetoricians and compositionists can communicate a different perspective: change of faith does not necessarily mean loss of faith. Toward this end, one point worth underscoring for religiously committed students is that vernacular religious creativity does not necessarily conflict with the continuity of religious traditions.

Stephen Carter speaks to this idea in *God's Name in Vain* when he defines religion as "a narrative activity, a story a people tells itself and its issue about its relationship to God over time" (174). Carter is careful to say that religion's emphasis on tradition does not mean it is "unchanging": "the very ability of a religion to accommodate itself to the world is crucial to its survival; those that cannot evolve, die" (174). He then adds that religions can evolve without forfeiting their "sacred truths" (174). Carter's point—a crucial one when it comes to understanding vernacular religious creativity as potentially contributing to constructive evolution of religious faith versus destructive unmooring—is that religious traditions like Christianity have room for change and adaptation.

As I pointed out in Chapter 2, though, not everyone will agree on what amounts to a sacred truth. So, for instance, I discussed Amanda and Katie, both of whom cited C. S. Lewis's *The Last Battle* as a book that authorized their shift from Christian exclusivism toward Christian inclusivism. For many contemporary evangelical Christians, this shift would not represent what Burke calls demoralization because it does not undercut their faith to the point where it loses all salience. Rather it represents an adaptation, arrived at via vernacular religious creativity, wherein individuals are able to come to terms with how to live their faith in relation to diverse human contexts. For many other evangelicals, though, this shift would be anathema: relinquishing the requirement for expressed faith in Jesus Christ as a requirement for salvation opens the door for a slew of other adjustments that could lead to demoralization. Vernacular religious creativity can be a slippery slope. I am not a theologian, and so I cannot comment on the rightness or wrongness of shifting toward a version of Christian inclusivism. What I can conclude, however, is that both Amanda and Katie made this shift as a result of interpreting their faith in relation to their pluralistic contexts and of reading a writer who is respected in many Christian circles. As I argued in Chapters 2 and 3, this is part of the process of vernacular religious creativity—responding to one's human context and drawing on available social, cultural, and religious resources in order to make sense of one's religious commitments and reassemble them by way of bricolage into a vernacular construction of lived religion.

In DePalma's terms, Amanda and Katie both became something different as a result of their vernacular religious creativity, though they did so in ways that, at that point in time, allowed them to adjust their relationship to their faith rather than abandon it completely. The same can be said of Austin, Kimberly, and Eloise as result of their enactments of vernacular religious creativity. While all three changed in largely subtle ways, none of them evidenced loss of faith, at least as far as I could tell from my case studies. Arguably, Austin and Eloise changed more than Kimberly did (more on Kimberly below). By stretching core beliefs to accommodate the views of non-Christians, Austin alters his faith in ways that make it more possible for him to accept as legitimate the beliefs of others, even when those beliefs don't correspond with his evangelical Christianity. If Austin continues thinking along these lines, he could find himself unmoored from his original principle. Instead of believing Christianity represents universal truth, he could come to see it as one legitimate option among many. Much the same could be said for Eloise's enactment of translation. By changing the way she speaks about her faith from universal into personal terms, Eloise similarly alters her relationship to her faith. Like Austin, she could ultimately come to espouse a perspective of religious pluralism, one wherein she perceives multiple paths to heaven or salvation as legitimate. And while scholars and teachers of rhetoric and writing might not balk at such a prospect, it might represent a position to which Eloise does not aspire.

Indeed, some theologically conservative evangelical Christians would see such an accommodation as undercutting key truths of Christianity. I would argue, though, that such a position, if arrived at consciously, would be far less troubling than arriving unawares at the perspective Christian Smith and Melinda Denton call moralistic therapeutic deism (162–63). For Smith and Denton, moralistic therapeutic deism is a belief system that somewhat resembles Christianity but that lacks any of the substance or content of that or any other faith tradition. Its core tenets include the beliefs that good people go to heaven and that, while God exists and created the world, God does not demand much of people; God wants people to be nice to each other and to feel good about themselves and is also available to help out when people encounter problems (Smith and Denton 162–63). As I noted in Chapter 1, theologian Kenda Creasy Dean aligns moralistic therapeutic deism with what she calls the "Church of Benign Whatever-ism," and, given its emphasis on feeling good about oneself rather than on self sacrifice and commitment, there is not much commendable in such an outlook. I imagine few rhetoricians and compositionists would hope that their students would ascribe to a perspective that has more in common with American self-help discourse than with any recognizable religious or ideological commitment that actually demands something of adherents.

At the same time, the conversation about religiously committed students in rhetoric and composition suggests that few scholars and teachers of rhetoric and writing would hope that their students come to embrace their commitments in fundamentalist ways. Thus while compositionists and rhetorical educators may want to talk with religiously committed students about the potential risks that correspond with vernacular religious creativity, they certainly don't want to be mistaken for encouraging such students to become (or remain) fundamentalists. Fortunately, Dean helps us see that the dangers of moralistic therapeutic deism don't have to be counterbalanced by the equally problematic perspective posed by fundamentalism—the antidote to moralistic therapeutic deism is not religious bigotry. On the contrary, Dean suggests that the answer rests in appreciating the "multitextured truth" that any faith tradition, Christianity among them, espouses (191). In a passage aimed at her audience of youth pastors and parents that should nonetheless resonate with scholars and teachers of writing and rhetoric, Dean writes, "Young people looking to us for meaning ... need us to model a theology marked by patience, determination, and, above all, humility as postmodern Christians honestly confront historical, biological, cultural, and sociological research that may challenge who we thought we were" (191). The parallels between Dean's point and Steiner's faithful witness model of evangelical civic engagement are clear—both emphasize humility, both emphasize self-reflection, both see aspects of postmodernism as beneficial for Christian faith. And the upshot of Dean's point is that while religiously committed students in the twenty-first century do need to come to terms with the extent to which they are always in the process of becoming something different, they don't need to conclude that such processes mean they're losing their faith. Between the poles of entrenched fundamentalism and shallow moralistic therapeutic deism, millennial evangelicals and other religiously committed students can find ways to reconcile their commitments within a pluralistic, globalized world. This is an important point to convey to our religiously committed students like Austin and Eloise who are attempting to negotiate their faith across differences of belief.

But what about Kimberly? As I noted above, Kimberly does not appear to evidence as much change in her beliefs as Austin or Eloise. Much of this has to do with the fact that she engaged in values articulation, a form of vernacular religious creativity that I see as flexible and thus reversible. The values hierarchies Kimberly enacts for her personal morality and for her argument in favor of the HPV vaccine can coexist with each other because she is aware that one works for her own life while the other applies to a public problem. Indeed, I noted in Chapter 5 that one of the differences between Kimberly and Austin is that Kimberly seemed more aware of how she was drawing on her beliefs and values than was Austin. Kimberly's awareness is evidenced by the comment she made while writing her essay that she wanted to make sure she was making an argument that aligned with her beliefs. And that might be what we want religiously committed students to know about any form of vernacular religious creativity: if they know it's happening and if they're able to reflect on it—in Burke's terms, if they're able to understand it as a methodology and not just a method (*Attitudes* 230)—then they have a far better chance of negotiating their faiths in ways that correspond with their desired senses of self.

Implications for Scholarship in Rhetoric and Composition

As the previous sections suggest, the implications of vernacular religious creativity for scholarship in rhetoric and composition are significant: because vernacular religious creativity demands that scholars rethink key assumptions concerning evangelical Christian and other religiously committed students, the research questions scholars pose about such students and the religious discourses they enact should similarly change. Moreover, my discussions of Austin, Kimberly, and Eloise also prompt researchers to ask questions about religiously committed student writers that we have not yet asked. Before exploring those questions, though, it's worth making a comment about methodology itself. The findings I was able to present in this book result from an intentionally designed study aimed at examining the relationship between millennial evangelical Christian students and the academic writing they produce, and I suggest that this study reveals the importance of doing just that—designing intentional studies that get at these phenomena rather than reacting to the writing of religiously committed students when we happen upon it. My point here tracks closely with what Emily Cope and I have argued elsewhere (Cope and Ringer) and with what Heather Thomson-Bunn and Catherine Matthews Pavia each has argued separately. That argument basically calls for composition scholars to design research projects that adopt a broad range of methodologies in order to study the complex intersections of religious faith and student writing.

To date, much of the scholarship about religiously committed students in rhetoric and composition derives from a teacher-research paradigm. In her study, Pavia found that more than half (fifteen out of twenty-seven) of the studies she analyzed employed teacher research (358). While there's nothing wrong with teacher research (I have used it and often require graduate students to use it), there's a problem if any single methodological perspective dominates a scholarly conversation (Cope and Ringer; Pavia; Thomson-Bunn). What results in the case of studying religiously committed students is a narrow portrayal of a diverse, complex population. By virtue of the fact that writing instructors tend to initiate teacher research in order to reflect on problems that arise when working with religiously committed students, the overwhelming reliance on teacher research has led to the reification of "evangelicals as 'problem students'" (Cope and Ringer 106). Diversifying our methodologies for investigating the rhetorical action of such students would lead to representations that are more diverse, more complex, and more nuanced. As Thomson-Bunn puts it so well, "If we want to understand religious rhetorics more fully—as sources of conflict, elements of diversity, shapers of culture, dimensions of writing and critical thought, and influences on social/political movements—we should interrogate and expand our methodological repertoire for approaching them" (126). We have begun to do this, but I suggest that we need more scholarship along these lines that intentionally sets out to explore the complex relationships that exist among student faith, rhetorical education, religious creativity, academic practice, and civic engagement (see Cope; Cope and Ringer; Marzluf; Pavia; Thomson-Bunn).

Working from an expanded methodological repertoire can help rhetoric and composition scholars better answer the kinds of questions that vernacular religious creativity prompts us to ask. Those questions should reflect the likelihood that our religiously committed students are undergoing processes of development and change. So instead of asking why millennial evangelical

Christian students integrate faith in ways that defy expectations of academic writing, we might expand that question to ask how such writing potentially represents students' attempts to negotiate their faith with perspectives that differ from their own. We might also ask how such negotiations amount to forms of vernacular religious creativity, forms that may reflect the three versions I discussed in this book (casuistic stretching, values articulation, and translation) or that offer insight into how students negotiate their faith in relation to diverse contexts. Asking such questions might help us perceive new strategies whereby religiously committed students attempt to communicate their faith across difference and accommodate their audience's perspectives. It is likely that there are many more forms of rhetorical action grounded in vernacular religious creativity than I have named in this book. Defining these rhetorical strategies would help scholars and teachers of rhetoric and writing better understand the rhetorical possibilities of vernacular religious creativity.

The prevalence of vernacular religious creativity also prompts researchers to look for a different kind of friction than we have previously noticed. Whereas existing scholarship tends to look at the gaps between academic discourse and the religious discourses of our students, the prevalence of vernacular religious creativity prompts us to consider how our religiously committed students might be using their academic writing to work out the frictions they perceive between themselves and their faith communities, their personal faith histories, the historical development of their faith traditions, popular or media representations of their faith, and so forth (M. Williams 339–43). That's not to say we shouldn't concern ourselves with the frictions that exist between religious and academic discourses—we still should. But vernacular religious creativity prompts scholars to ask how religiously committed students might be engaged in processes of negotiating vernacular constructions of faith that differ from popular representations. Researchers might do this by looking not only for evidence of discursive features that align student writers with a particular religous tradition (e.g., biblical citation or testimony), but also for those instances wherein student writers are engaging in some form of bricolage or assemblage. Where, for instance, do we see evidence of grafting, a version of bricolage that reflects what Elizabeth Vander Lei calls the "patched-together nature" of many of our students ("'Where'" 780)? Where do we see examples of students not just enacting religious discourse, whether Christian, Muslim, Mormon, or otherwise, but making or refashioning that discourse via vernacular religious creativity? If sociologist Nancy Ammerman is right when she argues that studying lived religion entails paying attention to the ways that religious beliefs are "improvised in new circumstances," then perhaps coming to terms with the full range of vernacular religious creativity of our student writers demands that we look for such improvisations in their rhetorical action (*Sacred* 8).

Relatedly, we might begin asking how student writing that integrates faith in ways that defy academic expectations might reveal not only who our students are in relation to their faith, but also who they aspire to be. Eloise is instructive toward this end: the activism paper she wrote anticipated her public writing in a manner that clearly shows her development as an evangelical Christian rhetor. Eloise's experience invites researchers to investigate how student writing might function to reveal the aspirational goals of student writers. I see this line of inquiry as appropriate for religiously committed students and for students who ascribe to no faith at all. How might we see within students' early attempts to grapple with new or unfamiliar discourses the potential for the development of hybridized identities or of deeper, more reflective commitment (Lecourt; Perry)? Might even the writing that strikes us as the most firmly entrenched within its particular ideology represent potential engagement with difference? Asking such questions would demand that scholars take the long view: we'd have to think about a piece of student writing not as a solitary text but rather as connected to the writing or rhetorical action that precedes and follows it. In an article I published in *College English* that looks at the consequences of Austin's casuistic stretching, I argued that our scholarship could benefit from longitudinal studies that consider how students' beliefs change as a result of their interactions within writing and rhetoric classrooms (Ringer, "Consequences" 295). I remain convinced of the need for such studies, but even if researchers aren't able to follow students for two or four years—or even for a semester—they might be able to perceive subtle rhetorical-religious development of students by looking at multiple papers in succession.

Researchers also might begin asking questions about the writing of religiously committed students that bears no explicit trace of that student's faith. This is work that is beginning to emerge in rhetoric and composition but that demands further attention (see Cope; Cope and Ringer). Designing studies aimed specifically at uncovering students' motives for including or not including faith in their academic practice could reveal a range of motives that might have bearing on civic engagement. Kimberly's experience in particular prompts scholars of rhetoric and composition to ask why religiously committed students opt against referencing their faith in academic writing. Some students may do so as a result of strictures against religious perspectives similar to the one Kimberly's instructor established in class; others might do so because, also like Kimberly, their prior educational experiences conditioned them to assume that religion is not germane to academic practice. But my case studies suggest that there also might be religious motives that lead to such cloaking of one's faith: Austin's desire to be an effective witness prompted him to remain silent following Chris's disparaging comment about religion, while Eloise grew more silent later in the semester in order to work out a new way of speaking as an evangelical Christian in class. Might there be occasions in academic and public contexts when making a conscious decision to conceal one's faith is appropriate not only in terms of the rhetorical situation in question, but also because doing so aligns with religious motives? Such a line of questioning suggests that there is room for scholarship that joins discussions about religiously committed students with theories related to rhetorics of silence (Glenn).

Implications for Public Discourse

Of course, the notion of silence is a particularly fraught one when it comes to the historical relationship between religion and public discourse in the United States: citizens and politicians of various stripes wish that religious believers would either keep their mouths shut or at least voice their perspectives in ways that correspond with liberal principles of rationality and tolerance (Carter, *Culture*, *God's Name*; Crowley; DePalma, Ringer, and Webber; Hansen; Heclo; Wolfe, *Transformation*, "Whose"). While I do not hope to resolve that issue here, I do wish to comment on the implications that the vernacular religious creativity of millennial evangelical students like Austin, Kimberly, and Eloise might have for public discourse. One implication I have suggested throughout this book is that vernacular religious creativity can make such discourse more civil, especially if we follow Wayne Booth, Sharon Crowley, Patricia Roberts-Miller, and Mark Allan Steiner, among others, as defining civil discourse as discourse that features respect and tolerance for other perspectives even in the face of disagreement. As I have attempted to show through my case studies, the strategies Austin, Kimberly, and Eloise adopt to communicate with people who disagree with them evidence civility: all three go to great lengths to accommodate the perspectives, values, and beliefs of their audiences, even when those perspectives differ markedly from their own. In doing so, Austin, Kimberly, and Eloise show themselves as students who are willing to negotiate with others; they value communicating across difference rather than simply proclaiming what they believe to be true.

Consequently, Austin, Kimberly, and Eloise evidence many of the features of Steiner's faithful witness model of evangelical civic engagement. They all, for instance, ultimately avoid the trap of proclaiming their own rightness while declaring others to be wrong (Steiner 311). When Chris made his comment about the nonexistence of God in class, Austin went so far as to remain silent so as not to come across as what he might call an "ineffective witness." Kimberly, on the other hand, demonstrated an ability to rearticulate her values depending on the context, a form of vernacular religious creativity that allowed her to sidestep the common pitfall that many evangelicals have a hard time avoiding: assuming that their take on morality is the one right way. And while Eloise certainly started off communicating with her peers in a moralistic fashion, she ultimately changed her way of speaking because she realized the extent to which she was alienating herself from her peers. Austin and Eloise in particular also came to recognize what Steiner calls "the importance of *ethos*"—they realized that they needed to foster trust with their peers who did not share their faith in order to earn "the right to be heard" (310, original emphasis). As I have argued throughout this book, such attitudes toward alternative perspectives and the interlocutors who hold them can go a long way toward constituting the conditions necessary for deliberative discourse. Such attitudes evidence a desire to communicate across difference. They also suggest that at least some millennial evangelical Christian students possess the "willingness to be addressed by an other" that Crowley locates at the center of civil discourse (29).

In addition to making civil discourse more civil, vernacular religious creativity also offers hope for making deliberative discourse possible. As I argued in Chapter 3, deliberative rhetoric does not just happen; it must be called into being or constituted by the interlocutors involved. Following Hauser, I have argued that the main precondition for achieving deliberative discourse is intersubjectivity, a shared perspective wherein interlocutors see each other as equal members of a public who hold legitimate views that exist within a common reference world. Each of the rhetorical strategies grounded in vernacular religious creativity I have discussed in this book—casuistic stretching, values articulation, and translation—can foster the intersubjectivity that makes deliberative rhetoric possible. Austin attempts to constitute this intersubjectivity by accommodating values he knows his non-Christian audience holds to be true; he goes so far in doing this that he ultimately stretches his own faith subtly but significantly. Kimberly's rhetorical strategy of values articulation holds potential for fostering intersubjectivity because she is able to reprioritize values depending on the context, a flexibility that can allow rhetors to establish common ground with audiences across differences of belief without giving up core convictions. And through writing "In My Own Words," Eloise aims to constitute a social reality wherein she and her non-Christian peers share a common reference world. The creative ways whereby Austin, Kimberly, and Eloise connect their faith to their academic practice and public writing could function to constitute the social conditions necessary for deliberative discourse.

Of course, it's important to point out here that attempts to foster intersubjectivity won't always succeed. Intersubjectivity requires that all parties to discourse perceive each other as legitimate and as sharing the same reference world, such that the efforts to foster intersubjectivity on the behalf of religiously committed students might fail due to a lack of reciprocity—Chris, after all, might not want to sit down and talk with Austin. Nonetheless, I maintain that rhetoricians and compositionists who care about the state of our public discourse should be encouraged by the religious creativity of students like Austin, Kimberly, and Eloise. These millennial evangelical Christian students demonstrate an aptitude for communicating across difference and respecting the views of others in ways that, as Crowley points out in *Toward a Civil Discourse*, has been lacking in American public discourse. And as I have attempted to show throughout this book, their motives for fostering intersubjectivity often are religious—Austin wants to be an effective witness, while Eloise aspires to be a quiet, humble evangelical like her boyfriend Daniel. And Kimberly's ability to rearticulate her values in contingent hierarchies is linked to her belief that decisions about abstinence and faith are matters of personal choice and commitment. The vernacular religious creativity of millennial evangelical Christian students suggests that Steiner might be right when he argues that evangelicals acting as faithful witnesses are "uniquely positioned to show the way to public discourses that are more edifying, more productive and more humane" (291). Indeed, perhaps encouraging the inclusion of religious voices like those of Austin, Kimberly, and Eloise will help foster the civic, civil discourse that many compositionists and rhetoricians rightly desire.

This point begs a larger question, though: what kind of publics do we envision when we think about the religious creativity of our students, and what is or should be the proper role for religion within such publics? Many scholars and teachers of rhetoric and writing would likely answer that the publics we envision should be inclusive; we should persuade our students to envision publics wherein citizens of all stripes, religious or otherwise, can speak freely, openly, and respectfully about their own and others' perspectives. As Roberts-Miller reminds us, though, inclusion is a god-term that, while it sounds appealing and is frequently invoked in rhetoric and composition, often obscures as much as it reveals (188–89). I have argued, for instance, that translation amounts to a rhetorical strategy grounded in vernacular religious creativity that can foster intersubjectivity across differences of belief. And while Habermas promotes his translation proviso as a means by which religious citizens can speak their perspectives in public arenas in terms that would make sense to others, such a proviso communicates the reality that not all perspectives can be included as is. Scholars ranging from Judith Butler and Charles Taylor to Hugh Heclo and Stephen Carter all register varying degrees of dissatisfaction with the need for religious citizens to translate their perspectives into terms more appropriate for liberal politics.

Should a public sphere that purports to be inclusive of religious perspectives welcome those perspectives in their untranslated form? While it might be easy to answer such a question in the abstract, considering it in light of my participants' experiences reveals just how complex of an issue it is. All three of my participants recognized or came to recognize that speaking openly as an evangelical Christian in a public university context entails significant risk—to the individual's reputation, standing in the class, legitimacy among a group of peers, and so forth. Austin sensed that if he had spoken out after Chris made his disparaging comment about religion, he might have alienated himself from the class and, more important to his concerns, come across as less than an effective witness. How do we analyze this situation in terms of inclusivity? Do rhetorical educators who see the rhetoric and writing classroom as a public-in-training welcome a comment like Chris's or censure it? Or in the wake of a comment like Chris's, do we invite alternative perspectives that might challenge the perceived hegemony of such an absolutist position? In doing so, we might risk embarrassing students by asking them to reveal their faith-based identities, knowing that some of our religiously committed students would rather not be known as such. Even if Austin did speak out as an evangelical Christian in favor of religious education at that moment, how might the dynamic of the class have changed? As rhetorical educators, we would hope that Chris and Austin would arrive at some degree of common ground, even if it amounts to agreeing to disagree. And yet there are any number of other scenarios that could have played out: Austin could have been shot down, the discussion could have devolved into name calling, other students in the class could have been silenced or hurt. Perhaps the worst-case scenario is that Austin might have entrenched himself in his perspective and failed to do what he eventually did in his writing: engage thoughtfully with a perspective that differed radically from his own.[1]

As I noted in Chapter 1, Stephen Carter might prompt rhetorical educators to pursue a different line of questioning when thinking about the publics we envision: what role, if any, might prophetic discourse enacted by students play in the protopublics of college writing and rhetoric classrooms? To my knowledge, no scholarship in rhetoric and composition has taken up this particular question, though much has been written about the rhetorical dimensions of the prophetic in general (see Duffy; Gutterman; Houck and Dixon; Zulick). Moreover, scholars like Shari Stenberg and Keith Gilyard have drawn parallels between prophetic religious discourse and the social justice goals that align with progressive forms of rhetorical education. The absence of scholarship that explores student enactments of prophetic rhetoric could derive from any number of reasons: contemporary college students do not enact prophetic discourse, writing instructors are unable to perceive it as such when they do, researchers don't wish to deal with the potentially thorny social, political, cultural, and religious implications of prophetic discourse when it emerges from religiously committed students, and so forth. And yet, in Carter's estimation, the best relationship religious voices can have with public discourse is to "stand outside the corridors of power" in order to "call those within to righteousness" (*God's Name* 22). While this prospect sounds appealing on some levels—Carter reminds us of the many prophetic religious voices during the Civil Rights movement that called American citizens and politicians to account for racial injustice—it's no doubt one that would make many contemporary rhetoricians and compositionists uncomfortable. And in fact, that might be the purpose of prophetic discourse: to stimulate discomfort with the aim of bringing about lasting social, political, and perhaps even spiritual change.

That said, my discussion about vernacular religious creativity raises an important question about prophetic rhetoric: do the motives that prompt vernacular religious creativity—motives that in general seek to adapt religious faith to socio-historical contexts—undermine the possibility of prophetic rhetoric? My case studies lead me to believe that vernacular religious creativity can function either to promote or undermine prophetic rhetoric. For example, if Kimberly were able to write from her ethos as a millennial evangelical Christian who values life over abstinence, she could come to be a prophetic voice within evangelical enclaves that tend to hold abstinence as more important than vaccination. In that instance, vernacular religious creativity would be informing a prophetic stance: Kimberly could speak from a different values hierarchy than the one many evangelicals espouse in order to call attention to matters of life and death. On the other hand, there's a chance that Eloise early in the semester was speaking prophetically—prophets, after all, are rarely welcome in society due to the radical nature of their messages, and Eloise clearly was not accepted as a result of the way she spoke from her faith-based perspective. If she was speaking prophetically, there's a chance that her rhetorical strategy of translation undercut her attempts to do so. And while such a concern might not be germane to rhetoric and writing classrooms, it is germane to public discourse in general—prophetic voices can be vital to the cause of justice in democratic societies (Carter, *God's Name*; Duffy; Gilyard; Houck and Dixon; Stenberg). Thus the relationship between vernacular religious creativity and prophetic rhetoric as it relates to civil discourse demands further attention.

Finally, my discussion about how the faith of individual students can change begs a larger question related to public discourse: are the microchanges made by Austin, Kimberly, and Eloise part of a larger pattern of change, one wherein American evangelicalism itself is in the process of becoming something different? Given that I am neither a sociologist of religion nor a religious historian, it is impossible to answer this question with any degree of certainty. And yet such a shift would not be outside of the realm of possibility. In *The Making of Evangelicalism*, historian Randall Balmer explores four large-scale shifts within the history of American evangelical Christianity. Those shifts, he argues, correspond with cultural and political changes within the social, cultural, and political realities of the United States. And while Balmer doesn't comment on whether the religious creativity of ordinary citizens played any role in the formation of those larger shifts, it's likely that it did. As collections like David Hall's *Lived Religion in America* and Ammerman's *Everyday Religion* suggest, the history of religious practice in the United States and abroad is marked by lived religion and vernacular religious creativity. And as I discussed in Chapters 2 and 3, Leonard Primiano sees vernacular religious creativity as functioning bidirectionally, shaping both the faith of individual believers and those believers' wider human contexts. Perhaps when Mark Alan Williams describes our religiously committed students as makers of discourses, he's referring not only to the ways students shape their own personal faith but also to the potential they hold for shaping public discourse itself.

And as I have attempted to show throughout this book, the vernacular religious creativity enacted by Austin, Kimberly, and Eloise aligns with larger trends as depicted in the National Study of Youth and Religion (NSYR). Those trends reveal millennials as more welcoming and appreciative of diversity than previous generations, even when it comes to differences of religious beliefs (Smith and Snell 80–81). Whether those trends will amount to another major shift within American evangelicalism and its relationship with public discourse—and whether the vernacular religious creativity of millennial evangelical Christians like Austin, Kimberly, and Eloise reflect or even constitute such a shift—remains to be seen. Additionally, while Balmer points to the 2008 election of Barack Obama and the decline of the Religious Right as laying "the groundwork for yet another turning point in evangelicalism" (80), more recent events suggest not much has changed. As I write, Kim Davis continues to make headlines for her religiously grounded refusal to issue marriage licenses to same-sex couples in Rowan County, Kentucky. Meanwhile, Bernie Sanders, a socialist from Vermont who is vying to be the presidential nominee for the Democratic Party, spoke at the late Jerry Falwell's Liberty University, where his audience of largely politically conservative evangelical and fundamentalist Christian students responded coolly at best to his argument that economic injustice represents a moral issue worthy of their concern. If the negotiations Austin, Kimberly, and Eloise made in their public university classroom contexts are part of a larger shift, then that shift seems to be coming in fits and starts. Even Balmer, himself a devout Christian, is careful to explain that evangelicals "stand at the cusp of … another turning point, a critical juncture. We can continue the narrow, petrified policies of the recent past. Or we can chart a new course, one that more fully embraces both the teachings of Jesus as well as the best of evangelicalism's history" (84).

Implications for Rhetorical Education

Finally, what are the implications of this study for rhetorical education? As I noted earlier, the prevalence of vernacular religious creativity should give rhetorical educators a measure of hope because it suggests that religiously committed students like millennial evangelicals are capable of adapting the way they communicate their beliefs in order to accommodate different perspectives. One of the primary goals of rhetorical education is that of fostering rhetorical awareness, the ability to size up situations in order to communicate effectively. Vernacular religious creativity, due to its emphasis on adjusting beliefs in relation to diverse human contexts, offers a way for rhetorical educators to think about how students' religious beliefs and identities might facilitate rather than constrain the development of such awareness. However, the rhetorical resources grounded in students' processes of vernacular religious creativity remain untapped in composition pedagogy and rhetorical education. I thus argue that the rhetorical possibilities of vernacular religious creativity should prompt composition instructors and rhetorical educators to rethink the role of religion in the classroom: instead of ignoring it, we should teach religiously committed students how to leverage its resources for deliberative ends. And to do so, we need to place students' beliefs and values at the center of rhetorical education.

As I have noted several times throughout this book, multiple scholars have called for the inclusion of religious perspectives in rhetorical education and composition instruction (DePalma; Dively, "Censoring"; Hansen; Swearingen, "Hermeneutics"). This argument proceeds as follows: because religious discourse is central to many of our students' lives and to the public discourse of the United States, ignoring religion in rhetorical education does our students, ourselves, and our public discourse a major disservice. I agree wholeheartedly with this argument, but I also suggest that vernacular religious creativity adds an important dimension to it: because our religiously committed students likely engage in vernacular religious creativity that trends toward recognizing and appreciating diverse perspectives, we do our students, ourselves, and our public discourse a major disservice if we fail to help them learn how to harness that creativity for deliberative ends. As I argued in Chapter 5, if we don't encourage our religiously committed students to articulate their faith with matters of public concern, we run the risk of missing out on opportunities to help millennial evangelical Christian students like Kimberly speak as "nonfundamentalist religious" citizens and potentially become "transformative force[s] in the center of a democratic civil society" (Habermas 25).

Of course, scholars and teachers of rhetoric and writing who are leery of welcoming religious discourse into the classroom might object to this argument on the basis that Kimberly already seemed to be a nonfundamentalist when she entered her first-year writing classroom. Teaching someone like her to leverage vernacular religious creativity for deliberative ends would work well enough, but what about those students who evidence fundamentalist ways of thinking and believing? Might welcoming their faith into the classroom lead to more problems than possibilities? The short answer is yes, it could, and I certainly agree that inviting religious perspectives into the classroom won't always succeed. Some students may not evidence vernacular religious creativity at all—when confronted with perspectives other than their own, they'll remain entrenched within their fundamentalist perspectives or even go so far as to withdraw completely from the academic contexts they see as posing a challenge to their faiths and identities (see Goodburn; Hunt; Montesano and Roen; Perkins, "'Attentive'"; Perry; Vander Lei, "'Where'"). Other students may evidence vernacular religious creativity in ways that hinder rather than foster deliberative discourse. As I noted in Chapter 2, Primiano assumes vernacular religious creativity can challenge the status quo or perpetuate it, and it is important to remember that not all instances of vernacular religious creativity will lead to the kind of civic civil discourse that many rhetoricians and compositionists desire.

While I agree that these risks are legitimate, I contend that they are risks we must take. When it comes to teaching rhetoric and writing, we always run the risk that our students, regardless of religion or ideology, will resist our efforts to convince them to think rhetorically, either because they're not persuaded by our rhetorical authority or because their belief systems are too densely articulated—or both (Bizzell, "Beyond"). Religion, though, isn't necessarily the problem: I have certainly taught students who were so entrenched in their religious beliefs that they were unwilling to consider perspectives other than their own, but I have also taught non-religious students who were entrenched within their political, social, or ideological perspectives in ways that prohibited rhetorical thinking. Of course, densely articulated religious beliefs can exacerbate or even be the root cause of such resistance, but so can densely articulated beliefs that have nothing to do with religion. And while students who come into our classrooms with densely articulated belief systems of any sort can be frustrating to work with (I remember cringing every time I heard one student refer to undocumented immigrants simply as "illegals"), the job of a rhetorical educator as I see it is to engage with these students at the level of their beliefs in order to disagree with or even challenge their perspectives when necessary. What we can't do is ignore such perspectives or wish they would go away. Roberts-Miller reminds us that a "perfectly inclusive public sphere … means that one must be willing to have" the same argument over and over again (226). If we want to model what an inclusive public sphere might look like in our classrooms, then we must be willing to invite in perspectives that depart from our own—religious and otherwise—and respond to them out of our own values and beliefs with patience, grace, and humility. And we must be willing to do this not once or twice, but semester after semester.

Moreover, my case study with Eloise suggests that even students we perceive as having densely articulated belief systems are capable of change—change that, as was clear in Eloise's case, resulted from proclaiming her faith openly as an evangelical Christian and then coming to the realization that she needed to translate her faith into personal terms. If Eloise had been discouraged from speaking or writing as a religiously committed student in the classroom—if she had faced a stricture similar to the one that Kimberly faced—then she might not have come to terms with the need to adjust her manner of speaking. If religiously committed students don't have the opportunity to explore their faith in protopublics like rhetoric and writing classrooms, then they might not have opportunities elsewhere to engage in an exchange of ideas that could help them develop civil positions. I agree with Roberts-Miller when she argues that deliberative democracy requires citizens to talk outside of their enclaves, and I see rhetoric and writing classrooms as ideal places in which to learn how to do so. These are contexts wherein ground rules for discussion can be established and made explicit in ways that can help foster deliberative exchange; they are also places where the very nature of civic discourse—what it is, what leads to it, and what can constrain against it—can be the subject of explicit discussion (Roberts-Miller 200–07).

But if we want to help students leverage their vernacular religious creativity for deliberative ends, then we must also see rhetoric and writing classrooms as places where religiously committed students can reflect on their faith actively and intentionally. Instead of ignoring religious beliefs or prohibiting religious perspectives from the classroom, we need to encourage students to think about how their beliefs and values might intersect with the rhetorical concepts they are learning and with the topics they are writing about. Doing so could amount to a powerful form of rhetorical invention, one that would be particularly appropriate for students like Kimberly who are writing about public issues that feature a religious dimension. While Kimberly was encouraged to think about her audience's views as a source of invention for her argument, she was not encouraged to think about how her own beliefs and values might give rise to "rhetorical lines of force" that could be particularly powerful for her argument (Crowley 61). Failing to encourage students to articulate their own beliefs in relation to the topics about which they write represents a significant blindspot for rhetorical education, especially given the potential of vernacular religious creativity. Because students are often unaware of their religious creativity, taking advantage of its rhetorical and deliberative possibilities demands that students pay keen attention to their own beliefs and values when writing arguments or engaged in other forms of deliberative rhetorical action (Perkins, "'Attentive'" 75). If students are asked to think about their own beliefs, values, and assumptions as sources of invention, they might be able to see how their religious creativity or vernacular constructions of faith can open up lines of argument that are unavailable to rhetors who do not share their beliefs or belong to their religious communities (Bizzell, "Faith-Based"; Lessl; Swearingen, "Rhetoric"). Mining one's own beliefs should not supplant attention to audience, genre, discourse community, or other sources of rhetorical invention. But it should play a role in how students of any faith or commitment come to name and develop arguments that are available to them.

Rhetorical educators and composition instructors who seek to help students leverage their vernacular religious creativity for rhetorical ends can do so by first introducing students to the concept of vernacular religious creativity—what it is, how it functions, the forms it takes in daily life, and its potential for fostering deliberative discourse. Teachers of writing and rhetoric could do this by asking students to read scholarship about lived religion from many of the scholars I have cited here—for instance, Nancy Ammerman, Alan Wolfe, Robert Orsi, Leonard Primiano, David Hall, and Christian Smith and Patricia Snell. They also might ask students to read excerpts from my discussions of Austin, Kimberly, and Eloise or examples of vernacular religious creativity I listed in Chapter 2. I have found that vernacular religious creativity is not a difficult concept for undergraduates to understand, and once students are introduced to it, they tend to see it everywhere—in their peers, their churches, their families, their friends, and, yes, even in themselves. In fact, two of the examples of vernacular religious creativity I provided in Chapter 2 came from students in a religious rhetorics class I taught recently. After introducing students to the concept of casuistic stretching as a form of vernacular religious creativity, I asked them to respond to our discussion through freewriting. What did they think about casuistic stretching? Had they enacted it in their own lives? Had they seen it in others? The examples I included from Esther and Rachel suggest that they understood casuistic stretching as a form of vernacular religious creativity and were able to name examples of how they enacted such creativity as a result of their own experiences within diverse human contexts.

A next step in the process of teaching vernacular religious creativity as a form of invention would be to ask students like Esther and Rachel to identify the beliefs, values, and assumptions operative in their enactments of religious creativity. Which beliefs or values are they stretching, rearticulating, or translating? Which perspectives are they attempting to accommodate? Why are they doing so? Naming their processes of vernacular religious creativity and the motives undergirding such processes could be revealing for such students, as it could illuminate the frictions they experience between themselves and the religious institutions to which they belong. It could also serve to highlight emerging values and beliefs that could motivate rhetorical action that serves to open up deliberative possibilities. Rachel, for instance, points to her belief in an inclusive God as the higher abstraction that allows her to reconcile her faith with her support for gay marriage. Once she has arrived at this understanding, Rachel could then be encouraged to think about how this higher abstraction might serve as a premise for an argument related to gay rights. Following from my discussion of Kimberly, Rachel could also be encouraged to think about how well such arguments might be suited for audiences who identify as evangelical Christian and those who don't. In other words, part of Rachel's inventional process could involve thinking about whether her arguments would best foster deliberative discourse within her religious enclaves or outside of them—or both.

For example, in a persuasive writing course I taught recently, an evangelical Christian student I'll call "Kristen" wanted to initiate dialogue within her church and campus ministry about how other members of her evangelical Christian enclaves might rethink their stance on gay rights and the LGBTQ community. Kristen's position was a nuanced one marked by vernacular religious creativity: while she was committed to her faith—and while the religious communities she belonged to tended to oppose LGBTQ rights—she was attempting to negotiate her own faith in relation to the LGBTQ community because she had a family member who had recently come out as gay. For her project, Kristen ended up writing an open letter to the other members of her campus ministry and a personal letter to the pastor of her church. Her communication with me after publishing these pieces within her enclaves suggests that she was able to get people talking productively: instead of shutting her down, they engaged with her in dialogue about an issue that mattered to her deeply as a religious citizen and as someone who had a gay family member. Kristen also communicated her views outside of her enclaves by publishing a letter to the editor that elicited significant response in a regional newspaper. In that letter, she attempted to foster intersubjectivity with her readers by writing openly as an evangelical Christian who sought to support gay rights and religious freedom, a vernacular construction of faith not unlike the one Rachel demonstrated. Kristen's efforts provoked responses from other readers who shared her faith and from those who didn't. Her rhetorical action got people talking, both inside of and outside of her religious enclaves. And Kristen engaged in such rhetorical action not in spite of her religious faith, but rather because of it: she wanted to make sense of her faith in relation to her changing human context, and she wanted to write in ways that reflected her developing sense of faith.

And that's the rhetorical potential of vernacular religious creativity: because our religiously committed students live in a rapidly changing world, they're always engaged in processes of figuring out how to fashion their religious commitments in, through, and against their social, cultural, and political commitments. There's energy is such negotiations, creative energy that can be directed toward rhetorical action that gets people talking across differences of belief and identity. As I see it, then, our task as rhetorical educators is to acknowledge the vernacular religious creativity of our religiously committed students and to teach them how to tap into its energy for deliberative ends. If we can do that, then we might find—or help our students of faith find—paths of invention that could help bridge the ideological divides that currently mark American public life. But to achieve this, we'd have to recognize our religiously committed students for what they are: complex, rhetorically savvy believers who are always in the process of becoming something different.

Note

1. See TJ Geiger's "Unpredictable Encounters" for an excellent discussion of the possibilities (and pitfalls) that can arise from a pedagogical practice he refers to as the "free exercise of rhetoric."

Appendix A
Methodology

The brief overview of my methodology in Chapter 1 offers just that—a brief overview. Here, I offer a fuller description of my methods along with a rationale for them. Readers might also want to consult "Coming to (Troubled) Terms: Methodology, Positionality, and the Problem of Defining 'Evangelical Christian,'" which I co-wrote with Emily Murphy Cope. In that essay, which I draw on heavily here, we discuss issues that arise when studying evangelical Christian students and discourse. It features some of the same voices of students I discuss in this book and offers further insight into why I went about this study the way I did.

Why Interview-Based Case Studies?

To begin, I want to answer the question as to why I adopted the interview-based case study for this project. The short answer to that question is that I wanted to get students talking. When I began this research in 2007, several articles and book chapters existed that offered compositionists suggestions for how to interact productively with evangelical Christian students. Few of them, though, featured the voices of the students themselves, and those that did still tended to depict evangelicals as "problem students" who didn't quite fit within the imagined geography of composition studies (Cope and Ringer 106; DePalma and Ringer, "Introduction"; Thomson-Bunn 125; Vander Lei, "'Where'"). Thus I saw interview-based case studies as a means by which to allow a frequently maligned population of students to voice their perspectives—about their writing, their academic contexts, their faith, and the interrelatedness of all three.

In some ways, then, my motives parallel those of Jonathan Alexander and Susan C. Jarratt. In "Rhetorical Education and Student Activism," Alexander and Jarratt discuss their interviews with five Muslim student activists in order to raise questions about the limits and potentials of rhetorical education. Alexander and Jarratt begin their conclusion by noting that they chose to focus on the voices of the Muslim students they interviewed in part because of "the richness of the archive [they] discovered and created through these interviews" (541). But they also decided to do so because, in general, "the deck of public discourse and opinion is heavily stacked" against the perspective their Muslim students shared (541). They go on to say that "[t]he very minimal scholarship about Muslim students, students who have emigrated from the Middle East, and students engaged in activism in resistance to the occupation of Palestine led us to attend as carefully and as fully as possible in an academic essay to the voices of these five students" (541).

I need to make it very clear here that I don't take the position that evangelical Christian students in the United States represent a similar minority to that of Muslim students—not at all. The former have far larger representation on many of our college campuses, not to mention in wider public discourse. And in composition scholarship, much more work has been done on evangelical Christian students than on Muslim students; some of the few exceptions include Bronwyn Williams's "The Book and the Truth: Faith, Rhetoric, and Cross-Cultural Communication" and Amber Engelson's more recent "The 'Hands of God' at Work: Negotiating between Western and Religious Scholarship in Indonesia." In fact, Mike DePalma and I argue in "Charting Prospects and Possibilities for Scholarship on Religious Rhetorics" that this is an area of scholarship that demands far more attention in rhetoric and composition than it has received (277).

At the same time, though, Alexander and Jarratt's words do apply to my research with evangelical Christian students, albeit with some caveats. First, like Alexander and Jarratt, I still marvel at "the richness of the archive" I encountered through my students' interviews: the transcripts from my sixteen hours of interviews with Austin, Kimberly, and Eloise number roughly four hundred pages, such that there are reams of material in that archive I don't report on here. More importantly, though, while evangelical Christian students have been featured in composition scholarship more than Muslim students, the number of studies that feature their voices as a primary data set still tends to be rather few. Exceptions include Shannon Carter's "Living inside the Bible (Belt)," DePalma's "Re-envisioning Religious Discourses as Rhetorical Resources in Composition Teaching," and my own "Consequences of Integrating Faith Into Academic Writing." As Elizabeth Vander Lei has recently pointed out, though, composition scholarship still tends to treat the voices of religiously committed students as "monstrous," prompting us to assume they exist outside of the confines of composition studies—or wish that they would ("'Where'"). As Brownyn Williams put it, evangelical Christianity in the early twenty-first century is rife with "cultural baggage" (qtd. in Pavia 352).

Vander Lei's and Williams's views are backed up by a survey conducted by the Institute for Jewish and Community Research (IJCR) about the religious beliefs and behaviors of American university faculty. A 2007 report by the IJCR features the following among their main findings:

1 Faculty feel warmly about most religious groups, but feel coldly about evangelicals and Mormons.

2 Faculty feel most unfavorably about evangelical Christians.
3 Faculty are almost unanimous in their belief that evangelical Christians ... should keep their religious beliefs out of American politics. (Tobin and Weinberg 2)

Regarding the second of these three points, IJCR researchers Gary A. Tobin and Aryeh K. Weinberg note that evangelical Christianity "is the only religious group about which a majority of non-evangelical faculty have negative feelings" (2). Later in their report, they note their own surprise regarding "the level of negativity faculty showed for Christian fundamentalists and Evangelicals. If not outright prejudice, faculty sentiment about the largest religious group in the American public borders dangerously close" (15). Tobin and Weinberg go on to pose a question that pertains to my concerns here: "What are the implications of the negativity that faculty feel about Evangelical Christians?" (15). The implications, I think, are that we tend to impose upon such students—and their voices—a limited set of possibilities for how they think and what they can achieve rhetorically, critically, civically. Thus Tom Newkirk's words from *The Performance of Self in Student Writing* still resonate today: the presence of "evangelical Christians in the writing class" remains "a topic that deserves more sensitive attention than it has been given" (15). My decision to feature these students' voices represents an attempt to answer Newkirk's call—though I would argue that, as evangelicalism continues to change and adapt, more work needs to be done.

Interview-based case studies, then, allowed me to turn the focus of my research more squarely on students' voices and perspectives. But because my focus here is on a question that remains as of yet unresearched in regards to evangelical Christian students—namely, how their faith might inform or align with a kind of creativity that offers hope for civic engagement—the case study methodology offers a means of providing an initial answer to that question (MacNealy 47). Anne Beaufort in *College Writing and Beyond* notes that while her case study with "Tim" is "not generalizable," it does allow her "the potential for refining a conceptual framework for writing expertise that could be tested in other settings" (26). My focus here is not on writing expertise—Beaufort is talking about her five-part model of discourse community, writing process, rhetoric, subject matter, and genre. And yet, my case studies with Austin, Kimberly, and Eloise have pointed me toward phenomena that, prior to this research, had gone unnoticed in composition scholarship regarding religiously committed students. Those phenomena include vernacular religious creativity (see Chapter 2) and the rhetorical possibilities that can result from such creativity (see Chapter 3)—phenomena that, like Beaufort's model of writing expertise, can and should be "tested in other settings." In other words, this study opens up as many questions as it answers, and my hope is that future scholarship will take up the question of how and when these forms of creativity emerge in student academic writing for deliberative ends.

Let me return, though, to Beaufort's idea that a single case study (or three) cannot be generalizable. This assumption is one that Tom Newkirk interrogates in "The Narrative Roots of the Case Study." For Newkirk, such an assumption is questionable because it misses the point of case study research, the authority of which does not derive from findings that might apply to all or even most first-year writing students, but rather from "the cultural values embedded in various narrative plots" (133). While Newkirk doesn't discount methodology, he critiques what he calls the "great god of Methodology" invoked by researchers to "protect" themselves "from charges of storytelling," to the extent that "the account appears as the almost inevitable output of a methodological machine. The researcher didn't write the study; the method did" (133–34). According to Newkirk, case studies are valuable or authoritative insofar as they tap into "a core of mythic narratives—deeply rooted story patterns that clearly signal to the reader the types of judgments to be made" (135). "Transformative narratives," those in which an "individual experiences some sort of conflict and undergoes a qualitative change in the resolution of that conflict," function as an example of such mythic narratives (134). Such a pattern undergirds my case studies of Austin, Kimberly, and Eloise. Each student experienced a type of conflict (e.g., How do I reconcile my Christian beliefs with my academic writing and context?) that they then negotiated through a "qualitative change" as represented by identifiable patterns of vernacular religious creativity.

My goal in adopting case study methods—and, indeed, of writing my findings as case studies—was to tap into their experiences as narratives and thus to tell the stories of at least some evangelical Christian students that have not yet been told in rhetoric and composition. In doing so, I am certainly complicit as a storyteller: I'm looking through a particular lens, that of a white, heterosexual male who grew up in a Pentecostal, evangelical Christian family in the northeastern United States and who eventually migrated to the Episcopal Church while in graduate school. As I discuss with Emily Cope, that vantage afforded me the opportunity to position myself as an "insider" to evangelical Christian faith and discourse with my participants, both in the interviews I conducted for this study and in the materials I used to recruit participants (Cope and Ringer 112–14, 119). This move allowed me to achieve a degree of trust that is essential to in-depth case study research, especially when it deals with facets of identity and belief as sensitive and emotionally laden as religious faith (Cope and Ringer 119; Thomson-Bunn 135). As the same time, that positionality also poses a risk, not the least of which is the possibility of "projecting [my] experiences onto others or misinterpreting what [my] participants wrote or said" (Cope and Ringer 103). Narratives, as Debra Journet remind us, are not necessarily more authentic than other modes of reporting research, especially when they're told by someone else.

What, then, allows for any degree of validity within case studies such as these? In *Interviewing as Qualitative Research*, Irving Seidman offers a potential answer. First, he underscores the fact that his three-part interview structure affords researchers the ability to identify instances of internal consistency—moments, say, in the third interview that reiterate something said in the first or second interview (Seidman 28). Given that I adapted Seidman's structure into five interviews, I'm able to identify even more instances of internal consistency. But I'm also able to cross-check what students say with what they wrote—the informal, heuristic writing they completed prior to each interview and the formal, academic writing they produced for their writing courses. The second point Seidman makes about his interview structure and validity is that of external consistency, or the ability to "relate" particular experiences "to a broader discourse on the issue" (29). I'm able to do this in two ways. In line with Heather Thomson-Bunn's suggestions about empirical hybridity (134–45), I put my participants' voices in conversation with scholarship in rhetoric and composition. But because much of that conversation involves my participants challenging or extending assumptions in composition, arguably the more important "discourse on the issue" to which I connect my data is contemporary sociological findings about millennial religious faith, most significantly the National Study of Youth and Religion (NSYR) data as reported on in Christian Smith and Patricia Snell's *Souls in Transition*. As I discuss more fully in Appendix B, my participants fit squarely within the age range of the thousands of "emerging adults" described by the NSYR data.

Of course, that's not to say that the experiences of Austin, Kimberly, and Eloise are necessarily representative. Not every millennial evangelical Christian student will engage in vernacular religious creativity in the same manner as the three students I feature here—though the nationally representative NSYR data indicate it's likely that millennial evangelicals will make at least some effort to adjust their religious beliefs in relation to their pluralistic contexts. As Newkirk reminds us, though, that's not the point of case study research. The point is to tell stories that, to borrow Beaufort's phrase, "ring true" (32). If I've done that—and if the research I report on here opens up paths of invention for future scholarship and for a more civil discourse—then I'll consider the project a success. I would attribute that success, though, to Austin, Kimberly, and Eloise. It was their courage, their intelligence, their willingness to talk with me and invite me into their struggles to reconcile faith commitments with academic writing in pluralistic contexts that pointed me toward vernacular religious creativity. Without them, these ideas would remain latent within their experiences and unrecognized in rhetoric and composition.

Methods

With that rationale in mind, I offer a fuller discussion of my methods, including participant selection, interview protocols, and data analysis.

Participants

My case studies took place at the pseudonymous Northeast State University (NESU) during the fall of 2008 and spring of 2009. I located my participants via affiliation with campus ministries (Cope and Ringer 111–14). Specifically, I talked with directors of various campus ministries, explained my project to them, and asked if they knew incoming first-year (FY) students who might be interested in participating. From there, I would email students, explain my project, and invite them to participate. In this initial email, I was careful to avoid terms like "evangelical," "fundamentalist," or "conservative Christian" when describing my study. Given the post-Christian, northeastern context of the study, I feared that some students who fit the criteria of evangelical based on their practices, beliefs, and subcultural affiliations would nevertheless seek to distance themselves from such politically loaded terms. Of course, because I was purposefully avoiding using these terms, I ran the risk of locating participants who did not fit my definition of evangelical Christian. To mitigate this risk, I initially designed a brief questionnaire that I planned to give to students in order to gauge their attitudes toward characteristics of evangelical Christianity. I wanted to ensure that they "fit" the category as I defined it. After talking with several colleagues about my proposed method, though, I began to feel that the questionnaire might come across as something akin to an inquisition, which Kathleen Norris in *Amazing Grace* defines as a question to which the answer is already known (217). Instead, I decided to have an initial discussion with potential participants to introduce myself, explain my research, and get a sense of their religious and educational backgrounds. Again, in these pre-interview discussions, I would avoid the use of terms like evangelical unless they brought it up themselves.

Because I was identifying FY students who were voluntarily attending evangelical campus ministries, I felt safer about assuming they fit the definition of evangelical. I was also communicating with various campus ministers about my project, and they would refer students to me whom they felt fit my description. By the time I contacted any of the students, they had already been through two informal "screening" processes. Still, I would arrange an informal meeting to talk with each prospective participant and get a better sense of who they were. In that meeting, I positioned myself as an insider to evangelical Christian discourse (Cope and Ringer 103) by telling them about my background—that I grew up in a Pentecostal Christian family in the Northeast, graduated from an evangelical Christian college in the South, attended a local Episcopal church, and participated in various initiatives via NESU's chapter of InterVarsity Christian Fellowship (IVCF). I also asked them about their backgrounds, their involvement with their campus ministry, the kinds of churches they had attended, and so forth. Though I did not plan to work with students from the same campus ministry, all three of my participants ended up coming from NESU's chapter of IVCF, one of the largest national evangelical Christian collegiate parachurch ministries. I did not know any of them through my involvement with IVCF, but more likely than not my numerous connections via IVCF helped me gain access to and recruit them (see Seidman 47–50). As I noted in Chapter 1, all three participants also attended Greenville Evangelical Church (GEC), a nondenominational evangelical church close to campus that attracted a large number of college students—and which I had also attended prior to their arrival at NESU. Telling students in our initial conversation that I had attended GEC and had friends who were involved there afforded us a point of contact that fostered trust (see Cope and Ringer; Thomson-Bunn).

Interviews

Each case study consisted of five interviews spread out over a period of roughly two months. I adapted Seidman's suggestions for conducting multiple interviews by stretching his three-interview structure into five. Though Seidman recommends no more than two weeks between interviews, conflicting schedules, semester breaks, and unplanned contingencies sometimes disrupted that regularity. Though the specifics of each case study vary from individual to individual, I did follow a stable progression in terms of the focus of each of the five interviews. That progression derives from Seidman, who suggests that the first interview focus on "the participant's experience in context by asking him or her to tell as much as possible about him or herself in light of the topic up to the present time," what Seidman would call each participant's "focused life history" (21). The first interview centered on student faith up to the present time, while the second turned the focus toward educational background and experiences. The next two interviews in my sequence correspond to Seidman's "Interview Two: The Details of Experience." Seidman recommends that this second interview "concentrate on the concrete details of the participants' present lived experience in the topic area of study" (21). The "concrete details" that interest me involve student writing—I wanted to analyze their writing and their "talk about writing" (Mortensen 105)—so interviews three and four were text-based interviews that focused on the writing produced by my participants. Finally, I stuck close to Seidman's suggestion for my final interview, wherein I asked students to reflect on the meaning of their experiences (Seidman 22), both in terms of their academic writing and practice as evangelical Christians and in terms of the study itself.

Because my focus was student writing, I asked students to respond to heuristic writing prompts prior to or at the beginning of each interview. These prompts, which I describe below, corresponded to the focus of each interview. For interviews after the first, I also provided students with a series of excerpts from something they wrote or said in or for a previous interview. This allowed me the opportunity to ask students to clarify something they had said, a move that aided in achieving internal consistency in each transcript. In some cases, it also afforded me the opportunity to "try out" my interpretations with my participants. While not a full-blown version of member checking, this move did allow participants to respond to my burgeoning analysis of the data (Thomson-Bunn 136). Finally, having these "textual artifacts" helped build continuity from interview to interview, especially in cases where interviews were separated by more than two weeks.

For the first interview, which focused on students' religious and educational backgrounds, each participant responded to the following prompt:

> Write a brief letter (1–2 pages) to someone in your FYW/FYE class—either professor or peer—and describe yourself as a Christian. Some questions you might consider: What does your faith mean to you? What aspects of Christianity are most important to you? How does your faith influence who you are on a daily basis? How did you come to be a Christian?

I asked students to email me their letter at least 24 hours prior to our interview. Using a set of standard interview questions as a guide, I would then formulate specific questions based on what the student wrote. For example, Kimberly wrote in her first writing prompt that she "grew up in a household where faith in God was a given." One of the guiding questions I wanted to ask each student in the first interview was how they had come to be a Christian. Kimberly's written response partially answered this question, but prompting her to talk more about the idea that "faith in God was a given" was a way of getting her to explore her religious background and her early conversion more fully. In this way, most of the questions I asked in the actual interview, though based on the guiding questions I developed, were unique to each participant.

The writing prompts for the next two interviews also remained consistent across all participants. The second interview explored students' current educational contexts, and they did so by responding to the following writing prompt:

> Write a brief letter (1–2 pages) in which you describe—to the same person you wrote to last time—what it's like to be a Christian in your FYW/FYE course. Some questions you might consider: What challenges have you faced? How has your faith made things easier/better/more difficult for you? How does your faith influence what you say, how you say it, and when you choose not to say anything?

There are a few reasons why I asked students to respond by writing a letter. One was that I agree with Sue Dinitz and Toby Fulwiler when they write that "[l]etter writing is as natural and easy as writing ever gets" (vii). I also agree with them that, because "letters usually have a clearly defined purpose and audience," they tend to elicit "focused, clear writing" (Dinitz and Fulwiler viii; see also Booth, "Rhetorical"). I wanted students to think about and write for a particular audience, and I wanted it to be someone with whom they had had contact while negotiating their academic and evangelical identities.

I also wanted students to recall concrete experiences as much as possible. Writing letters to their professors or peers seems to have done this. Though I did have to prompt students to go into further depth in each interview, the letters often illustrate the extent to which each students' evangelical and academic trajectories intertwined in her or his "nexus of multi-membership" (Wenger 158). Austin, for instance, chose to write his second letter to Chris, the student in class whose outspokenness about his distaste for religion constituted the exigency that prompted Austin to write a defense of religious education. In fact, it was that letter that alerted me to that moment in class—a moment that might have gone unnoticed had Austin not been asked to write a letter wherein he described his faith to someone in his FYW class. Eloise followed a similar tack by writing to a student with whom she did not see eye to eye in regards to faith. Though the level of authenticity varied from participant to participant, writing letters did seem to imbue their responses with a sense of focus and purpose and ground their responses in concrete social situations—situations that played a significant role in how students negotiated their evangelical identities in pluralistic contexts.

Even though letters can be easier to write than other genres, they are still time consuming. And because all of my participants had busy educational and social lives outside of our study, I didn't want to overburden them with preparing for each interview. For the third and fourth interviews, then, I asked students to do a directed freewrite for ten minutes at the beginning of the interview. The prompts for these interviews reflected the focus of each interview. For example, interview three was a text-based interview; my goal in this interview was to initiate "conversation in which speakers attend to text or the processes of creating text" (Mortensen 105). In it, I talked with each participant about one or more pieces of academic writing they had written for their FYW course. I had each participant email me the sample academic writing as soon after the second interview as possible so I would have time to read it and formulate questions. In the freewriting prompt I gave them at the beginning of their interview, I asked them to "[t]ake about 10 minutes and freewrite about how (or if) your identity as a Christian influenced how you wrote this. What does this essay mean to you as a Christian?" I would sometimes change this prompt to reflect each student's submitted work. For example, I would include the title of each student's paper in the prompt.

The fourth interview served as a follow-up to the third in that its focus remained on what Peter Mortensen would call each student's "talk about writing" (105). I tailored the heuristic writing prompts to each student based on their writing and on what took place in the third interview. My first interviewee was Austin, and I asked him to freewrite in response to the following prompt:

> I'm interested to hear more about how your faith and identity as an evangelical Christian informs this paper. How does what you know

> as a Christian and how you know as one shape what you say in "Christian Schools"? Another way to think about it: What are you able to say in this paper that someone who isn't evangelical would not be able to say?

In this way, I was asking Austin to think about his paper as a nexus of what Mortensen calls intertextuality and intersubjectivity—how his essay, for instance, bears the traces not only of other texts (e.g, the Bible), but also of other subjectivities, other voices—the shared "social space" and its attendant "common resources" that "enable [writers] to communicate" (Mortensen 118–19). In a way, Mortensen's assumptions about intertextuality and intersubjectivity constituted my motives for both text-based interviews: I wanted my participants to talk about their texts and processes of writing those texts in ways that would offer insight into the various resources, religious, academic, and otherwise, that informed what they wrote and how they wrote it.

The aim of my fifth interview resonated with Seidman's final interview in his three-part structure (22–23). I wanted students to "reflect on the meaning" of their experiences, both as evangelical Christians in their academic contexts and as participants within the study itself. The letter I asked students to write prior to this interview evidences that reflective component:

> Write a brief letter (1–2 pages) to one of your spiritual mentors—maybe a pastor, parent, sibling, friend, campus minister, or youth pastor—and tell her or him how you see your faith as shaping your education and your education as shaping your faith. Feel free to reference anything you and I have talked about over the first four interviews—your religious and educational backgrounds, your current educational context, your academic writing, and your reflection on others' experiences.

My goal here was to help my participants see their academic practice from both a spiritual and academic vantage. It was also, as the prompt indicates, aimed at helping students reflect on the different threads of the study itself—what they had thought about and talked with me about over the course of their participation. The questions I asked in the interview were contingent upon each student's response and our discussion to that point.

I recorded each interview using a digital audio recorder. Though I often took notes during the interview, I relied primarily on the recordings for the transcriptions. Shortly after each interview, I would transcribe it as fully as necessary—that is to say, I would transcribe fully those sections that pertained to my research while only taking notes on those sections that did not pertain (see Daniell, *Communion* 22). Given that I ended up with sixteen hours of interviews to listen to and transcribe, this helped save time, though I still ended up with well over four hundred double-spaced pages of interview transcriptions. On some occasions, I found it necessary to go back and fully transcribe a section for which I initially had only taken notes.

Data Analysis

I used an emergent coding scheme for analysis of the interview transcripts and student writing. Initially, this coding scheme came from composition research related to writing and identity (see Ivanič; LeCourt). This analysis helped me write a very different version of Chapter 4, a *College English* essay on Austin called "The Consequences of Integrating Faith into Academic Writing: Casuistic Stretching and Biblical Citation." Readers familiar with this essay will know that, in that piece, my focus is somewhat different than my focus in this book—that is to say, I'm looking mostly at the risks of stretching faith, not the possibilities. As I thought about that argument, though, and as I considered Austin's move towards what Perry calls multiplicity, I began to question if that was the only story to tell. In this process, I was influenced by a question Elizabeth Vander Lei had asked me several years ago, one that had to do with why I had chosen to focus on the consequences or risks that might arise when student faith intersects with academic practice, rather than on the possibilities. I didn't have a good answer for her at the time, but that thought continually resurfaced in my consciousness. What if there was another story to tell? What might those possibilities look like?

That's when I came across the work of Leonard Primiano and Robert Glenn Howard, folklorists (the latter also a rhetorician) who concern themselves with vernacular faith. Reading their work, I started to formulate a new terministic screen with which to see the rhetorical and civic possibilities latent within the transcripts and writings of Austin, Kimberly, and Eloise. I then started to rethink their stories in terms of vernacular religious creativity and the possibilities it might have for opening up discourse rather than closing it down—and did so while also reading Smith and Snell's *Souls in Transition* and work on lived religion by sociologists Nancy Ammerman and others. That work and their terms constitute much of the coding scheme I used for the present study, though I also still draw on the terms provided by Ivanič, LeCourt, and others concerning identity and writing when necessary.

Limitations

Any study has its limitations, and this one is no different. I focus here on three students from a single university in a particular regional context. Even with my ability to contextualize the writing and thinking of Austin, Kimberly, and Eloise in larger, nationally representative studies like the NSYR, the fact that I focus on a small sample of students in very specific writing contexts—and zero in on one or two assignments they wrote—limits the extent of my generalizations. Not every millennial evangelical Christian student will approach even similar assignments in ways that correspond to the strategies that Austin, Kimberly, and Eloise adopted. Also, for reasons I outlined above, I focus primarily on these students' perspectives of their experiences. There are other voices I could have included, not the least of which are the students' instructors and peers such as Chris in Austin's class and Michaela in Eloise's class, both of whom played significant roles in what those participants wrote and how they approached their assignments. I also didn't conduct observations, though gaining access to Eloise's living and learning class would have been difficult. Moreover, by the time I identified participants, key exigencies, such as Eloise's manner of proclaiming as an evangelical and Chris's comment to Austin, had already passed. I made every attempt to identify participants prior to the semester starting—I even contacted youth pastors in the region over the summer of 2008 to ask if they knew of students attending NESU as freshmen in the fall—but turned up no leads. Thus I had to wait until midsemester before interviewing any of them, and by then my presence in a classroom of twenty students might have changed classroom dynamics significantly.

At the outset of this Appendix, I cited Alexander and Jarratt's words about "the richness of the archive [they] discovered and created through these interviews" (541). Writing this book has been a study in just how rich of an archive I gained from Austin, Kimberly, and Eloise. Equally important, it's a testament to just how rich an archive each of our students is, religious or otherwise. I hope this book helps us appreciate that richness in all of its various manifestations.

Appendix B
The National Study of Youth and Religion as Context

The National Study of Youth and Religion (NSYR) is a national-scale, multi-stage research project funded by the Lily Endowment and spearheaded by sociologist Christian Smith, one of the foremost experts on trends within American religious practice. According to the project's website, the purpose of the NSYR is as follows:

> [T]o research the shape and influence of religion and spirituality in the lives of American youth; to identify effective practices in the religious, moral, and social formation of the lives of youth; to describe the extent and perceived effectiveness of the programs and opportunities that religious communities are offering to their youth; and to foster an informed national discussion about the influence of religion in youth's lives, in order to encourage sustained reflection about and rethinking of our cultural and institutional practices with regard to youth and religion. ("Research Purpose")

The project began in 2001 and, according to the NSYR's website, is funded by the Lily Endowment through the end of 2015.

The project involves multiple "waves" of data collection, with the first commencing in the summer of 2002 and the fourth and final ending in late 2012. *Soul Searching: The Religious and Spiritual Lives of American Teenagers*—the first major publication from NSYR data—reported on American youth ages 13–17. Data collection for *Soul Searching* came from the first wave of data collection—telephone interviews with over 3,000 participants that occurred between July 2002 and April 2003 and follow-up interviews with 267 teenagers during the spring and summer of 2003. A second study, *Souls in Transition: The Religious and Spiritual Lives of Emerging Adults*, was published in 2009 and focuses on the next highest age bracket: "emerging adults," who are 18 to 23 years old. The methods for this study likewise involved a telephone survey of over 2,000 members and follow-up interviews with more than 200. The survey took place between September 2007 and April 2008, while the personal interviews occurred between May and September 2008.

To my knowledge, Austin, Kimberly, and Eloise did not participate in any wave of this national study, but their ages align with the population researched: in 2003, they would have been at or close to age 13. Thus the results from *Soul Searching* offer a national backdrop within which to contextualize the religious identities of my participants. And given that my three participants were traditional first-year students in the fall of 2008 at or close to the age of 18, they align with the youngest bracket of the NSYR's emerging adult population profiled in *Souls in Transition*. The upshot of this is that while I report here on case studies with only three participants, the NSYR study allows me to contextualize their faith and experiences within larger, nationally representative trends among similarly aged teens and young adults who were living at the same historical moment.

Here I comment on how Austin, Kimberly, and Eloise match up with the population of students Smith and Snell define in *Souls in Transition*. I focus on that study because the age group reported on in that book aligns with the population of students that would most likely show up in a first-year writing class. Smith and Snell divided their respondents into four religious types: Devoted, Regular, Sporadic, and Disengaged (259). As one could imagine, the latter two categories identify a population that attends religious services sporadically or never and for whom faith is relatively unimportant. Given their regular involvement with InverVarsity, weekly attendance at Greenville Evangelical Church, and daily Bible or devotional reading, my participants fit well within the category of the "Devoted," which Smith and Snell define as follows:

- Attend religious services weekly or more often.
- Faith is very or extremely important in everyday life.
- Feel very or extremely close to God.
- Pray a few times a week or more often.
- Read scripture once a week or twice a month or more often. (259)

Given my method of identifying participants via their participation within a campus ministry and the recommendation of a campus ministry leader (see Appendix A; see also Cope and Ringer), the fact that my three participants align with Smith and Snell's Devoted should come as little surprise. But what other data exist that locate Austin, Kimberly, and Eloise within the category of the Devoted? The following brief excerpts help provide a sense of these students' faith. For instance, Austin, a white, male, first-year student who spent his early childhood in the South but had lived in the Northeast for most of his life, said the following over the course of our interviews:

- I've experienced God on nearly a daily basis in prayer. Just feeling the comfort and knowing he's there. I just know.
- Like, my decisions that I make are based on my faith, or I try to make them—I mess up like everyone else—but when I do make a decision, I want it to be lined up with the Word, like, more than anything.

- I couldn't go a day without reading my Bible. [...] Everyday I'll get up in the morning and read a devotion.
- Throughout this past month of school God has really put on my heart, like, just wanting to reach campus and reach those around me.
- I've been talking to a couple of guys [at Greenville Evangelical Church] about going on a men's retreat. And, um, the church is awesome. Like, they're so supportive of the NESU students.
- The Bible tells us we need Christian fellowship. I believe strongly in that. I never had that before, before I came here. Through [InterVarsity] I've been able to have such strong friendships with the people there. Like, so God-inspired it's ridiculous.

Over the course of our interviews, Kimberly, a Jamaican American first-year student from a nearby state in the Northeast, said the following:

- The one concern that really—about coming to NESU—was me not being able to go to church. And, um, I was like, what am I gonna do? Like, I just can't sleep in on Sundays and not go to church. So, I started going to like these Christian groups on campus and met a couple people and they said, "You know, we take a van out to church on Sundays. So why not?" So, it's just become part of my routine now.
- Some of [my sorority sisters] just come to me and say, "You know, Kimberly, I have a prayer request," or, "Can you just pray for this for me?" And it's like, definitely.
- Usually I just wake up—or before to go to bed—I pray. Just like being in a college setting gets kind of hectic, so, I'm not able to read my bible on a daily basis as I would like to. So, um, I've gotten into the thing where I'm gonna do a book at a time before bed—I'll try to do that. And then within my sorority I'd do like Bible study and I led that last week. So just that once a week if anything I'll be able to be getting that. And, um, leading personal bible studies with my sisters. Like, one on one type of thing. I'm able to read my bible and at least just do that special time with God.
- Like, I just had a Bible study and my thing was to, um, write—um, just summarize the chapter and write, um, just break it up and summarize it into parts. And writing it out definitely helps in allowing me to see, um, what I'm taking from the Scripture, and what the key elements that I see.
- I feel like when I don't read the Bible, I don't know what my motivation is. I don't know what to do with myself. And then um just seeing that, you know, God is always there. He has a will and purpose for my life. So I'm gonna—so reading the Bible does that for me. It allows me to get through the day and pick up on what I need to do to fulfill that purpose, that role.

Finally, Eloise, a female first-year student of partial Iranian descent who converted to evangelical Christianity while in high school, said the following over the course of our interviews:

- I spend my time on the more important things in life. Going to church every Sunday and InterVarsity meeting on Tuesdays, Thursdays and Sundays is something I look forward to every week. Even waking up twenty minutes earlier than I have to so that I can devote some time to my quiet time is another aspect of being a Christian that I enjoy, for it truly starts my day off right.
- I have the Word of Life Bible Institute quiet time. It's a book, and it gives you—I think it's around ten verses a day. And you just read them and then, two questions are the same every time. It's, "What is the writer trying to tell you?" and "How do you apply this to your life?"
- [E]ven if I'm just walking to class, like, I'll start praying and being thankful for stuff.

Based on these data, it's clear that Austin, Kimberly, and Eloise mostly fit the category of Devoted. I say "mostly" because there are some minor inconsistencies—Kimberly's admission that it can be difficult while in college to engage in daily Bible reading, for instance. Smith and Snell do allow for mixed categories, such that an individual could be somewhere between Devoted and Regular. Again, though, based on the interview data, all three of my participants lean towards Devoted if they don't fit squarely within it. Why, though, is this important? What's the significance of categorizing Austin, Kimberly, and Eloise as Devoted? Based on the NSYR findings, only five percent of emerging adults fit the Devoted category, the significance of which has to do with attitudes related to civic engagement. According to Smith and Snell, religious devotion correlates strongly with higher levels of "giving and volunteering" (262); increased engagement with "organized activities" (263); greater appreciation of various marginalized groups (264); and stronger senses of "purpose and gratitude" (268). All of which again suggests that highly devout evangelical Christian millennials like Austin, Kimberly, and Eloise might be perfectly positioned to intervene productively and deliberatively in public discourse.

Bibliography

Alexander, Jonathan, and Susan C. Jarratt. "Rhetorical Education and Student Activism." *College English* 76.6 (2014): 525–44. Print.

Ammerman, Nancy T., ed. *Everyday Religion: Observing Modern Religious Lives.* New York: Oxford UP, 2007. Print.

———. "Introduction: Observing Religious Modern Lives." Ammerman, *Everyday* 3–18. Print.

———. *Sacred Stories, Spiritual Tribes: Finding Religion in Everyday Life.* New York: Oxford UP, 2014. Print.

Anderson, Chris. "The Description of an Embarrassment: When Students Write about Religion." *ADE Bulletin* 94 (Winter 1989): 12–15. Print.

Anson, Chris. "Response Styles and Ways of Knowing." *Writing and Response: Theory, Practice, and Research.* Ed. Chris Anson. Urbana: National Council of Teachers of English, 1989. 332–66. Print.

Aristotle. *Rhetoric.* Trans. W. Rhys Roberts. Rpt. in *The Rhetoric and Poetics of Aristotle.* New York: Modern Library, 1984. 1 218. Print.

Austin. First interview. 7 Oct. 2008.

———. Second interview. 21 Oct. 2008.

———. Second letter. 21 Oct. 2008.

———. Third interview. 30 Oct. 2008.

———. Fourth interview. 14 Nov. 2008.

———. Fifth interview. 8 Dec. 2008.

Balmer, Randall. *The Making of Evangelicalism: From Revivalism to Politics and Beyond.* Waco: Baylor UP, 2010. Print.

Banks, Adam. *Digital Griots: African American Rhetoric in a Multimedia Age.* Carbondale: Southern Illinois UP, 2011. Print.

Bartkowski, John P. "Connections and Contradictions: Exploring the Complex Linkages between Faith and Family." Ammerman, *Everyday* 153–66. Print.

"The Barna Millennials Project." *Barna.org.* The Barna Group. Web. 27 Jan. 2015.

Baumlin, James S. "Introduction: Positioning *Ethos* in Historical and Contemporary Theory." Baumlin and Baumlin xi–xxxi. Print.

Baumlin, James S., and Tita French Baumlin, eds. *Ethos: New Essays in Rhetorical and Critical Theory.* Dallas: Southern Methodist UP, 1994. Print.

Beaufort, Anne. *College Writing and Beyond: A New Framework for University Writing Instruction.* Logan: Utah State UP, 2007. Print.

Bebbington, David W. *Evangelicalism in Modern Britain: A History from the 1730s to the 1980s.* Oxford: Oxford UP, 2004. Print.

Bellah, Robert, et al. *Habits of the Heart: Individualism and Commitment in American Life*. Berkeley: U of California P, 1985. Print.

Berlin, James A. "Rhetoric and Ideology in the Writing Class." *College English* 50.5 (September 1988): 477–94. Print.

Berthoff, Ann E. "Introductory Remarks." Interchanges: Spiritual Sites of Composing. *College Composition and Communication* 45.2 (May 1994): 237–38. Print.

Bielo, James S. *Emerging Evangelicals: Faith, Modernity, and the Desire for Authenticity*. New York: New York UP, 2011. Print.

Bizzell, Patricia. "Beyond Antifoundationalism to Rhetorical Authority: Problems Defining 'Cultural Literacy.'" *College English* 52.6 (1990): 661–75. Print.

———. "Faith-Based World Views as a Challenge to the Believing Game." *The Journal of the Assembly for Expanded Perspectives on Learning* 14 (2008–09): 29–35. Print.

———. "Rationality as Rhetorical Strategy at the Barcelona Disputation, 1263: A Cautionary Tale." *College Composition and Communication* 58.1 (2006): 12–29. Print.

Booth, Wayne C. *The Rhetoric of RHETORIC: The Quest for Effective Communication*. Malden: Blackwell, 2004. Print.

———. "The Rhetorical Stance." *College Composition and Communication* 14.3 (1963): 139–45. Print.

Brandt, Deborah, et al. "The Politics of the Personal: Storying Our Lives against the Grain." *College English* 64.1 (2001): 41–62. MLA *International Bibliography*. EBSCO. Web. 4 May 2010.

Buley-Meissner, Mary-Louise, Mary McCaslin Thompson, and Elizabeth Bachrach Tan, eds. *The Academy and the Possibility of Belief: Essays on Intellectual and Spiritual Life*. Cresskill: Hampton P, 2000. Print.

Burke, Kenneth. *Attitudes toward History*. Berkeley: U of California P, 1984. Print.

———. *A Grammar of Motives*. Berkeley: U of California P, 1969. Print.

———. *A Rhetoric of Motives*. Berkeley: U of California P, 1969. Print.

Butler, Judith, et al. "Concluding Discussion." Mendieta and VanAntwerpen 109–17. Print.

Calhoun, Craig. "Afterword: Religion's Many Powers." Mendieta and VanAntwerpen 118–34. Print.

Canada, Geoffrey. *Fist, Stick, Knife, Gun: A Personal History of Violence in America*. Boston: Beacon P, 1995. Print.

Canagarajah, A. Suresh. "Introduction: New Possibilities for the Spiritual and the Critical in Pedagogy." *Christian and Critical English Language Educators in Dialogue: Pedagogical and Ethical Dilemmas*. Ed. Mary Shepard Wong and A. Suresh Canagarajah. New York: Routledge, 2009. 1–18. Print.

Carlson, Cheree. "Creative Casuistry and Feminist Consciousness: The Rhetoric of Moral Reform." *Quarterly Journal of Speech* 78 (1992): 16–32. Print.

Carter, Shannon. "Living inside the Bible (Belt)." *College English* 69.6 (July 2007): 572–95. Print.

Carter, Stephen. *The Culture of Disbelief: How American Law and Politics Trivialize Religious Devotion*. New York: Anchor Books, 1993. Print.

———. *God's Name in Vain: The Rights and Wrongs of Religion in Politics*. New York: Basic Books, 2000. Print.

Cary, Lorene. *Black Ice*. New York: Knopf, 1991. Print.

Charland, Maurice. "Constitutive Rhetoric: The Case of the *Peuple Quèbèçois*." *Quarterly Journal of Speech* 73.2 (1987): 133–50. Print.

Cope, Emily Ann. “The Academic Writing of Evangelical Undergraduates.” Diss., U. of Tennessee, 2015. Print.

Cope, Emily Murphy and Jeffrey M. Ringer. “Coming to (Troubled) Terms: Methodology, Positionality, and the Problem of Defining ‘Evangelical Christian.’” DePalma and Ringer 103–24. Print.

Crowley, Sharon. *Toward a Civil Discourse: Rhetoric and Fundamentalism*. Pittsburgh: U of Pittsburgh P, 2006. Print.

Daniell, Beth. *A Communion of Friendship: Literacy, Spiritual Practice, and Women in Recovery*. Studies in Writing and Rhetoric. Carbondale: Southern Illinois UP, 2003. Print.

———. “More in Heaven and Earth: Complicating the Map and Constituting Identities.” DePalma and Ringer 243–61. Print.

———. “Whetstones Provided by the World: Trying to Deal with Difference in a Pluralistic Society.” *College English* 70.1 (September 2007): 79–88. Print.

Dean, Kenda Creasy. *Almost Christian: What the Faith of Our Teenagers Is Telling the American Church*. New York: Oxford UP, 2010. Print.

DePalma, Michael-John. “Re-envisioning Religious Discourses as Rhetorical Resources in Composition Teaching: A Pragmatic Response to the Challenge of Belief.” *College Composition and Communication* 63.2 (December 2011): 219–43. Print.

DePalma, Michael-John, and Jeffrey M. Ringer. “Charting Prospects and Possibilities for Scholarship on Religious Rhetorics.” DePalma and Ringer 262–87. Print.

———. “Introduction: Current Trends and Future Directions in Christian Rhetorics.” DePalma and Ringer 1–13. Print.

———, eds. *Mapping Christian Rhetorics: Connecting Conversations, Charting New Territories*. Routledge Studies in Rhetoric and Communication. New York: Routledge, 2014. Print.

DePalma, Michael-John, Jeffrey M. Ringer, and Jim Webber. “(Re)Charting the (Dis)Courses of Faith and Politics, or Rhetoric and Democracy in the Burkean Barnyard.” *Rhetoric Society Quarterly* 38.3 (July 2008): 311–34. Print.

Dinitz, Sue, and Toby Fulwiler. “Introduction.” *The Letter Book: Ideas for Teaching College English*. Eds. Sue Dinitz and Toby Fulwiler Portsmouth: Boynton/Cook, 2000. vii–xii. Print.

Dively, Ronda Leathers. “Censoring Religious Rhetoric in the Composition Classroom: What We and Our Students May Be Missing.” *Composition Studies* 25.1 (Spring 1997): 55–66. Print.

———. “Religious Discourse in the Academy: Creating a Space by Means of Poststructuralist Theories of Subjectivity.” *Composition Studies* 21.2 (Fall 1993): 91–101. Print.

Downs, Douglas. “True Believers, Real Scholars, and Real True Believing Scholars: Discourses of Inquiry and Affirmation in the Composition Classroom.” Vander Lei and kyburz 39–55. Print.

Duffy, William. “Transforming Decorum: The Sophistic Appeal of Walter Rauschenbusch and the Social Gospel.” DePalma and Ringer 222–39. Print.

Durst, Russell K. *Collision Course: Conflict, Negotiation, and Learning in College Composition*. Urbana: NCTE, 1999. Print.

Ehrenreich, Barabara. *Nickel and Dimed: On (Not) Getting by in America*. New York: Metropolitan, 2001. Print.

Elbow, Peter. *Vernacular Eloquence: What Speech Can Bring to Writing*. New York: Oxford UP, 2012. Print.

Eloise. First interview. 3 Nov. 2008.
———. First letter to Michaela. 3 Nov. 2008.
———. Second interview. 10 Nov. 2008.
———. Second letter to Michaela. 10 Nov. 2008.
———. Third interview. 17 Nov. 2008.
———. Fourth interview. 3 Dec. 2008.
———. Fifth interview. 10 Dec. 2008.

Emerson, Michael O., and Christian Smith. *Divided by Faith: Evangelical Religion and the Problem of Race in America*. New York: Oxford UP, 2000. Print.

Engelson, Amber. "The 'Hands of God' at Work: Negotiating Between Western and Religious Sponsorship in Indonesia." *College English* 76.4 (2014): 292–314. Print.

Farmer, Frank. *After the Public Turn: Composition, Counterpublics, and the Citizen Bricoleur*. Logan: Utah State UP, 2013. Print.

Fleming, David. *City of Rhetoric: Revitalizing the Public Sphere in Metropolitan America*. Albany: SUNY P, 2009. Print.

———. "The Very Idea of a *Progymnasmata*." *Rhetoric Review* 22.2 (2003): 105–20. Print.

Freitas, Donna. *Sex and the Soul: Juggling Sexuality, Spirituality, Romance, and Religion on America's College Campuses*. New York: Oxford UP, 2008. Print.

Geiger, T. J., II. "Unpredictable Encounters: Religious Discourse, Sexuality, and the Free Exercise of Rhetoric." *College English* 75.3 (2013): 250–71. Print.

Gere, Anne Ruggles. "Articles of Faith." Brandt, et al. 46–47. Print.

Gilyard, Keith. *Composition and Cornel West: Notes Toward a Deep Democracy*. Carbondale: Southern Illinois UP, 2008. Print.

Glenn, Cheryl. *Unspoken: A Rhetoric of Silence*. Carbondale: Southern Illinois UP, 2004. Print.

Gogan, Brian. "Expanding the Aims of Public Rhetoric and Writing Pedagogy: Writing Letters to Editors." *College Composition and Communication* 65.4 (June 2014): 534–59. Print.

Goodburn, Amy. "It's a Question of Faith: Discourses of Fundamentalism and Critical Pedagogy in the Writing Classroom." *JAC* 18.2 (1998): 333–53. Print.

Gutterman, David S. *Prophetic Politics: Christian Social Movements and American Democracy*. Ithaca: Cornell UP, 2005. Print.

Habermas, Jürgen. "'The Political': The Rational meaning of a Questionable Inheritance of Political Theology." Mendieta and VanAntwerpen 15–33. Print.

Hall, David D., ed. *Lived Religion in America: Toward a History of Practice*. Princeton: Princeton UP, 1999. Print.

Hansen, Kristine. "Religious Freedom in the Public Square and the Composition Classroom." Vander Lei and kyburz 24–38. Print.

The HarperCollins Study Bible: New Revised Standard Version. San Francisco, CA: HarperSanFrancisco, 2006. Print.

Hauser, Gerard A. *Introduction to Rhetorical Theory*. 2nd ed. Long Grove, IL: Waveland P, 2002. Print.

———. *Vernacular Voices: The Rhetoric of Publics and Public Spheres*. Columbia: U of South Carolina P, 1999. Print.

Heclo, Hugh. *Christianity and American Democracy*. Cambridge: Harvard UP, 2007. Print.

hooks, bell. *Teaching Community: A Pedagogy of Hope*. New York: Routledge, 2003. Print.

Houck, Davis W. and David E. Dixon, eds. *Rhetoric, Religion and the Civil Rights Movement, 1954–1965*. Waco, TX: Baylor UP, 2006. Print.

Howard, Robert Glenn. *Digital Jesus: The Making of a New Christian Fundamentalist Community on the Internet*. New York: New York UP, 2011. Print.

Hunt, Doug. *Misunderstanding the Assignment: Teenage Students, College Writing, and the Pains of Growth*. Portsmouth, NH: Boynton/Cook, 2002. Print.

Hunter, James Davison. *To Change the World: The Irony, Tragedy, and Possibility of Christianity in the Late Modern World*. New York: Oxford UP, 2010. Print.

Hyde, Michael, ed. *The Ethos of Rhetoric*. Columbia: U of South Carolina P, 2004. Print.

Investigations Course Syllabus. Fall 2008. First-Year Experience Program, North East State University.

Ivanič, Roz. *Writing and Identity: The Discoursal Construction of Identity in Academic Writing*. Philadelphia: Benjamins, 1998. Print.

Jarratt, Susan, and Nedra Reynolds. "The Splitting Image: Contemporary Feminisms and the Ethics of *êthos*." Baumlin and Baumlin 37–64. Print.

Johnson-Eilola, Johndan, and Stuart Selber. "Plagiarism, Originality, Assemblage." *Computers and Composition* 24.4 (2007): 275–403. Print.

Journet, Debra. "Narrative Turns in Writing Studies Research." Nickoson and Sheridan 13–24. Print.

Juzwik, Mary M. "American Evangelical Biblicism as Literate Practice: A Critical Review." *Reading Research Quarterly* 49.3 (2014): 335–349. Print.

Juzwik, Mary M. and Cori McKenzie. "Writing, Religious Faith, and Rooted Cosmopolitan Dialogue: Portraits of Two American Evangelical Men in a Public School English Classroom." *Written Communication* 32.2 (2015): 121–49. *SAGE Complete*. Web. 6 May 2015. Print.

Katie. Personal interview. 22 July 2006.

Kimberly. First interview. 7 April 2009.

———. First letter. 7 April 2009.

———. Second interview. 14 April 2009.

———. Third interview. 22 April 2009.

———. Fourth interview. 28 April 2009.

———. Fifth interview. 12 May 2009.

———. Fifth letter. 12 May 2009.

Kinneavy, James L. "The Basic Aims of Discourse." *College Composition and Communication* 20.5 (1969): 297–304. JSTOR. Web. 15 Sept. 2015.

Kirsch, Gesa. "From Introspection to Action: Connecting Spirituality and Civic Engagement." *College Composition and Communication* 60.4 (2009): W1-W15. JSTOR. Web. 3 Dec. 2014.

Kirsch, Gesa, and Patricia A. Sullivan, eds. *Methods and Methodology in Composition Research*. Carbondale: Southern Illinois UP, 1992. Print.

LeCourt, Donna. *Identity Matters: Schooling the Student Body in Academic Discourse*. Albany: SUNY P, 2004. Print.

LeFevre, Karen Burke. *Invention as a Social Act*. Carbondale: Southern Illinois UP, 1987. Print.

Lessl, Thomas M. "Civic Engagement from Religious Grounds." *Journal of Communication and Religion* 32 (Nov. 2009): 195–98. Print.

Lewis, C. S. *The Last Battle*. The Chronicles of Narnia. Vol. 7. New York: Harper Trophy, 1994. Print.

Lindsay, D. Michael. *Faith in the Halls of Power: How Evangelicals Joined the American Elite*. New York: Oxford UP, 2007. Print.

Lövheim, Mia. "Virtually Boundless?: Youth Negotiating Tradition in Cyberspace." Ammerman, *Everyday* 83–100.

Mackenzie, Debora. "Will Cancer Vaccine Get to All Women?" *New Scientist* 186.2495 (2005): 8–9. *Academic Search Premier*. Web. 4 May 2010.

MacNealy, Mary Sue. *Strategies of Empirical Research in Writing*. Boston: Allyn and Bacon, 1999. Print.

Magolda, Peter and Kelsey Ebben Gross. *It's All about Jesus! Faith as an Oppositional Collegiate Subculture*. Sterling: Stylus, 2009. Print.

Marsden, George M. *The Outrageous Idea of Christian Scholarship*. New York: Oxford, 1997. Print.

Martel, Yann. *Life of Pi*. New York: Harcourt, 2001. Print.

Marzluf, Phillip. "Religion in U.S. Writing Classes: Challenging the Conflict Narrative." *Journal of Writing Research* 2.3 (2011): 265–97. Web. Directory of Open Access Journals. Journal of Writing Research. 10 Feb. 2015.

McLaren, Brian D. *A Generous Orthodoxy*. Grand Rapids, MI: Zondervan, 2004. Print.

Meghan. First-Year Writing Syllabus. Fall 2008. English Dept., North East State University.

Mendieta, Eduardo and Jonathan VanAntwerpen, eds. *The Power of Religion in the Public Sphere*. New York: Columbia UP, 2011. Print.

Montesano, Mark and Duane Roen. "Religious Faith, Learning, and Writing: Challenges in the Classroom." Vander Lei and kyburz 84–98. Print.

Morris, Leon. *The Gospel According to John*. Rev. ed. Grand Rapids: Eerdmans, 1995. Print.

Mortensen, Peter L. "Analyzing Talk about Writing." Kirsch and Sullivan 105–29. Print.

Mortenson, Greg, and David Oliver Relin. *Three Cups of Tea: One Man's Mission to Fight Terrorism and Build Nations, One School at a Time*. New York: Viking, 2006. Print.

"The Mt. Oread Manifesto on Rhetorical Education 2013." *Rhetoric Society Quarterly* 44.1 (2014): 1–5. Print.

Neulieb, Janice. "Spilt Religion: Student Motivation and Values-Based Writing." *Writing on the Edge* 4.1 (1992): 41–50. Print.

Newbigin, Lesslie. *The Gospel in a Pluralist Society*. Grand Rapids: Eerdmans, 1989. Print.

Newkirk, Thomas. "The Narrative Roots of the Case Study." Kirsch and Sullivan 130–52.

———. *The Performance of Self in Student Writing*. Portsmouth: Boynton/Cook, 1997. Print.

Nickoson, Lee, and Mary P. Sheridan, eds. *Writing Studies Research in Practice: Methods and Methodologies*. Carbondale: Southern Illinois UP, 2012. Print.

The NIV Study Bible. Grand Rapids: Zondervan, 1985. Print.

Norris, Kathleen. *Amazing Grace: A Vocabulary of Faith*. New York: Riverhead, 1998. Print.

Ono, Kent A., and John M. Sloop. "The Critique of Vernacular Discourse." *Communication Monographs* 62 (March 1995): 19–46. Print.

Orsi, Robert A. "Everyday Miracles: The Study of Lived Religion." Hall 3–21. Print.

Pally, Marcia. "The New Evangelicals." *New York Times*. 9 December 2011. Web. 27 May 2014.

Palmeri, Jason. *Remixing Composition: A History of Multimodal Writing Pedagogy*. Carbondale: Southern Illinois UP, 2012. Print.

Pavia, Catherine Matthews. "Taking Up Faith: Ethical Methods for Studying Writing in Religious Contexts." *Written Communication* 32.4 (October 2015): 336–67. *SAGE Complete*. Web. 16 Sept. 2015.

Perelman, Chaïm and L. Olbrechts-Tyteca. *The New Rhetoric: A Treatise on Argumentation*. Notre Dame: U of Notre Dame P, 1969. Print.

Perkins, Priscilla. "'Attentive, Intelligent, Reasonable, and Responsible': Teaching Composition with Bernard Lonergan." Vander Lei, et al. 73–88. Print.

———. "'A Radical Conversion of the Mind': Fundamentalism, Hermeneutics, and the Metanoic Classroom." *College English* 63.5 (May 2001): 585–611. Print.

Perry, William G., Jr. *Forms of Intellectual and Ethical Development in the College Years: A Scheme*. New York: Harcourt Brace Jovanovich, 1968. Print.

Pollitt, Katha. "Virginity or Death!" *Nation* 280.21 (2005): 9. *Academic Search Premier*. EBSCO. Web. 4 May 2010.

Primiano, Leonard Norman. "Vernacular Religion and the Search for Method in Religious Folklife." *Western Folklore* 54 (1995): 37–56. Print.

Rand, Lizabeth A. "Enacting Faith: Evangelical Discourse and the Discipline of Composition Studies." *College Composition and Communication* 52.3 (February 2001): 349–67. Print.

"Religion Among the Millennials." Pew Forum on Religion & Public Life. *Pewforum.org*. 17. Feb. 2010. Web. 27 Jan. 2015.

Regnerus, Mark. *Forbidden Fruit: Sex and Religion in the Lives of American Teenagers*. New York: Oxford UP, 2007. Print.

"Research Purpose." *National Study of Youth and Religion*. University of Notre Dame, 2015. Web. 29 Sept. 2015.

Ringer, Jeffrey M. "The Consequences of Integrating Faith into Academic Writing: Casuistic Stretching and Biblical Citation." *College English* 75.3 (January 2013): 272–99. Print.

———. "The Dogma of Inquiry: Composition and the Primacy of Faith." *Rhetoric Review* 32.3 (Summer 2013): 349–65. Print.

Roberts-Miller, Patricia. *Deliberate Conflict: Argument, Political Theory, and Composition Classes*. Carbondale: Southern Illinois UP, 2004. Print.

"'Safe Sex' for the Whole Nation: Why Mandating the HPV Vaccine is Not a Good Idea." *Chrsitianity Today*. Christianitytoday.com. 22 March 2007. Web. 27 Jan. 2015.

Schwyzer, Hugo. "Christianity Today, the HPV Vaccine, and the Myth That Sex is Ever Safe." Hugoschwyzer.net. 23 March 2007. Web. 27 Jan. 2015.

Seidman, Irving. *Interviewing as Qualitative Research: A Guide for Researchers in Education and the Social Sciences*. 4th ed. New York: Teachers College P, 2013. Print.

Shaver, Lisa J. "The Deaconness Identity: An Argument for Professional Churchwomen and Social Christianity." DePalma and Ringer 203–21. Print.

Simonson, Peter. "Reinventing Invention, Again." *Rhetoric Society Quarterly* 44.4 (2014): 299–322. Print.

Smart, Juanita. "'Frankenstein or Jesus Christ?' When the Voice of Faith Creates a Monster for the Composition Teacher." Vander Lei and kyburz 11–23. Print.

Smith, Christian. *American Evangelicalism: Embattled and Thriving*. Chicago: U of Chicago P, 1998. Print.

———. *The Bible Made Impossible: Why Biblicism is Not a Truly Evangelical Reading of Scripture*. Grand Rapids: Brazos P, 2012. Print.

Smith, Christian, and Melinda Lundquist Denton. *Soul Searching: The Religious and Spiritual Lives of American Teenagers*. New York: Oxford UP, 2005. Print.

Smith, Christian, and Patricia Snell. *Souls in Transition: The Religious and Spiritual Lives of Emerging Adults*. New York: Oxford UP, 2009. Print.

Smitherman Trapp, Joona. "Religious Values and the Student: A Plea for Tolerance." *Dialogue: A Journal for Writing Specialists* 6.1 (Fall 1999): 14–22. Print.

Sprigg, Peter. "Pro-Family, Pro-Vaccine—But Keep it Voluntary." Editorial. *The Washington Post* 15 July 2006: A21. *LexisNexis*. 5 May 2010. Print.

Steensland, Brian, et al. "The Measure of American Religion: Toward Improving the State of the Art." *Social Forces* 79 (2000): 291–318. Print.

Steiner, Mark Allan. "Reconceptualizing Christian Public Engagement: 'Faithful Witness' and the American Evangelical Tradition." *Journal of Communication and Religion* 32 (Nov. 2009): 289–318. Print.

Stenberg, Shari J. "Liberation Theology and Liberatory Pedagogies: Renewing the Dialogue." *College English* 68.3 (January 2006): 271–90. Print.

Stephanie. First-Year Writing Syllabus. Spring 2009. English Dept., North East State University.

Swearingen, C. Jan. "The Hermeneutics of Suspicion and Other Doubting Games: Clearing the Way for Simple Leaps of Faith." Buley-Meissner, Thompson, and Tan 137–152.

———. "Rhetoric and Religion: Recent Revivals and Revisions." *Rhetoric Society Quarterly* 32.2 (2002): 119–37. Print.

Taylor, Charles. "Language and Society." Communicative Action. Ed. Axel Honneth and Hans Joas. Cambridge, MA: MIT P: 23–35. *EBSCO eBook Collection*. Web. 19 July 2015.

———. "Why We Need a Radical Redefinition of Secularism." Mendieta and VanAntwerpen. 34–59. Print.

Thieme, Katja. "Constitutive Rhetoric as an Aspect of Audience Design: The Public Texts of Canadian Suffragists." *Written Communication* 27.1 (2010): 36–56. *SAGE Journals*. Web. 12 Feb. 2015.

Thomson-Bunn, Heather. "Empirical Hybridity: A Multimethodological Approach for Studying Religious Rhetorics." DePalma and Ringer 125–40. Print.

Tobin, Gary A., and Aryeh K. Weinberg. *Religious Beliefs & Behavior of College Faculty*. Vol. 2. San Francisco: Institute for Jewish & Community Research, 2007. Print.

Toulmin, Stephen. "From *The Uses of Argument*." *Teaching Argument in the Composition Course: Background Readings*. Ed. Timothy Barnett. Boston: Bedford/St. Martin's, 2002. 121–32. Print.

Vander Lei, Elizabeth. "'Ain't We Having Fun Yet?': Teaching Writing in a Violent World." Vander Lei, et al. 89–104. Print.

———. "Coming to Terms With Religious Faith in the Composition Classroom: Introductory Comments." Vander Lei and kyburz 3–10. Print.

———. "'Where the Wild Things Are': Christian Students in the Figured Worlds of Composition Research." DePalma and Ringer 65–85. Print.

Vander Lei, Elizabeth, and bonnie lenore kyburz, eds. *Negotiating Religious Faith in the Composition Classroom*. Portsmouth, NH: Boynton/Cook, 2005. Print.

Vander Lei, Elizabeth, and Lauren Fitzgerald. "What in God's Name? Administering the Conflicts of Religious Belief in Writing Programs." *Writing Program Administration* 31.1/2 (2007): 185–95. Print.

Vander Lei, Elizabeth, et al., eds. *Renovating Rhetoric in Christian Tradition.* Pittsburgh: U of Pittsburgh P, 2014. Print.

Webber, Robert. *The Younger Evangelicals: Facing the Challenges of the New World.* Grand Rapids: Baker, 2002. Print.

Wenger, Etienne. *Communities of Practice: Learning, Meaning, and Identity.* New York: Cambridge UP, 1998. Print.

West, Cornel. *The American Evasion of Philosophy: A Genealogy of Pragmatism.* Madison: U of Wisconsin P, 1989. Print.

———. "Prophetic Religion and the Future of Capitalist Civilization." Mendieta and VanAntwerpen. 92–100. Print.

Williams, Bronwyn T. "The Book and the Truth: Faith, Rhetoric, and Cross-Cultural Communication." Vander Lei and kyburz 105–20. Print.

Williams, Mark Alan. "Transformations: Locating Agency and Difference in Student Accounts of Religious Experience." *College English* 77.4 (2015): 338–63. Print.

Wilson, William A. *The Marrow of Human Experience: Essays on Folklore.* Logan: Utah State UP, 2006. Print.

Wolfe, Alan. *The Transformation of American Religion: How We Actually Live Our Faith.* New York: Free P, 2003. Print.

———. "Whose Christianity? Whose Democracy?" Heclo 185–208. Print.

Zulick, Margaret D. "Prophecy and Providence: The Anxiety over Prophetic Authority." *Journal of Communication and Religion* 26 (2003): 195–207. Print.

Index

Night Wraps the Sky

Night Wraps the Sky

Writings by and about

Mayakovsky

Edited by Michael Almereyda

Farrar, Straus and Giroux

New York

Farrar, Straus and Giroux
18 West 18th Street, New York 10011

Distributed in Canada by Douglas & McIntyre Ltd.
Printed in the United States of America
First edition, 2008

Owing to limitations of space, all acknowledgments for permission to reprint previously published and unpublished material can be found on pages 271–72.

Library of Congress Cataloging-in-Publication Data
Night wraps the sky : writings by and about Mayakovsky / edited by Michael Almereyda. — 1st ed.
p. cm.
ISBN-13: 978-0-374-28135-9 (hardcover : alk. paper)
ISBN-10: 0-374-28135-1 (hardcover : alk. paper)
1. Mayakovsky, Vladimir, 1893–1930. 2. Mayakovsky, Vladimir, 1893–1930—Translations into English. 3. Poets, Russian—20th century—Biography. I. Almereyda, Michael. II. Mayakovsky, Vladimir, 1893–1930. Selections. English. 2008.

PG3476.M312N54 2008
891.71'42—dc22

2007046662

Designed by Jonathan D. Lippincott

www.fsgbooks.com

10 9 8 7 6 5 4 3 2 1

For Susan Kismaric

Contents

3. SOUL ON A PLATTER (1913–16)

4. AN EXTRAORDINARY ADVENTURE (1917–26)

5. NIGHT WRAPS THE SKY (1927–30)

List of Illustrations

Editor's Note

All poems are by Vladimir Mayakovsky, with two exceptions (by Andrei Voznesensky and Frank O'Hara) near the end of the book. Assembled poems, essays, excerpts, and commentaries are followed by their original publication dates. Passages from Mayakovsky's autobiography, *I Myself*, are scattered throughout. The remaining material—by Rachel Cohen, Val Vinokur, Christopher Edgar, and myself—was written for this volume.

M.A.

Introduction

by Michael Almereyda

*Mayakovsky was better known as a person, as an action, as an event.**

Even at this distance—more than seventy-five years after his death and nearly twenty years after the collapse of the government he fervently promoted—it remains difficult to account for the phenomenal nature, the sheer outlandishness, of Vladimir Mayakovsky. As unofficial poet laureate of the Russian Revolution ("my revolution," he called it) Mayakovsky had unrivaled authority and glamour, taking on multiple responsibilities and roles—orator, playwright, magazine editor, stage and film actor, poster maker, jingle writer—with a singular mix of self-mockery and martyrdom.

Photographs of the poet—particularly the glowering, shaved-head portraits taken by Aleksandr Rodchenko in 1924, when Mayakovsky was thirty-one—display a kind of proto-punk ferocity, a still-burning aura of tough-guy tenderness, soulful defiance. The poems are virtually inseparable from this persona, as Mayakovsky

*All quotes in italics are from Viktor Shklovsky, *Mayakovsky and His Circle*, 1940; English edition translated and edited by Lily Feiler (New York: Dodd, Mead and Company, 1972).

made theatrical appearances in his verse and made a spectacle of his personal life. "He felt the need," his friend Viktor Shklovsky wrote, "to transform life." And so it followed that for Mayakovsky, poetry itself was transformative. He channeled experiences directly into his work while being convinced that the resulting poems could pace and project the ideals of a new social order.

He was calm, massive, and he stood with his feet slightly apart, in good quality shoes that had metal reinforcements and tips.

It may be bewildering, now, to imagine a poet expecting his words to translate into an active force for change, but this conviction was at the center of Mayakovsky's life and work, and it was shared by a generation of artists coming of age in the revolution's early, ecstatic wake. (Auden's famous circumspect assertion that "poetry makes nothing happen" would have been greeted by Mayakovsky with a howl of derision. Rodchenko and his typographical counterpart, El Lizzitsky, would have whipped up terrific corroborating posters.)

Mayakovsky was born in Bagdadi, Georgia, southern Russia, on July 7, 1893. His father, a forest ranger, died from blood poisoning when Vladimir was twelve, and the remaining family—Mayakovsky's mother and two older sisters—moved to Moscow, where Vladimir went to high school. He had an early start in anti-czarist sentiment: incited by a pamphlet brought home by his sister, he participated in a pro-Bolshevik demonstration the year before his father's death, became an active Party member at age fourteen, and was arrested twice before being jailed for aiding the escape of a political prisoner from Novinsky Prison. He was locked up for seven months, much of the sentence served in solitary confinement. His first arrest, the previous year, had followed from his involvement with an underground printing press—solidifying the link in Mayakovsky's mind, you might guess, between printed matter and high-stakes consequences, between language and action. In jail, at any rate, he began to write poems.

Once released, Mayakovsky enrolled in art school in Moscow, nurturing a strong if conventional skill as a draftsman, but his gift with words took precedence when his older friend, fellow student and provocateur David Burliuk, heard Mayakovsky recite a poem during an evening stroll. Burliuk declared Mayakovsky a genius. This opinion, which Mayakovsky promptly adopted, carried the poet through a quick apprenticeship and led to the formation, with Burliuk and other young accomplices, of a Russian division of Futurism, a willfully scandalous bohemian/literary project. Like their Italian predecessors, Russian Futurists were enraptured by city life, by machine-age energy and speed, and they matched a hunger for new forms with a well-publicized contempt for artistic tradition, for contrived sentiment, for bourgeois complacency and decorum. In the words of Bruce Chatwin, the Futurists "saw themselves as a wrecking party which would unhinge the future from the past."* Despite or, as likely, because of the movement's anarchic clowning, its embrace of the inexplicable and the absurd, Mayakovsky came to absorb and enact a central Futurist ambition: to bring art closer to life.

For a long time, Mayakovsky had been buffeted and tossed around. He knew how to use his elbows.

Futurism's self-promotional spirit was manifested in Mayakovsky's glaring yellow-orange blouse, worn proudly during a traveling cabaret, a virtual two-year reading tour that began in St. Petersburg in

*"George Costakis: The Story of an Art Collector in the Soviet Union," in Bruce Chatwin, *What Am I Doing Here* (New York: Viking Penguin, 1989).

1913 and swept through broad patches of Russia. Accompanied by Burliuk and a handful of fellow Futurists, Mayakovsky became a supremely commanding performer, having conjured within himself a remarkable arsenal of poems, and having perfected a confident style for reciting them in, a booming voice, at once laconic and fearsome:

> He stands upright, hands in his pockets . . . His cap pushed to the back of his head, cigarette moving in his mouth. He smokes nonstop. He sways on his hips, examining the public with cold flashing eyes.
>
> "Quiet, my kittens." He keeps people under control.*

The 1912 Futurist manifesto, "A Slap in the Face of Public Taste," may now seem tamer than its title suggests, but the slap of Mayakovsky's early poems can still carry a sting. They clash irony and sincerity, lyricism and violence, and they are uniquely pitched in a mode that James Schuyler later described as "the intimate yell." Notable among these early outbursts are two sensationally sustained longer pieces: an eighteen-page verse play written when the poet was twenty, *Vladimir Mayakovsky: A Tragedy* (goofily derived from *Hamlet*), and then, two years later, the breathtaking *A Cloud in Pants*,† an unclassifiable, delirious declaration of anguish, an apocalyptic love song. In both works the central protagonist shares the poet's name and is essentially the same towering, raw-nerved character who, in the course of an eventful career, converses equably

*Sergei Spassky, in *Mayakovsky and His Fellow Travelers* (Leningrad, 1940), in Wiktor Woroszylski, *The Life of Mayakovsky*, trans. Boleslaw Taborski (New York: Orion Press, 1970).

†Mayakovsky's most famous poem, *Oblako v Shtanakh*, is best known in English as *A Cloud in Trousers*; Matvei Yankelevich's tough-minded translation recognizes that the Russian title does not feature an internal rhyme and *shtanakh* signifies clothing of an untailored everydayness, making *pants* more fitting than *trousers*. All the same, when cited by earlier writers throughout this volume, the poem wears the more traditional title.

with the Eiffel Tower, Pushkin, the sun, the Brooklyn Bridge, and (in what became Mayakovsky's suicide note) "the ages, history, all creation."

The Mayakovsky persona was intact from the start, a voice at once seductive and hectoring, casual and elevated—a versatile voice employing the language of the streets, encompassing the immediacy and messiness of an engaged life. Mayakovsky was working outward from a love of words and an implicit political commitment that evolved alongside current events. By 1914 his anarchic/Futurist fury converged with a heightened recognition of the horrors of the First World War. And when at last the Bolshevik Revolution broke out, in 1917, the shift from smart-ass cultural iconoclasm to a seething political conscience to a revolutionary demand for the overthrow of the entire social order—this evolution came to seem inevitable, requiring merely a few brave forward steps. Mayakovsky took these steps, redefining Futurism to accommodate the emerging Soviet state, what Theodore Dreiser, among many contemporaries, regarded as "the most tremendous government experiment ever conducted."* While the experiment remained open, Mayakovsky addressed and was welcomed by a vast proletarian audience. It was a time of wrenching change, wild chances, blinding hope.

The lady of the house, with her large face and beautiful eyes, hunching her slender shoulders, looked at Mayakovsky as if he were not quite tamed lightning.

Mayakovsky liked company and crowds, but by definition he was a poet, an individual spending a great deal of time alone with lan-

*Theodore Dreiser, *Dreiser Looks at Russia* (New York: Horace Liverright, 1928).

guage. He understood loneliness as an index of conscious existence, and he recognized poetry as a way to break through loneliness.

Central to this effort, and to Mayakovsky's enduring personal mythology, was the poet's off-kilter romance with Lili Brik, who remained married to Mayakovsky's publisher, patron, and friend, Osip Brik, for the entirety of their relationship. (Mayakovsky met the couple in 1915 and shared living quarters with them for most of his adult life.)

The Mayakovsky-Brik alliance can be considered emblematic of a generation's impulse to break with convention, but it would be hard to name another sustained literary ménage so brazenly lived out in public and confided in print. Lili Brik's efficacy as icon and muse can be traced through Mayakovsky's career, but it is most conspicuous in *About This* (1923), dedicated "for Her and Me" and first published alongside eight tumultuous photo collages by Rodchenko. Rodchenko's cover famously displays Lili's detached and staring sphinx-like head, and half the other illustrations show her looming over smaller figures and landscapes. What did this woman have to do with the forging of a new national consciousness, the future of socialism, the common good? The question is caught in the center of this poem, and indeed the center of Mayakovsky's life, like a kite whirling in a high wind.

About This was, among other things, a willed respite from the poet's ongoing effort to establish a coercive, public, "revolutionary" voice. He'd spent nearly three years (1919–22) illustrating and supplying slogans for thousands of propaganda posters for the Russian Telegraph Agency. Working with Rodchenko in 1923, he devised jingles and entire ad campaigns for state-manufactured goods. ("There have never been, nor are there now, better pacifiers. They are ready for sucking until you reach old age.") Following Lenin's death, in 1924, Mayakovsky produced his longest poem, *Vladimir Ilich Lenin*, a monumental funeral procession, a bronzed tract celebrating Lenin as myth and messiah. The poem, full of topical references and foreshortened political theory, was a nominal hit, read before huge congregations of workers. *Very Good!*, commemorating the revolution's tenth anniversary in 1927, nearly matches *Lenin* in length and stridency. Throughout these didactic epics, Mayakovsky reliably smuggled in an element of cartoon exaggeration, a measure of mock heroism rising through the solemnity, but the poet's radically personal lyricism was checked at the door. In his autobiography he described abandoning a novel during this period, admitting disgust with his own imagination, a preference for "names and facts." John Berger's assertion that poetry was a system of exchange for Mayakovsky, that the poet and his work depended on a circuit of immediate and measurable interactions, finds a sharp confirmation in a seldom-anthologized piece, "My Best Poem" (also 1927). In it, Mayakovsky portrays himself at a reading, responding to "questions / and barbed requests" when a newspaper editor rushes to the podium, interrupting the poet with a whispered announcement, which Mayakovsky translates to his audience with a thundering voice:

> "Comrades,
>   the workers and troops of Canton
> have occupied
>   Shanghai!"

Elated and humbled, Mayakovsky takes in the answering ovation, fifteen minutes long—"as if / they were mangling tin / in their palms." It's what he really craved: poetry as uproarious breaking news.

But hindsight grants a blood-soaked historical view of the Revolution's final costs, and Mayakovsky's bluntest propaganda now feels particularly hollow, unconvincing, and coarse. (Or rather, that's how it registers in the English translations I've come across. You will not find much outright agitprop in this book.)

Love was set as a distant goal, and the road leading to that goal was the same as the great goal itself.

Mayakovsky was always writing about the future. Resurrection and immortality were constant twin motifs. (Suicide was the other side of the coin.) In the last stretch of *About This*, the poet exhorts a scientist in the far future to restore him to life:

Your thirtieth century
    will abolish
        the trifles that tore our
            hearts.
Will return
    what we
        had not time
            to love properly
                of future nights
                    countless
                        stars.
Revive me,
    if for nothing else,
        because I,
                a poet,
                    cast off the heap of everyday
                trash,
                        to wait for you.

But as the consequences of the revolution became increasingly clear and dire, Mayakovsky found it impossible to wait for a diminishing future, and he chose to escape into a darkness always swimming near the surface of his poems. On the morning of April 14, 1930, at age thirty-six, he took his life with a self-administered bullet to the heart.

It was a death foretold in the poems, but its impact was convulsive. Few chronicles of Soviet history fail to mention Mayakovsky's suicide as a turning point, on the heels of Trotsky's banishment to Central Asia and Stalin's Five Year Plan (the forced collectivization of Soviet agriculture, resulting in famine and an estimated ten million deaths between 1928 and 1931). Even so, by 1935, Mayakovsky's posthumous reputation was in the shadows, and Lili Brik enlisted a new lover who had government connections to help engineer an improbable proclamation, issued by Stalin: "Mayakovsky was and remains the best and most talented poet of our Soviet Epoch." The opinion carried an ominous addendum: "Indifference to his memory and to his work is a crime."

And so Mayakovsky's second death, as Boris Pasternak defined it, went into effect. To this day, a good many citizens of the former empire, force-fed Mayakovsky in school, can count themselves guilty of this crime. Similarly, selections in this book tend to veer away from Mayakovsky's unalloyed agitprop. For all his originality and intransigence, and even as he grew increasingly embattled and embittered, facing repressive government policy and vicious personal attacks, Mayakovsky had become a Soviet mascot and shill. The final burden of his self-reproach was, clearly, staggering.

But he staggered valiantly, up to the last. In his only poem completed the year of his death—commonly titled in English, "At the Top of My Voice," but presented here in Ron Padgett's impudent translation as "Screaming My Head Off"—the poet again addressed readers of the future, ideally workers redeemed at last by the triumph of communism, readers for whom a crazed Mayakovsky could reassert his unrepentant individuality, his status as a tough case, a "blabbermouth," an untamable beast:

I've had every kind
    of bullshit
        up to here! . . .

For you,
    you who can afford
        to be healthy,
I've had to sing
    with the big blue tongue
        of death.
To you I must look
    like some flying
        prehistoric lizard.

Well, yes and no. For this reader, Mayakovsky remains extraordinarily human, and his best poetry has stayed fascinating and urgent; and in a way even Auden would approve, it continues to make things happen. The last stretch of this book reaches past the poet's death to give a sampling of his posthumous influence.

He played billiards with utter involvement and integrity, losing again and again, creating his own rules. He never paid, for instance, for the last game, and never asked others to. This was a rule he valued greatly.

As few English translations of Mayakovsky are currently in print, the chief aim here is to reintroduce the poet to English-speaking readers, stitching together a suitable patchwork of documents, photographs, posters, and other imagery, foregrounding new translations of seminal work. A good many primary sources are extracted from Wiktor Woroszylski's lovingly researched, definitive choral biography, *The Life of Mayakovsky*, first published in 1966 and long out of print. (Interested readers are urged to rummage and exhume a copy of this epic work.)

Russians have warned me, passionately, or with a serene note of pity, that Mayakovsky is untranslatable. This is irrefutably true, up to a point, as all great poets are untranslatable. The compounded problem here, as I understand it, radiates from Mayakovsky's irreverent virtuosity when employing rhyme schemes, and from his habit of dirtying poetic diction with slang, puns, and an unpredictable vernacular rawness, an assaultive energy in every taut or terraced line.

All the same, the translations offered here have managed to capture, to my non-Russian ear, more spark and grit and fire than most versions of Mayakovsky encountered elsewhere, and they purge the texts of a starched British idiom adhering to many earlier English incarnations. For this I owe deep thanks to three young Russian-born New York–based writers: Val Vinokur, Matvei Yankelevich, and Katya Apekina.

It's a great thing, a very difficult thing, to relate to the past not only through memories, and not only through love for one's own youth.

At the conclusion of the exit ramp in Moscow's V. V. Mayakovsky State Museum, there stands a jumbled collection of portrait busts and small statues—a Mayakovsky bestiary. There he is looking like Elvis, like Mussolini, like Beethoven, like Jean-Paul Belmondo. The touseled proletariat superhero coexisting with the scowling punk prophet; the worker coexisting with the movie star; the man of thought coexisting with the man of action; the national monument coexisting with the Cloud in Pants. This book has been assembled with the hope that multiple Mayakovskys can face themselves in one volume, mingling with a few close friends, and that the resulting conversation, in more or less plain English, can carry past the spiked fences of politics, nationalism, provincial history, space and time.

1. Overview

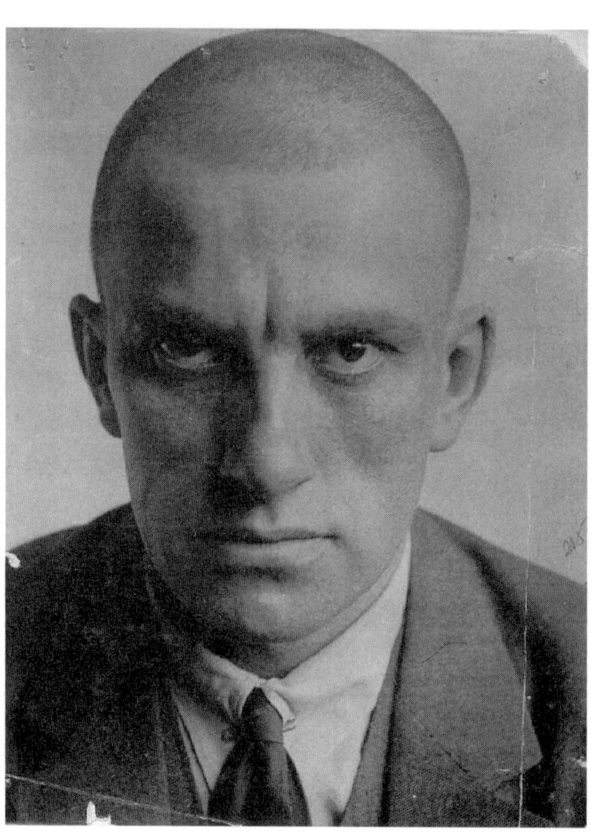

Screaming My Head Off (1930)

You people
of the future,
Running back
over the past,
Shining a light
back over your shoulder,
You'll probably
want to learn
about me,
Mayakovsky.
Your scholars will say
the veins stood
out on my neck
And I was pissed off!
Hey Perfesser,
get that bicycle
off your nose!
Here's my story:
I'm a health inspector
and water boy
Swimming in blood before
I was wet behind the ears.
My tears had fallen
on my poems

Vladimir Mayakovsky in April 1924. One of six portraits made by Aleksandr Rodchenko in the photographer's Moscow apartment.

that bloomed
Like flowers,
like Mary's flowers in
"Mary Mary Quite Contrary
how does your garden grow?"
Some poets dribble
and others serve towels
with their showers:
Six of one and a half dozen
of the other.
They keep rolling
along
And those mandolins again:
da-di da-di da-di.
So what if a statue of me
grows out from a big rose
in a square
Where whores with rough trade
and the clap
spit pa-tooey!
I've had every kind
of bullshit
up to here!
Give me one love song:
They're nice
and they get the money.
Anyway I thought
I was smart
Putting my foot
in my own mouth.
Get that!
Straight from the blabbermouth!

Great scream of poetry,
my books are going straight
toward you.
Together you will speak
back and forth.
I'll be there soon,
a mad Communist,
Not
like a Prince Charming
out of Esenin.
My poems
will fly over the ears
of our time,
The heads of state!
My poems
will come
Not
like the frail arrow
leaving Cupid's bow,
Not
as the penny comes
to the trembling coin collector,
Not
like the light
from a dead star.
They will come
hard and heavy as
a giant jaw
Cut out of rock,
The way an aqueduct
goes on forever.
You'll come across them

in the used book store,
Lines hard and straight
as an ionic column.
My poems do not powder
the ears
or nibble
The earlobes
of some pretty young girl.
Shit no! My poems
jump out
like mad gladiators.
"Kill!"
they cry.
Hand to hand
and head to head!
And the words fly out
like bullets
exploding
In your brain.
You see!
I'm giving it all away,
everything to you,
Workers of the world.
Any friend of yours
is a friend of mine,
too bad for the rest!
You can move
hard and fast
When you're starving
and blood is flying.
Books by Marx and Engels
were great

But we didn't have to read them
because we knew
where we stood.
Don't give me Hegel
and his dialectic!
It smashed its heads
together
And the sound
of the skulls cracking
was poetry!
Like fame and genius
going down
the same drain!
OK! Poems go
down drain
too!
Hundreds of trillions of people
down the drain
into heaven!
To hell with statues
and monuments.
We're famous enough.
Our monument is built
with moving blood:
socialism.
So go look them up
in your dictionary:
jack off
mutation
underground.
For you,
you who can afford

to be healthy,
I've had to sing
with the big blue tongue
of death.
To you I must look
like some flying
prehistoric lizard.
Well, Life, let's go,
go talking our
heads off
About the Five Year Plan.
I don't have
a red cent
And the furniture
never came,
but all I need
Is a clean shirt.
I couldn't care less
When I show up
in Tsikaka,
Radiant and
in the future,
I'll raise
all the books
of my poems
Over the heads
of the creeps!

Adaptation by Ron Padgett

From *"The Bedbug" and Selected Poetry* (1960)

PATRICIA BLAKE

Everybody is right about Mayakovsky. In the thirteen volumes of his complete works, about one-third consists of fulminations on patriotic and political themes. Another third is composed of serious "revolutionary" poems which are quite original in their genre and which still today can evoke some of the fervor of the early years of the Bolshevik Revolution. What remains are his satiric plays and his lyrics on the themes that were central to Mayakovsky's life: a man's longing for love and his suffering at the hands of the loveless; his passion for life and his desolation in a hostile and inhuman world; his yearning for the absolutes of human experience and his rage at his impotent self.

From the introduction to *"The Bedbug" and Selected Poetry*, ed. Patricia Blake (Bloomington: Indiana University Press, 1975). First published in 1960, Blake's collection stands as the finest compact assemblage of Mayakovsky in English.

On the Captain's Bridge (1940)

LEV KASSIL

The Moscow Polytechnical Museum is besieged. Queues surging in disorder. Barriers are quaking. Crowd-pressure brushes all posters off the walls. The administrator is in a stew . . . he pops in and out of his box-office pigeon-hole like a bald cuckoo. He repeatedly requests the militia to clear the vestibule. Glass quivers. The door-springs moan. Hubbub. And Mayakovsky himself can't get into his own reading. It turns out he is held in ransom by the besiegers. They demand a price from him: 50 entrance tickets . . . all right, 20! . . . Then they'll release him. But he's already given away dozens of free passes and tickets. He has none left . . . cleaned right out. So Mayakovsky begins to force his way through to the entrance. He begins to push, heave, ram like a hemmed-in icebreaker. Then suddenly he passes through the very press of the crowd with remarkable ease.

"He went through them like a hot iron through snow," remarked Shklovsky.

The hall is overcrowded. The public in the front rows is complaining. People are sitting in the gangways, on the stairways, on the edge of the stage, on each other's knees.

Not another ticket left. That's definite.

Mayakovsky fills the tiny dressing room to overflowing. It quivers as he paces to and fro. He is cramped. He has great wide shoulders. In the corner of his mouth—a fag-end. Chewed like a bit.

Up the stairs comes the noise of the siege:

MA-YA-KOV-SKY! . . .

PLEASE—LET-US-IN! . . .

Vladimir Vladimirovich says to me, almost in confusion: "Kassilchik, please . . . go to the administrator. I haven't got any more cheek. There's some Komsomols waiting, members of poetry study circles. I promised them. Get him to let five of them in . . . maybe . . . eight, well . . . say ten. Beat your chest, pull your hair, break your heart, and swear that these are the last. He'll believe you. He's believed it nine times already!"

By now the refractory audience is stamping impatiently. And Mayakovsky comes on. His appearance on the stage brings forth a burst of merry and welcoming clapping from the crater of the hall. Friends and companions in arms escort him on to the stage.

In one hand he holds a portfolio, in the other a glass of tea. The stage trembles under his steps. He shifts the table. Lays down his books in order. Poems. Paper. Watch. The spoon tinkles in the glass. He makes himself at home. Takes his bearings, and is eyed by the public. He throws back the lapels of his jacket, sticks his hands behind in his belt: taking on an almost sportive pose.

"Tonight," he begins, "I (he roars) . . . shall . . . (and then announces the programme of the evening) . . . after the lecture there will be an interval for me to rest and for the public to express its delight."

"But when will you read your poems?" mincingly some girl asks.

"Aha, you want the most interesting stuff to start right away?" Mayakovsky replied in a similar mincing tone, but with a bass voice.

The first peal of subdued laughter rolled through the hall. But the audience stores up its still hidden pleasure. And Mayakovsky rumbles through his lecture. Though really it isn't a lecture. It's a brilliant discussion, a most convincing story, a stormy monologue, a fiery speech. Full of the most interesting information, facts, raging demands, happiness, indignation, daring assertions, curiosities, aphorisms, parodies, epigrams, keen thoughts, provoking jokes, striking examples, blazing attacks and acute formulas. Murderous deadly-aimed definitions and lashing jokes fall onto the heads and shoulders of the knights of philistine art; the stern indignation of the poet crashes upon them. Mayakovsky speaks. Stenographers write: "Laughter and applause . . . general laughter . . . stormy applause."

Notes fly down to the stage from all corners of the hall. Offended ones shout. Others hiss them. The offended ones are insulted. "Commotion in the hall," the stenographers record.

"Don't get frisky, comrades," replies Mayakovsky. He doesn't raise his voice a bit. But the thunder of his bass easily covers the noise of the whole meeting. "Don't get frisky . . . once I've begun speaking, it means I shall end speaking. There isn't a man yet born who could out-shout me. You'll sit here like the damned and listen . . . Hey, you there, in the third row, don't wave your gold tooth so threateningly. Sit down. And you put away that newspaper at once or leave the hall. Here you've got to listen to me, and not read. What? You're not interested? Here you are then, here's a tanner for your ticket. You may consider yourself at liberty. And you there—shut your door. What's the idea, flapping your jaw open like that. You're not a man, you're a cupboard."

Mayakovsky is warm. He takes off his jacket, and folds it accurately. Puts it on the table. Hitches up his trousers.

"I'm at work here. I'm hot. Have I the right to improve my conditions of work? Undoubtedly."

A certain shocked dame cries almost hysterically: "Mayakovsky! What are you pulling up your trousers like that for? It's disgusting to look at."

Mayakovsky asks politely, "And if they drop, they'll be pleasant for you to look at, eh?"

Lightning-like answers strike all those attempting to catch the poet.

"Your jokes don't reach my understanding," bristles up a non-understanding one.

"You—are a giraffe," exclaims Mayakovsky. "Only a giraffe can wet his feet on Monday and not catch a cold till Sunday."

His opponents wilt. Stenographers put down a grammalogue meaning general applause of whole meeting.

Suddenly a bold young man jumps up.

"Mayakovsky," he cries challengingly, "do you take us all to be idiots, then?"

"Now, now . . ." says Mayakovsky in surprise, "why all? So far I only see one standing before me."

Someone in horn-rimmed glasses and glittering tie mounts the stage and, without asking permission, declares heatedly and complainingly that "Mayakovsky is already a corpse and no poetry can be expected of him." The hall is indignant. The orator, unconfused, continues to slay Mayakovsky.

"That's strange," Mayakovsky said thoughtfully. "I'm the corpse, yet it's he that stinks."

That put the lid on that orator. When the laughter died away, in one of the corners of the hall someone else began to shout in dissatisfaction.

"If you're going to make so much noise," said Mayakovsky persuasively, "it'll be the worse for you: I'll let loose the last orator on to you."

A fat little fellow clambers on the stage, bumping people aside in the process. He charged Mayakovsky with gigantomania.

"I must remind Comrade Mayakovsky," he said heatedly, "remind him of an old adage, which was known even to Napoleon: from the sublime to the ridiculous is but one step . . ."

In that very second, lifting his leg elephant-like, Mayakovsky silently took one great stride covering the distance between himself and the now bewildered chatterer.

"From the sublime to the ridiculous just one step!" and the hall bursts with laughter.

The conversation then turned, as it always does, to the classics, to their critical assimilation.

Someone from the Rights shouts scathingly:

"Aha! Mayakovsky's been grabbed by the backside!"

"Well, and what are you crowing about?" replied Vladimir Vladimirovich. "Sure for us that's a backside. But, for you—it takes the place of your literary face."

A critic, "A," who all the time has been passing remarks, shouting from his seat and demanding the floor, suddenly gets it . . . when it turns out that he has "changed his mind, and in general wasn't prepared . . ."

Mayakovsky states triumphantly: "Owing to wet weather, fireworks postponed indefinitely."

Then he reads his poems. The whole hall, opponents and supporters, cools into an attentive, tense silence. With unrivalled mastery Mayakovsky recites. His famous voice rings out bold and sincere, filling every nook and cranny of the museum hall. Even the attendants, who have heard many, many things in that hall, listen spellbound. The militiaman and fireman on duty stand with mouths agape.

Mayakovsky recites: "Very Good."

The excited hall thunders madly. They clap, stamp, shout, cheer . . . die down, thunder again . . . then Mayakovsky reads on . . . again the hall is stock-still. When, suddenly, from the second row a certain fat and bearded individual gets up noisily and marches through the hall to the exit. His great beard lies on his fat chest like on a tray. Unperturbed by the hissing around him he makes his way out.

"What's that bearded personage making his exit for?" Mayakovsky asks threateningly. But the personage continues unceremoniously to carry his beard to the exit. And suddenly Mayakovsky says in absolute seriousness, and almost as if apologising: "The citizen has gone for a shave."

The hall splits with laughter. The bearded one, now quite dispirited and indignant, disappears through the door. Even the stenographers clap. And all around even the most stolid people are laughing to tears, almost in hysterics. . . .

Afterwards Mayakovsky replies to questions. With amazing ruthless and inexhaustible wit he replies to the stinging questions of his opponents, to the questions of the curious philistine, to the queries of the literary fan.

"Mayakovsky! How much do you get paid for this evening's meeting?" "And what's it to do with you? You won't get a penny out of it anyway . . . Next."—"What is your real name?" Mayakovsky, with a secretive air, bends towards the public: "Shall I tell?—Pushkin . . ." —"Could a second Mayakovsky appear, say in Mexico?" "Hm . . . why not . . . I may go there again, maybe marry . . . then a second Mayakovsky might appear."—"Your poems are too topical. Tomorrow they'll be dead. You'll soon be forgotten. Immortality won't be your lot." "Well, you come and see me in a thousand years' time. Then we'll see."—"Your last poem was too long." "Well, shorten it. You can stick your own name on the cut-out."—"Mayakovsky, you said that from time to time you must clean yourself free of adhering traditions and habits. If you must clean yourself, then you must be dirty." "And you don't wash yourself and think yourself clean, eh?" —"Mayakovsky, it's about time you chucked out those sitting behind your back." Mayakovsky quickly turned his back to the audience: "There, now I completely agree with the proposal," he laughed over his shoulder.—"What's this? Ah, a familiar handwriting. I was waiting for this. At last it comes: 'Your poems are not understood by the masses.' So you're here. I've been waiting a long time to pull your ears. I'm just about fed up with you. Here's another: 'My comrades and I read your poems and didn't understand anything.' You must choose more clever comrades."—"Mayakovsky, with what part of you do you think you're a poet of the revolution?" "In the place diametrically opposite to where that question was born."—"Mayakovsky, you consider yourself a proletarian poet-collectivist, and you're always writing I, I, I." "Well, what do you think. Nicholas the Second, was he a collectivist? He always wrote, We. We, Nicholas the Second . . ."

And then in a break between bursts of laughter, he again continues, seriously and untiringly, the fight for the political poetry of our day.

The evening has ended. The Polytechnical Museum has emptied. We are riding home. Vladimir Vladimirovich is tired. He is full of impressions and written questions. Pieces of paper stick out from all his pockets.

"Gets one tired," he said, "I'm knocked out. Trousers got nothing to hang on to! But it's interesting. I love it. Love to talk . . . and the public—no matter their ages, they all come: they respect me; they know, the devils! That evening-class student in the balcony . . . surprisingly true grasp! It's a pleasure. Fine lads . . .

"Didn't I get a good one over that fellow with the beard? Eh?"

From *Mayakovsky Himself* (Moscow, 1940); in Herbert Marshall, ed. and trans., *Mayakovsky* (New York: Hill and Wang, 1965). Lev Kassil (1905–70) became a successful writer of books for and about Soviet adolescents.

Mayakovsky: His Language and His Death (1975)

JOHN BERGER WITH ANYA BOSTOCK

> Jackals used to creep right up to the house. They moved in large packs and howled terribly. Their howling was most unpleasant and frightening. It was there that I first heard those wild piercing howls. The children could not sleep at night and I used to reassure them, "Don't be afraid, we have good dogs, they won't let them come near."

Thus Mayakovsky's mother described the forest in Georgia, Russia, where Vladimir and his sisters were brought up. The description is a reminder at the start that the world into which Mayakovsky was born was very different from our own.

When a man in good health commits suicide it is, finally, because there is no one who understands him. After his death the incomprehension often continues because the living insist on interpreting and using his story to suit their own purposes. In this way the ultimate protest against incomprehension goes unheard after all.

If we wish to understand the meaning of Mayakovsky's example—and it is an example central to any thinking about the relation between revolutionary politics and poetry—we have to work on that meaning. A meaning embodied both in his poetry and in the destiny of his life, and death.

Mayakovsky with his family in the Georgian town of Bagdadi (later renamed Mayakovsky), 1900

Let us begin simply. Outside Russia, Mayakovsky is known as a romantic political legend rather than as a poet. This is because his poetry has so far proved very hard to translate. This difficulty has encouraged readers to return to the old half-truth that great poetry is untranslatable. And so the story of Mayakovsky's life—his avant-garde Futurist youth, his commitment to the Revolution in 1917, his complete self-identification as poet with the Soviet state, his role during ten years as poetic orator and proselytizer, his apparently sudden despair and suicide at the age of 36—all this becomes abstract because the stuff of his poetry, which, in Mayakovsky's case, *was* the stuff of his life, is missing. Everything began for Mayakovsky with the language he used, and we need to appreciate this even if we cannot read Russian. Mayakovsky's story and tragedy concern the special historical relation which existed between him and the Russian language. To say this is not to depoliticize his example but to recognize its specificity.

Three factors about the Russian language.

1. During the nineteenth century the distinction between spoken and written Russian was far less marked than in any Western European country. Although the majority were illiterate, the written Russian language had not yet been expropriated and transformed to express the exclusive interests and tastes of the ruling class. But by the end of the century a differentiation between the language of the people and the new urban middle class was beginning to become apparent. Mayakovsky was opposed to this "emasculation of the language." Nevertheless it was still possible and even natural for a Russian poet to believe that he could be the inheritor of a living popular language. It was not mere personal arrogance which made Mayakovsky believe that he could speak with the voice of Russia, and when he compared himself with Pushkin it was not to bracket two isolated geniuses but two poets of a language which might still belong to an entire nation.

2. Because Russian is an inflected and highly accented language, it is especially rich in rhymes and especially rhythmical. This helps to explain why Russian poetry is so widely known by heart. Russian poetry when read out loud, and particularly Mayakovsky's, is nearer to rock than to Milton. Listen to Mayakovsky himself:

> Where this basic dull roar of a rhythm comes from is a mystery. In my case it's all kinds of repetitions in my mind of noises, rocking motions, or in fact of any phenomenon with which I can associate a sound. The sound of the sea, endlessly repeated, can provide my rhythm, or a servant who slams the door every morning, recurring and intertwining with itself, trailing through my consciousness; or even the rotation of the earth, which in my case, as in a shop full of visual aids, gives way to, and inextricably connects with the whistle of a high wind.*

These rhythmic and mnemonic qualities of Mayakovsky's Russian are not, however, at the expense of content. The rhythmic sounds combine whilst their sense separates with extraordinary precision. The regularity of the sound reassures whilst the sharp, unexpected sense shocks. Russian is also a language which lends itself easily through the addition of prefixes and suffixes, to the invention of new words whose meaning is nevertheless quite clear. All this offers opportunities to the poet as virtuoso: the poet as musician, or the poet as acrobat or juggler. A trapeze artist can bring tears to the eyes more directly than a tragedian.

3. After the Revolution, as a result of the extensive government literacy campaign, every Soviet writer was more or less aware that a vast new reading public was being created. Industrialization was to enlarge the proletariat and the new proletarians would be "virgin"

*V. V. Mayakovsky, *How Are Verses Made?* (London: Cape, 1970; New York: Grossman, 1970).

readers, in the sense that they had not previously been corrupted by purely commercial reading matter. It was possible to think, without unnecessary rhetoric, of the revolutionary class claiming and using the written word as a revolutionary right. Thus the advent of a literature proletariat might enrich and extend written language in the USSR instead of impoverishing it as had happened under capitalism in the West. For Mayakovsky after 1917 this was a fundamental article of faith. Consequently he could believe that the formal innovations of his poetry were a form of political action. When he worked inventing slogans for the government's propaganda agency, ROSTA, when he toured the Soviet Union giving unprecedented public poetry readings to large audiences of workers, he believed that by way of his words he would actually introduce new turns of phrase, and thus new concepts, into the workers' language. These public readings (although as the years went by he found them more and more exhausting) were probably among the few occasions when life really appeared to confirm the justice of his own self-appointed role. His words were understood by his audiences. Perhaps the underlying sense sometimes escaped them, but there in the context of his reading and their listening this did not seem to matter as it seemed to matter in the interminable arguments he was forced to have with editors and literary officials: there the audience, or a large part of it, seemed to sense that his originality belonged to the originality of the Revolution itself. Most Russians read poetry like a litany; Mayakovsky read like a sailor shouting through a megaphone to another ship in a heavy sea.

Thus the Russian language at that moment in history. If we call it a language *demanding poetry* it is not an exaggerated figure of speech, but an attempt to synthesize in a few words a precise historical situation. But what of the other term of the relation, Mayakovsky the poet? What kind of poet was he? He remains too original to be easily defined by comparison with other poets, but perhaps, however crudely, we can begin to define him as a poet by examining his own view of poetry, always remembering that such a definition is made without the pressures to which he was subject throughout his life: pressures in which subjective and historical elements were inseparable.

This is how, in his autobiographical notes, he describes becoming a poet:

> Today I wrote a poem. Or to be exact: fragments of one. Not good. Unprintable. "Night." Sretensky Boulevard. I read the poem to Burliuk. I added: written by a friend. David stopped and looked at me. "You wrote it yourself!" he exclaimed. "You're a genius!" I was happy at this marvellous and undeserved praise. And so I steeped myself in poetry. That evening, quite unexpectedly, I became a poet.

The tone is laconic. Nevertheless he is saying that he became a poet because he was called upon to become one. Obviously the potential of his genius already existed. And would probably have been released in any case. But his temperament insisted that the release should come *through a demand*.

Later, he continually refers to poetry as something which must meet "a social command." The poem is a direct response to that command. One of the things which his early, marvelously flamboyant Futurist poetry has in common with his later political poetry is its form of address. By which we mean the poet's stance towards the *you* being addressed. The *you* may be a woman, God, a party official, but the way of presenting the poet's life to the power being addressed remains similar. The *you* is not to be found in the life of the *I*. Poetry is the making of poetic sense of the poet's life for the use of another. One might say that this is more or less true of all poetry. But in Mayakovsky's case the notion that poetry is a kind of exchange *acting between* the poet's life and the demands of other lives is specially developed. In this idea is implanted the principle that the poetry will be justified or not by its reception. And here we touch upon one of the important conflicts in Mayakovsky's life as a poet. Its starting point is the existence of language as the primary fact; its finishing point is the judgment of others towards his use of that language in a set of particular circumstances. He took language upon himself as though it were his own body, but he depended upon others to decide whether or not that body had the right to exist.

One of Mayakovsky's favorite comparisons is between the production of poetry and industrial factory production. To explain this metaphor just in terms of a Futurist admiration for modern technology would be to miss the point. Poetry for Mayakovsky was a question of processing or transforming experience. He speaks of the poet's experience as the *raw material* for poetry, the finished product being the poem which will answer the social command.

> Only the presence of rigorously thought-out preliminary work gives me the time to finish anything, since my normal output of work in progress is eight to ten lines a day.
>
> A poet regards every meeting, every signpost, every event in whatever circumstances simply as material to be shaped into words.

What he means there by preliminary work is the inventing and storing of rhymes, images, lines which will later be useful. The "manufacture" of the poem, as he explains with unique frankness in *How Are Verses Made*?, goes through several stages. First there is the preliminary work: the casting into words of experience and the storing of these relatively short word-units.

> In about 1913, when I was returning from Saratov to Moscow, so as to prove my devotion to a certain female companion, I told her that I was "not a man, but a cloud in trousers." When I'd said it, I immediately thought it could be used in a poem . . . Two years later I needed "a cloud in trousers" for the title of a whole long poem.

Then comes the realization that there is "a social command" for a poem on a particular theme. The need behind the command must be fully understood by the poet. Finally comes the composition of the poem in accordance with the need. Some of what has been cast into words can now be used to its ideal maximum. But this requires trial and retrial. When it is at last right, it acquires explosive power.

Comrade tax inspector,
        on my honor,
A rhyme
        costs the poet
                a sou or two.
If you'll allow the metaphor,
                a rhyme is
                        a barrel.
A barrel of dynamite.
        The line is the fuse.
When the fuse burns up
        the barrel explodes.
And the city blows into the air:
        that's the stanza.
What is the price tariff
        for rhymes
Which aim straight
        and kill outright?

It could be that
    only five undiscovered rhymes
        are left
In all the world
    and those perhaps in Venezuela.
The trail leads me
    into cold and hot climates.
I plunge,
    entangled in advances and loans.
Citizen,
    make allowance for the cost of the fare!
Poetry—all of it!—
    is a voyage into the unknown.
Poetry
    is like mining for radium.
The output an ounce
    the labor a year.
For the sake of a single word
        you must process
Thousands of tons
    of verbal ore.
Compare the flash-to-ashes
        of such a word
With the slow combustion
    of the ones left in their natural state!
Such a word
    sets in motion
Thousands of years
    and the hearts of millions.*

*This is a literal translation by Berger and Bostock.

When the poem is written, it needs to be read. By readers themselves, but also by the poet out loud. At his public readings Mayakovsky was a man showing what the things he had made could do: he was like a driver or test pilot—except that his performance with the poems took place, not on the ground or in the air, but in the minds of his listeners.

We should not, however, be deceived, by Mayakovsky's desire to rationalize the making of verses, into believing that there was no mystery in the process for him. His poetic vision was passionate, and continually rocked by his own astonishment.

The universe sleeps
And its gigantic ear
Full of ticks
That are stars
Is now laid on its paw.

Yet he saw poetry as an act of exchange, an act of translation whose purpose was to make the poet's experience usable by others. He believed in an alchemy of language; in the act of writing the miraculous transformation occurred. When he wrote about Esenin's suicide in 1925 he was unable to give any convincing reason why Esenin should have gone on living—although he judged that this was what the social command required. It is early in the poem that he makes his real point: if only there had been ink in the hotel bedroom where Esenin cut his wrists and hanged himself, if only he had been able to *write*, he could have gone on living. To write was simultaneously to come into one's own and to join others.

In the same poem Mayakovsky speaks of the Russian people "in whom our language lives and breathes," and he castigates all timid, academic usage of this language. (Esenin, he says, would have told the conformist orators at his funeral to stuff their funeral orations up their arse.) He admits that it is a difficult time for writers. But what time hasn't been? he asks. And then he writes:

> Words are
> the commanders
> of mankind's forces.
> March!
> and behind us
> time
> explodes like a landmine.
> To the past
> we offer
> only the streaming tresses
> Of our hair
> tangled
> by the wind.*

To clarify what we are saying, it may be helpful to compare Mayakovsky with another writer. Yannis Ritsos, the contemporary Greek poet, is like Mayakovsky an essentially political poet: he is also a Communist. Yet despite their common political commitment, Ritsos is precisely the opposite kind of poet to Mayakovsky. It is not from the act of writing or processing words that Ritsos's poetry is born. His poetry appears as the *consequence* of a fundamental decision which in itself has nothing to do with poetry. Far from being the finished product of a complicated production process, Ritsos's poetry seems like a by-product. One has the impression that his poems exist for him *before* their accumulation of words: they are the precipitate of an attitude, a decision already taken. It is not by his poems that he proves his political solidarity, but the other way

*From "To Sergei Esenin" in Mayakovsky, *How Are Verses Made?*

around: on account of his political attitude, certain events offer their poetic face.

Saturday 11 a.m.

The women gather the clothes from
  the clothes line.
The landlady stands in the doorway
  of the yard.
One holds a suitcase.
The other has a black hat on.
The dead pay no rent.
They have disconnected Helen's
  telephone.
The doughnut man shouts on
  purpose: "Doughnuts,
  warm doughnuts." The young
  violinist at the window—
  "warm zero-round doughnuts,"
  he says.
He throws his violin down on the
  sidewalk.
The parrot looks over the baker's
  shoulder.
The landlady tinkles her keys.
The three women go in, shut the
  door.*

There can be no question of quoting Ritsos against Mayakovsky, or vice versa. They are different kinds of poets writing in different circumstances. Ritsos's choice, of which his poetry (given his poetic

*Yannis Ritsos, *Gestures*, trans. Nikos Stangos (London: Cape Goliard, 1971; New York: Grossman, 1970).

genius) is the by-product, is a choice of opposition and resistance. Mayakovsky considered that it was his political duty to celebrate and affirm. One form of poetry is public, the other clandestine. Contrary, however, to what one may expect, the former may be the more solitary.

To return now to Mayakovsky. Before the Revolution and during its first years, one can say that the Russian language was *demanding* poetry on a mass scale; it was seeking its own national poets. It is impossible to know whether Mayakovsky's genius was actually formed by this demand or only developed by it. But the coincidence between his genius and the state of the language at that moment is crucial to his life's work, and perhaps to his death. It was a coincidence which lasted only for a certain time.

From the period of NEP* onwards, the language of the Revolution began to change. At first the change must have been almost imperceptible—except to a poet-performer like Mayakovsky. Gradually words were ceasing to mean exactly what they said. (Lenin's will-to-truthfulness was exceptional and his death, in this respect as in others, now appears as a turning point.) Words began to hide as much as they signified. They became double-faced: one face referring to theory, the other to practice. For example the word *Soviet* became a designation of citizenship and a source of patriotic pride: only in theory did it still refer to a particular form of proletarian democracy. The "virgin" reading public became, to a large degree, a reading public that was deceived.

Mayakovsky was dead before the devaluation of the Russian language had extended very far, but already in the last years of his life, in works like *Very Good!*, "The Bedbug," *The Bath-house*—all of which were badly received—his vision became increasingly satirical.

*The New Economic Policy, decreed on March 21, 1921, required farmers to yield raw agricultural products to the government.

Words were loaded with a meaning that was no longer just or true. Listen to the Producer in the third act of *The Bath-house*:

> All right now, all the men on stage. Kneel down on one knee and hunch your shoulders, you've got to look enslaved, right? Hack away there with your imaginary picks at the imaginary coal. Gloomier there, gloomier, you're being oppressed by dark forces.
>
> You there, you're Capital. Stand over here, Comrade Capital. You're going to do us a little dance impersonating Class Rule . . .
>
> The women on stage now. You'll be Liberty, you've got the right manners for it. You can be Equality, doesn't matter who acts that does it? And you're Fraternity, dear, you're not likely to arouse any other feeling anyway. Ready? Go! Infect the imaginary masses with your imaginary enthusiasm! That's it! That's it! That's it!

Meanwhile, what was happening to Mayakovsky himself? A woman he was in love with had abandoned him. His work was being subjected to more and more severe criticism, on the grounds that its spirit was far from the working class. The doctors had told him that he had damaged his vocal cords irrevocably by straining his voice when reading. He had dissolved his own avant-garde group (LEF, renamed REF) and had joined the most official, "majority" association of writers, which had always been highly critical of him (RAPP): as a result, he was snubbed by them and treated as a renegade by his former friends. A retrospective exhibition of his life's work—poems, plays, posters, films—failed to make the impact he had hoped. He was thirty-six, next year he would be the same age as Pushkin when he met his death. Pushkin had incontestably been the founder of the language of modern Russian poetry. Yet what was happening to the language of revolutionary poetry which Mayakovsky had once believed in?

If a writer sees his life as raw material waiting to enter language, if he is continually involved in processing his own experience, if he sees poetry primarily as a form of exchange, there is a danger that, when he is deprived of an immediate audience, he will conclude that his life *has been used up*. He will see only its fragments strewn across the years—as if, after all, he had been torn to pieces by the jackals. "Don't be afraid, we have good dogs, they won't let them come near." The promise was broken. They came.

From John Berger, *The Sense of Sight* (New York: Pantheon Books, 1985).

2. Wake Up Comrade

(1893–1912)

From ***I, Myself*** (1922)

Mayakovsky's sole exercise in outright autobiography, I, Myself *was written in 1922. The entries are terse and impressionistic, alternating hectic recall with dry sarcasm. Mayakovsky grants his father's death little more than a single line. His first encounter with Lili and Osip Brik warrants a solitary notation (albeit a celebratory one). The prevailing sense is of a man in a rush giving a hurried look over his shoulder, occasionally laughing. The headlong style clouds a little when the narrative is resumed in 1928, filled out for inclusion in the first book of Mayakovsky's ten-volume* Collected Works. *Later entries (not all included here) became weighted with polemical self-justification, the embattled author writing with his back to the wall.*

1ST MEMORY

Concept of images. Unknown place. Winter. Father subscribed to the magazine *Homeland. Homeland* has a "humor" supplement. The funnies are discussed and eagerly waited for. Father walks around singing his constant "Allons enfants de la by four."* *Homeland* arrives. I open it (picture) and begin to shout: "How funny! A man and a woman are kissing." Laughter. Later, when the supplement actually arrives and there was truly something to laugh about, it turned out that before—they were only laughing at me. Thus our understanding of images and humor diverged.

*A pun mangling the opening words of the "Marseillaise."

2ND MEMORY

Concept of poetry. Summer. Crowds arrive. A tall, handsome student—B. P. Glushovsky. He draws. A leather-bound notebook. Glossy paper. On the paper is a tall pantsless person (or maybe the pants are just very tight) standing in front of a mirror. The person is named "Eugene Onegin." Boris was tall and the one in the picture was tall. It all became clear. I understood Boris to be this "Eugene Onegin." I held this opinion for about three years.

3RD MEMORY

Practical concept. Night. Mom and Dad's constant whispering in the other room. About a piano. I couldn't sleep all night. One phrase kept nagging at me. In the morning I burst in on my father: "Dad, what is an installment plan?" I thoroughly enjoyed the explanation.

BAD HABITS

Summer. An amazing number of guests. Birthdays have accumulated. Father brags about my memory. For each birthday I have to learn a poem. I remember the one I learned especially for Dad's birthday:

> There was once a time before a crowd of
> Congeneric hills . . .

"Congeneric" irritated me. Who this was, I didn't know, but in life he never bothered introducing himself to me. Later, I found out that this was "poetic" and began to quietly detest it.

ROOTS OF ROMANTICISM

The first house is clearly remembered. Two floors. The top one—ours. The bottom one—a winery. Once a year—carts of grapes. Pressed. I eat. They drink. All of this in the territory of the most ancient Georgian fortress near Bagdadi. Around the fortress a rectangular old wall. In the corners—stands for cannons. Inside the walls, turrets. Beyond the wall, trenches. Beyond the trenches, forests and jackals. Above the forests, hills. I grew older. Ran to the highest peak. The hills got lower toward the north. On the north side is a cliff. I daydreamed—this is Russia! Its pull on me was intense.

THE UNUSUAL

Around the age of seven. Father began to take me on horseback on his rounds through the forest. A pass. Night. Enshrouded in fog. Even my father is invisible. The path is extremely narrow. Father must have bumped a sweetbriar branch with his sleeve. The branch swung back at me, thorns lodged in my cheeks. Squealing slightly, I removed the thorns. The fog disappeared immediately along with the pain. Below us, as the fog cleared—a glowing sky. Electricity. The rivet factory of Count Nakashidze. After electricity, I lost all interest in nature. An unperfected thing.

LEARNING

Taught by Mother and various female cousins. Arithmetic seemed implausible. Have to count the apples and pears, given out to boys. Everyone always gave, and I always gave to everyone else without such calculations. There was more than enough fruit to go around in the Caucasus. I took great pleasure in learning how to read.

THE FIRST BOOK

Some *Agafia of the Aviary*. If more books like this had come my way—would have stopped reading entirely. Thankfully, the second one was *Don Quixote*. Now that's a book! I made a wooden sword and some armor and attacked everything in sight.

EXAM

Moved. From Bagdadi to Kutaisi. Entrance exam to the gymnasium. I passed. Was asked about the anchor (on my sleeve)—easy enough. But the priest asked—what is an "oko." I answered: three pounds (that's in Georgian). The kindly examiners explained that "oko" means eye in ancient Church Slavonic. I almost failed because of that. That's why I immediately began hating everything ancient, everything ecclesiastical and everything Slavic. It's possible that my Futurism, my Atheism, and my Internationalism originated from this.

SECONDARY SCHOOL

Preparatory, 1st and 2nd years. Top of the class. All A's. Reading Jules Verne. And in general everything Fantasy. Some bearded guy began to notice my artistic abilities. Gave me free lessons.

JAPANESE WAR

An increased number of magazines and newspapers at home. *The Russian Chronicle*, *The Russian Word*, *The Russian Wealth*, and so on. Read everything. Inexplicably wound up. Impressed by post-cards of cruisers. Enlarged them and copied them over. The word "proclamation" appears. Proclamations were hung by Georgians. Georgians were hung by Cossacks. The Georgians were my comrades. I began to despise the Cossacks.

ILLICITNESS

My sister moved back from Moscow. She was ecstatic. Secretly gave me leaflets. Enjoyed it: very risky. Can still remember. The first:

> Wake up comrade, wake up, brother
> Throw your rifle to the ground.

And also, something with the ending:

> The only other way—
> To the Germans with your son, your wife and your
> mother . . .

(About the Tsar.)

This was the revolution. This was poetry. Poetry and the revolution somehow united in my head.

1905

Other things to do than study. Got F's. Graduated to the fourth year only because my head got bashed in with a rock (got into a fight by the Rion)—on the makeup examinations they took pity on me. For me, the revolution started like this: My friend, the priest's cook, Isidor, jumped from joy, barefoot onto the stove—they'd killed General Alihanov. Georgia's "pacifier." Protests and mutinies began. I also went. Good. Absorb it chromatically—the anarchists in black, the Socialist-Revolutionaries in red, the Social Democrats in blue, the federalists in all the other colors.

SOCIALISM

Speeches, newspapers. Lots of unfamiliar phrases and words. Demand understanding from myself. Leaflets in the windows. "Burevestnik."* I got all of them. Get up at six in morning. Read insatiably. First: "Down with Social Democrats." Second: "Conversations on Economics." For my whole life I've been amazed at the Socialists' abilities to untangle facts, systematize the world. "What to Read?"—by Rubakin, I think. Reread all the recommended reading.

Don't understand a lot of it. Ask about it. They took me into a Marxist circle. Got there when they were in the middle of the Erfurt Programme. About the "lumpenproletariat." Began to consider myself a Social Democrat: Stole my dad's rifles and brought them to the committee.

Took a liking to LaSalle as a figure. It must have been because he didn't have a beard. Youthful. I confused him in my head with

*"The stormy petrel." From a Maxim Gorky poem heralding the coming revolution.

Mayakovsky in a school uniform, with his family, 1905, the year he declared himself a socialist

Demosthenes. Hung around Rion. Gave speeches, my mouth full of pebbles.

REACTION

I think everything began like this: In a panic during the demonstrations in Bauman's memory, I (having fallen) was hit on the head by an enormous drum. Scared, I thought I myself had split.

1906

Father died. Pricked his finger (sewing book bindings). Blood poisoning. Since then can't stand pins. Prosperity ended. After Father's funeral we had three rubles. Feverishly and instinctively sold all of our tables and chairs. Moved toward Moscow. Why? We didn't know anyone there.

MOSCOW

Not enough to eat. Pension—10 rubles a month. My two sisters and I are studying. Mom had to rent out the rooms. The rooms were shitty. The students that lived there were poor. Socialists. I remember—the first "Bolshevik" I met was Vasya Kandelaky.

THE PLEASANT

Sent for kerosene. 5 rubles. In the colonial shop they accidentally gave me 14 rubles and fifty kopeks; 10 rubles of pure profit. My conscience pricked at me. Circled the store twice. Who lost money on this, the owner or the worker? I quietly asked the clerk. The owner! Bought and ate four fruit buns. The rest I spent riding around on a boat in the Patriarchal Ponds. Haven't been able to stand the sight of fruit buns since.

WORK

The family has no money. Had to make crafts and draw. I especially remember the Easter Eggs. Round, they spin and creak like doors. Sold the eggs at a crafts shop on Neglinski Street. 10–15 kopeks each. Since then I eternally detest Russian folk art and crafts.

THE FIRST HALF POEM

The third high school published an illegal little journal, *The Surge*. Hurt; others are writing, but I can't?! Began scribbling. The result was totally revolutionary, and equally terrible. Similar to Kirrilov's current work. Don't remember a single line. Wrote a second one. Turned out very lyrical. Didn't consider such outpouring of the heart compatible with my "socialistic dignity," abandoned it completely.

THE ARREST

Caught in a raid in Gruzini. Our illegal printing press. Ate the notebook. A bound one with addresses. Presnenskaya station. Secret Police. Suschevskaya station. Investigator Voltanvosky (appar-

ently, considering himself so clever) forced me to take dictation: I was being accused of writing proclamations. I was blatantly misspelling everything. Wrote: "sosheal-dimokratik." They fell for it. They let me off with a reprimand. Read "Sanina," with some puzzlement. For some reason it was in all the stations. Apparently it's soul-saving.

Released. A year of party work. And again a brief imprisonment. The revolver was seized. Mahmudbekov, a friend of my father's and then an assistant to the director of the Crosses,* accidentally arrested during my ambush. Declared the revolver was his, and I was released.

SECOND ARREST

Our lodgers were digging a tunnel under the Taganka.† Freeing female convicts. Succeeded in setting up a breakout from the Novinsky Prison. They took me in. Didn't want to be in there. Tantrumed. Transferred from station to station—Bassmanya, Meshchanskaya, Myasnitskaya, etc.—and finally—Butyrki. Solitary confinement No. 103.

Translated by Katya Apekina. (As are all subsequent selections from I, Myself.*)*

*A prison in St. Petersburg.

†A Moscow prison.

Report of the Prison Governor (August 17, 1909)

Confidential. Vladimir Vladimirovich Mayakovsky, held under guard in the prison under my administration, by his behavior incites other prisoners to disobedience with regard to prison officers, insistently demands of guards free access to all cells, purporting to be the prisoners' leader; whenever he is let out of his cell to go to the lavatory or washroom, he stays out of his cell for half an hour, parading up and down the corridor. Mayakovsky does not pay attention to any of my requests concerning order . . . On August 16, when permitted to go to the lavatory at 7:00 PM, he began to walk up and down the corridor, going up to the other cells and demanding that the guard open them; when asked by the guard to go back to his cell, he refused. In order to be able to let others go to the lavatory one by one, the guard began to ask him categorically to go into his cell. Mayakovsky called the guard a lackey and began to shout in the corridor so that he could be heard by all prisoners, "Comrades, a lackey is driving your leader to his cell." In this way he incited all the prisoners, who in their turn became noisy. I arrived there with the officer on duty and restored order.

I wish to inform the Security Department of this incident and

МОСКОВСКОЕ ОХРАННОЕ ОТДѢЛЕНІЕ.

Фотографіи въ 1/7 натур. величины.
Ретушированіе не допускается.

МАЯКОВСКІЙ ВЛАДИМІР

ОПИСАНІЕ ПРИМѢТЪ.

Возрастъ по нар. виду 17–19 Годъ и мѣс. рожденія 7 Июля 1893 г.
Ростъ 1 метръ сант. Полнота Тѣлосложеніе Объемъ въ поясѣ
1) Волосы: Цвѣтъ Волнистость Густота Лысина
2) Борода и усы: Цвѣтъ Форма Густота Особ.
3) Лицо: Цвѣтъ Полнокровіе Выраженіе Особ.
4) Лобъ: Высота Накл. Морщины Форма головы
5) Брови: Цвѣтъ Форма Густота Расположеніе Особ.
6) Глазныя впад. (орбиты): Величина Глубина Особ.
7) Глаза: Цвѣтъ райка Классъ Особ. Разст. между глазъ
8) Носъ: Спинка Основаніе Выст. Длина Шир. Особ.
9) Ухо: Форма Оттопыренность Велич. Особ.
Ухо: 10) борд.: Нач. Верх. Низ. 12) Противо-коз: Накл. Проф. Вып.
11) мочка: Накл. Форма Приростаніе 13) Внутр. скл.: Вып. Велич.
14) Губы: Форма Высота Толщина Выступаніе Особ.
15) Подбородокъ: Длина Накл. Форма Полнота Особ.
16) Плечи: Ширина Накл. Шея Особен.
17) Руки: Величина Привычка держать Особен
18) Ступни ногъ: Длина (№ обуви) 10–11 Особенность формы ногъ
19) Осанка (выправка корпуса, Манера держаться):
20) Походка:
21) Особ. въ жестикуляціи, гримасы, мимика, и т. п.

3) Во весь ростъ, стоя, въ въ томъ самомъ головномъ уборѣ верхн. платьѣ и обуви, въ кото былъ задержанъ. Если носитъ очки, то одѣть.

Mayakovsky at age fourteen. Registration card in the files of the Okhrana (the Russian secret police), Moscow, 1908.

humbly beg for an order authorizing the transfer of Mayakovsky to another prison.

From Wiktor Woroszylski, *The Life of Mayakovsky* (New York: Orion Press, 1970).

From ***I, Myself***

11 MONTHS OF BUTYRKI*

The most important time for me. After three years of theory and its practical application—I threw myself into literature.

Read all the newest stuff. Symbolists—Bely, Balmont. Piqued by innovations in form. But it was foreign to me. Themes, images not from my own life. Tried to write as well, but about other things—impossible. It turned out maudlin and trite. Something like:

In gold and purple the forests were dressed,
The sun on the church tops played
I awaited: but days got lost in months,
Hundreds of languishing days.

Filled a whole notebook with this sort of thing. A thank-you to the guards—they took it away at my release. Otherwise I would have published it!

Having read all the contemporaries, I collapsed onto the classics. Byron, Shakespeare, Tolstoy. The last book—*Anna Karenina*. Didn't finish it. They called me at night and told me to gather my things. Still don't know what ended up happening to those Karenins.

I was released. Was supposed to (according to the secret police) do three years in Truchansk.† My father's friend, Mahmud-bekov, interceded for me in Karlov.

*The Moscow prison where Mayakovsky was incarcerated.

†In Siberia. A prime spot for banished revolutionaries.

While doing time, I was tried for the first offense—guilty, but I was a minor. Released under police surveillance and parental supervision.

THIS SO-CALLED DILEMMA

All worked up when released. Those whom I'd read are so-called greats. But it's not at all hard to write better than them. I already have the right attitude toward life. I just need experience in art. Where do I get it? I'm completely ignorant. I need to go through serious schooling. And I'd been expelled from high school, even from Stroganovsky. If I were to remain in the Party—I'd have to become an outlaw. As an outlaw, it seemed to me, I wouldn't be able to complete my studies. Perspective—spend my whole life writing leaflets, laying out thoughts from books that were correct, but not my own inventions. If one were to shake out of me everything I'd read, what would be left? Marxist method. But did this weapon not fall into a child's hands? It's easy to handle when equipped only with your own thoughts. But what do you do when confronted with an enemy? Since, after all, I can't actually write better than Bely. He knew how to get his jollies—"I sent a pineapple up into the sky," as I'm whining—"a hundred languishing days." The other Party members are lucky. They at least had university. (I held higher education—I didn't know what it was yet—in high regard back then!)

What contrast could I create to the old aesthetic that was burying me? Wouldn't the revolution demand serious schooling? I dropped by Medvedev's, a friend from the Party. Want to make Socialist art. Seriozha laughed for a long time: "You haven't got the guts."

I think that he underrated my guts.

I ended Party work. Sat down to my studies.

BEGINNING OF MASTERY

Thought—I can't write poetry. My attempts were pitiful. Began painting. Studied with Zhukovsky. Painted little silver tea sets with some ladies. After a year, figured out I was making handicrafts. Went to Kelin. Realist. A good draftsman. Best teacher. Firm. Adjusting.

Requirement—mastery, Holbein. Had no patience for prettiness.

Respected the work of poet Sasha Chornoy. Happy with the anti-aestheticism.

THE LAST SCHOOL

Got into the School of Painting, Sculpture and Architecture: the only place that accepted you without a certificate of good conduct. Worked well.

Surprised: imitators were encouraged and innovators were bullied. My revolutionary instinct put me behind the bullied ones.

DAVID BURLIUK

Burliuk appeared at the school. Had an arrogant air about him. Lorgnette. Frock coat. Walks around humming. I began picking on him. We almost came to blows.

Mayakovsky as art school student at the Stroganoff Institute, Moscow, 1910

IN THE SMOKING ROOM

Social event. Concert. Rachmaninov. *Isle of the Dead*. Ditched it because of the unbearably melodic boredom. A minute later so did Burliuk. We both had a good laugh about it. We left to go for a walk together.

MEMORABLE NIGHT

A conversation. From the Rachmaninov boredom, we went on to academic boredom, and then from academic boredom to all the other classic boredoms. David has the anger of a master that has surpassed his contemporaries, I have the pathos of a Socialist, knowing the inevitability of the collapse of old ways. Russian Futurism was born.

NEXT

I made a poem during that day. That is—fragments. Bad ones. Published nowhere. Night. Sretensky Boulevard. Read lines of it to Burliuk, adding that they were from a friend of mine. David stopped. Looked me over. Barked: "But you wrote this yourself. You are a genius." Applying such a grandiose and undeserved epithet to me made me giddy. I immersed myself fully in poetry. That evening, completely unexpectedly, I became a poet.

BURLIUK'S STRANGENESS

Already that morning. Burliuk, introducing me to someone, announced: "You don't know? My brilliant friend. The famous poet

Mayakovsky." I gave him a shove, but Burliuk was undeterred. He even growled at me, taking a step back: "Now write. Otherwise you're going to make me look bad."

THUS DAILY

Had to write. And I wrote my first one (my first professional, printable one)—"Red and White," as well as others.

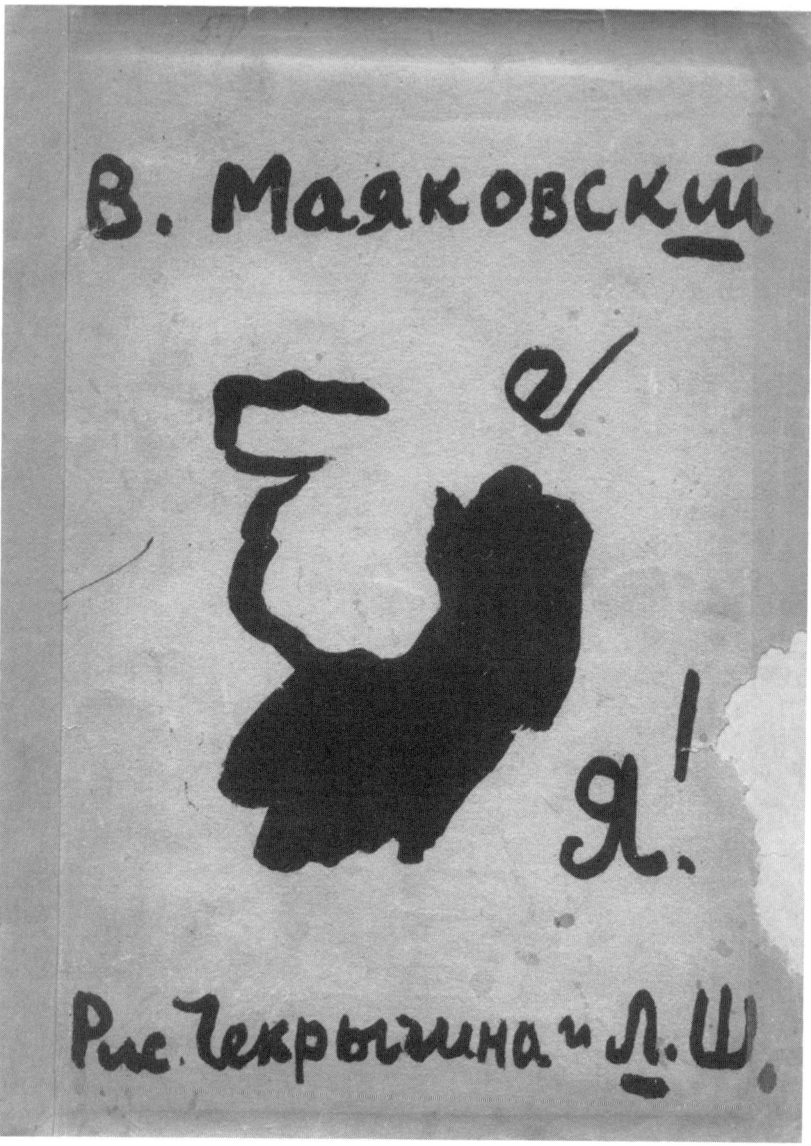

Front cover of Mayakovsky's first book of poems, *I*, 1913, designed and drawn by Mayakovsky

Port (1912)

Bedsheets of water under the belly
torn to waves by a white tooth.
The howl of a horn—as if pouring
love and lust through copper pipes.
The lifeboats cradled, suckling the
teats of their metal mothers.
In the deaf ears of the steamboats
the anchors' earrings glistened.

Translated by Katya Apekina

From ***I, Myself***

WONDERFUL BURLIUK

Always with great love I think about David. A wonderful friend. My true teacher. Burliuk made me into a poet. Read French and German writers to me. Buried me in books. Walked around talking endlessly. Never let me out of his sight. Gave me a daily allowance of fifty kopeks so I could write without going hungry.

On Christmas he took me to his house in Novaya Mayachka.

A SLAP IN THE FACE

Came back from Mayachka. If with unfocused views, then with a sharpened temperament. Khlebnikov's* in Moscow. His quiet brilliance had been completely eclipsed by roaring David. And whirling here was the futuristic Jesuit Kruchenykh.†

After a few nights of lyricism we birthed a joint Manifesto. David put it together, copied it, titled it, and published it—"A Slap in the Face of Public Taste."

*Velimir (Viktor) Khlebnikov (1885–1922). One of Futurism's most radical experimenters, fusing Slavic folklore, numerology, and a visionary imagination into a "transrational" form called *zaum*. ("Language," he wrote, "is like a face with a hat pulled low on its eyes.") After serving in the Red Army, Khlebnikov contracted typhoid and died in the wake of the famine of 1921. Mayakovsky eulogized him as "a most magnificent and honest knight in our poetical struggles."

†Aleksei Kruchenykh (1886–1968). Cofounder of *zaum*; conductor of ecstatic explorations of sound and non-sense, producing daring punctuation-free linguistic/typographical experiments. Cited in Mayakovsky's 1916 "Lilichka!" (page 115.)

From **"A Slap in the Face of Public Taste"** (1912)

D. BURLIUK, ALEKSEI KRUCHENYKH,
V. MAYAKOVSKY, VIKTOR KHLEBNIKOV

To the Readers of our First New Unexpected.

We alone are the *face* of *our* time. Through us the horn of time blows through the art of the word.

The past is too tight. The Academy and Pushkin are less intelligible than hieroglyphics.

Throw Pushkin, Dostoyevsky, Tolstoy etc., etc. overboard from the Ship of Modernity.

. . .

From the heights of skyscrapers we gaze down at their insignificance!

We order that poets' rights be preserved!

1. **To enlarge the *scope* of the poet's vocabulary with arbitrary and derivative words (word-novelty).**
2. **To feel an insurmountable hatred for the language existing before their time.**
3. **To push with horror off their proud brow the Wreath of cheap fame you have made from bathhouse switches.**
4. **To stand on the rock of the word "we" amidst the sea of boos and outrage.**

And if *for the time being* the filthy slogans of your "Common sense" and "good taste" are still present in our lines, these same lines *for the first time* already glimmer with the Summer Lightning

of the New Coming Beauty of the Self-sufficient (self-centered) Word.

Moscow, December, 1912

Translated by Anna Lawton and Herbert Eagle

3. Soul on a Platter

(1913–16)

Mayakovsky the Futurist, 1914

From ***I, Myself***

THINGS GET GOING

Exhibits of "Jack of Diamonds." Disputes. Impassioned speeches, mine and David's. Newspapers began to fill up with Futurism. The tone wasn't all too polite. For example, they simply called me a "Son of a Bitch."

THE YELLOW BLOUSE

I never had any suits. Had two blouses—hideous things. There's a tried-and-true method to sprucing up any outfit—a tie. No money. Took a yellow ribbon from my sister. Tied it around myself. A huge to-do. Therefore, the most noticeable and beautiful thing about a person is . . . a tie. Apparently, the bigger the tie, the bigger the to-do. And, as the size of a tie has its limitations, I went about things with some cunning—I made a shirt out of ties, and a tie out of shirts.

The impression it made was irresistible.

NATURALLY

The board was getting indignant. Count Lvov, the director of the Institute. Suggested we stop the criticism and agitation. Refused.

Council of "artists" expelled us from the school.

A FUN YEAR

Traveled around Russia. Parties. Lectures. The authorities were wary. In Nikolaev, they suggested we stay off the topic of the authorities, and Pushkin. The lectures often ended abruptly in mid-sentence, broken up by the police. Vasia Kamensky* joined the gang. A real old Futurist.

For me these years were about—formal work, mastery of the word.

The publishers wanted nothing to do with us. Their capitalistic noses smelled our volatility. No one bought a single line.

Returning to Moscow—mostly I lived on the boulevards.

This time was concluded with the tragedy *Vladimir Mayakovsky.* Put on in Petersberg. Luna Park. People hissed holes in it.

*Vasily Kamensky (1884–1961). A former aviator, he performed in Futurist guise with the image of a crashed plane inked on his forehead. Developed a mode and theory of "ferroconcrete" poetry, visually arranged verse experiments sharing some affinity with the calligrams of Apollinaire. An excerpt from his 1940 *Life with Mayakovsky* appears on page 107.

SIx Futurists, 1913. Standing: Nikolai Burliuk, David Burliuk, Mayakovsky; seated: Viktor Khlebnikov, Mikhail Kuzmin, S. Dolinsky.

From ***Vladimir Mayakovsky: A Tragedy*** (1913)

CHARACTERS

VLADIMIR MAYAKOVSKY, a poet (twenty to twenty-five years old)

THE ENORMOUS WOMAN, his lady friend (fifteen to twenty feet tall; she does not speak)

OLD MAN WITH SCRAWNY BLACK CATS (several thousand years old)

MAN WITH ONE EYE AND ONE LEG

MAN WITH ONE EAR

MAN WITHOUT A HEAD

MAN WITH A LONG DRAWN-OUT FACE

MAN WITH TWO KISSES

CONVENTIONAL YOUNG MAN

WOMAN WITH A TINY TEAR

WOMAN WITH A TEAR

WOMAN WITH A GREAT BIG TEAR

NEWSBOYS, CHILD KISSES, ETC.

[OLD MAN WITH ONE SHORN CAT]

PROLOGUE

(spoken by **MAYAKOVSKY)**

Can you understand
why I,
quite calmly,
through a hailstorm of jeers,
carry my soul on a platter
to be dined on by future years?
On the unshaven cheek of the plazas,
trickling down like a useless tear,
I
may well be
the last poet there is.
Have you noticed,
dangling
above the pebbled paths,
the striped face of boredom—hanged?
And on lathery necks
of rushing rivers,
bridges wringing their iron hands?
The sky is weeping—
uncontrollably,
loudly;
a cloud,
its little mouth twisted, is looking wry,
like a woman expecting a baby,
to whom God has tossed an idiot blind in one eye.
With swollen fingers sprouting reddish hairs,
the sun has caressed you with a gadfly's persistence:
in your souls, a slave has been kissed to death.
I, undaunted,

have borne my hatred for sunlight through centuries,
my soul stretched taut as the nerves of a wire.
I
am king of lights!
Come to me,
you who ripped the silence,
you who howled
because the nooses of noon were too tight!
I will reveal to you,
with words
as simple as bellowing,
our new souls—
humming
like the arcs of streetlights.
I shall merely touch your heads with my fingers,
and you
will grow lips
for enormous kisses,
and tongues
native to all peoples.
Then I, my shabby soul hobbling,
shall go off to my throne
with the starry holes in the worn-out dome.
I'll lie down,
radiant,
clothed in laziness,
on a soft couch of genuine *dreck*;
and quietly,
kissing the knees of the crossties,
the wheel of a locomotive will embrace my neck.

Mayakovsky at the Neptune studios, Moscow, 1918

EPILOGUE

(spoken by* MAYAKOVSKY*)

**I wrote all this
about you—
poor drudges!
It's too bad I had no bosom: I'd have fed
all of you, like a sweet little old nanny.
But right now I'm a bit dried up—
and a little bit touched in the head.
On the other hand,
who'd
have given his thoughts such inhuman latitude?
Who, and where?
It was I
who stuck my finger into the sky:
I proved that He's
a thief!
Sometimes it seems to me
that I'm a Dutch rooster,
or else
a Pskovian king.
But at other times, what pleases me
more than anything
is my own name:
Vladimir Mayakovsky.**

(Curtain)

From *Mayakovsky—Plays*, trans. Guy Daniels (New York: Washington Square Press, 1968).

From *The Futurist Moment* (1986)

MARJORIE PERLOFF

Mayakovsky not only produced, directed, and starred in his play: he also insisted that the other roles—the Man with One Ear, the Man with One Eye, and so forth—be played by university students rather than by professional actors so that he could coach them and bring their puppet figures into close conjunction with his own role . . .

Vladimir Mayakovsky: A Tragedy was originally called *The Revolt of Objects*, and indeed the play presents us with a world in which subject and object, self and world is curiously obliterated . . . "The poet," says Viktor Shklovsky, "dissects himself on stage, holding himself between his fingers as a gambler holds his cards."

From Marjorie Perloff, *The Futurist Moment: Avant-Garde, Avant Guerre, and the Language of Rupture* (Chicago and London: University of Chicago Press, 1986).

From ***I, Myself***

BEGINNING OF '14

I feel the mastery. Can own a subject. Fully. Pose a question around the subject. A revolutionary one. Think over *Cloud in Pants*.

Fop's Jacket (1913)

I will sew myself black trousers
from the velvet of my voice.
A yellow jacket out of three lengths of sunset.
Down the Nevsky *monde*, down its polished latitudes,
I'll step along like Don Juan in profile.

Let the earth cry out, all sissy soft from slumber:
"You're off to rape green spring herself!"
As for the sun, I'll offer an obnoxious grin and say:
"See how the pavement rolls me along like a French *r*!"

And isn't it because the sky is blue,
and the earth is my lover girl in birthday clothes,
that I can give you poems, jolly ones, like be-bi-bo,
and sharp and needful ones, like toothbrushes!

Ladies, lovers of my prime cuts, and that
girl who's looking at me like I was her brother,
bury me in tossed smiles—
I'll sew your garlands into a fop's jacket.

Translated by Val Vinokur

A Few Words About Myself (1913)

I love to watch children dying.
You noticed the crashing surf of hazy laughter
behind boredom's long gray trunk?
But me—
my reading room is in the streets—
there, so often I've leafed through coffin lids.
Midnight
with its soaked fingers
groping me and the battered fence.
And droplets of rain on the cupola's bald spot
galloped with the crazy cathedral.
I see Christ running out of an icon,
the slush crying and kissing at his billowing shirt.
I scream at the bricks,
my frenzied words thrusting a dagger into
the sky's swollen pulp:
Sun!
My father!
You, at least, have some pity! Don't torture me so!
It is you who has spilled my blood, it runs toward the
horizon!
That is my soul
tufts of a shredded cloud
in the burnt-out sky
over the rusty cross of the bell tower.
Time!
At least you,

you limping icon painter,
scrawl the image of me
and lock it in the glass case
as a monster for the ages.
I am lonely, like the last eye
of a man going blind.

Translated by Katya Apekina

From a sequence of four poems with the general title I, making up Mayakovsky's first published "book"—a lithographed pamphlet with a print run of three hundred, paid for by the author, who personally delivered the work to booksellers.

Listen! (1914)

Listen!
Well, if stars are lit
doesn't it mean—there is someone who needs that?
doesn't it mean—there is someone who wants them there?
doesn't it mean—that someone
sees those specks of spit
as pearls?

And, struggling through
whirlwinds of afternoon dust
he bursts in on God,
worried he's late
whimpering and kissing at God's
sinewy hands.
He begs God
for a star.
He swears up and down,
that he just can't bear such starless torture.
Afterward,
he paces anxiously,
though outwardly he's calm.
He tells someone:
"Well, it's not so bad now?
Not so scary?
Yes?"

Listen!
Well, if stars
are lit
Doesn't it mean—there is someone who needs that?
Doesn't it mean—it's of utmost importance
that every evening
above the rooftops
there be at least one blazing star.

Translated by Katya Apekina

For You! (1915)

**You, wasting away from orgy to orgy,
owning a bathtub and heated toilet,
aren't you ashamed, scanning through St. Giorgy's
Awards* in the columns of newspapers?**

**Do you, talentless masses, thinking only
of stuffing your faces, ever consider that
maybe, just now, the legs of Petrov the Lieutenant
are being torn off by a bomb?**

**And what if he, delivered for slaughter,
in shreds, suddenly saw
your meat-greased lips
lasciviously humming Severyanin?†**

**To give a life for you,
lovers only of food and fucking—
I'd rather serve pineapple liquor
to whores at the bar.**

Translated by Katya Apekina

*A military decoration
†Igor Severyanin (1887–1941). Slick, pompadoured rival Ego-Futurist poet, former tour partner with Mayakovsky; left Russia after the revolution. Severyanin also gets kicked to the curb in *A Cloud in Pants*, p.79.

From *Safe Conduct* (1958)

BORIS PASTERNAK

He sat in a chair as on the saddle of a motorcycle, leant forward, cut and quickly swallowed his Wiener Schnitzel, played cards, turned his eyes all ways without turning his head, strolled majestically along the Kuznetsky, intoned hollowly in his nose like fragments of a liturgy particularly significant extracts from his own and other people's stuff, frowned, grew, rode and made public appearances, and in the depths behind all this, as behind the straightness of a skater at full speed, there glimmered always his one day preceding all other days, when this amazing initial take-off was made, straightening him so boldly and independently. Behind his manner of bearing himself, something like decision took one by surprise, decision when it is already put into action and its consequences can no longer be averted. His genius was such a decision, and a meeting with it had once so amazed him that it became his theme's prescription for all times.

Boris Pasternak, *Safe Conduct: An Autobiography and Other Writings*, trans. Robert Payne (New York: New Directions, 1958). One of the most gifted poets of his generation, Pasternak (1890–1960) met Mayakovsky in 1913. Their poems were first published together in *Nov* (*Virgin Soil*), November 20, 1914.

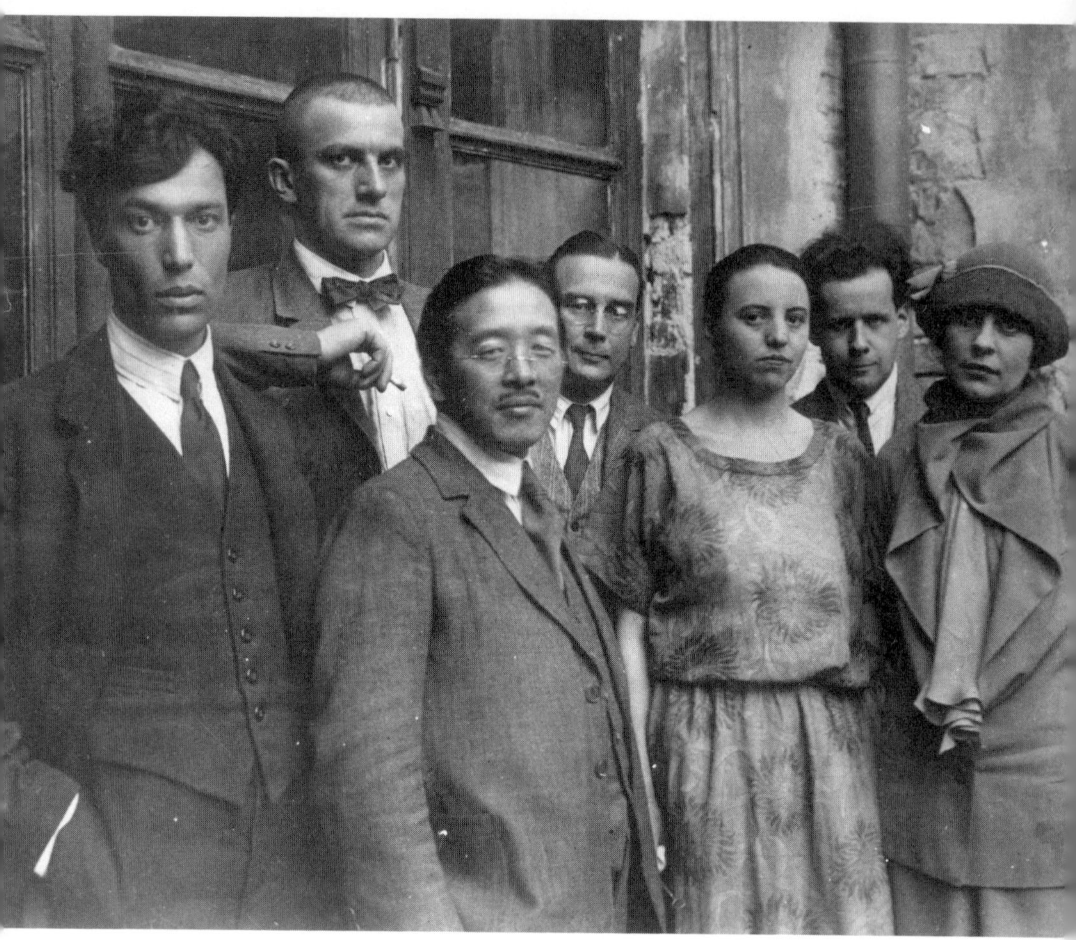

Boris Pasternak, Mayakovsky, T. Naito (a Japanese journalist), A. Voznesenskaya, O. Tretiakova, Sergei Eisenstein, and Lili Brik at a meeting of the Soviet Community of International Cultural Relations, Moscow, 1924

A Cloud in Pants (1915)

Tetraptych

PROLOGUE

I'll tease your thought
on the blood-soaked shred of a heart
as it daydreams on a brain beaten to softness
like a blown-out intern on a grease-stained sofa.
Cocky and caustic, I'll mock you till I've had enough.

Not a single strand of gray streaks the hair of my soul,
there's no old-fogy tenderness in me!
The might of my voice shakes up the world
as I walk, a beautiful
twenty-two-year-old.

Tender ones!
You jam love on violins.
A hick lays love out on a cymbal.
But you can't turn yourself inside out
like I do, to be all lips!

Come learn from me,
officious officialette of the league of angels,
dressed in your dining-room cambric.

And you who leaf through kisses listlessly
like a maid strumming the pages of a cookbook.

If you want
I'll go meat-mad
—and, like the sky, its hues changing—
if you want,
I'll be irreproachably tender,
not a man, but—a cloud in pants!

I don't believe in the Nice of flowers!
Rumpled as a hospital, men,
and women, tattered like proverbs,
sweet-talk themselves to glory in me again.

1.

You think I'm delirious with malaria?

It was
in Odessa, back then.

"I'll see you at four," said Maria.

Eight.
Nine.
Ten.

Even evening
has left the window
into night's horrific filth,
grim,
Decemberish.

The candlesticks cackle and snort
at my wasted back.

No one could recognize me now:
an enormous sinewy sack
moaning,
agonizing.
What could this clod want?
But the clod wants a lot!

Who gives
if he's bronzed
or if his heart's like a cold scrap of metal.
At night you want
to hide your clang in softness,
in femme.

And now,
immense,
I hunch in the window,
melting the pane with my forehead.
Will there be love or no?
What kind—
big or mini?
Where would such a body get it:
must be a little,
pacific lovey.
She jumps back from the cars' honking.
Loves the tiny bells of horse-drawn buggies.

On and on,
pressing into the rain

my face flush against its pockmarked face,
I wait,
sprayed by the thunder of urban waves.

Midnight, pacing with knife in hand,
caught up and
flayed him—
Get out!

The twelfth hour has fallen,
like the head off an executioner's block.

On the windowpane,
howling as one, gray droplets of rain
gargantuated a grimace,
as if chimeras howling
on the Parisian Cathedral of Notre Dame.

Damned woman!
What—isn't that enough?
Soon screaming will shred my mouth.

Listen:
quiet,
like a sick man from his bed,
a nerve jumps to.
And out—
first leisurely walking,
step by step,
then races,
getting worried,
exacting.

Now, joined by a new pair,
back and forth in a desperate soft shoe it paces.

The plaster collapses one floor below.

Nerves—
big ones,
little ones,
myriad!—
jumping mad,
and straightaway
their nerve-legs give out beneath them.

But night mires and mires around the room—
the eye, heavy-laden, can't pull itself out of the filth.

Suddenly the doors trembled
as if the hotel
had teeth to chatter with.

You walked in,
blatant, like "take it!"
torturing your gloves' suede.

"You know something—
I'm getting married."
Well then, get married.
I'll be ok.
See—how calm I am!
My pulse
a dead man's.

Remember?
You used to say:
"Jack London,
money,
love,
passion"—
and all I saw was
you—a Gioconda
that's got to be stolen!

And it was.

In love again, I'll go out gambling,
blasting fire on the bends of brows.
What of it!
Sometimes homeless hobos
live in a burnt-out house!

You're teasing?
"You've got fewer emeralds of madness
than a pauper kopeks in his pocket."
Remember this!
Pompeii perished
when Vesuvius was mocked!

Hey!
Ladies and Gents!
Amateur collectors
of blasphemies,
crimes,
carnage—
have you seen

what's most frightening of all—
my face
when I am
absolute calm.

And I sense—
I've grown out of
"I."
Somebody's stubbornly trying to break out of me.

Hi!
Who is it?
Mommy?
Mom!
Your son is wonderfully ill!
Mom!
His heart's on fire.
Tell my sisters, Lyuda and Olya—
he's done for.
Every word,
even a wisecrack,
that belches from his smoldering hole,
like a naked whore throws herself
out of a blazing bordello.

The crowd sniffs it out—
smells like a barbecue!
Rounded some up.
They glitter!
In helmets!
Boots aren't allowed!
Tell the firemen:

a burning heart is climbed in caresses.
I'll do it myself.
My teary eyes I'll pump out by the bucket.
Let me lean up against my ribs.
I'll leap out! Out! Out! Out!
Collapsed.
You can't leap out of a heart.

From the crack of lips
on a smoldering face
a charred kissy-kiss rose up to spring.

Mom!
I can't sing.
The choir loft in this heart's little church is ablaze!
From my skull,
like children out of a burning tenement,
come burnt little figures of words and numbers.
So fear
outstretched
the *Lusitania*'s flaming hands
to grab the sky by the collar.

The hundred-eyed blaze tears from the pier to reach
out to the people trembling
in apartment quiet.
The final screech—
you, at least,
moan out, into the centuries, that I am on fire!

2.

Glorify me!
Between me and the greats there's no comparison.
I put "nihil"
over all that's been done.

Never
do I want to read, and nothing.
Books?
What about them!

Before, I thought
books are made as follows:
a poet ambles,
loosens his lips nice and easy,
and straight off the inspired dope breaks out in song—
there you have it!
But, before the singing kicks in,
it turns out—
you've got to walk awhile, work up calluses from pacing,
while quietly, it flounders in the mire of the heart,
the stupid saltcod of the imagination.
While, fiddling rhymes, they boil down
some kind of stew out of loves and nightingales,
the languageless street makes awful faces—
it's got nothing to shout with or make conversation.

Our Babylonian towers,
we raise again, full of pride,
while god
our cities to pastures

razes,
mixing the word.

The street towed along torment in quiet.
The scream stood straight out of the gullet.
Fat yellow cabs and skinny rickshaws
bristled, lodging in its craw.
My chest's outtrampled by pedestrians.
Flatter than whooping cough.

With darkness the city locked up the road.

And when—
finally!—
shoving off the church threshold that stepped on its throat,
onto the square it spat up the crush,
it dawned on me:
in choruses of an archangelic chorale,
god, robbed blind, is coming to punish!

And the street squatted, screaming:
"Let's chow!"

The city gets a makeover from Krupps and Krupplets*
into a wrinkling of menacing brows,
while little corpses
decompose in the mouths of dead words,
only two live on, bloating—
"scum"

*The Krupp family. German steel magnates, producers of arms and munitions. —M.Y.

and another one,
seems like “borscht.”

Poets,
wet with crying and sobbing
tore away from the street, mussing their dos:
“With just these two
how will we sing
the lady
and love,
the tiny flower under the dews?”

And following the poets—
several thou of the street:
students,
prostitutes,
sales reps.

People!
Hold it!
You’re not the poor,
don’t you dare beg for handouts!

We, healthy giants,
with our yardstick stride,
must quit listening and rip them to shreds—
them,
sucker-stuck like a free accessory
to every queen-size bed!

Should we humbly ask them:
“Help me out!”

Beg them for an anthem,
or a public gab!
We're ourselves creators in the fiery hymn—
in the noise of factories and labs.

What's Faust got to do with me,
in a fury of fireworks
sliding with Mephistopheles over the heavenly parquet!
I know—
the nail in my boot's much more
terrible than the fantasies of Goethe.

I,
golden-mouthiest,
whose every word
gives the body birthdays
and births the soul anew,
say to you:
the tiniest dust-speck of the living
is worth more than anything I did or will do!

Listen up!
Pacing and moaning,
a present-day Zarathustra
preaches through screaming lips!
We've
got a face like a sheet that's slept on,
with lips heavy-hung like a chandelier,
we,
camp-laborers of a city of leprosy
where gold and dirt brought our sores to the top,
we are cleaner than Venetian azure
that's been washed by the suns and seas.

It ain't spit
that Homer and Ovid
have no one to match us,
people in pockmarks of soot.
I know—
the sun would grow dim if it
but saw our soul's golden spread.

Truer than prayer—sinew and muscle.
Is it our lot to beg for time's charity?
We
hold the reins of entire worlds—
each of us—
in our five-fingered extremities!

We were brought to the Golgothas of lecture halls
in Petrograd, Kiev, Odessa, and Moscow,
and there wasn't one
among you all
who wouldn't shout:
"Crucify him,
crucify him!"
But to me—
people,
even you that insult me,
you're closer and dearer to me than all else.

Did you see
how a dog licks the hand that beats it?!

Laughed at by the tribe of today
like a crude and
long-winded joke,

I
see the one that no one else can
walking over mountains of time.

Where the limited eye of man falls short,
in revolutions' wreath of thorns,
at the head of hungry hordes,
the year of '16 draws on.

Among you—I'm his precursor;
That's me—everywhere where pain is;
on every drop of the teary river
I crucified myself on a cross.
Now nothing can be forgiven.
I burned away souls in which kindness was nurtured.
That's tougher than taking
the Bastille a thousand times over!

And when,
announcing
his arrival with riots,
you come out to greet your savior—
I'll drag out
my soul for you,
stomp it flat,
so that it's giant!
and, blood-soaked, bestow it—a banner.

3.

Hey, what's this,
where'd it come from,
this thrust of dirty fist
into our fair fun!

It came in,
covered my head with despair—this
idea of mental institutions.

And—
as if diving into wide-open hatches
to escape choking fits
in the *Dreadnought* disaster—
Burliuk crawled, going mad
through his eye
torn apart to a howl.
Nearly bludgeoning his tear-soaked eyelids
crawled out,
stood,
walked on,
and with softness surprising for a fat man,
went and blurted:
"It's good!"

It's good—for the protection of the soul
from sidelong glances—to wrap it in a yellow shirt!
It's good,
when thrown into the gnash of the scaffold,
to belt out:
"Drink only Van Gutten's hot chocolate!"

This booming
Bengal-fireworks
second,
I wouldn't trade for a thing,
not a thing . . .

Through cigar smoke,
stretched like a shot glass,
the mug of a lush—Severyanin.

How dare you call yourself Poet,
and chirp like a grouse—so dull!
Today
with brass knuckles
you've got to
cut open the world in your skull.

You,
worried by one thought only:
"do I dance gracefully?"—
look how I'm enjoying
myself—
a cardsharp
and a pimp on the city square!

From you
who were drenched with falling in love,
from whom
into the centuries the tear flows,
I'll walk away,
into a wide-open eye
inserting the sun as my monocle.

Unbelievably gussied up,
around the world I'll strut
to burn and be liked,
and in front
on a chain, I'll walk Napoleon like a mutt.

All the world will lie down a woman for me,
thrashing her flesh about, but giving;
things come alive—
the lips of the thing
blabbering:
"gimme, gimme, gimme!"

Now
the clouds
and the other overcasts
tilted the sky into a fantastic tumult,
like white workers, angry with the sky,
declaring a general walkout.

Going wild, thunder clambered out of the clouds,
blew condescending its nostrils gigantic,
and for a split second the sky's face frowned
with the fierce grimace of an iron Bismarck.

And someone
stretched his arms out toward the café,
tangled in cloudy confusion—
ladylike,
as if to be tender,
and similar to the gun-carriage for a cannon.

You think so—
that's the sun
preciously patting the café on its cheek?
Not, it's General Galliffet* come
to shoot down the rioters in the street!

Take your hands out of your pockets, pedestrians,
take a rock, a knife, or a bomb,
and if one of you don't have no hands,
then use your head if you've got one!

Onward, my hungry ones,
little sweaty ones,
little defeated,
gone sour in a flea-infested muckiness!

Onward!
We'll paint Mondays and Tuesdays
with blood into holidays!
With your knives make the earth remember
who it tried to rub in the dirt!
The earth,
grown fat like a lover,
that's been loved by a Rothschild till it hurt.

So that the flags flap in the heat of gunfire
like at every respectable holiday—
you, lampposts, hoist higher
the bloodied carcasses of hawkers.

*The Marquis de Galliffet (1830–1909), a French general, aided in the suppression of the 1871 Paris Commune. —M.Y.

I cussed them out,
I pleaded
slashed,
crept after some guy
to sink my teeth in his sides and gnash.

In the sky, the sunset, Marseillaise red,
gave a shudder, growing cold as the dead.

It's already madness.

There'll be nothing left.

Night will come,
bite right through it,
eat the rest.

You see it—
the sky doing Judas
with its handful of betrayal-bespattered suns?

It's here.
Resting its ass
on the city; it feasts like a Hun.
This is a night our eyes can't shoulder,
as black as a double agent.

I scrunch, tossed like a rag into pub corners,
pour wine over both soul and tablecloth,
and find:
in a corner—my eyes popping—
the Madonna, her eyes gnawing into my heart.

What's the use of bestowing on pub crawlers,
this hack-painted glow!
You see that? Once more
they prefer Barabbas over
that spat-on Golgothnik.

Maybe I do it on purpose
so that in this hash of humanity
my face is newer than no one's.
I
may be
the most beautiful
of all your sons.

Give them,
grown over with mold in their happiness,
the swift death of time,
so that children should grow up,
boys—become fathers,
girls—become pregnant.

And let the cheek-turning gray of the magi
overgrow those who are newly born,
and they'll come—
and their children they'll baptize
with the names of my poems.

Singing the praises of England and machinery,
I may simply be
the thirteenth apostle
in the most ordinary of gospels.

And when my voice
lewdly bellows—
from one hour to the next,
round the clock,
Jesus Christ might get a whiff of
my soul's forget-me-nots.

4.

Maria! Maria! Maria!
Maria, let me in!
I can't stand it out on the streets!
Don't want to?
You're waiting
for my cheeks to cave into a ditch,
for that day when, tried by everyone,
tasteless,
I'll come to you,
and toothlessly lisp
that today I'm
"surprisingly honest."

Maria,
Look—
my shoulders have already begun to stoop.

In the streets
folks will punch holes in the fat of four-story tumors,
and stick out their beady eyes,
rubbed dry in a forty-years' drag,

to giggle back and forth rumors
that stuck in my teeth
—once again!—
is the crusty roll of yesterday's caresses.

The rain's sobbed up the sidewalks,
dripping wet, a con man in the tight squeeze of puddles
licks the cobblestoned corpse of the streets,
and on his gray lashes—
for sure!—
on lashes of frosty icicles
tears out of eyes—
for sure!—
from the downcast eyes of the drainpipes.

The rain's muzzle has sucked on every pedestrian,
while in carriages fat athlete shleps after fat athlete:
people popped open,
gorged through and through to the bone,
and bacon seeped through the cracks,
and the regurgitated mush of week-old burgers
with their sucked-out breading,
flowed off the carriages in a muddy river.

Maria!
How can I fit a quiet word into an overfed ear?
The bird
begs with a song,
sings,
hungry, ringing.
But I'm just a human, Maria,
plain,

spit up by the tubercular night into the grimy hand of the Presnya.*

Maria, you want one like me?
Maria, let me in!
With my fingers' frightening seizure, I'll choke the iron throat of your bell!

Maria!

The streets' fenced pastures have gone wild.
My neck shows the scab of stampeding fingers.

Open the door!

It hurts!

Look—my eyes are stuck
full of ladies' hatpins.

She let me in.

Little one!
Don't be afraid
just because I've got sweaty-bellied women
sitting on my oxen back like a wet mountain—
all my life I've had to drag around
millions of tremendous pure loves, as well as
little dirty lovelettes by the millions of millions.
Don't be afraid

*A working-class Moscow neighborhood. —M.Y.

that once more,
in betrayal's blahs,
I'll cloyingly cling to a thousand cute faces
who "love Mayakovsky!"—
it's no more than a dynasty
of princesses who've ascended a lunatic's heart.

Closer, Maria!

Whether in naked shamelessness,
or in quivers of dismay,
but give me the unfaded beauty of your lips:
me and my heart have never lived to see May,
and only the hundredth April exists
in what life I've managed to live.

Maria!
The poet sings sonnets to Tiana,*
while I—
made up of meat,
human in every shred—
but ask for your body
like the Christians plead:
"Give us this day
our daily bread."

Maria—give it to me!

Maria!
I'm afraid to forget your name,

*From a Severyanin poem. —M.Y.

like a poet's afraid to forget
some word or other
born in the torment of night
and equal to god in its greatness.

This body of yours
I will love and cherish,
like a soldier
whom war has severed,
unneeded,
alone,
will hang on to his only leg.

Maria—
don't you want me?
You don't want me!

Well!

So it is—again,
darkly and lowly
I'll take my heart,
with the drizzle of my tears,
to carry it,
like a dog
that into its kennel
carries
the paw a train's run over.

With the blood of my heart I cheer up the road,
sticking in flowers by the dust of my tunic.
A thousand times the sun will dance for Herod

around the earth—
the head of the Baptist.

And when it has danced out to the end
the number of my years—
the path to my father's house will spread
with a million bloody tears.

I'll come out
filthy (from nights spent in ditches),
stand side by side with him,
lean over
and whisper in his ear:

Listen to me, mister god!
Aren't you bored
of every day dabbing your eyes grown over-kind
with the clouds' fruit-concentrate gel?
Let's—you know what?—
shall we conjure a carousel
on the tree of the knowledge of good and evil!

Omnipresent one, you'll be in every cupboard,
and we'll set out such wines on the table
so even the gruff apostle Peter
will want to kick up a ki-ka-pu.
Little Eves again we'll settle in paradise:
command it—
tonight
the most gorgeous girls from every boulevard
I'll dredge up for you.

Would you like that?

You wouldn't?

Shake your head, unkempt one?
Wrinkling your gray-streaked brow?
You're thinking—
this winged one,
the one standing behind you,
knows what love really is?
I'm also an angel, I was one—
peeking into their eyes like a sugary lamb,
but no more will I give to old mares
vases crafted from the torments of Sevres.
Almighty one, you dreamed up a pair of hands,
made it
so each one has a head—
but why didn't you think
to make it so one could kiss and kiss and kiss
without being tormented?!

I thought you were an all-powerful godful,
but you're only a minuscule godlette, a dropout.
Watch me: I bend down,
and get the knife of a cobbler
from out of the top of my boot.

Winged lowlifes!
Crowd in your heaven!
Ruffle your feathers quaking in horror!
You, stinking of incense, I'll cut you open
from here to Alaska.

Let me in!

You can't stop me.
I lie,
or maybe I'm legit,
but I can't get any calmer.
Look now—
the stars once again decapitated,
and the sky is all bloodied with slaughter!

Hey, you!
Sky above!
Take your hat off!
Here I come!

I can't hear . . .

The universe sleeps,
laying upon its paw,
tick-laden with stars, its enormous ear.

Translated by Matvei Yankelevich

AN ENCOUNTER WITH MAXIM GORKY

As novelist, editor, playwright, and ideologue, Maxim Gorky (1868–1936) stands as one of the towering figures in Russian literature, with a posthumous reputation matching the oscillations of Soviet politics. Gorky's endorsement of Mayakovsky and Futurism had a propulsive effect, granting validation to a movement attempting to position itself beyond the need of validation.

•

Volodya, swaying slightly, as if he were standing on board ship, began to recite slowly in his deep bass the prologue to *A Cloud in Trousers* . . .

I noticed that Gorky received with a kind of astonishment and joy the powerful timbre of Mayakovsky's voice and the clear striking rhythm of his manly verse . . . Gorky rose and embraced Mayakovsky with tears in his eyes.

Mayakovsky went on reciting poems; he recited a lot and in an excellent way.

—Vasily Kamensky, *Life with Mayakovsky* (Moscow, 1940).

•

There is no Russian Futurism. There are just Igor Severyanin, Mayakovsky, Burliuk, V. Kamensky. There can be no doubt that there are among them men of talent, who—once the dross is thrown away—will in the future become a valuable quantity. They do not know much, they have seen little, but they will undoubtedly learn, work, and improve themselves.

—Maxim Gorky, "On Futurism," *Zhurnal Shurnolalov* 1 (April 15, 1915)

•

A Cloud in Trousers had just come out in an orange cover. He was telling me about the new friends to whom he was taking me, about his acquaintance with Gorky, about how the social theme was taking an increasing part in his projects and allowing him to work in a new way, spending fixed times over allotted tasks.

—Boris Pasternak, *Safe Conduct: An Autobiography and Other Writings* (1958)

•

When I told him that in my opinion a great, though not easy, future awaited him, he replied gloomily, "I want the future now." . . . He spoke with two voices, as it were: with pure lyricism, and then again—in tones of sharp satire. One felt that he did not know himself and was afraid of something. At the same time he showed an addiction to playing with words.

—Maxim Gorky, letter to Ilya Gruzdyev, 1915, excerpted in Woroszylski's *The Life of Mayakovsky*

•

Went to Mustemaki. M. Gorky. Read him fragments of *Cloud.* Moved, Gorky wept all over my vest. Upset him with my poems. I was almost proud, but soon it turned out that Gorky weeps over every poetic vest.

Still, I hold on to the vest. I could lend it to someone for an exhibit in some provincial museum.

—Vladimir Mayakovsky, *I, Myself*

From *Poet on the Screen: Mayakovsky the Film Actor* (1958)

ALEXANDRA REBIKOVA

One day Vladimir Vladimirovich presented me with his poem *A Cloud in Trousers.* We were in a droshky, I think, when I told him that there were many places in the poem I did not understand. I opened the book, read some of them and laughed. "You don't understand anything," said Mayakovsky with a grim smile. "I am the greatest modern poet. One day you will realize this." He then snatched the book from my hands and tore it to shreds, which he threw away on the Kuznetsky Bridge.

From Max Polonovsky, *Poet on the Screen: Mayakovsky the Film Actor*, 1958, translated in Woroszylski's *The Life of Mayakovsky.* Alexandra Rebikova appeared with Mayakovsky in *The Lady and the Hooligan* (she was the lady) and in *Fettered by Film* (playing a jealous Gypsy, second fiddle to Lili Brik).

From ***I, Myself***

HAPPIEST DATE

July, 1915. Met L.Y. and O.M. Brik.

From "Mayakovsky's Last Loves" (2002)

FRANCINE DU PLESSIX GRAY

There was a strong streak of masochism in Mayakovsky, and the woman he fell in love with in 1915 seems to have been invented to satisfy it. Her name was Lilia (Lili) Yurevna Brik, née Kagan, and she would serve as his muse longer than any other woman.

The daughter of a prosperous Jewish jurist, the handsome, erotically obsessed, highly cultivated Lili grew up with an overwhelming ambition prevalent among women of the Russian intelligentsia: she dreamed of being perpetuated in human memory as the muse of a famous poet. When she was twenty, she married Osip Brik, the learned son of a wealthy jeweler whose politics, like hers, were ardently Marxist. The two made a pact to love each other "in the Chernyshevsky manner"—a reference to one of nineteenth-century Russia's most famous radical thinkers, who was an early advocate of "open marriages." Living at the heart of artistic bohemia and receiving the intelligentsia in the salon of his delectable, red-haired wife, Osip Brik, true to his promise, calmly accepted Lili's infidelities from the start. In fact, upon hearing his wife confess that she had gone to bed with Mayakovsky Brik exclaimed, "How could you refuse anything to that man!"

Mayakovsky's sexual relationship with Lili lasted only approxi-

Mayakovsky's drawing of Lili Brik, 1916

mately from 1915 to 1923. But his close friendship with Osip, a noted literary scholar and a pioneer of formalist criticism, created a bond with both Briks that far transcended any sexual attachment. For the rest of his life, "Osia" Brik remained the poet's most trusted adviser, his most fervent proselytizer, and also a co-founder, with Mayakovsky, of the most dynamic avant-garde journal of the early Soviet era, *Left Front of Art*, which published artists and writers such as Sergei Eisenstein, Aleksandr Rodchenko, and Isaac Babel. In 1918, when Mayakovsky and the Briks became inseparable, he simply moved in with them. Throughout the rest of his life, he made his home at a succession of flats that the Briks occupied. He also had a tiny studio space next to the old Lubianka prison, where he worked and carried on his numerous liaisons with other women.

Osip Brik enjoyed his own occasional flings, and the ménage à trois seemed to prosper on these arrangements. The two men rose ahead of Lili in the mornings, and had long conversations over breakfast. Before leaving the flat, Mayakovsky came up to Osip and kissed him on the top of the head, saying, "I kiss your little baldness." The Briks offered Mayakovsky both independence and the stability of a family life, which he had not enjoyed since childhood. In return, the poet, who by 1918 had become a popular idol, became the Briks' principal breadwinner. The substantial publishing royalties and lecture fees the poet earned in Russia and abroad supplemented the meager income the Briks made through literary criticism and occasional work that Lili found in films . . .

Mayakovsky's liaison with Lili, however, was as tormented as his friendship with Osip Brik was serene. Mutual friends remained amazed, throughout the following years, by the despotic manner in which she treated him and the fearful obsequiousness with which this dynamic, seemingly powerful man catered to his mistress's every wish. ("If I'm a complete rag, use me to dust your staircase," he wrote her in one particularly self-abasing letter.) For years, with her tacit approval, his poems publicly lamented her heartlessness and inconstancy—in "The Backbone Flute," of 1915, he likens her rouged lips to "a monastery hacked from frigid rock." The poet's unrequited passion for Lili even incited him to flirt with death, in 1916, by playing Russian roulette.

Published in slightly revised form in *Them: A Memoir of Parents* (New York: Penguin Books, 2005). The book contains two discriminatingly detailed chapters on Mayakovsky, as du Plessix Gray's mother, Tatiana Yakovleva, entered into a passionate, increasingly impossible romance with the poet in 1928. In tracking this intimate history, which preceded but inevitably haunted her own life, du Plessix Gray deftly defines Mayakovsky's attachment to his previous muse.

Lilichka! (1916)

(*Instead of a letter*)

May 26, 1916, Petrograd

Tobacco smoke ate away the air.
The room—
a chapter in Kruchenykh's hell.
Remember—
behind that window
the first time
I frenziedly caressed your arms.
Today you sit there,
your heart metallic.
Any day now—
you'll kick me out,
maybe even cursing me.
In the bleary front hall,
my arm, broken by trembling,
doesn't fit into the sleeve.
I'll run out,
throw my body into the street.
Feral,
crazed,
lacerated by despair.
Let's not have this,
my darling,
my sweet,
let's say goodbye now.
And anyway,
my love
weighs heavily

on you
no matter where you run.
Allow me a final wail
to expel the last of my bitter woes.
If you work a bull to exhaustion,
he'll go,
and sink into the cold waters.
Besides your love,
I have
no ocean,
and from your love
even a tearful plea won't grant me peace.
If a tired elephant wants rest—
he'll sprawl majestically in the fiery sand.
Besides your love,
I have
no sun,
and I don't know where you are, or who you're with.
If you had tortured a poet like this,
he would
trade in his beloved for money and fame,
but for me,
not a single sound brings me joy
but the ring of your lovely name.
I won't throw myself down a stairwell,
or drink poison,
or pull the trigger on the gun pressed to my temple.
Besides your sharpened gaze
the blade of any other knife
is powerless.
Tomorrow you'll forget
I had crowned you,

I had charred my blossoming soul with love,
and the whirling carnival of cluttered days
will ruffle the pages of my books . . .
and my words, dead leaves, will
stop you, as you
gasp for air?

At least let me,
with a last tenderness, pave
your departing path.

Translated by Katya Apekina

"Lilichka!" was unpublished until 1934, four years after Mayakovsky's death. Not that the relationship with Lili Brik was remotely secret. Mayakovsky attached printed dedications to Lili to most of his long poems, including *A Cloud in Pants* (written in 1914, before they met; published by Osip Brik in 1915), "The Backbone Flute" (1915), and *About This* (1923). In 1921, playing at anonymity for his *150,000,000*, Mayakovsky left his name off the general edition but asked the printer to issue three copies—for himself, Lili, and Osip—containing the dedication to Lili.

LIFE WITH LILI

Everybody spurned the poet, wounded him . . . And here, at last, home and a contract with Brik: half a ruble for every line, forever, and tomorrow he publishes . . .

Lili Brik cut Mayakovsky's hair, told him to wash himself, gave him a change of clothing. He began to carry a heavy stick . . .

Lili has brown eyes, a large head, is beautiful, redhaired, light, wants to become a dancer.

—Viktor Shklovsky,* *Mayakovsky and His Circle* (1940)

•

Volodya would put on a top hat, I, a large black hat with feathers, and we would go to the Nevsky, for instance, to buy a pencil for Osia . . .

*Viktor Shklovsky (1893–1984) was Mayakovsky's exact contemporary and one of the most sharp-eyed witnesses of the era. As a literary theorist, age twenty, he aligned himself with the Futurists in 1913. His exceptional prose style—elliptical detail alternating with dazzling metaphor—both invites and resists piecemeal quotation. His book on Mayakovsky sustains a tone of astringent lyricism, gathering intimate, fragmentary images into an expansive historical panorama. Shklovsky's other books, equally rich and unique, include *Zoo or Letters Not About Love* (1923), tracking the author's roundabout courtship of Lili Brik's sister, Elsa Triolet (1896–1970), who, in the course of deflecting Shklovsky, found her own voice as a writer.

Mayakovsky and Lili Brik in *Fettered by Film*, 1918. Only a fragment of the film survives.

At night we walked along the seafront. In the darkness it looked as if the ships did not emit smoke but sparks.

Volodya said, "They don't dare emit smoke in your presence."

—Lili Brik, *Almanac with Mayakovsky* (Moscow, 1934)

•

I remember how one day Mayakovsky came with Lili Brik to the Comedian's Inn. They went out together. Soon Mayakovsky came back in a hurry.

"She left her handbag behind," he said, and found a small black handbag on a chair.

At the table was sitting Larissa Reisner, young, beautiful. She looked at Mayakovsky sadly.

"You have now found your handbag and will carry it all your life."

"I can carry this handbag in my mouth, Larissa Mikhailovna," the poet replied.

—Viktor Shklovsky, *Mayakovsky and His Circle* (1940)

4. An Extraordinary Adventure

(1917–26)

Mayakovsky's poster for the 1918 film (now lost) *Not for Money Born.* "In the lead role of the poet is the magnificent Poet Futurist Vladimir Mayakovsky"

Revolution (1999)

PATRICIA BLAKE

The revolution was a psychological imperative. He was a born rebel. It was in his temperament. At the same time, he was alienated. He felt desolate, and he needed some certitudes. I would say that much of his life was spent in the search for refuge from this pain that hounded him, and he sought it in the absolutes of his time: the revolution, communism, and, when they failed him, in death.

This and all further Patricia Blake commentary was supplied for a BBC 3 radio program on communism and the arts, "The Red Flag and the Red Mask," broadcast in January 1999.

From ***I, Myself***

CALLED UP

Drafted. Now I don't want to go to the front. Pretended to be a draftsman. Learning at night from some engineer how to draft autos. With printing, things are even worse. Soldiers are forbidden to publish. Only Brik makes me happy. Buys all my poems at 50 kopeks a line. Printed "Backbone Flute" and *Cloud. Cloud* came out very wispy. The censors blew on it. About six pages worth of dotted lines.

Since then, I've despised dotted lines. And commas too.

OCTOBER

To accept or not to accept? This question didn't exist for me or for the other Moscow Futurists. My revolution. Went to the Smolni Institute. Worked on anything that came my way.

Getting Along with Horses (1918)

Hooves struck.
Like song:
—Clip.
Clop.
Clep.
Clup.—

The wind stripped
street, an ice
shod slide.
A horse crashed
on its rump, and
right away
one slack-jaw after another
came down Kuznetsky
in bell-bottoms to have a look—
                                        see,
crowding round,
a jingle jangle of laughter:
—Horse fell!—
—Fallen horse!—
All Kuznetsky Street laughed,
Except for me,
I didn't mix my voice into that howl.
I walk up
and I see
the horse eyes . . .

The street toppled over,
flowing how it likes . . .
I walk up and I see
drop from drop
rolling down its face,
burrowing in its hide . . .

And some kind of common
animal anguish
splashed and poured out of me
and dissolved in a rustle.
"Horse, please, don't.
Listen to me, horse—
do you think you're any less than they are?
Little one,
all of us are horses, sort of,
every one of us a horse in his own way."
Maybe the old nag
didn't need a nanny,
maybe she thought my notion seemed a little
stale,
but
the horse
gave a jerk,
stood on its legs,
neighed
and off she went.
Flicking its tail.
Chestnut, childlike.
Came home cheerful,
stood in its stall.
And the whole time she felt

like a colt,
and life was worth living,
and work worthwhile.

Translated by Val Vinokur

MAYAKOVSKY ON FILM

JANUARY

Stopped by in Moscow. Perform. At night in the "Poet's Café" in Nastasinskom. The revolutionary grandmother of today's little poet-café salons. Write screenplays. Star in them. Draw movie posters. June. Again Petersburg.

—Vladimir Mayakovsky, *I, Myself*

•

I have seen the early films in which Mayakovsky acted. Not films really—only a few fragments have been preserved. It is strange to see them: fluttering, pale like water, images almost absent. On them—the face of young Mayakovsky—sad, passionate, evoking immense compassion, the face of a strong and suffering man.

—Yuri Olesha,* "Literary Diaries," in *Literary Moscow* (1956)

•

I once asked Mayakovsky when he found time to write his poems. He used to spend days filming, evenings—in cafés . . . or some-

*Olesha (1899–1960) was a poet and short-story writer, acclaimed (and, in time, officially vilified) for the delicate psychology of his 1927 satiric novella, *Envy*.

where else . . . Mayakovsky replied that when he felt like writing he would find time and nothing could stop him.

It soon happened that in a crucial moment in the filming, which was going on all the time, day after day, Mayakovsky did not appear at the Samarsky Alley.

They looked for him in his apartment, in the apartments of all his friends, asked for him in all the places he used to frequent . . . But they did not succeed in finding Mayakovsky in Moscow.

The actors gathered in the morning at the studio, the proprietors were flustered, all work stopped, people wandered around with nothing to do . . .

But the poet soon appeared at the studio, ready to continue filming.

"Where have you been, Vladimir Vladimirivich? Where did you get to?"

"I worked. I had the need to write a poem, so I found the time. I warned you, remember?"

—Evgeny Slavinsky* (1958), from Max Polonovsky's *Poet on the Screen*, translated in Woroszylski's *The Life of Mayakovsky*

*Evgeny Slavinsky (1877–1950) served as director and cinematographer on *The Lady and the Hooligan* (1918). The poem accounting for Mayakovsky's absence was "Getting Along with Horses," one of his enduring hits.

The Heart of the Screen

MICHAEL ALMEREYDA

Early on, through David Burliuk's tutelage, Mayakovsky found poetic precursors in the rhapsodic aggression of Rimbaud and in the caustic public manner of Baudelaire. (Compare the preamble of *Les Fleurs du Mal*, "To the Reader," with Mayakovsky's scorching "To You!") But as he hit his stride, Mayakovsky consciously identified with Walt Whitman, who provides a fair index for measuring Mayakovsky's swagger, the physicality of his language, his openness and generosity of spirit. All the same, the force and range of the Russian's distinguishing effects—the jolting, telescoping metaphors, mixed tenses and tones, abrupt shifts of scale, time, and space—all add up to something singularly *Mayakovskian*.

It is also worth remarking that these effects are notably *cinematic*—but in fact they anticipate a film language that didn't quite exist at the time. Is it overreaching to insist (as Viktor Shklovsky has) that Mayakovsky's verse anticipated and influenced dramatic innovations unleashed by the great Russian filmmakers of the 1920s? Mobile points of view, rapid-fire editing rhythms, startling transitions, an urge to find cosmic connections in factual, physical detail—it was as if a shared current were flowing between Mayakovsky's poems and the brains and editing rooms of Dziga Vertov,

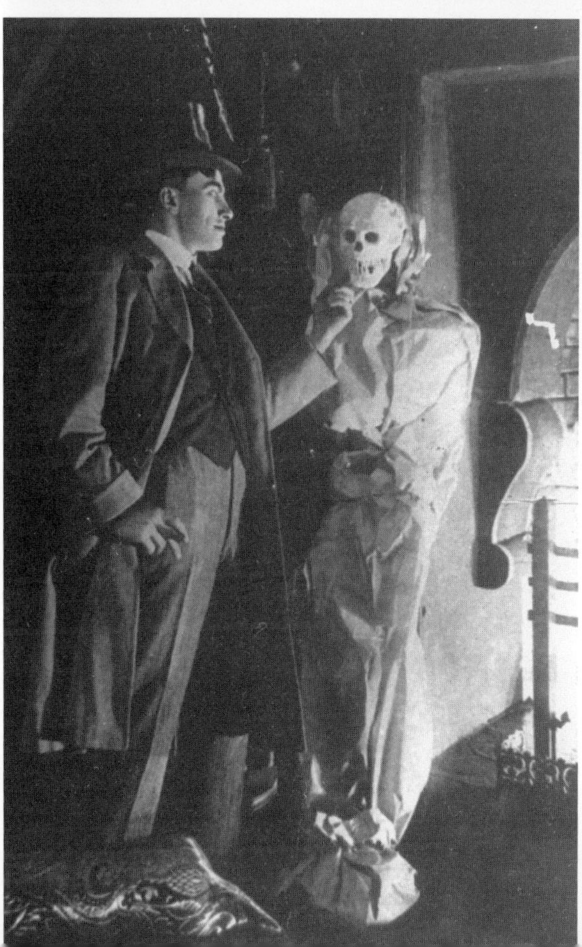

Two stills from *Not for Money Born*, 1918. Mayakovsky as the poet Ivanov.

Sergei Eisenstein, Alexander Dovzhenko. In 1923, at any rate, the third issue of *LEF* (edited by Mayakovsky and Osip Brik) featured Eisenstein's seminal essay "Montage of Attractions" alongside Vertov's manifesto "Kino-Eye." Eisenstein's astonishing first films, *Strike* and *Battleship Potemkin*, were two years away, though Vertov had been working full tilt on weekly newsreels (from 1918 to 1919), and his *KinoPravda* series commenced in 1922—documentary experiments that culminated with Vertov's dazzling, decidedly Mayakovskian 1929 masterpiece, *Man with a Movie Camera.*

But Mayakovsky's most direct interaction with the medium came several years earlier and was curiously limited. In 1918, the twenty-four-year-old poet landed a veritable three-picture deal with the fledgling Neptune studios. Of his three starring vehicles, only *The Lady and the Hooligan** survives, the sole directorial effort of cameraman Evgeny Slavinsky. The script, improvised from an 1892 Italian novel, is credited to Mayakovsky, who plays a "hooligan" enraptured with a prim schoolteacher, but the thin story hardly accounts for the film's charm and power, which has everything to do with its sharp visual design and with Mayakovsky's potent screen presence. Lanky and alert, surrounded by oafish peasant archetypes, he gives off an unforced Brando-ish intensity that seems imported from another era.

Mayakovsky also scripted *Not for Money Born*, a story grafted from Jack London's *Martin Eden* and shot almost back-to-back with *The Lady and the Hooligan.* Again, he plays the central role—a poet tempted by riches and fame. Surviving stills suggest that the picture was, like *Hooligan*, another example of melodramatic hokum. But in *Fettered by Film*—the apparent standout of the three—Mayakovsky crafted a fittingly imaginative vehicle for his own personal mythol-

*The film, titled *La Demoiselle et le Voyou*, is crisply preserved on a French DVD issued by Bach Films, paired with Alexander Medvedkin's antic *Le Bonheur.*

ogy. He played a bored married painter who goes to the movies and is entranced by a ballet dancer on-screen. The dancer was Lili Brik, whose memory of Mayakovsky's screenplay is richly specific.* The painter's longing conjures the dancer out of the movie and into the dark and dingy real world. A skittish courtship ensues, but the dancer soon longs for home. "She throws herself at anything white that reminds her of the screen, strokes the tile stove and the tablecloth." Meanwhile, the dancer has vanished from all the movie screens in the city and—as in Woody Allen's *The Purple Rose of Cairo*, made more than sixty years later—fellow movie characters are confounded by their colleague's disappearance, stirred into a revolt. The film concludes with Mayakovsky's painter losing the dancer but locating the name of a mythical filmland listed in fine print at the bottom of a poster. He sets off to find her.

Mayakovsky continued to pursue an elusive cinematic muse for the rest of his life. In 1926 he returned to *Fettered by Film*, reshaping it into a new script, *The Heart of the Screen.* Herbert Marshall's *Mayakovsky* casually mentions that the poet wrote thirty other screenplays.

*As recounted by Max Polonovsky in Woroszylski's *Life of Mayakovsky.*

From ***I, Myself***

’18

RSFSR* has no time for art. But that is precisely what I have the time for.

Why am I not in the Party? The Communists were working in the front lines. But with art—they were willing to compromise. I wish they’d just send me to catch fish in Astrakhan.

25TH OF OCTOBER, 1918

Completed *Mystery.*† Recited. There’s a lot of talk. Meyerhold and K. Malevich produced it. Everyone was weeping like crazy. Especially the Communist intelligentsia. Andreeva did everything in her power. To get in the way. They performed it three times—then it was torn down. Then came the Macbeths.

*Russian Soviet Federated Socialist Republic, a.k.a. the U.S.S.R.

†*Mystery-Bouffe*, Mayakovsky’s second play, written to commemorate the first anniversary of the Bolshevik takeover. There is not adequate space in this book to consider Mayakovsky’s work for the stage, but it’s worth noting that he was particularly lucky with his collaborators. Vsevolod Meyerhold (1874–1940) directed *Mystery-Bouffe*; Kasimir Malevich (1878–1935) designed the sets. Both men were among the most brilliantly innovative artists of their generation, a generation for which brilliance seems almost commonplace. Meyerhold also directed Mayakovsky’s *The Bedbug* (1928) and the bitterly satiric *The Bathhouse* (1930). Both plays featured musical scores by Dmitri Shostakovich.

On *Mystery-Bouffe* (1999)

PETER CONRAD

The hyphen in the title splices together a medieval mystery play and an opera buffa, solemn biblical lore and irreverent satire. The revolution brings about a deluge like Noah's flood, which spares the unclean proletarians. Evacuated in the ark, they are visited by Christ; Mayakovsky played the role himself in Meyerhold's production. The savior strolls across frothing water in the vicinity of Ararat and updates the sermon he once delivered on another mount . . . The proletarians decide that they prefer Petrograd to this dreary idyll [heaven], but before leaving they grab God's thunderbolts, now deployed in the Russian campaign of electrification. They tramp back to their commune with its fuming chimneys and bountiful crops: this is their kingdom come, an earth "washed by revolution and dried in the heat of the new suns." They plait sunbeams into dazzling brooms with which they clear away the debris of history, and they pave their streets with stars.

From Peter Conrad, *Modern Times, Modern Places* (London: Thames and Hudson Ltd., 1999).

From ***I, Myself***

'19

My friends and I travel to the factories with *Mystery* and other pieces. A cheerful welcome. In the Vyborg district a Futurist commune springs up, we publish *Art of the Commune*. The Academies are creaking and rattling. In the spring I move to Moscow.

I was struck with *150,000,000*. Went to do agitation work for ROSTA.*

*Abbreviation for the Russian Telegraph Agency.

Mixed Media

MICHAEL ALMEREYDA

As civil war raged from 1919 to 1921, the Russian Telegraph Agency issued a stream of posters widely disseminated throughout the U.S.S.R.—propaganda relating to matters of public health, safety, morale. The posters, called "windows," tended to be displayed in the windows of famine-emptied stores. As Edward J. Brown put it, the poster/windows "served the double purpose of concealing from the pedestrian's eye the evidence of an economy in ruins while turning his thoughts to the struggle against enemies of the revolution and to the great hope of the communist future."* Mayakovsky formalized a comic-strip format initiated by his friend Mikhail Cheremnykh: linked images—four to six per poster—were matched with rhymed texts centering on one topic. By his own estimate, Mayakovsky generated 3,000 of these posters; 635 of them were included in the third volume of his *Collected Works*.

As with many extraordinary literary practitioners (from Blake to Cocteau to Flannery O'Connor), Mayakovsky's graphic talent centered on a decisive use of line, shadowless contours, a cartoon

*Edward J. Brown, *Mayakovsky: A Poet in the Revolution* (Princeton, N.J.: Princeton University Press, 1973).

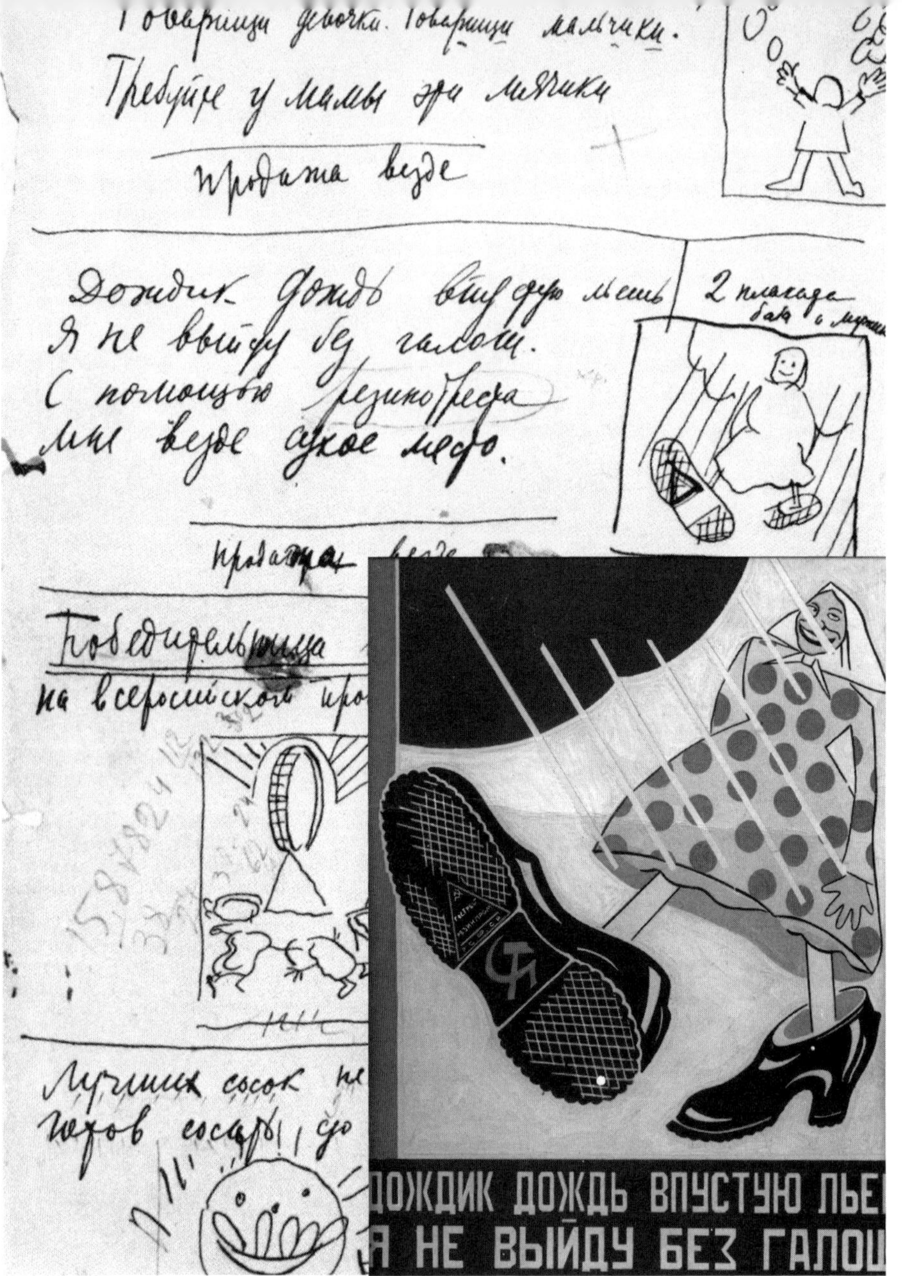

Mayakovsky's sketches and captions for state-sponsored ads co-created with Rodchenko. Inset: Rodchenko's finished poster. "Rain, rain, you fall for nothing / I won't go out without my galoshes."

depthlessness. Cocteau's aphorism applies: "Drawing is handwriting unwound in new directions." Mayakovsky provided cover art for his first book, worked up posters for two of his films, sketched costume designs for his plays, and decorated letters with doodled self-portraits (for Lili Brik, he pictured himself as a puppy; for Tatiana Yakovleva, an ox). The feverish assembly-line production for ROSTA gave rise to a fresh and vivid cartoon style (for which the artist picked up a prize in Paris in 1925), but the things he depicted—balloon-shaped, top-hatted capitalists, superheroic workers, soldiers massed in spiky silhouettes—amount to a boisterous collection of clichés. It may be fitting to note a measure of self-knowledge in Mayakovsky's decision to almost never illustrate his less public verse, as if he recognized his adventures in language to be something separate and, finally, unmatchable.

ROSTA (1934)

LILI BRIK

We drew on newspaper cuttings, then stuck rough edges together. If something was not quite right, instead of rubbing it out, we simply stuck something else on top.

We followed this technique: Mayakovsky drew in charcoal; I colored the drawing; then he finished it and polished it off.

We worked in an unheated place. The only source of heat to warm freezing paints and glue was burning newspapers in an old stove.

Mayakovsky composed up to eighty captions in verse daily.

We worked almost without sleep. Cheremnykh* did fifty posters per night. Sometimes he would doze off in the course of working from sheer fatigue. He maintained that upon waking up he found that the work had been completed by inertia.

There was an inspection in our department. They decided that Cheremnykh was a Futurist and had to be removed. Mayakovsky was not accused of Futurism. He ardently defended Cheremnykh and managed to save him.

From Woroszylski's *The Life of Mayakovsky*.

*Mikhail Cheremnykh (1890–1962), painter and cartoonist, originator of the ROSTA poster.

Two ROSTA posters. This page: "1. Each truancy 2. is joy to the enemy. 3. And each labor's hero 4. is a blow to the bourgeois."

"1. The last enemy is ready! 2. It will slowly release the older enlistees. 3. The soldiers will return to their homes, 4. and will take up work for Russia's prosperity. 5. One thing you shouldn't forget—capitalism lives in 3/4 of the world. 6. Be ready!"

An Extraordinary Adventure That Happened to Vladimir Mayakovsky One Summer at a Dacha (1920)

Sunset swarmed in a hundred forty suns,
as summer rolled into July;
there was the heat,
the swimming heat—
this all happened in the countryside.
Pushkino's foothill, humpbacked
with Akulova,
and below the hill—
there was a village
a crust of crooked roofs.
Beyond the village—
was a hole,
and in that hole, most likely,
the sun sank down each time,
so faithfully and slowly.
But tomorrow
once again
to flood the world
the sun would rise up scarlet.
And day by day
this very thing
began
to make me
furious.
And one time so enraged was I
that all things paled in fear,
I shouted at the sun point-blank:

David Burliuk's woodcut illustrating "An Extraordinary Adventure," 1920

"Get over here!
Stop your loafing in that pitch-hole!"
I shouted at the sun:
"Old sponger!
caressed by clouds you are,
while here—winter, summer,
I sit and draw these posters."
I shouted at the sun:
"Just you wait!
Listen here, goldenbrow,
instead
of setting aimlessly,
come by,
have tea with me!"
What have I done!
I'm dead!
Coming toward me
of his own good will,
the sun himself,
in wide beaming strides,
strode across the field.
Don't want to show I'm scared,
I saunter backward, casual.
His eyes are in the garden now,
in windows,
doors,
through cracks, he came,
piled in, a sunny mass,
poured in;
and with a deep breath,
he spoke in basso:
"I drive the fires back

for the first time since creation.
You called me?
Boil some tea,
poet, spread out some jam, I say!"
Tears in my eyes—
out of my mind from heat,
but I showed him
to the samovar and said:
"Well then, have a seat, you
luminary!"
Devil made me, raked my arrogance,
to shout at him like that,—
confused,
I sat on a bench corner,
scared—things could get worse!
But, from the sun, a strange radiance
streamed,—
and formalities
forgotten,
I'm sitting, chatting
with the luminary freely.
I talk of this,
of that,
how I've been swallowed up by poster-work,
but the sun says:
"All right,
don't get fired up,
just look at things more simply!
Take me, you think it's
easy
shining on like this?
Go ahead and try it!—

You move along the sky—
since move you must,
you move—and shine your eyeballs out!"
We blabbed like that til it got dark—
til what was night once, that is.
For what darkness was there here?
We were familiar with each other,
easy, free.
And soon, since friendship never melts,
I slap him hearty on the back.
And the sun does me the same:
"Me and you, comrade,
quite a pair we make!
Let's get out there, poet,
let's dawn
and sing
before this gray mess of a world.
I'll pour my sunny heart out,
and you—your own,
in verse."
A wall of shades,
a jail of nights
fell under the double-barreled suns.
A stir of rays and verse—
shine all you've got!
And if he gets tired,
and wants a night of rest,
dull sleepyhead,
that's when I
shine with all my might—
and day rings out again.
Shine all the time,

shine everywhere,
until the plunging end of days,
to shine—
to hell and back!
Here is my motto for you—
my slogan and the sun's!

Translated by Val Vinokur

Poetry for Everyone (1922)

OSIP MANDELSTAM

When Mayakovsky purged the poets in alphabetical order at the Polytechnic Museum, there were young people in the audience who volunteered, when their turn came, to read their own poetry, so that Mayakovsky's task was made easier. This is only possible in Moscow, for nowhere else in the world are there people who, like Shiites, are ready to prostrate themselves so that the chariot of the stentorian voice might drive over them.

Highly knowledgeable about the richness and complexity of world poetry, Mayakovsky, in establishing his "poetry for everyone," had to send everything incomprehensible to the devil, that is, everything that presupposed even the tiniest bit of poetic education in the audience. To read poems to an audience that is completely uneducated in poetry is just as thankless a task as trying to sit on a spiked fence . . . And yet Mayakovsky writes poetry, and very cultivated poetry . . . Thus, Mayakovsky impoverishes his poetry in vain. He is in danger of becoming a poetess, something which has already partially happened.

From Jane Gary Harris, ed., *Mandelstam: The Complete Critical Prose and Letters*, trans. Jane Gary Harris and Constance Link (Ann Arbor, Mich.: Ardis, 1979). Osip Mandelstam (1891–1938) was a primary member of the Acmeist school, favoring a poetry that was notably interior, allusive, dense. He died in transit to a labor camp near Vladivostok after having been arrested for harboring anti-Soviet sentiments. An edition of Mandelstam's collected poems was not legally available to Soviet citizens until 1973. Posterity grants him immense stature among twentieth-century writers.

From "The Red Flag and the Red Mask" (1999)

PATRICIA BLAKE

Mayakovsky usually managed to retain his originality, even in his crudest polemics and his broadest satires. In *150,000,000*, a poem written during the American intervention in the Russian Civil War, the colossal peasant Ivan, who has 150,000,000 heads, an arm as long as the Neva River, and heels as big as the Caspian steppes, wades across the Atlantic to fight a hand-to-hand battle with a Woodrow Wilson resplendent in a top hat as high as the Eiffel Tower.

From **150 Million** (1920)

150,000,000 is master of this poem.
Bullet-rhythm.
                Rhyme-fire spreading from building to building.
150,000,000 speak through my lips.
It is on the circular steps
                in the cobblestone squares
that this edition is printed.

Who'll ask the moon?
                Who'll pull an answer from the sun?
                        Are you fixing the nights and days?!
Who will name the lands of the brilliant author?
And so,
                for my poem

                                there is no author.

And it has but one goal—
                        to shine through to the new tomorrow.

In this very year,
                on this day and hour,
                        underground,
                                on the earth,
                                        in the skies,
                                                and higher—

billboards,
flyers,
posters,
have appeared:

"EVERYONE!
EVERYONE!
EVERYONE!
Everyone,
who can't take it anymore!
Gather
together
and go!"
. . .
And all of these
hundred and fifty million people
billions of fish,
trillions of insects,
animals,
pets,
hundreds of provinces,
with everything that's been built there,
that stands there,
that lives there,
everything that moves,
and everything that doesn't move,
everything that was barely moving,
slithering,
crawling,
floating—
All of this erupting,
Pouring out like lava!

. . .
And now
Russia
isn't a raggedy orphan,
nor piles of rubble,
nor charred buildings—
Russia is
fully
united into Ivan,
and his arm—
is the Neva,
and his heels—the Caspian steppes.

Let's go!
Letsgoletsgo!
Not walking, but flying!
Not flying, but lightning bolting!
Souls washed by breezes!
Past
the bars and bathhouses.
Beat the drum!
Drum the drums!
. . .
Now
Let's turn the wheel of inspiration.
A new rhyme and meter.
This part's lead character—Wilson.
The setting—America.

The world,
gathering itself into a quintet,
bestowed them with supernatural force.

A city in it stands
      on just one screw,
all electro-dynamo-mechanical.

In Chicago
    there are 14,000 streets
       rays of the town square suns.

From each one—
       700 alleys
         a yearlong train trip.
It's great for a person in Chicago!
In Chicago
    sunlight
       is no brighter
         than a penny candle.
In Chicago
    even raising an eyebrow
       requires electric current.
. . .
Of course,
    the scientists
       were drawn here by
           the theory of the flood.

The artists
    by some
       magnificent
           école des beaux arts

Nothing of the sort!

                                        Everyone has gathered
                                                            just to
go shopping.
Every morning
          all of these
                    lovers of muses and glory
load up on baskets,
                    and go to the market
carrying back
                    meat
                              and butter.
Some king of their poets,
                              Longfellow
                                        lugs along a hundred jars of cream.
Wilson stuffs his maw,
          cultivating his lard,
                    his stomachs grow,
                              the rolls rising story by story.
. . .
And so,
for quite a while
everyone was busy with
their leisure time.
But already
an hour ago
something
began to change.
Barely audible,
but by the tip of one's soul,
some sort of whistling.
In the windless ocean
                    splashing waves begin to form.

What's going on?
What's this about?
And in the morning
by the glimmer of lightning,
the ATA
(American Telegraphic Agency)
shocked the city with this broadcast:
"A terrible storm raging on the Pacific.
The monsoons and trade winds have gone mad.
Fish have been caught off the coast of Chicago.
Very strange ones.
Covered in fur.
With large noses."

Sleepily, people emerged from their homes,
but before they have the chance to discuss these occurrences,
the radio
had another
rush of announcements:
"Information regarding the fish was untrue.
The fisherman was a local drunk.
The monsoons and trade winds are doing just fine.
But there is a storm.
It's even worse than we thought.
Causes unknown."

. . .

What Ivan?
Which Ivan?
Where Ivan?
Why Ivan?
How Ivan?

The situation could not have been more confusing.
There were no explanations that
were convincing
or sensible.
The presidential cabinet
stayed up all night worrying.
. . .
The sword shrieked.
Slicing
from the shoulder
down
four yards.
Wilson gets up and waits—
there should be blood
but from
the wound
a person suddenly crawls out.
And how they all began to come!
People,
houses,
battleships,
horses,
all squeeze through the narrow slit.
They come out singing.
All musical.
Good grief!
They've sent from northern Troy
a person-horse stuffed with rebellion!

Translated by Katya Apekina

COMRADE LENIN

FROM A NOTE TO ANATOL LUNACHARSKY, MAY 6

Aren't you ashamed to vote for the publication of 5,000 copies of Mayakovsky's *150 Million*?
This is absurd, stupid, monstrously stupid, and pretentious.
In my opinion only one in ten of such pieces should be printed and not more than 1,500 copies for libraries and eccentrics.
And Lunacharsky should be whipped for Futurism.

—V. I. Lenin (1921), from Woroszylski's *The Life of Mayakovsky*

•

Mayakovsky as a thinker is not an eagle, and he is all for effect . . . Can we say, however, that Mayakovsky finds it difficult to be Mayakovsky? Is it not clear to any objective observer that Mayakovsky has immense resources of images and words? Writing flows out of him as water from a fountain or a hot spring. He finds it very easy to be himself. He is elemental.

—Anatol Lunacharsky,* review in *Pyechat' I Revolutsya* (1921)

*Anatol Lunacharsky (1875–1933), an early and steadfast supporter of Mayakovsky, served as Soviet Commissar of Enlightenment, responsible for culture and education, generating a campaign of agitprop between 1919 and 1922.

•

Yesterday I came across a poem by Mayakovsky by chance in the *Izvestia** on a political theme. I do not count myself among the admirers of his poetic talent, though I fully admit my lack of competence in that sphere. But it is a long time since I have felt so satisfied from a political and administrative point of view. In that poem, the poet utterly derides meetings and mocks the Communists because they confer and debate all the time. I do not know whether it is good poetry, but I promise you he is absolutely right from a political point of view.

—V. I. Lenin, speech at the Metal Worker's Congress, March 6, 1922

*A Soviet newspaper. Mayakovsky's "Re: Conferences," his first contribution to the paper, pictures the poet barging into an office full of bodies severed from the waist down—Party members who have split themselves in two to attend continuous, simultaneous meetings.

From ***I, Myself***

’20

Finished *A Hundred and Fifty Million.* Print it anonymously. Want everyone to add onto it and improve it. Nobody did this, but everyone knew who the author was. It doesn’t matter. I’m printing this under my own name.

Day and night ROSTA. Write and draw. Made about three thousand posters and six thousand captions.

’21

Breaking through all the red tape, pettiness, bureaucracy and stupidity—I put on a second version of *Mystery.* Plays in Theater #1 RSFSR—directed by Meyerhold and the art by Lavinsky, Hrakovsky, Kiseliov and in the circus in German for the Third Congress of the Comintern. Put on by Granovsky with Altman and Ravdel. Had a run of about a hundred shows.

Began writing for *Izvestia.*

’22

Organize the publishing house MAF. Gather together Futurists—communes. Aseyev, Tretiakov, and other comrades in arms came from East Asia. Began to record the third year of “Fifth International.” Utopia. They’ll be showing this five hundred years from now.

Frame from a newsreel, June 10, 1929

’23

Organizing LEF.* LEF embraces a large socialist subject using all the tools of Futurism. This definition, of course, does not exhaust the issue—to those interested I offer a look at our numbers. Tightly united: Brik, Aseev, Kushner, Arvatov, Tretiakov, Rodchenko, and Lavinsky.

Wrote *About This.* With personal motifs about universal topics. Began thinking over the poem *Lenin.* One of the slogans, one of the big conquests of LEF—the de-aestheticization of manufactured art, Constructivism. Poetic application: *agitka* and household *agitka*—advertisements. Despite poetic hollering, consider “Nowhere but in Mosselprom”† to be poetry of the highest caliber.

*LEF: Left Front for the Arts. Both a literary group and a magazine edited by Mayakovsky and Osip Brik. The magazine ran from 1923 to 1925.

†“Nowhere but in Mosselprom” was Mayakovsky’s concise promotional zinger, plastered throughout Moscow, assuring consumers that the state-owned store could supply them with everything needed or known.

From ***About This*** (1923)

PROLOGUE
(*for her and for me*)

ABOUT WHAT—ABOUT THIS?

In this theme,
**   so private,**
**   so petty,**
sung over
**   before and again,**
I've spun round, a poetical squirrel,
and want to keep spinning some more.
This theme
**   now is**
**   both Buddha's prayer**
and a slave's knife itching for Master's neck.
And on Mars
**   if there is even one human heart,**
it will
**   scribble and**
**   scrape**
**   at the very same thing.**
This theme will come
**   grab a cripple by the elbow,**
drag him to a piece of paper,
**   and command:**
**   Scratch away!**

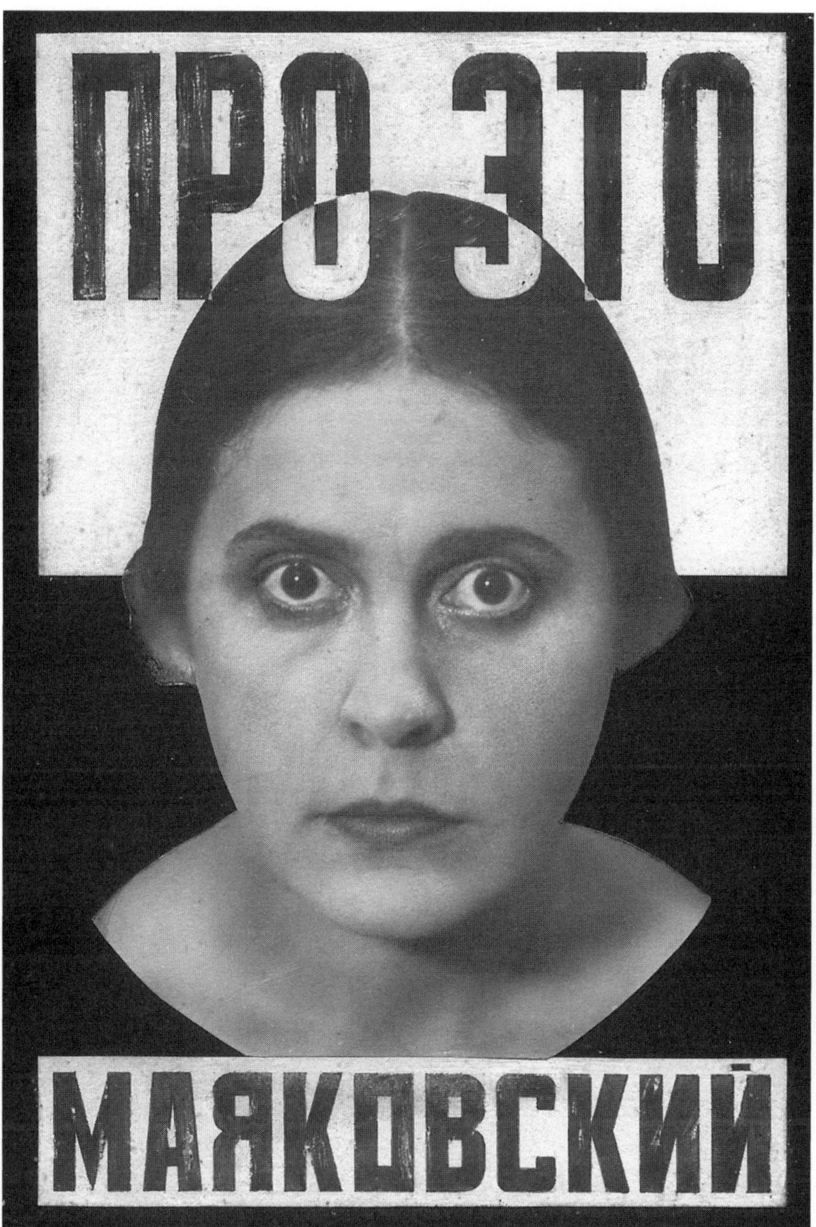

Lili Brik on the cover of *Pro Eto* (*About This*), 1923. Photomontage by Aleksandr Rodchenko.

And the cripple
soars from the page
like an eagle,
screeching bitter lines of song into the sun.
This theme will come,
ring at the kitchen door,
Turn back,
vanish like clover,
and then a giant
will sprout, stand for a second,
then crumble
and sink beneath a rippling sea of notes.
This theme will come
and order:
Veritas!
This theme will come
decreeing:
Beauty!
And even if
you find yourself splayed on a cross,
your lips will find themselves humming a waltz.
This theme runs laps round your dizzy alphabet book—
but why bother, you thought, with something so plain!—
as it angles your
"A"
like sheer Mount Kazbek.
You'll get muddled,
forget about bread, about sleep.
This theme will come,
still fresh after decades,
just to say:
From now on, look only at me!

And you look at her,
and walk along with her banner,
a red silken flame flickering over the earth.
This theme is crafty!
It dives under what happens,
ready to pounce out of secret instincts,
—and just you try and forget her—
its fury will shake
our souls out of their hides.
This theme turned up at my place raging,
commanding me:
Hand over
the reins!
Took one look at my daily cares, started making faces,
and scattered everything and everyone in a storm.
This theme came along,
rubbing out any others,
and alone
became near and dear.
This theme put a knife to my throat.
Like a blacksmith's hammer
ringing from heart to skull.
This theme darkened my day, and tells me:
Strike the dark with lines pulled from your brow.
The name
of this
theme is:
..................!

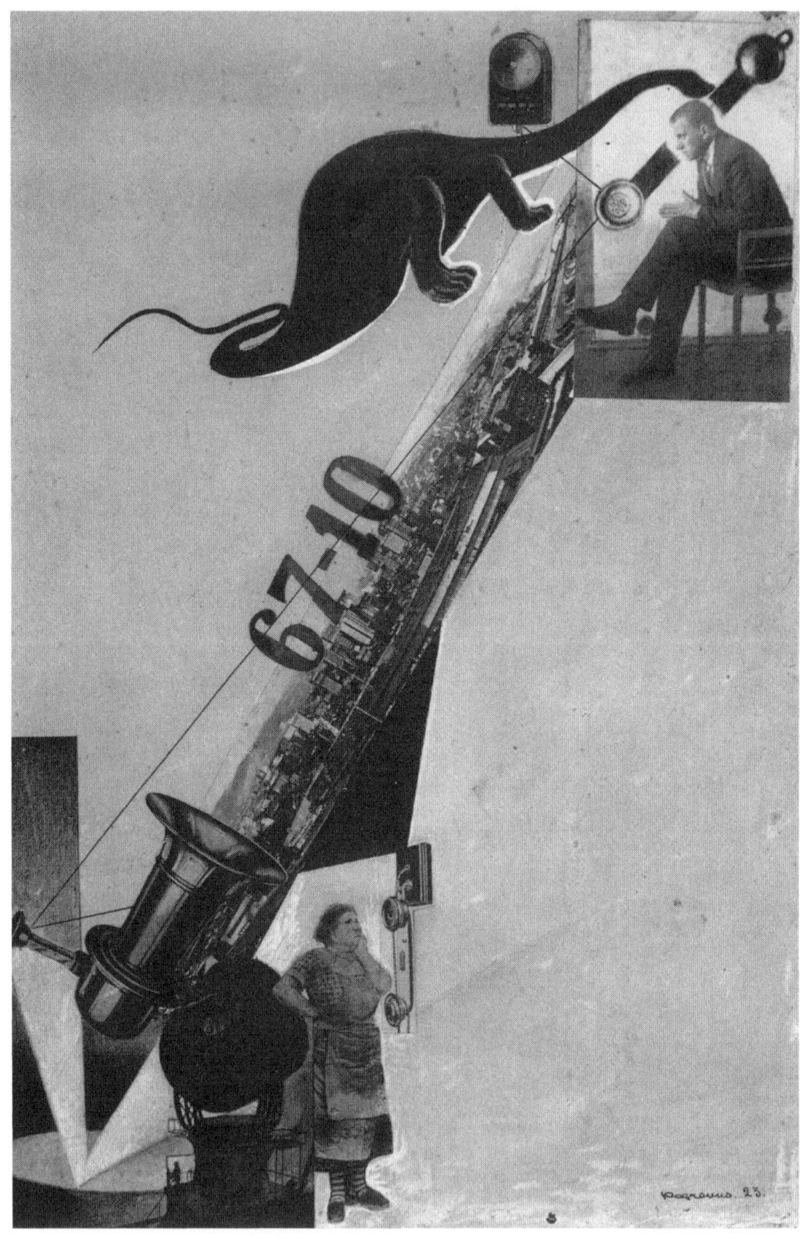

One of eight Rodchenko photomontages illustrating *Pro Eto*, 1923 (". . . out of the crowd / came jealousy crawling, / a cave-dwelling monster, / a troglodyte . . .")

I: THE BALLAD OF READING GAOL*

I stood—I remember.
It gleamed.
And it was called
the Neva then.
—Mayakovsky, "Man"

The fad for ballads is not young,
but if the words hurt
and if the words say they hurt,
then even the ballad fad grows young.
Lubyansky Drive.
Vodopyany Lane.
Set
and
Scene.
She.
Lying in bed.
He.
Telephone on the table.
"He" and "She," that's my ballad.
Not terribly new.
What's terrible is
"He" is "Me"
and "She"
has to do with me.
Why jail?
It's Christmas.
All bustles.

About this ballad
and
about any ballads

*See Oscar Wilde's poem of the same title. —V.V.

No bars on these windows.
But never mind that.
Like I said—jail.
The table.
On the table, a reed.

I touch it, barely—and blisters flare.
The horn flies from my hands.
Out of the trademark stamp
two bright arrows
shoot telephone lightning.

A number
released
through the cable

And next door.
From one room over,
drowsy:
"When, what?
Where's the stuck pig?"
The ringer already squealing from burns,
the phone molten-white.
She's sick!
In bed!
Run!
Quick!
It's time!
My flesh is smoking, a smothered searing.
Lightning running up and down my body.
Pressed and clutched by a million volts.
My lip bumps into the telephone furnace.
And through the drill holes
of the house,
Plowing up
Myasnitsky St.,
ripping apart
the cable,

the number
flies like bullet
to the switchboard girl.
Her eyes are drowsy—
holidays you work double.
Another red light.
She's calling!
The lamp goes out.
And all the sudden
a blinking impish play,
the whole network shreds.
—67–10!
Connect me!
Vodopyany Lane!
Quick!
Oh boy!
Or else the electricity builds up—
and on the night before Christmas
you'll be blown sky-high
along with
your whole
telephone station.
Once upon a time there was an old man who lived
on Myasnitskaya for a hundred years—
and for that hundred years
he would tell
his grandchildren
about this.
—It was—a Saturday . . .
before a Sunday . . .
Out for a bit of ham . . .
Wanted to buy it cheap . . .

Then someone, somewhere, somehow: crack! . . .
An earthquake . . .
My feet are hot . . .
boot-soles shake! . . . —
The kids don't buy it,
the who
and the where
and the how of it.
An earthquake?
In winter?
At the Central Post Office?!

Squeezing a miracle through its shoelace-thin   The telephone
cord,   pounces
the ear horn stretches, gaping,   on all
a ringing thunder smothers the silence,
a belch of lava beneath the telephone jangle.
This shrill
ringing drill
scorched its way into the walls
trying to blow up what's left.
Pealing echoes,
thousands of them,
ricochet
off the walls,
rolling under the chairs,
under the bed.
The abominable bell leaps from the ceiling
and smacks the floor.
And then again,
like a slaphappy basketball
bounces against the ceiling from the floor,
and a ringing rain of splinters falls.

Every windowpane
and every fireplace damper
were moved to harmonize in telephone tone.
Shaking
the house
like a rattle,
a telephone drowning in its own ringing flood.

Call for a second

Sleep swollen
pinpoint eyes
prickling through fired cheeks.
The cook gets up, sluggish,
walks over,
grunting and groaning.
Her head like a stewed apple.
Her brow wrinkled by thinking.
—Who?
Vladim Vladimych?!
Oh!—
Waddles off, slippers flapping.
Walks.
Measuring paces, like a proper second.
Her footsteps recede . . .
Hardly hear them . . .
And the rest of the world steps aside
as the unknown takes aim at me
down the barrel of a telephone.

Enlightening
the world

Conference panelists of the world
freeze in mid-gesture.
Just like that,
mouths gaping
in my direction

at the Christmas to end all Christmas.
Seems like they live
squabble to squabble.
Their home
a daily blah.
They look at me
like a mirror,
and wait for the single combat of my deadly love.
The howling sirens turn to stone.
The spinning wheels and footsteps cease.
Just the clearing for the duel,
and doctor-time standing by
with the endless bandage of all-healing death.

Translated by Val Vinokur

The final Rodchenko photomontage appearing in *Pro Eto*, 1923 (". . . She too loves beasts, / She'll come to see the zoo.")

About *About This*

MICHAEL ALMEREYDA

> For many of them what mattered was not physical survival but sacrifice, not preservation of life but its complete transcendence, not the fragile human existence in this world, but collective happiness in the other world.
>
> —Svetlana Boym, *Common Places: Mythologies of Everyday Life in Russia*, 1995

> All questions of world peace have been decided. Embassy cigarettes are the best.
>
> —Vladimir Mayakovsky, 1923

About This was written over a two-month period during which Mayakovsky and Lili Brik agreed to live separately, commencing late in 1922. The poet sequestered himself in his studio apartment, determined to grapple with "this"—the role of love in his life—in relative isolation, but the split accommodated frequent phone calls and almost daily letters. ("My beloved, kind, dearest little sun Lili! . . . Today I learned that you are sulking a bit. Don't, my little Sunshine!")

Disenchantment with the compromises of everyday life, an awareness of an ebbing of revolutionary intensity, had infected Mayakovsky's relationship with Lili. Or rather, it might be fair to say that the inconsistencies of the relationship contributed to a sense of anxiety that collided squarely with the ragged pieties of *byt*—the Russian word for daily life and, by extension, the tired and complacent domestic routines that postrevolutionary culture was supposed to cancel or leave behind. According to Christina Kiaer (in *Imagine No Possessions*, an enchantingly specific study of Constructivist fashion, advertising, and design, published in 2006), *About This* is nothing less than an indictment of *byt*. Throughout the poem, the literal and symbolic ingredients for domestic bliss are presented as embodiments of an oppressive force, referred to as "the endless hum-drum morass" or, more simply, "domestic shit." (The problem of *byt* persisted, of course, past the perimeter of this poem. Mayakovsky's final poetic statement—his suicide note—features this central line: *"Lyubovnaya lodka razbilas o byt."* Love's boat has smashed against the daily grind.)

Considering Lili's prominence in Aleksandr Rodchenko's photomontages, and given the poem's reputation as one of Mayakovsky's major lyrical works, *About This* features less intimate reporting on the Mayakovsky-Brik relationship than might be expected. In fact, the poem is less a love story than a manic cartoon adventure in which the narrator, identified as Mayakovsky, spends only part of the poem pining for an unspecified "she." Early on, the poet is transformed, werewolf fashion, into a bear. Then, with time alternately slowed, frozen, or fast-forwarded, this Mayakovsky bear rides through a sequence of set pieces, propelled by associative jumps, jolts, and special effects. Traveling by ice floe, he visits a figure strapped to a bridge overlooking the Neva—Mayakovsky's suicidal double last seen in his 1916 poem "Man," a revolutionary martyr now crying for help "with my own voice":

Vladimir,

stop!

Don't go off and leave me!

Without much strict sense, this double urges Mayakovsky to enlist Christmas revelers to relieve him of his torture, a rescue operation whereby he imagines

Love
the savior
comes
and my spirit arouses.

But the narrator-bear is swept along under the bridge and whirled to Moscow's snowy Petrovsky Park. There follows a respite during which Mayakovsky shaves off his bearish beard before visiting his mother on Christmas Eve. His own family can't be persuaded to rescue the man on the bridge. Mayakovsky moves on, carrying presents in his paws, to a parlor where "she" is glimpsed playing the piano as cardplaying maggots crawl out from under the bed and bureau, greeting the narrator with hollow enthusiasm. Mayakovsky recognizes another version of himself among the insects, while Jesus and Marx beam from picture frames on the wall.

For all its madcap energy, the poem reveals a fundamental despair. Already, in 1923, Mayakovsky is airing the suspicion that his younger, fiercer self has been compromised, that conventional success is meaningless, that a world of objects can crowd out a more difficult and generous way to live. At length, with comic cheer, the poet pleads to be transported to a hypothetical future, the thirtieth century, where he hopes to be employed as a street sweeper in a zoo, if zoos still exist. The presence of simple animals, the consolation of fellow creatures, appears more satisfactory than the complications of his avowed subject, the tangles and torments of romantic love. Nonetheless, he rallies and requests that "she" join him at the zoo, and Mayakovsky ends the poem with a grand rhetorical flourish, invoking a utopian time of universal comradely compassion:

> With love no more a sorry servant
>   of matrimony,
>   lust
>   and daily bread.

About This served as the centerpiece for the inaugural issue of *LEF* and was issued a few months later in an edition of three thousand—a one-poem pamphlet with Rodchenko's cover and interior photomontages printed on heavy paper and glued into the binding. It was the first such volume illustrated with photomontages, and it kicked off a trend, sending standard graphic illustration into a widespread retreat.

In a trilingual edition published in Berlin in 1994, art historian Aleksandr Lavrent'ev—Rodchenko's grandson—offers a sharp description of the photomontages in *About This*, defining them not merely as literal illustrations but as visual equivalents matching Mayakovsky's themes, motifs, and prismatic formal approach. In *Imagine No Possessions*, Christina Kiaer extends Lavrent'ev's analysis and further elucidates how Mayakovsky and Rodchenko's conflict with *byt* was pursued and embodied in ads executed directly after they collaborated on the poem. They formed a two-man agency called Reklam-Konstruktor (Advertising-Constructor) in the summer of 1923, and the team provided posters and packaging for state-manufactured goods that were not inherently "revolutionary"—caramels, cigarettes, cookies, pacifiers. With contemporary academic lingo breezily partaking of a touch of Soviet earnestness, Kiaer argues that the best of these ads promoted "a more conscious relation to socialist commodity objects" while also presenting "a crisp diagramming of the excess of desire that defines capitalist consumption." Perhaps.

In any case, some eighty years later, capitalist consumption rages on, and the team's advertising work has proved remarkably durable. On any given weekend in lower Manhattan you can find street vendors selling T-shirts featuring non-copyrighted Mayakovsky-Rodchenko designs. And just recently the pop band Franz Ferdinand's latest CD was launched with a Rodchenko homage, a candid rip-off of the poster showing Lili Brik with her amplifying hand held up to a mouthful of remarkably even white teeth, shouting an endorsement for the state-run publishing house.

Rodchenko's collaboration with Mayakovsky had another reverberating consequence. After recruiting Abram Shterenberg to supply photos for his *About This* illustrations, Rodchenko elected to take up a camera himself. His first formal portrait sitting was, in fact, with Mayakovsky in April 1924, a session resulting in a sequence of six images. In the book accompanying a 2001 Rodchenko retrospective at New York's Museum of Modern Art, Peter Galassi deemed "the unadorned directness" of these portraits to be "virtually without precedent in photographic art." It's as if a trained athlete took hold of a baseball bat for the first time and proceeded to slam every pitch out of the park. Rodchenko's subsequent photographic output constitutes one of the glories of the medium.

Rodchenko, Viktor Shklovsky, Mayakovsky, 1926. Rodchenko is credited with originating the shaved-head haircut.

From **a Letter to Lili Brik** (Paris, November 9, 1924)

I terribly want to go to Moscow, if I wasn't ashamed before you and the editorial boards I'd leave today. Although—what is there for me to do in Moscow, I cannot write, and as for who you are and what you are I still have absolutely, absolutely no idea. Because there is really no way to console myself, you are dear to me and I love you, but all the same you are in Moscow and you're either someone else's or not mine. Forgive me—but I feel so wretched.

From Bengt Jangfeldt, ed., *Love Is the Heart of Everything: Correspondence Between Vladimir Mayakovsky and Lili Brik, 1915–1930*, trans. Julian Graffy (Edinburgh: Polygon, 1986).

Lili and Osip Brik, Roman Jakobson, and Mayakovsky, Berlin, 1923

Some Stage Sets for Mayakovsky

RACHEL COHEN

They believed there would be a future reader to whom their life would seem strange, even unknowable. In the play *The Bedbug*, Mayakovsky imagined a Russian like himself but named Prysypkin, who, together with a bedbug, was unfrozen half a century into the future and caged at a future zoo. Mayakovsky said in the stage directions that the cage should look like a standard-issue Soviet apartment: *"In the top of the cage, a lamp with a yellow shade. Above Prysypkin's head, a radiant halo consisting of postcards arranged fanwise."* Prysypkin and the bedbug would live under the light of the yellow lamp, and the people of the future would come to stare. Viktor Shklovsky wrote of how Moscow looked when Mayakovsky first arrived: "Above Moscow ran wires, cutting across the slim necks of the bell towers. The narrow Sobolevak, the prostitutes' quarter, merged with the ring of the Sadovayas. Above it, the streetcar wires crossed their sparks." The future reader would like to be familiar with the places where they lived but feels that they were probably right, that this is unknowable, and she tries not to be an American peering down through the crossed wires at the Moscow zoo.

In Petersburg, before the revolution, Osip and Lili Brik lived on

Zhukovsky Street in an apartment that had an empty doorframe between its rooms, and once Mayakovsky stood in the doorway and leaned against the frame and recited *A Cloud in Pants*. Lili Brik said they had been feeling that "all the poetry around seemed pointless—the wrong people were writing on the wrong subjects in the wrong way," and then, hearing Mayakovsky, "suddenly the right person was writing in the right way about the right subject." Her sister, Elsa Triolet, who had known Mayakovsky first and brought him to the Briks, wrote of the power of Mayakovsky's recitations, "I've only seen one man, I've only seen Mayakovsky 'possess' a room, play with it, tease it, provoke it like a bull, and always make it go where he wanted." Triolet remembered hearing that when Mayakovsky read parts of *A Cloud in Pants* to Maxim Gorky in 1913 or 1914, the older writer was "overcome by the reading, he cried from emotion and joy in front of this discovered genius," and she added a recollection of "the first reading of *War and the Universe* in Lili's apartment, in Petersburg, in 1916. Viktor Shklovsky, weeping, his head resting on the piano, a sort of collective frisson, what troops marching toward the front feel for the drum, that silence hammered by the rhythmic step, the despair, the heart in rags."

At the house on Zhukovsky Street they loved to play cards. Mayakovsky invented games everywhere he went, and always played for money if he could. Triolet told of his taking bets on whether he could throw his cane over the gilded sign on the side of a funeral home in Montmartre. He won: "he had an eye and arm of great precision." When the Briks were really playing cards, they would hang a sign on the door that said "The Briks are not receiving today," and if Gorky came over, he played, too. Mayakovsky was in love with Lili Brik and later would live with the Briks. Shklovsky said:

> We will find, together with mankind, the only simple and happy answer.

That was the way they lived on Zhukyovskaya Street 7. The war went on, dragging us along.

Though Gorky was not a Futurist, Mayakovsky and Shklovsky and Osip Brik all worked for Gorky's journal *The Chronicle*, and at the same time Shklovsky and Brik put together "collections on the theory of poetic language" for the publishing house OMB, which stood for Osip Maksimovich Brik. Around Osip Brik there was always publishing: *A Cloud in Pants*, a single issue of the magazine *Took*, later *LEF* and *New Lef*, where the early stories of Isaac Babel appeared.

Drawn by Mayakovsky, Boris Pasternak began coming to the Briks, too. He had been expected to have a fight with Mayakovsky; everything was arranged by the Novators, a group to which Pasternak belonged, for various arguments about literature and prominence to be decided by a young poets' brawl at a café, but instead Pasternak "watched Mayakovsky uninterruptedly," and by the time they left the café, he "was crazy about Mayakovsky and was already missing him." In this way, "the antagonists we should have annihilated went away unvanquished," and a pattern began: "While he existed creatively," Pasternak wrote, "I spent four years getting used to him and did not succeed." Not long after the February Revolution, Pasternak went to the rooms where Mayakovsky was staying in Moscow: "He was just getting up and as he dressed he read me the new parts of his *War and the Universe*." Thirty years later, Pasternak would write of Mayakovsky's language: "The fragments of Church canticles and lessons are dear to Blok, Mayakovsky, and Esenin in their literal sense, as fragments of everyday life, in the same way as the street, the house, and any words of colloquial speech are dear to them." Mayakovsky, coauthor of the Futurist manifesto "A Slap in the Face of Public Taste"—who entered the public eye tromping onstage in an orange shirt to recite under a suspended piano—might have objected to being included in this list of gentler poets: Aleksandr Blok, a Symbolist he meant to overthrow, and Sergei Esenin, lyricist of village Russia, whom Mayakovsky saw as a rival.

"Mayakovsky entered the Revolution as he would his own home," was how Shklovsky saw it. In 1917 the Briks moved to a six-room apartment on the same staircase in Zhukovsky Street. Mayakovsky, filming in Moscow, used to visit Petersburg, and he brought Lili Brik a rug with an embroidered scene of ducks on it. Shklovsky described how OPOYAZ, the organization of the Formalists, had its first meeting in the Briks' old apartment, "the abandoned apartment in Zhukovsky Street. We used books to make a fire, but it was cold and Pyast kept his feet in the oven." OPOYAZ met every week "in virtual darkness, by the light of the tiny round yellow flame of a night lamp."

At this time the Futurists and the Formalists were close, even overlapping, and they and the Acmeists were all in fairly respectful rebellion against the Symbolists, Blok and Andrei Bely. The Acmeists—chiefly Osip Mandelstam, Anna Akhmatova, and her husband, Nikolay Gumilyev, shot in 1921 by Soviet authorities for alleged counterrevolutionary acts—had as their earliest slogan "Down with Symbolism! Long live the living rose!" Mandelstam wanted the handmade poetry of Acmeism to resist the great mechanizing sweep of Futurism, explaining that they hoped for "a man-centered poetry and poetics, with man as master of his own home, not man flattened into a wafer by the horrors of pseudo-Symbolism." Acmeism understood "the warmth of the hearth experienced as something sacred."

But these differences might not have been decisive. Nadezhda Mandelstam remembered the Symbolists welcoming the Futurists with open arms; Pasternak saw Blok listening with great joy to Mayakovsky's recitation. And, as Nadezhda Mandelstam wrote in *Hope Abandoned*, "When Mayakovski came to Petersburg in 1912 or so, he struck up a friendship with M. [Mandelstam], but they were quickly separated and dragged off in opposite directions." Before the revolution, the poets staged battles, but later these opposite directions grew more irrevocable; she felt, and events bore her out, that Osip Brik was one of the first to see that after the revolution there would be official recognition for only one of the groups, and he "fought for this monopoly against numerous competitors."

Petersburg was more the home of the Acmeists, Moscow of the Futurists. In Petersburg in about 1920 many people took up residence in what Shklovsky remembered as "a large building that overlooked the Moyka, the Nevsky and the Morskaya." What they called the House of the Arts was in the dining room; Shklovsky and Pyast lived downstairs, and "Mayakovsky stayed in the big library when he came to town; the library had red bookcases with green glass doors, and very few books." Once, Mayakovsky read poems in this library, and when an old servant, Yefim, who had worked there before the revolution, brought in tea, Mayakovsky said, "Say, your people can't write that way, can they?" But, as Shklovsky told the story, "Yefim had been thoroughly and personally trained by the poets" and said, " 'Personally, Vladimir Vladimirovich, I prefer the Acmeists.' And he made his exit with great dignity." That evening Mayakovsky heard the Acmeist ballads and liked them.

In Moscow, Mayakovsky had a study on Lubyansky Passage. Across the passage were two men who had a razor, a Gillette razor, and Mayakovsky would go over in the morning to borrow it. Elsa Triolet stayed in the room in Lubyansky Passage in 1925, when Mayakovsky was traveling to Mexico and the United States and Paris. She described it: "a single window onto the courtyard, the paper on the walls dark, like the great desk perpendicular to the window, the light to the left, and a narrow cot, covered by a black, slippery oilcloth. The place was warm and harsh, and it always smelled a little of a grocery." This room, which Mayakovsky called his "boat," was also where they held the meetings of the Moscow Linguistic Circle (in Moscow the home of Formalism, as OPOYAZ was its home in Petersburg). Shklovsky remembered:

> A small narrow room that looked like a blunt-nosed boat, and a fireplace.
>
> This was the little boat in which Mayakovsky was sailing.
>
> An unhappy little boat.
>
> There in the fireplace, I burned up cornices and the cases of the butterfly collection, but still did not get warm.

Most of the time, Mayakovsky lived with the Briks on Poluektov Lane, which was also the headquarters for *LEF* magazine. Shklovsky, who had an architectural mind, said, "The entrance was from the yard, if my memory does not betray me, in a white separate wing of the building. A white wing, three steps, a staircase, and next to the staircase, a red-haired dog called Shchen [puppy]." The Briks thought that Mayakovsky and this dog, a red-haired setter, were like each other, and when Mayakovsky wrote to the Briks, he drew a little picture at the end of the letter and signed "Shchen." For *LEF*, Mayakovsky and Brik made a list of the Futurists and included Mayakovsky, Esenin, Pasternak, Khlebnikov, and Brik. Clarifying his dissociation, Pasternak said, "In spite of my announcement about my resignation from *LEF* and my ceasing to be a member of their circle, my name continued to appear among the names of contributors." In the list, Mayakovsky and Brik did not put Shklovsky, who had been a Futurist but was now more a Formalist and did not always agree with LEF's positions, writing, "*LEF* erred in its theory and spoke in a contrived, conspiratorial language; it spoke about art as though apologizing for it, as though justifying itself." By this time, "Brik was against prose and against poetry. / He said things like: 'Poetry is not needed, anyway.' "

Censorship was not only in the streets but inside their apart-

Lili Brik and Mayakovsky in the Crimea, 1926

ments. The revolutionary Victor Serge—who was friendly with Mayakovsky and especially with Esenin—wrote, "Multiple censoring deformed and killed books. First, before taking a manuscript to the publisher, the writer brought together his friends, read them his work, and we all asked ourselves together if certain pages would 'pass.' " In Nadezhda Mandelstam's account, confirmed by Edward Brown's study of Mayakovsky, "Brik had turned his apartment into a place where his colleagues in the Cheka (including Agronov) could meet with writers and sound out public opinion." Agronov was one of the Briks' connections in the GUP, the precursor to the KGB; these connections were helpful later in getting Osip Brik's defense of Mayakovsky onto Stalin's desk. Nadezhda Mandelstam thought the name "internal émigré," which Brik came up with for her husband and Akhmatova, "played an important part in their subsequent fate."

Is it necessary to remember that the red-haired dog named Shchen was at Poluektov Lane? Yes, because at that time Esenin was still alive, as he was when the Briks and Mayakovsky found their two rooms in Vodopyany Lane. Shklovsky: "Directly at the entrance, to the left stood the piano, and on the piano—a telephone." The telephone was communal, so the tenants in the rear "could quietly listen to the conversations between Lubyansky Passage and Vodopyany Lane." Esenin hanged himself in 1925 at the Hotel d'Angleterre, having written with blood from his wrists his last lines:

> Dying is nothing new in this life
> But then, living is nothing new either.

Victor Serge: "We carried, through the night and the snow, the body of Sergei Esenin. It was not an era of dreams and lyricism." After the suicide, Mayakovsky wrote a poem that seemed to some to elbow Esenin out of the way:

Dying
in this life
is not hard.
Making life
is much harder.

Farther into the poem are the poet's fear of his own suicidal inclinations and a tenderness that finds its way into Esenin's last room:

Maybe
if there'd been ink
in that room in the Angleterre,
You wouldn't have had to
cut open
your veins.

Mayakovsky and the Briks left Vodopyany Lane; he traveled. Elsa Triolet last saw him in a hotel room in Paris in 1929. "I remember how, sitting on the ground, a pad of paper balanced on the bed, he was writing letters to Moscow. Have you noticed how children always choose the most uncomfortable position in which to read or write? They stay for hours in a position that they seem to have taken just for an instant . . . Mayakovsky was like that."

In Moscow, Pasternak did not come to the Briks anymore. Shklovsky:

> They started on Pasternak.
> For a long time, Mayakovsky had loved Pasternak.
> Pasternak broke away.
> "They've snatched one," said Mayakovsky.

These divisive forces, never named, seem to have become almost part of the air. Gorky and Mayakovsky were separated, too, though,

Shklovsky said, "it was impossible to alienate Gorky and Mayakovsky on literary grounds. Gorky had said that *150,000,000* was a titanic work." Shklovsky wrote about Gorky and Mayakovsky—the brackets are the cuts of the censors of the 1964 edition: "Had they been together [not in the museums but in life] both would have been happier [and the course of the history of Soviet literature would have been different]."

At the end, the Briks and Mayakovsky moved to Gendrikov Lane. In her memoirs, Lili Brik described this apartment: "The principle according to which the flat was decorated was the same one that had been used for the printing of the first edition of *A Cloud*—nothing superfluous." They left the walls bare except for two blankets Mayakovsky had brought back from Mexico and the embroidered ducks. Lili Brik: "There was a bath, which we had been deprived of for so long, and which we loved as if it were a living creature. It was so small that it's amazing that Vladimir Vladimirovich could get into it." This house was the last literary salon of the Briks. Shklovsky "quarreled with L. Brik in the house on Gendrikov Lane about some utterly petty nonsense . . . Literary salons no longer had a reason to exist. We were unaware of this and constantly cross with one another." Later, this house was made into a Mayakovsky museum, and later still, when it was important for the purity of the revolution to establish the legend of Mayakovsky apart from the Jewish Briks, this museum was moved to the Lubyansky Passage, where it took up four floors.

Shklovsky remembered "a striped wool Mexican scarf in soft colors" hanging near Mayakovsky's body in Lubyansky Passage, when Mayakovsky shot himself. Pasternak came then and saw how all along the staircase people were "hurled and splashed against the walls by the destructive force of the event." Pasternak could not weep until he heard again the voice he knew in the grieving of Mayakovsky's sister: "Mayakovsky's own voice cried out indignantly, strangely transmuted by his sister's contralto. 'To make it more amusing. They laughed. They called for him—And this is what was happening to him. Why didn't you come to us, Volodya?' "

Even after the end, in the worst of the thirties, the Mandelstams went to the Shklovskys' apartment. Nadezhda Mandelstam remembered what Shklovsky said when the family was assigned an apartment in a new building for writers: " 'Now,' he said to the other lucky persons who had been allotted space in the same building, 'we must pray God there won't be a revolution.' He couldn't have said a truer word: they had achieved the height of good fortune and wanted nothing more than to make the best of it." The Shklovskys' apartment was "the only place where we felt like human beings again." If the Shklovskys were away when they arrived, the children would invite them into the kitchen and feed them and tell them about their schoolwork and the birds the son Nikita kept in his room:

> He told us that songbirds always learned to sing from certain older birds that were particularly good at it. In the Kursk region, once famous for its nightingales, the best songsters had all been caught, and young birds had no way of learning any more. The Kursk "school" of nightingales was thus destroyed because of the selfish people who had put the best songsters in cages.

It was dangerous to open the door to the Mandelstams in the 1930s, and they stayed away to try to protect their friends, but Viktor's wife, Vasilisa Shklovsky, cried tears of joy when they came again.

They lived in small, cold rooms through the Russian winters; they drank coffee made from grilled barley. Specialists in Persian literature found ways of frying horsemeat in soap. Mayakovsky had liked cigars when he could get them. Acmeism was an apartment with a window that looked out on an imagined green and blue landscape from Italy, and an old library with very few books; Futurism was a house with a red-haired dog, a Mexican blanket, and thin paper for printing magazines. At the home of Formalism they burned butterfly cases, and even the exiled felt cheerful. There are dark shapes building fires, there seem to be people painting on the floor, but looking again, the rooms are empty. Later, there were very few of them left.

SOURCES

Brik, Lili, and Vladimir Mayakovsky. *Love Is the Heart of Everything: Correspondence Between Vladimir Mayakovsky and Lili Brik, 1915–1930*. Edited by Bengt Jangfeldt, translated by Julian Graffy. Edinburgh: Polygon, 1986.

Brown, Edward J. *Mayakovsky: A Poet in the Revolution*. Princeton, N.J.: Princeton University Press, 1973. [Translations of poems by Esenin and Mayakovsky included here are Edward Brown's.]

Mandelstam, Nadezhda. *Hope Abandoned*. Translated by Max Hayward. New York: Atheneum, 1974.

———. *Hope Against Hope*. Translated by Max Hayward. New York: Modern Library, 1999.

Mandelstam, Osip. *The Complete Prose of Osip Mandelstam*. Edited by Jane Gary Harris, translated by Jane Gary Harris and Constance Link. Ann Arbor, Mich.: Ardis, 1979.

Mayakovsky, Vladimir. *The Complete Plays of Vladimir Mayakovsky*. Translated by Guy Daniels. New York: Washington Square Press, 1968.

Pasternak, Boris. *I Remember: Sketch for an Autobiography*. Translated with a preface and notes by David Magarshack. Cambridge: Harvard University Press, 1983.

———. *Safe Conduct: An Autobiography and Other Writings*. Translated by Robert Payne. New York: New Directions, 1958.

Serge, Victor. *Memoires d'un revolutionnaire et autres ecrits politiques, 1908–1947*. Edited and annotated by Jean Riere and Jil Silberstein. Paris: Robert Laffont, 2001. Translated to English by Rachel Cohen.

Shklovsky, Viktor. *Mayakovsky and His Circle*. Translated and edited by Lily Feiler. London: Pluto Press, 1974.

Triolet, Elsa. *Malakovsky: poète russe*. Paris: Pierre Seghers, 1945. Translated to English by Rachel Cohen.

Osip and Lili Brik and Mayakovsky, Moscow, 1929

From *Mayakovsky* (1965)

HERBERT MARSHALL

1925, May

Mayakovsky first broadcast his poems over the Moscow Radio. When he entered he pointed to the microphone and said: “Are there many listeners?” The reply was: “the whole world.” Mayakovsky answered, “Well, I don’t need any more.”

From *Mayakovsky*, ed. and trans. Herbert Marshall (New York: Hill and Wang, 1965).

Mayakovsky reading from *Very Good!*, commemorating the tenth anniversary of the October Revolution, October 24, 1927

Passionate Machines

VAL VINOKUR

Comparing Mayakovsky to, say, Eminem, can yield more than a glib generalization about the rappable *physicality* of Mayakovsky's verse. The two share not only a grandiose and overexposed lyrical sensibility but also a relentlessly mechanical style. They are passionate machines. There is nothing "free" about the way either of them composes or recites. Listen to Mayakovsky's recordings. His pronunciation and cadence are so deliberate, his references so precise and even arcane. Eminem's lyrics—internally and multisyllabically rhymed, often mechanical anapests—sound like rhythmic by-products, the syllables sticking out like gear teeth. "I have become a human machine," declares Volodia, the insufferable young Communist superman in *Envy*, Yuri Olesha's satirical novella of Moscow in the 1920s. But Mayakovsky's Futurist verse and Eminem's "verses" suggest that we have always been human machines, our hearts and lungs driving us beyond our senses and reason.

From ***How Are Verses Made?*** (1926)

I walk along, waving my arms and mumbling almost wordlessly, now shortening my steps so as not to interrupt my mumbling, now mumbling more rapidly in time with my steps.

So the rhythm is trimmed and takes shape—and rhythm is the basis for any poetic work, resounding through the whole thing. Gradually, individual words begin to ease themselves free of this dull roar.

Several words just jump away and never come back, others hold on, wriggle and squirm a dozen times over, until you can't imagine how any word will ever stay in its place (this sensation, developing with experience, is called talent) . . .

Where this basic dull roar of a rhythm comes from is a mystery. In my case it's all kinds of repetitions in my mind of noises, rocking motions, or in fact any phenomena with which I can associate a sound. The sound of the sea, endlessly repeated, can provide my rhythm, or a servant who slams the door every morning, recurring and intertwining with itself, trailing through my consciousness, or even the rotation of the earth, which in my case, as in a shop of visual aids, gives way to and inextricably connects with the whistle of a high wind.

Rhythm is the fundamental force, the fundamental energy of verse. You can't explain it, you can only talk about it as you do about magnetism and electricity. The rhythm can be the same in a lot of poems, even in the whole oeuvre of the poet, and still not make the work monotonous, because a rhythm can be so complex, so intricately shaped, that even several long poems won't exhaust its possibilities . . .

It's a good idea to write a poem about the first of May in November or December, when you feel a desperate need for May.

In order to write about the tenderness of love, take Bus No. 7 from Lubyansky Square to Nogin Square. The appalling jolting will serve to throw into relief for you, better than anything else, the charm of a life transformed. A shake-up is essential, for the purposes of transformation.

Vladimir Mayakovsky, *How Are Verses Made?* trans. G. M. Hyde (London: Jonathan Cape, 1970).

Brooklyn Bridge (1925)

Hey, Coolidge,
shout for joy!
I've got to hand
it to you—
with compliments
that will make you blush
like my country's flag
no matter how United
States of America
you may be!
As a madman
enters a church
or retreats
to a monastery,
pure and austere,
so I,
in the haze
of evening
humbly approach
the Brooklyn Bridge.
Like a conqueror
with cannons
tall as giraffes
entering a besieged
city, so, drunk
with glory,

Mayakovsky in New York City, 1925

higher than a kite,
I cross
the Brooklyn Bridge.
Like a painter
whose smitten eyes pierce
a museum Madonna
through the glass of a frame,
so I look at New York
through the Brooklyn Bridge
and see the sky and the stars.
New York,
hot and humid
until night,
has now forgotten
the daily fight,
and only the souls
of houses rise
in the serene
sheen of windows.
Here the hum
of the El
can hardly be heard,
and only by this hum,
soft but stubborn,
can you sense the trains
crawling
with a rattle
as when dishes clatter
in a cupboard.
And when from below,
a merchant transports sugar
from the factory bins,

the masts
passing under the bridge
are no bigger than pins.
I'm proud of just this
mile of steel.
My living visions here
stand tall:
a fight for structure over style,
the calculus of beams of steel.
If the end of the world should come,
wiping out the earth,
and all that remains
is this bridge,
then, as little bones, fine as needles,
are assembled into dinosaurs
in museums,
so from this bridge
the geologists of the future
will reconstruct
our present age.
They will say:
This paw of steel
linked seas and prairies.
From here,
Europe rushed to the West, scattering
Indian feathers
to the wind.
This rib
reminds us of a machine—
imagine having the strength,
while standing
with one steel leg
in Manhattan,

to pull Brooklyn
toward you
by the lip!
By these cables and wires
I know we have retired
the age of coal and steam.
Here people screamed
on the radio,
or flew in planes.
For some life was a picnic;
for others a prolonged
and hungry howl.
From here desperate men
jumped to their deaths
in the river.
And finally I see—
Here stood Mayakovsky,
composing verse, syllable by syllable.
I look at you
as an Eskimo admires a train.
I stick to you
as a tick to an ear.
Brooklyn Bridge,
you're really something, aren't you?

Adapted by David Lehman (with assistance from Val Vinokur)

To Sergei Esenin (1926)

You have gone,
(as they say)
to a Better World.
Bullshit.
Built yourself
a stairway to the stars, didn't you?
No more publishers'
advances, no more bars.
Sobered up at last.

No, Esenin, this isn't a joke.
There's a lump of grief in my throat.
I can see you with your slit wrists
slinging up your bundle of bones.

STOP IT!
Come off it!
Are you crazy or what?
Smearing your cheeks with dead-white chalk?
You, who could do things with words
no one in the world
could do!
WHY? WHAT FOR?
None of us understands.
The critics
mutter:
"The reasons are these or
maybe those,

but mostly he didn't have enough rapport
with the working classes
because he drank too much beer and wine."
Fine.
Only what they mean is if you'd given up your artsy friends
for workers that would have been a good influence and you
would have been saved.

What the hell do you think
workers drink?
Lemonade?

What they mean is,
you'd have gotten a party-poet
assigned to your case, and output
would have outweighed
poetry:
you'd have had to write a hundred lines
a day, as dull and dopey
as the rest of them.

Before I'd have gone through
anything that dumb I'd have laid
hands on myself too.
Better to die of vodka—
if it was boredom, it's worse.

Neither that noose
or that knife
reveals the depth
of our loss. If the Angleterre had only had some ink,
you wouldn't have had to cut open
your veins.

Your imitators loved it. Encore!
A bunch of them
have done themselves in already.
What for?
Why increase the number of suicides?
Why not just increase the production of ink?
Your tongue is stopped in your mouth forever.
It's stupid,
uncalled for
to make things mysterious.
The word-workers' roaring
debauchee-in-training
is dead . . .
There's a lot to do
just to keep up.
First we have to remake life,
then we can write
poems about it.
These days are hard for the pen
and the poem—
But when,
where,
what great man
ever chose a path already beaten down
and easy?
Words are commanders
of humanity armies—
Forward, march!
Let time tear past us
like rocket shells
blazing in the air!
Let it carry away
to days gone by

only the wind
as it ruffles our hair.
Our planet
was poorly designed
for happiness.
We must snatch delight
from days to come.

In this life, death is not so hard.
To build new life, that's harder.

Translated by Paul Schmidt

From *The Stray Dog Cabaret: A Book of Russian Poems* (New York: New York Review Books, 2007).

From ***I, Myself***

'25

I finished the novel in my head, but never transferred it to paper, because while finishing it, was penetrated with disgust for the imagined and began demanding from myself that it be based on names and facts. Actually, this is also true for '26 and '27.

'26

I consciously try to be more of a newspaper journalist in my work. Article, headline. The poets ramble, but they can't write concise journalism, they just publish in socially irresponsible supplements. For me their lyrical bullshit is laughable, since it's so easy to do this sort of thing and no one takes any interest in it except their spouses.

Write for *Izvestia*, *Trudie*, *Rabochie Moskve*, *Zare Vostoka*, *Bakinskim Rabochiem* and others.

My second job—continuing in the interrupted tradition of minstrels and troubadours. Go from town to town giving readings. Novocherkassk, Vinnitsa, Kharkov, Paris, Rostov, Tiflis, Berlin, Kazan, Tula, Prague, Leningrad, Moscow, Voronezh, Yalta, Eupatoria, Vyatka, Ufa, etc. etc. etc.

Mayakovsky on the Road: Travels to North America

CHRISTOPHER EDGAR

Mayakovsky's experience during his three-month stay in Mexico and the United States in the late summer of 1925 must be cobbled together from disparate sources, of which the poet's own *My Discovery of America* figures as the most intriguing, richly detailed, and ultimately incomplete. This book, read alongside other accounts, provides a fascinating portal into the complexities of Mayakovsky's psyche and, by extension, the forces of change with which he was grappling.

By 1925 Mayakovky's literary fame had reached a zenith. He published widely in journals, and the State Publishing House had recently made a commitment to issue his collected works. The "handsome 22-year-old" of *A Cloud in Pants* had turned thirty, but he still cut a dashing figure, if one broader in girth and sometimes haggard in complexion. Indeed, the Mayakovskian persona, in public and in print, had swelled to near-mythological proportions. He was a figure of undeniable magnetism, an amalgam of colorful contradictions and extremes. As a writer who refused any connection with Russian poetry of the past, he adored Pushkin. A performer who could charm the most skeptical audience with his deep bass voice and sharp tongue, he could often be found, moments later, sitting gloomily in a corner. He was a rake wrapped around the finger of one woman (Lili Brik), and a lover of dogs harboring a deep dislike of children. These contrary sides of his personality often coexisted in a delicate balance, as exemplified by Roman Jakobson's description of Mayakovsky the gambler:

> Mayakovsky played fantastically, but was terribly nervous during the game. He would win; he was able to do so particularly at poker, a psychological game. He would clean out his opponent often. But afterwards—I was witness to this on several occasions . . . —he would walk up and down the room weeping, so overwrought were his nerves.

If tightly wound, Mayakovsky seemed to neutralize the discords within by subjugating all else to the twin pillars of his universe: Lili Brik and the revolution.

Abruptly, though, the sure footing these foundations provided had begun to slip. After the death of Lenin in 1924, the relative liberalism of the New Economic Policy would be cut short. The climate that allowed the great flowering of avant-garde experiment was vanishing. On a more personal plane, in the spring of 1925 Mayakovsky's ten-year affair with the capricious Lili had arrived at a cul-de-sac. The pair had made a pact to end the relationship if it showed signs of stagnation. "It seems to me that you love me far less, and I won't allow you to grow dull," Lili had written, and on her cue, they decided to end the affair. In practice, things changed little—Mayakovsky continued to share a Moscow apartment and a dacha in Pushkino with Lili and Osip Brik—yet to the poet, who had agreed to a platonic relationship with resignation, it must have seemed that prospects for a future with Lili were growing dim.

All the same, Mayakovsky was entering a new phase in his career: a grueling schedule of lectures and readings—long tours

Mayakovsky in Mexico, 1925

through Ukraine, the Crimea, the Urals, always under difficult traveling conditions—would leave him exhausted, his vocal cords strained. Perhaps more troubling was the fact that his public stature entailed a loss of creative freedom. The revolution was by necessity ongoing, and revolutionary poetry required appropriate subjects, presented with aggressive clarity. The mixed reception of *About This* (1923), the long, prismatic poem dedicated to Lili that was in many ways an attempt to resurrect the experimental lyricism of his earlier work, might have given Mayakovsky an inkling of what was to come. Soon he would be forced to disband LEF, his credentials as a proletarian writer would come under attack, and detractors would denounce his work as "anarcho-individualist." By 1925 he was feeling the strain, and travel—specifically, travel abroad—provided an outlet.

Since his early Futurist days, Mayakovsky had a keen desire to witness the world's most industrialized and modern society firsthand, particularly the skyscrapers, subways, and crowded streets of Manhattan. He was a fan of American movies, and Jack London and Walt Whitman had won his approval. (Whitman's Russian translator, Kornei Chukovsky, was impressed by Mayakovsky's enthusiasm for Whitman's verse, some of which he could recite from memory: "He singled out [those lines] nearest to his own heart at the time, e.g., 'The scent of armpits, aroma finer than prayer . . .' Mayakovsky asked me about Whitman's life, and it looked as if he were measuring it against his own.") The cartoonlike exoticism of America—land of cowboys, tycoons, Indians, flappers, gumshoes, and gangsters—likewise held great appeal for him. As it had for the Russian giant Ivan in Mayakovsky's *150,000,000*, America represented for the poet a political, social, and cultural rival that had to be vanquished.

Embarking on his transatlantic voyage, Mayakovsky ditched plans for a novel he'd been contemplating and set to work in a form that was new but natural to him: the travel journal. The resulting book is, like its author, a vivid, volatile mix of diverging aims and motives—one mostly sympathetic but at times difficult to swallow. Plainly an effort to wow the Soviet public with travel sketches à la Mark Twain, at once wide-eyed and satiric, *My Discovery of America* is also an unabashed propaganda tract. It would be fair to say that Mayakovsky, by dint of personality, was more successful as a caustic raconteur than as an authoritative reporter; his deployment of facts was decidedly cavalier. When asked, during a visit to Prague, why he loved to travel, Mayakovsky had answered, "Because of the details," but the problem with his travel book lies, ironically, in the willfully erratic choice of details.

The first half of *My Discovery of America* describes, in leisurely fashion, Mayakovsky's indirect journey to the United States: a crossing by boat (the *Espagne*) from Le Havre to Havana to Veracruz; then, by train, a visit to Mexico City before continuing to the border town of Laredo and, eventually, New York. Of the sea voyage, he reported on impromptu boxing matches between passengers, and rising tensions among the *Espagne*'s first, second, and third classes. A Cuban rainstorm occasions a jaunty aphoristic description: "What is rain? It is air with streaks of water. What is tropical rain? It is solid water with streaks of air." But perhaps the most striking detail in this early part of the book is the buried fact that Mayakovsky, poet of proletarian revolution, was traveling in first class.

His twenty-four-hour stay in Havana provided a brush with poverty, Prohibition, and Yankee hegemony, while serving up ample evidence of the harsh divide between rich and poor. Mayakovsky was fascinated by billboards for whiskeys: King George, White Horse, and Black & White—the latter providing the title for one of his poems. Exploring Havana's backstreets, Mayakovsky lost his way and befriended a street urchin who proudly declared himself a Bolshevik, prompting the two of them to break into a Communist anthem.

In Mexico City, Mayakovsky stayed with Diego Rivera and Frida Kahlo, but does not say much about them in *My Discovery*; in Laredo he obtained a U.S. visa and, after a celebratory night drinking with Russian émigrés, boarded a train at San Antonio bound for New York City.

Indeed, when Mayakovsky takes in New York for the first time, *My Discovery* momentarily catches fire. His bedazzled impressions of Manhattan were decidedly those of the innocent abroad and, to his home audience, must have read like science fiction. Mayakovsky was awed by the height of the buildings, the size of the crowds, the fact that one could travel horizontally and vertically, by subway or elevator, local and express. (Moscow in the 1920s was, after all, a city with trams and cars but no tall buildings or subway.) He was especially taken by the grid pattern of Manhattan streets, with its one iconoclastic diagonal:

> At six or seven, Broadway lights up. This is my favorite street, which, among streets and avenues that are straight as prison bars, is the only one that cuts, capriciously and insolently, across the others. To lose one's way in New York is more difficult than in Tula. Avenues run north–south, streets east–west. That's all you need to know . . .
>
> Lights do not go on all along the entire twenty-five-mile-long Broadway (here a man is not going to say, "Please drop by; we're neighbors, we both live on Broadway"), but only from 25th to 50th Streets, especially at Times Square—this is what Americans call the Great White Way.
>
> It really is white and impresses one that it is brighter at night than in the daytime, because there is light everywhere in the daytime, but this White Way, against the backdrop of the black night, is bright as day. The lights of street lamps, the jumping light of the advertisements, the glow of windows on

> shops that never close, the lights illuminating huge billboards, the lights from the marquees of cinemas and theaters, the rushing lights of automobiles and trolley buses, the lights of the subway trains glittering under one's feet through the glass pavements, the lights of inscriptions in the sky.
>
> Brightness, brightness, brightness.*

He can't play the neophyte for long, though, and soon assumes the air of an old hand:

> If you need an office, there's no need to rack one's brains over it.
>
> You just telephone any old thirty-story office building.
>
> "Hello. I need a six-room office, ready tomorrow. Twelve typists. A sign:
>
> Renowned and Esteemed Purveyor of Compressed Air for Pacific Submarines. Two boys in brown liveries—caps with starred ribbons, and 20,000 blank invoices with letterhead. Goodbye."
>
> The next day when you arrive, the two reception boys will greet you excitedly, "How do you do, Mister Mayakovsky."

After these initial excited encounters with Manhattan's Brave New World, however, *My Discovery* devolves into an excoriation of capitalism, occasionally perceptive, sometimes pat, and often hyperbolic. Only on Sundays, Mayakovsky writes, do the exhausted wage slaves in dingy bedsits have time to eat a real breakfast, after which the only available diversions are loitering by Grant's Tomb, escorting the missus to an automat, or taking a day trip to Coney Island, which the poet found positively macabre. Subjects for extended diatribes include the pervasiveness of racism (the Ku Klux Klan rules

*Translated by Christopher Edgar, as are all further translations within this piece.

the New York docks, as the Masons preside over Philadelphia) and the ingrained worship of the American dollar—"God is the dollar, the dollar is the Son, the dollar is the Holy Spirit."

According to *My Discovery of America*, the poet had no regrets when his three-month stay came to an end. Leaving New York Harbor on the *Rochambeau*, Mayakovsky rejoiced at the last sight of the Woolworth Building and the rest of the skyline. He was gladder still to reach the other side of the Atlantic. European soil was a far cry from home, but infinitely preferable to what he had come from:

> In comparison with America, [the houses] were wretched hovels. Every inch of land was the product of centuries of struggle, exhausted by centuries of a chemist's myopia for growing violets and salad greens. But even the contemptibleness of the homes and plots of land, each subject to centuries of feudal servitude, seemed to me incredibly cultured when compared with the bivouac-like growth and selfish character of American life.

Thus Mayakovsky returns home the victor, having said what he needed to say while playing his cards close to the vest. One of the great oddities of Mayakovsky's account is the fact that after he boards the train in San Antonio, all other people disappear. He makes no mention of his ostensive reason for his trip—the series of public readings and lectures he gave in New York and other cities—let alone who helped organize these events, whom he met, who fed and lodged him.

But there is a far more personal history of the poet in New York—a slim volume titled *Mayakovsky in Manhattan: A Love Story with Excerpts from the Memoirs of Elly Jones*, published in 1993—that reveals Mayakovsky's New York stay as far more social than the poet cared to admit. Three of his key contacts had gathered at the

Mayakovsky reunited with David Burliuk in New York, 1925. The boys are Burliuk's sons.

dock on East Fourteenth Street to see him off: Charles Recht, an American lawyer with Russian clients and socialist sympathies; David Burliuk, his old cohort from Futurist days, who had emigrated to the United States via Japan and was now living with his family in the Bronx; and Elly Jones, a tall twenty-year-old brunette, the daughter of Russian Mennonite parents. (Jones was living alone, partially supported by an English ex-husband, and working on occasion as a showroom model.)

Mayakovsky and Jones met at a party held in his honor at Charles Recht's East Side apartment during Mayakovsky's first week in Manhattan. Despite being warned of the towering Russian's reputation as a womanizer, Jones found herself next to him on the sofa. In a loquacious mood, Mayakovsky fetched her a drink, facetiously told her he was married, asked for her phone number, and invited her to join him for dinner. Jones awoke in the wee hours of the morning to find herself still in the company of Mayakovsky and her friend Lydia—in Mayakovsky's Fifth Avenue apartment. Allergic to alcohol, she had passed out. Mayakovsky suggested a taxi ride to the Brooklyn Bridge: "New York taxis must be prepared for anything—even taking a Russian poet and two Russian girls to the Brooklyn Bridge in the middle of the night."

Jones remembered how ecstatic he was, striding across the mile-long span in the moonlight. The night walk inspired the best of Mayakovsky's New World poems, "Brooklyn Bridge." To a photograph of himself on the bridge (taken later, in daylight) he added the inscription "Mayakovsky and the Brooklyn Bridge, with feelings of kinship."

The Mayakovsky-Jones romance was soon on the ascendancy. Elly decided to rent an apartment on East Twelfth Street to be closer to him. She would later write:

> I'm sure that in all his life he never had three months of complete freedom and the devotion of one woman. When we first

> knew each other, he said, "Let's just live for each other. This time, let's keep it to ourselves. It doesn't concern anybody. Just you and me."

This proved an impossibility, however. Money was tight. There were no admission charges for Mayakovsky's readings, the poet was not directly compensated, and Jones had to pursue her modeling work. Of Mayakovsky's ongoing public appearances, she wrote:

> He gave two big lectures. The first time was in a sort of East Side ballroom. There were a lot of young people. There must have been an awful lot of people in New York who knew Russian. As soon as he came in they began to sing the "Internationale," and he said, "Tovarishchi, tovarishchi, please. Please. Please. I had such trouble getting a visa. This must not turn into a political meeting."

In reality, Mayakovsky's presentations—which took the poet to Chicago, Pittsburgh, Detroit, Cleveland, and Philadelphia—were entirely political. They were also virtually the same at each venue. Mayakovsky would read a few agitprop poems such as "Our March" and then expound upon the virtues and greater equality of Soviet life. As might be predicted, the appraisal of the Chicago paper *Ruskii Vestnik* (*Russian Herald*) was shared by many:

> In older, better days all we knew about Mayakovsky was that he was a Futurist. Now we know that under the guise of literary lectures he is merely a propagandist for Soviet development and the glories of Soviet life.

Mayakovsky struck the pose that he couldn't care less about what his audiences thought. He even displayed open contempt for his promoters—most often Russian-Jewish trade unionists—whom he termed "the small fry." When one promoter addressed the audience in Yiddish, Mayakovsky commandeered the podium and launched into a torrent of Georgian, which caused an uproar once the baffled crowd realized that he had no intention of stopping. But this only underscores the poet's failure to connect with his American audiences, whether Russian or native-born, and seems an effort to conceal a wounded sense of pride.

A rift arose between Mayakovsky and Jones when Elly chanced upon a telegram from Lili Brik: "Where have you disappeared to? Write about how you are. With whom you are doesn't matter. I want to go to Italy. Arrange for me to get money." Elly was devastated. Mayakovsky explained about the "wife" to whom he was not actually married, and about Osip and all the rest. His words must have elicited some sympathy, as Elly would later write:

> He had been brought up by women. His mother and sisters idolized him. Perhaps that's why women were always so important in his life—some as lovers, and some as just friends. But to those on intimate terms with him, he was by nature tender, considerate, and caring.

Mayakovsky wired all the money he could to Lili and booked passage (third class, this time) on the next available ship to Europe. According to Elly, she and Mayakovsky made love the night before his departure. The next day, Elly, Burliuk, and Recht watched the *Rochambeau* set off without being able to board and say goodbye—the poet did not venture down the gangplank.

From Le Havre, Mayakovsky traveled directly to Berlin to meet Lili, who was returning from her Italian travels. He reserved rooms at the Hotel Kurfürsten, where they had shared happy times on previous visits. According to Lili, who described the reunion in an unpublished memoir (retold by her chronicler V. V. Katanian), Mayakovsky greeted her at the station in a tweed jacket "with an unprecedented chamois tie, dapper and radiant." Their hotel room was filled with flowers, and Mayakovsky lavished gifts on her from Mexico (wooden toys), Havana (colored cigarettes), and New York (a travel iron). The reunion was emotional on both sides, but Lili had resolved beforehand to keep some distance.

Upon their return to Moscow, Mayakovsky found lodgings of his own, apart from the Briks. His relationship with Lili remained close but was never the same. She would pursue other lovers, and he would follow suit. Soon Mayakovsky was on the road again, lecturing about the deficiencies of the United States and, within two months, reading from *My Discovery of America.* Published in record time after his return, his travel journal would receive very mixed reviews, particularly from more "proletarian" quarters. Among other things, the book was derided, perhaps not unfairly, as *khaltura* (hackwork) by dint of both the haste of its publication and public knowledge that the poet was well paid for it. This would prove a foretaste of things to come.

The New York interlude would have a rather more poignant epilogue. Before leaving New York, Mayakovsky told Jones to write to him care of his sister—he was worried that his mail would be read. Despite sending many letters, Elly received no reply. But she remained undeterred. Three years later she wrote to Mayakovsky that she would be in France that summer, and he arranged to meet her in Nice. He followed through, staying with her just a few days, the only time he saw the daughter Elly had conceived while he was in New York—Patricia Jones, later to become Patricia J. Thompson.

The allure of travel can be broken down to a set of elemental motives: occasionally we travel for the pure pleasure of it; sometimes we travel to escape; and most often we go to come back home again. For Mayakovsky in the New World, it was this third card that typically trumped the others. He could not resist the ties that bound him to his dual "wives," Lili and Russia, who made up so much of his identity. Once he tested his loyalties, it was time to dutifully return. His public reception in America must have been a disappointment, and we cannot underestimate the impact of the daily language barrier.

A final key to understanding Mayakovsky's New World travels is the suite of poems he composed en route. Generally, these mirror the first section of *My Discovery of America* in their excited impressions of new places and things. The two standouts are "Brooklyn Bridge" and "Homeward!," a poem Mayakovsky wrote on the *Rochambeau*. These poems—both of which profit immensely from the appearance of the Mayakovskian "I," rare in his later work—can be said to represent two poles of Mayakovsky's American experience. "Brooklyn Bridge" encapsulates the excitement of the encounter, in all its positive attributes. "Homeward!" on the other hand, expresses his homesickness and melancholy while on the road:

Why
                    in rainy foreign parts
am I to soak and rot—
                                        I really don't know.
I am lying
                    somewhere beyond the seas,
parts of my mechanism
                    are barely vibrating
I feel I am
                    a Soviet factory
producing happiness

[. . .]

I want my native country

to understand me—

and if it doesn't—

I will bear that too:

I will pass

sideways over

my country,

Like a side-

long

rain.

SOURCES

Brik, Lili. *Pristrastnye rasskazi* (*Biased Stories*). Nizhnyi Novgorod: Dekom, 2003.

Brown, Edward J. *Mayakovsky: A Poet in Revolution*. Princeton, N.J.: Princeton University Press, 1973.

Jakobson, Roman. *My Futurist Years.* Edited by Bengt Jangfeldt and translated by Stephen Rudy. New York: Marsilio Publishers, 1992.

Katanian, Vassily V. *Lilia Brik: Zhizn'* (*Lilia Brik: A Life*). Moscow: Zakharov, 2003.

Kerdimun, Boris. "Mayakovsky in America." In *Mayakovsky and the Book: Eight Decades.* New York: MJS Books and Graphics, 1989.

Mayakovsky, Vladimir. *Moe otkrytie Ameriki* (*My Discovery of America*). In *Izbrannye proizvedeniya* (*Collected Works*), Volume 1. Moscow: Khudozhestvennaya literatura, 1955. During the preparation of this manuscript, a fine translation appeared in English, translated by Neil Cornwell and published by Hesperus Press.

Shklovsky, Viktor. *Mayakovsky and His Circle.* Edited and translated by Lily Feiler. New York: Dodd, Mead and Company, 1972.

Thompson, Patricia J. *Mayakovsky in Manhattan: A Love Story with Excerpts from the Memoirs of Elly Jones.* New York: West End Productions, 1993.

Triolet, Elsa. *Maïkovski, poète russe.* Paris: P. Seghers, 1945.

Woroszylski, Wiktor. *The Life of Mayakovsky.* Translated by Boleslaw Taborski. New York: Orion Press, 1970.

5. Night Wraps the Sky

(1927–30)

Tatiana (2005)

FRANCINE DU PLESSIX GRAY

In Paris on October 25, 1928, returning from Nice, Mayakovsky met eighteen-year-old Tatiana Yakovleva in a doctor's office. The encounter was engineered by Lili Brik's sister, Elsa Triolet, as a way of deflecting the poet's potential attachment to Elly Jones and their three-year-old daughter, whom Mayakovsky had never met. Tatiana, instead, proved to be a deeper distraction—a central figure in the final chapter of Mayakovsky's life.

Upon one of the few occasions my mother mentioned Mayakovsky to me, she said that he insisted on taking her home in a cab [the morning they first met], spread his coat over her knees to keep her warm, and upon depositing her at the front door of her grandmother's flat fell on his knees to declare his love. ("Yes, on his knees on the sidewalk," Mother commented when telling the story, "and it wasn't even lunchtime yet.")

. . . Bolshevism didn't seem to pose a problem for the lovers in the nostalgic landscape of Paris's émigré community. Mayakovsky deliberately did not speak of world events to Tatiana, and her own anticommunist scruples were apparently absolved by the great narcissistic pleasure she took in the love of a famous poet. As for

Mayakovsky his infatuation had deepened when he discovered Tatiana's extraordinary knowledge of Russian poetry. Sitting with him at the various cafes they frequented—La Coupole, Le Voltaire, La Rotonde, Le Danton, La Closerie des Lilas—she recited poetry by the hour. How could he not have been seduced when he heard her speak out the whole of his own *A Cloud in Trousers*, some seven hundred lines long? He told all his friends that Tatiana had "absolute pitch" for poetry, in the way some musicians have for their medium. She replaced Lili as his confidante. He informed her of his domestic arrangements with the Briks, and notwithstanding her primness she seemed to take his ménage à trois in stride. She even helped him to find a dress for Lili and to purchase the four-cylinder gray Renault Lili had asked him to bring back from Paris.

The poet proposed marriage within the first fortnight, a suggestion Tatiana seems to have received in a mood of cool noncommittalness. Over lunch at the Grande Chaumiere in Montparnasse in November, he presented her with two poems he had composed and dedicated to her.

. . . "Letter to Comrade Kostrov"—the first poem he had ever dedicated to any woman other than Lili Brik—was the most passionate love lyric Mayakovsky had written in years, and it intimated that he had found the "very great, true love" that, as he'd told Roman Jakobson, might yet save him.

From *Them: A Memoir of Parents* (New York: Penguin Books, 2005).

Letter from Paris to Comrade Kostrov About the Essence of Love (1928)

Please forgive
            me,
                        Comrade Kostrov,
with your characteristic
            breadth of soul,
for blowing
            part of the lines
you allotted to Paris
                        on lyrics.
Just imagine:
            a beauty
                        enters,
wrapped
        in beads and furs.
I
    took this beauty
            and I said:
—did I say right
                    or wrong now?—
I come from Russia,
                    Comrade,
well-known in my land am I,
I've seen
      girls more beautiful
I've seen
      girls with better figures.
And girls

prefer poets.
'Cause I'm clever
and full-throated,
I can talk your teeth off—
if only
you agree to listen.
Can't snare
me
with crap,
with a passing
pair of whims.
Love
has wounded me
for good—
can barely drag myself about.
I can't
measure love
with weddings:
She's unloved me—
sailed away.
I mean it,
Comrade,
I couldn't give a spit
for cupolas.
So now we're getting into details,
right, enough jokes,
my beauty,
I'm not twenty,—
rather, thirty . . .
and then some.
Love
lies not

Tatiana Yakovleva in Paris, 1929

in harder boiling,
lies not
in burning coals,
it lies
in that which rises beyond hills of breasts
over
hair-jungles.
To love—
means this:
to run
deep into the yard
with a gleaming axe,
chop wood
until the rook-black night,
flaunting all
your
strength.
To love—
is to tear yourself
away from sheets torn
by insomnia,
jealous of Copernicus,
because he,
and not some Jane Doe husband
is
my
rival.
Love
for us
is no bushy paradise,
Love
for us

is a humming that tells us
that the stalled motor
of the heart
just got started up again.
You
broke the thread
to Moscow.
Years—
distance.
Just how
could I
explain
this situation to you?
Skyful of lights
upon the earth . . .
Hellful of stars
upon the deep blue sky.
If I were
not a poet,
I would be
an astrologer.
The square begins to buzz,
traffic spins,
I walk around,
scribbling poems
in a little notebook.
Cars
zip
along
without knocking me down.
The clever fellows
get it:

here is a man—
in ecstasy.
A crowd of sights
and insights
brimming
to the lid.
Here
even bears
might grow wings.
And so
out of some
greasy cafeteria,
once all this
comes to a boil,
from gut
to star
the word yawns
like a golden-born comet.
The tail
splashed
across a third of the sky,
its plumage
burns and sparks,
so that two lovers
could admire the stars
from their
lilac arbor.
So that weak eyes
could be lifted,
led,
and lured.
So that hostile

heads

could be sawed from shoulders

by this long-tailed

glittering sword.

As for myself—

'til the last thump inside my chest,

I will linger,

as though I'm on a date—

I overhear myself:

love will ever start and hum—

so simple,

human.

Hurricane,

fire,

water

rumble forward.

Who

could

control this?

Can you?

Go ahead, try . . .

Translated by Val Vinokur

From *Them: A Memoir of Parents* (2005)

FRANCINE DU PLESSIX GRAY

The last months of 1928 had marked the ascendance of Joseph Stalin to unchallenged power in the Communist Party hierarchy and the beginning of his violent transformation of Soviet society. This entailed, among other measures, the forced collectivization of Soviet peasantry, a series of "five-year plans" to run the management of all enterprises to the central government, a resumption of cultural isolation from the West and—most relevant to Mayakovsky—the imposition of strict Party control over education and culture . . .

This "Revolution from Above," as it is called, also enabled the Soviet Union's most oppressive literary faction, the Russian Association of Proletarian Writers (or RAPP), to gain ascendance over literature. In December of 1929, an editor in the Communist Party paper *Pravda* demanded that all Soviet writers support RAPP and adopt its edicts, which required a strict adherence to proletarian values and the elimination of all "bourgeois" and "deviationist" writing. This is the context within which Mayakovsky, in the early fall of 1929, was either denied a visa to return to Paris to resume his courtship of my mother or else warned that he should not even risk the political dangers of asking for one . . .

Mayakovsky's last months brought a succession of heartbreaks.

His play *The Bathhouse*, a violent attack on the increasingly rigid Soviet bureaucracy that, in his view, was betraying the 1917 Revolution, was received with what one eyewitness describes as "murderous coldness." But the public's animosity was becoming far more personal. Even though he seldom used the car he had sent back for Lili the previous year, and had to get her permission each time he wished to borrow it, he was being censured for owning such a luxurious possession. He was even criticized for the pen of foreign make he always carried on him—the Waterman that had been my mother's parting gift. His exhibition *Twenty Years of Work*, which opened on February 1, 1930—posters, paintings, graphics, diverse editions of his books—was boycotted by all official writers' groups, and was visited almost exclusively by students. He paced the empty rooms, with a "sad and austere face, arms folded behind him."

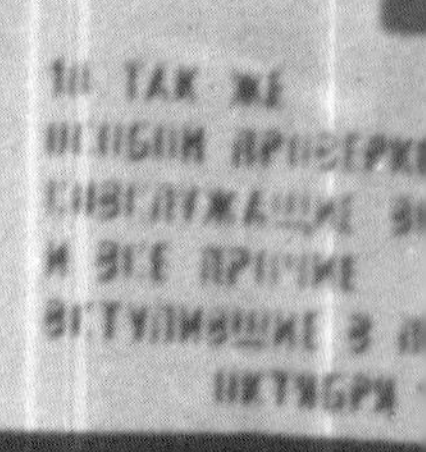
1. ТАК ЖЕ
И ВСЕ ПРОЧИЕ

АМЕРИКУ
ПРОСИТЬ

2. ПОМОГ

4. УЧИТЕСЬ Н
НА БЕЛОГ
ПРОТРЯСС

Twenty Years of Work (1940)

LEV KASSIL

Two days before New Year's, on December 30, 1929, the poet's comrades—writers, musicians, directors, poets, Chekists,* artists—arrive in the evening at Gendrikov Lane. They send Mayakovsky off to his Lubyanka study, and ask him not to appear before everything is ready . . .

On the ceiling they affix a big long sign, and red letters run above from wall to wall: "M-a-y-a-k-o-v-s-k-y." The little apartment gets more and more crowded. They bring costumes from the theater. Guests rummage in piles of brightly colored fabrics, dress up in scarves, raincoats, camisoles, and rehearse a funny jubilee cantata . . .

The door to the vestibule bangs and in walks Mayakovsky, dressed up, freshly shaven, and smiling. He stands his cane in the corner, hangs up his coat, and tosses his cap over the hook. They hug him and lead him into the dining room . . . We sing, standing in a semicircle . . .

Mayakovsky grabs a chair with one hand, lifts it up, turns it

*Secret police.

Mayakovsky with ROSTA posters at the *Twenty Years of Work* exhibition, Moscow, 1930 around backward, and straddles it. He puts on a big papier-mâché mask—the head of a goat.

"One should have the appropriate head of a celebrant, to go with all the jubilant bleating."

They strike up the cantata again. Kirsanov the poet conducts. Then the comedic farce begins.

Aseev plays one of those half-deaf critics who have long plagued Mayakovsky with their mindless presentations. He gives a long welcome speech, and only toward the end does it become apparent that the critic is confused and has come to honor an altogether different poet, not Mayakovsky . . .

Late at night they beg Mayakovsky to read something from his early poetry. He resists for a long time, complaining that his voice has given out, that his older works are no longer interesting. They beg him in a friendly chorus, plead and grovel. And with a loud sigh he gives in. First he reads "Getting Along with Horses." He stands up, rests his hand on the corner of the cupboard, surveys us with a slow, memorable gaze, and declaims quietly . . .

Suddenly everyone is serious. It's no longer a joke, not a joyous celebration of a poet, not a party of friends—everyone is immediately seized, as if by a chill running through the folds of their brains, by the hint that they should remember this moment.

And suddenly, with a very simple and unmistakable clarity that gripped the heart, an unuttered word was heard by everyone: History. And the walls either turned transparent or fell away altogether. We could see a great distance all around us. And time buzzed in our ears.

And he read, looking off somewhere through the walls.

"Horse, please, don't.
Listen to me, horse—
do you think you're any less than they are?

Mayakovsky with students at his *Twenty Years of Work* exhibition, Moscow, 1930

Little one,
all of us are horses, sort of,
every one of us a horse in his own way."

And he turns his yard-wide shoulders, as if strapped into an enormous harness, as if climbing a hill steeply . . .

And the whole time she felt
like a colt,
and life was worth living,
and work worthwhile.

Quieting the applause, immediately upon finishing, he says:

"This is all old! Old! I'm sick of it. I have new poems now just tumbling out. They'll really be poems! You'll see. Better than anything I've written."

And softly moving away, as if afraid to injure anyone, he goes into the other room and stands there for a long time, bent over his elbows on the bureau, clutching in his hand a glass of unfinished tea. A kind of helpless, lonely heartache has come over him, which no one yet understands.

Translated by Christopher Gilman

From Lev Kassil, *Mayakovsky Himself* (Moscow, 1940).

From *Them: A Memoir of Parents* (2005)

FRANCINE DU PLESSIX GRAY

On April 11, 1930, for the first time in his life, Mayakovsky failed to appear at a reading he had been scheduled to give. On April 13, he telephoned several friends to see who was free, and was pained to hear that they were all busy . . .

Volodia and Nora* spent the evening writing each other notes on little bits of cardboard torn out of a chocolate box, which Mayakovsky, who drank more than usual that night, tossed across the table to Nora with the gesture of a roulette player. At 3:00 a.m. they went to their respective homes. In the morning, Mayakovsky came by to pick her up and take her to his apartment. According to Nora's memoirs, they quarreled a great deal—he pressured her to remain with him, while she insisted that she had to go to rehearsal . . . At 10:15 a.m., barely able to free herself from her lover's grip, Nora ran out of his room. A few seconds later, as she was beginning to go down the corridor, she heard a pistol shot. She hastened back into his room. It was still filled with smoke.

*Veronica Polonskaya, called Nora, a young actress, was the last woman in Mayakovsky's life. His suicide note reads, in part: "Comrade Government—my family is: Lili Brik, mother, sisters, and Veronica Vitoldovna Polonskaya. / If you care to assure them a decent existence—I thank you. / Please give the unfinished poems to the Briks, they will get the hang of them."

Mayakovsky had been rehearsing this act in his poetry since his adolescence. "It might be far better for me / to punctuate my end with a bullet," he had written in 1915. Yet when the suicide actually occurred, it had the impact of a national disaster.

Pasternak's analysis of Mayakovsky's suicide is particularly lucid: "Mayakvosky shot himself out of pride because he had condemned something in himself . . . with which his self-respect could not be reconciled."

The poet's suicide was not as sudden as it initially seemed. He left a note, written in pencil in a large, clear hand on three pieces of white paper, which he'd apparently started composing two days before his death. "To All" (*"Vsem"*), it began. "Do not blame anyone for my death, and please, no gossip. The deceased always detested gossip. Mother, sisters, friends, forgive me—this is not the way (I do not recommend it to others), but there is no other way out for me."

Past One O'Clock . . . (1930)

Past one o'clock. You must have gone to bed.
The Milky Way streams silver through the night.
I'm in no hurry; with lightning telegrams
I have no cause to wake or trouble you.
And, as they say, the incident is closed.
Love's boat has smashed against the daily grind.
Now you and I are quits. Why bother then
To balance mutual sorrows, pains, and hurts.
Behold what quiet settles on the world.
Night wraps the sky in tribute from the stars.
In hours like this, one rises to address
The ages, history, and all creation.

Translated by George Reavey

From *"The Bedbug" and Selected Poetry*, edited and with an introduction by Patricia Blake (Bloomington: Indiana University Press, 1975).

From *Safe Conduct* (1958)

BORIS PASTERNAK

He lay on his side, his face turned toward the wall, somber, tall, a sheet covering him to his chin, his mouth half open as in sleep. Turning proudly away from us all, even when he was lying down, even in this sleep, he was going away from us in a stubborn endeavor to reach something. His face recalled the time, when he had spoken of himself as "beautiful in his twenty-two years," for death had ossified a mask which rarely falls into its clutches.

Suddenly there was a movement in the hall. Alone, apart from her mother and sister, who were already giving way to their grief inaudibly in the crowd, the younger sister of the dead man, Olga Vladimirovna, entered the flat. She entered possessively and noisily. Her voice floated into the room before her. Mounting the stairs alone she was speaking to someone in a loud voice, addressing her brother openly. Then she herself came into view, and walking through the crowd as through a rubbish pit, she reached her brother's door, threw up her hands and stood still. "Volodya!" she screamed in a voice which echoed through the whole house. A second flashed by. "He says nothing! He doesn't answer. Volodya. Volodya! How terrible!"

She was falling. They caught her up and quickly began to restore her to consciousness. She had hardly come to herself, when she moved greedily towards the body and sitting down at his feet, precipitately resumed her unexhausted dialogue. At last, as I had long desired, I burst into tears . . .

When I returned in the evening, he was already in his coffin. The faces which had filled the room during the day had given place to others. It was comparatively quiet. There was scarcely any more weeping.

Suddenly, outside, underneath the window I imagined I saw his life, which now already belonged entirely to the past. I saw it move away obliquely from the window like a quiet tree-bordered street resembling the Povarskaya . . . And it occurred to me then in the same irrelevant way, that this man was perhaps this State's unique citizen. The novelty of the age flowed climatically through his blood. His strangeness was the strangeness of our times of which half is yet to be fulfilled. I began to recall traits in his character, his independence, which in many ways was completely original. All these were explained by his familiarity with states of mind which though inherent in our time, have not yet reached full maturity. He was spoilt from childhood by the future, which he mastered rather early and apparently without great difficulty.

Mayakovsky's funeral procession, Moscow, April 17, 1930

From "The Red Flag and the Red Mask" (1999)

PATRICIA BLAKE

You may say that his suicide was one of those rare acts of definition in history, which strips clean a whole era, and lays open the future, mercilessly. Here was a poet who had tried to place his supremely individual gifts at the service of a collective society, and he now lay with a bullet through his heart. In fact, he would surely not have survived the thirties, the regimentation of literature. He was too undisciplined, insubmissive, anarchic. They would have killed him, as they completely disposed of some six hundred other writers. He may have had some presentiment of that. In a sense, you could say that he took his execution into his own hands.

Note to E. Yanitskaya, Formerly Typist to Mayakovsky (1963)

ANDREI VOZNESENSKY

Mayakovsky never paid you off.
I am honoring his debt.
Excuse him for not having lived long enough.

The sense of my life
is to pay for Lermontov, Lorca,
an everlasting debt.

Payable in blood
the terrible charges mount.

Fathers, forefathers, we have you to thank.
Wheel of the epoch, keep on turning . . .
But who will pay for me,
who will close the account?

Translated by Stanley Kunitz

From Patricia Blake and Max Hayward, eds. *Antiworlds, and the Fifth Ace: Poetry* by Andrei Voznesensky (London: Oxford University Press, 1967).

This Can't Be Death

MICHAEL ALMEREYDA

In government-sponsored reports as well as letters to Lili, Mayakovsky registered more scorn than affection for the United States, but a crop of American poets coming of age three decades after his death effectively fell in love with him, absorbing both a variety of technical stratagems—the broken long lines, the flexible use of "I" and "you"—and the example of a restless conscience broadcasting itself in a voice mixing politics and personality, confession and reportage. Allen Ginsberg, Kenneth Koch, and Frank O'Hara are the most conspicuous inheritors of Mayakovskian energy and style, but they were hardly alone. Jean-Luc Godard gave Mayakovsky a posthumous cameo in his 1963 film *Les Carabiniers*, a haunting comedy depicting the ravages of war. Toward the film's end, a delicate young woman is rousted from her hiding place in the woods, granted a cigarette, and asked if she has any final words. Her stoic reply: "I would like to recite this charming fable by Vladimir Mayakovsky."

Before being shot, she then speaks the following lines (as presented in English subtitles, translated from French):

> This can't be death.
> Why would she hang about here?

Aren't you ashamed to believe in a fable?
Someone has a party, creates a carnival,
invents this killing as he blinks his eyes.
She is charming, but like the cannons.
The gas mask is but a simple toy. See?
In her careful course she measures the heavens.
Has death slipped on the floor of the sky?

I've found these words impossible to track back to the *Collected Works of Mayakovsky.* Godard may, characteristically, have written them himself. The relevant fact is that one of the most searching filmmakers of his time chose Mayakovsky as the name to invoke, the most resonant source for a hapless/heroic flare of rhetoric in the face of barbaric gunfire.

Research for this book landed me in Moscow in the fall of 2004. It's not easy to imagine Vladimir Mayakovsky coexisting with the city's latest skyline, the inescapable capitalist spectacle: venerable architecture decked with corporate logos and wall-size portraits of Adrien Brody and other sleek young people celebrating the demise of communism. I buried myself in the cavernous Kremlin subway, rode two quick stops to Lubyanka Square, walked past the towering former headquarters of the secret police, on to Miasnitskaia Street, to visit Aleksandr Lavrent'ev, art historian and grandson of Rodchenko.

Sasha, as he's called, was cordial, relaxed, at once professorial and boyish. Over tea and cake, he presented himself as a neutral repository of information, a dispatcher of discreetly detailed facts. Lili Brik "lived to pour tea." Victor Shklovsky's encyclopedic pronouncements "were like stones that he carefully dropped." Mayakovsky, the Briks, Rodchenko, and his wife, Stepanova, loved to

---

Abram Shterenberg's portrait of Mayakovsky, 1923. Used in Rodchenko's photo collage for *Pro Eto*.

play mah-jongg in this very apartment, with tiles painted by Rodchenko, after Mayakovsky brought the game back from the United States in 1925. This was the year Stepanova gave birth to their only child, Sasha's mother, Varvara—the thin, frail woman sitting across the table, self-contained as a cat.

Varvara Aleksandrovna Rodchenko was nearly eighty years old. Her face was heart-shaped, dominated by thick-lensed glasses. She didn't speak English, didn't speak much at all, but watched me closely before bringing out an envelope containing a small photographic print of Mayakovsky—the portrait with the cigarette, the cover image for this book. She also handed over a slim blue-gray hardbound volume chronicling her mother's achievements as photographer, painter, designer—or rather, she attempted to hand it to me but, reaching across the table, dropped the book directly onto the cake, mashing lavender frosting onto the splayed pages. When she deflected this catastrophe with a big bright laugh, I laughed with her and felt smitten.

Sasha told me his grandfather had written at length about Mayakovsky three times, but at a distance, years after his friend had died. At Mayakovsky's funeral, Rodchenko went to great lengths to remove the flowers surrounding the open casket. "He cleared them out entirely because he wanted the finality of this death to be clear and unsentimental, without flowers, as Mayakovsky always strove to be clear and unsentimental." But something went wrong with Rodchenko's camera lens; the resulting photos, never published, were all out of focus. Meanwhile, more mourners—roughly 150,000 over three days—brought more flowers. A surviving picture, taken by another photographer, shows Mayakovsky horizontal in the casket, a border of flowers dividing him from the scrutiny of Osip and Lili Brik, Mayakovsky's mother, and anonymous others. The living and the dead all look carved from wax.

Gesturing at a wall, Sasha explained that the adjoining space had served as Rodchenko's first darkroom: "If you removed this, you could see the original pasteboard with seams taped to prevent light from leaking in." Here was an explanation for the visible backdrop, an odd grid, in two of the famous Mayakovsky portraits, which also show the poet in one of the Rodchenko-designed chairs we were all sitting in. I remember trying to ward off my own sentimental impulses while touching my chair's distinctive circular seat, reflecting on the routine fact that people tend to be more temporary than furniture, photographs, buildings, and books.

My pilgrimage continued in the Mayakovsky Museum, blocks away from the Rodchenko-Lavrent'ev household but a world apart. Mayakovsky's study on Lubyansky Passage was claimed by the Soviet state in 1974; the entire building was gutted, with only its wide iron-railed stairwell left intact, plus a single room on the fourth floor where Mayakovsky worked and where he shot himself. This room, partitioned by a velvet rope, is now nested within a series of hectic displays presenting the poet's life and legacy. Posters, papers, photos, and other artifacts jostle for attention with candidly contrived props—flying girders, a chair, a desk, a door—painted in primary colors and tilted and angled as if caught in hurricane winds. There's even, on one floor, a red biplane suspended under a zigzag formation of buzzing fluorescent tubes. (Despite his Futurist fervor for machines, Mayakovsky hardly ever traveled by air, and planes don't appear much in his poems.) Manuscripts and drawings—surely not the originals, but then again, why not?—are sandwiched in squares of transparent plastic, hung akimbo from every available surface. These exhibitions of convulsive energy, ecstasy, and upheaval are presided over by mute, hunched museum guards, women over sixty with hair dyed bronze and gold, installed one per room, most of them sitting in spindly chairs, hands clasped, elbows on knees.

I surveyed the clutter. The dustbin of history is overflowing with Soviet-era aesthetic debris of this approximate sort, but among monuments to great writers, is there anything quite like the Mayakovsky Museum? Its ostentatious lack of sobriety, its atmosphere of aggressive self-congratulation, even its dinginess, are magnificent. If nothing else, the place provides a sort of clearinghouse for the poet's outsize contradictions, a chaotic stage set framing a drama whose central actor plays all the parts but who has, in room after room, fled the scene.

I circled back to the study. The antique phone, the small couch fitted to the wall, and the solitary picture above the rolltop desk—a framed portrait of Lenin, compact enough to fit in your hand—were familiar from the KGB crime-scene photo I'd seen in *Talk* magazine (October 1999), where it appeared in print for the first time. The photo showed Mayakovsky's corpse—his stained chest, his open-mouthed, empty face—and it ran with an extended caption supplied by Francine du Plessix Gray, not yet asserting her identity as Tatiana Yakovleva's daughter and one of Mayakovsky's most ardent contemporary mourners. I chose not to include the photo here. (Who among you, mysterious readers, would like his or her bloody corpse displayed in a book?) The one surprise in the picture is that despite the early hour of his suicide, Mayakovsky is wearing a dress shirt replete with starched collar and bow tie—suggesting that he'd been playing an old-fashioned game of Russian roulette, adhering to the tradition of putting on a clean shirt before committing the ultimate gamble.

Often enough, in the course of my research, I encountered the claim that the KGB murdered Mayakovsky at Stalin's request, as the poet had become an inconvenience, a nuisance, a liability. But there were converging causes—deep losses and defeats—pressing in on him, and Mayakovsky's last days have been documented in humiliating detail. "He died," writes the ever-quotable Shklovsky, "having surrounded his death like a disaster area with warning lights." Suicide was a recurring theme and threat in the poems, and Mayakovsky's public repudiation of Esenin's suicide, five years before his own, can be understood as a harsh self-defense, the shout of a proud man pretending the same tide could never sweep him under. And how can you dismiss the anguished authority of Mayakovsky's suicide note, pragmatically adapted from a poem to Tatiana? Since when did the secret police dabble in poetry?

Despite Tatiana's forty-some years of entrenched Americanization in New York and Connecticut, an array of her letters, photos, and memorabilia spanning her post-Mayakovskian existence have found a secure resting place on the Mayakovsky Museum's uppermost floor. When I visited, the lights were dimmed but easily activated by an energetic guide, a woman in her sixties who explained that Tatiana was the poet's last muse, then launched into a recitation of "Letter from Paris to Comrade Kostrov About the Essence of Love," in Russian, of course, and in its entirety. She stood inches away from me, arms outstretched, her forehead pulsing to the movement of her lipsticked mouth.

This, I told myself, is not *my* Mayakovsky, though it could hardly be less valid than the patchwork I'd been assembling for publication on another shore, detaching the poet from his revolutionary era, his native tongue, and the political ideals that propelled and defeated him. Auden, again, supplies a primary aphorism: "The words of a dead man / are modified in the guts of the living." And so I tumbled out of the Mayakovsky Museum in the early part of the twenty-first century, my guts suitably unsettled while holding on to the suspicion that Mayakovsky will continue to speak to new readers, answering necessary and impossible demands to find a bridge between freedom and responsibility, poetry and conscience, art and life.

A True Account of Talking to the Sun at Fire Island

(1958)

FRANK O'HARA

The Sun woke me this morning loud
and clear, saying "Hey! I've been
trying to wake you up for fifteen
minutes. Don't be so rude, you are
only the second poet I've ever chosen
to speak to personally
                                        so why
aren't you more attentive? If I could
burn you through the window I would
to wake you up. I can't hang around
here all day."
                        "Sorry, Sun, I stayed
up late last night talking to Hal."

"When I woke up Mayakovsky he was
a lot more prompt" the Sun said
petulantly. "Most people are up
already waiting to see if I'm going

to put in an appearance."

I tried

To apologize "I missed you yesterday."

"That's better" he said. "I didn't

know you'd come out." "You may be wondering why I've come so close?"

"Yes" I said beginning to feel hot

and wondering if maybe he wasn't burning me

anyway.

"Frankly I wanted to tell you

I like your poetry. I see a lot

on my rounds and you're okay. You may

not be the greatest thing on earth, but

you're different. Now, I've heard some

say you're crazy, they being excessively

calm themselves to my mind, and other

crazy poets think that you're a boring

reactionary. Not me.

Just keep on

like I do and pay no attention. You'll

find that people always will complain

about the atmosphere, either too hot

or too cold or too bright or too dark, days

too short or too long.

If you don't appear

at all one day they think you're lazy

or dead. Just keep right on, I like it.

And don't worry about your lineage

poetic or natural. The Sun shines on

the jungle, you know, on the tundra

the sea, the ghetto. Wherever you were
I knew it and saw you moving, I was waiting
for you to get to work.

And now that you
are making your own day, so to speak,
even if no one reads you but me
you won't be depressed. Not
everyone can look up, even at me. It
hurts their eyes."
"Oh Sun, I'm so grateful to you!"
"Thanks and remember I'm watching. It's
easier for me to speak to you out
here. I don't have to slide down
between buildings to get your ear.
I know you love Manhattan, but
you ought to look up more often.
And
always embrace things, people earth
sky stars, as I do, freely and with
the appropriate sense of space. That
is your inclination, known in the heavens
and you should follow it to hell, if
necessary, which I doubt.
Maybe we'll
speak again in Africa, of which I too
am specially fond. Go back to sleep now
Frank, and I may leave a tiny poem
In that brain of yours as my farewell."

"Sun, don't go!" I was awake
at last. "No, go I must, they're calling
me."
"Who are they?"
Rising he said "Some
day you'll know. They're calling to you
too." Darkly he rose, and then I slept.

From Donald Allen, ed., *The Collected Poems of Frank O'Hara* (University of California Press, 1995). Found among O'Hara's papers after his death in 1966, the poem was dated "Fire Island, July 10, 1958."

Mayakovsky at a book bazaar with Red Army men, Moscow, 1929

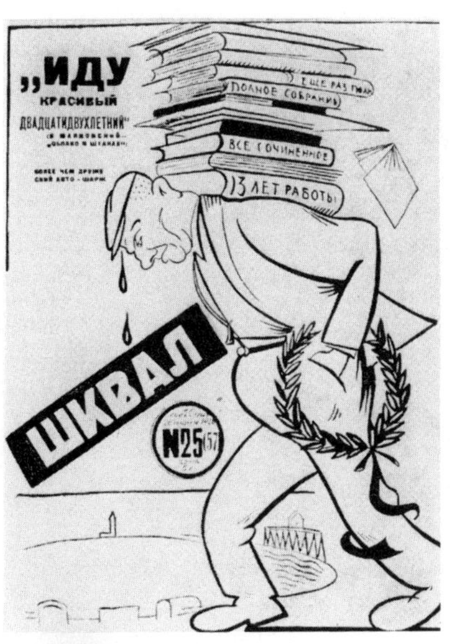

Mayakovsky's self-caricature for *The Squall*, an Odessa magazine, 1926

Caricature by "the Kukryniksy" (a trio of artists: Kuprianov, Krylov, Sokolov), 1928

Self-caricature, 1929

The Whole Shebang (1998)

JOSEPH BRODSKY

Mayakovsky behaved so very archetypically. The whole shebang: from avant-gardist to courtier to victim. And you're always consumed by the suspicion that maybe that's how it ought to be. Maybe you're too shut up inside yourself, whereas here was a genuine nature, an extrovert, doing everything on the grand scale.

If his poems are bad, there's good reason for it. Bad poems are a poet's bad days. And Mayakovsky did have quite a few bad days in his life, but when things got their absolute worst, he came up with some great poems. Of course, he let his tongue run away with him completely.

Mayakovsky was the first major victim, for he had a major gift.

From Solomon Volkov, *Conversations with Joseph Brodsky* (New York: The Free Press, 1998). Exiled from the U.S.S.R. in 1972, transplanted to American soil, Joseph Brodsky (1940–96) embarked on a second artistic life in English while remaining the last conspicuously great Russian poet of the twentieth century.

The bronze statue in Mayakovsky Square (later renamed Triumphalnaya), Moscow, unveiled in 1958. Viktor Shklovsky wrote of the statue: "It's made absolutely clear that he could step down, walk on the street, argue with people, give directions."

Rodchenko's portrait of Mayakovsky seated on a chair designed by Rodchenko, Moscow, 1924

Acknowledgments

Andrew Hultkrans, then editor of *Bookforum*, inadvertently prodded this book into being when he recruited me to review a 2001 reissue of Mayakovsky's 1923 collaboration with El Lissitzky, *For the Voice*. The assignment led to the simple conclusion that a more comprehensive English edition of Mayakovsky was overdue. I'm grateful to Colin Robinson, Robert Walsh, and Jonathan Galassi for embracing the idea when it was little more than a rough notion in my head. As editor, Lorin Stein provided an overarching sense of lucidity, discrimination, and patience over many years. Cara Spitalewitz, reviewing the manuscript in the last stretch, contributed equal measures of openness and discernment. The support and guidance of ace literary agent Denise Shannon telescoped beyond my expectations. Carolyn Mimran gathered the multitude of permissions with dazzling efficiency, and enlisted Keith Gessen, to whom I'm also grateful, for a diplomatic mission in Moscow. *Spasibo*, as well, to Svetlana Effimovna and her gracious colleagues at the V. V. Mayakovsky State Museum, supplier of scans for most of the illustrations. The works of Aleksandr Rodchenko are included courtesy of Aleksandr Lavrent'ev and Varvara Rodchenko, executors of the Rodchenko estate. I feel lucky to have met them on this road.

For additional encouragement, scanning, faxing, loaned books, translations, recommendations, and tips, I'm indebted to Yekaterina Apekina, John Ashbery, Marina Belozerskaya, John Berger, Patricia Blake, Miye Bromberg, Joshua Clover, Peter Galassi, Chris Gilman, Francine du Plessix Gray, Susan Kismaric, Chris Marker, Rose Swan Meacham, Jim Robison, Tom and Anna Roma, Peter Schjeldahl, Gary Shteyngart, and Cynthia Walker. Robert Walsh warrants an extra debt of gratitude for his fastidious final run through the galleys.

Lastly, redoubled thanks to new friends supplying new translations and texts: Katya Apekina, Rachel Cohen, Christopher Edgar, Val Vinokur, and Matvei Yankelvich—gifted writers lending their voices to this shared echo chamber of a book.

Permissions Acknowledgments

"Screaming My Head Off" by Vladimir Mayakovsky, adapted by Ron Padgett. Copyright © 1970 by Ron Padgett. Reprinted by permission.

"Past One O'Clock" and an excerpt from the Introduction to *"The Bedbug" and Selected Poetry* by Vladimir Mayakovsky, edited by Patricia Blake. Translated by Max Hayward and George Reavey. Copyright © 1960 by Harper & Row, Publishers, Inc. Reprinted by permission of HarperCollins Publishers.

Excerpt from *The Sense of Sight* by John Berger, copyright © 1985 by John Berger. Used by permission of Pantheon Books, a division of Random House, Inc.

Excerpt from "A Slap in the Face of Public Taste" by David Burliuk, Aleksei Kruchenykh, Vladimir Mayakovsky, and Viktor Khlebnikov from *Words in Revolution: Russian Futurist Manifestoes 1912–1928*, edited and translated by Anna Lawson and Herbert Eagle, published by New Academia Publishing, LLC, 2005.

Excerpt from *Mayakovsky—Plays*, translated by Guy Daniels. Reprinted by permission of Northwestern University Press.

Excerpt from *The Futurist Moment* by Marjorie Perloff reprinted by permission of University of Chicago Press.

Excerpts from *Safe Conduct: An Autobiography and Other Writings* by Boris Pasternak copyright © 1949, 1958 by New Directions Publishing Corp.

Excerpts from *Them: A Memoir of My Parents* by Francine du Plessix Gray, copyright © 2005 by Francine du Plessix Gray. Used by permission of The Penguin Press, a division of Penguin Group (USA) Inc.

Excerpt from *Mayakovsky and His Circle* by Viktor Shklovsky, copyright © 1985 by Varvara Shklovskaya-Kordi, reprinted by permission.

Excerpt from *Modern Times, Modern Places: Life and Art in the Twentieth Century* by Peter Conrad. Copyright © 1998 by Peter Conrad. Reproduced by permission of Thames & Hudson, Ltd., London.

Excerpts from *Mandelstam: The Complete Critical Prose and Letters*, edited by Jane Gary Harris, translated by Jane Gary Harris and Constance Link, reprinted by permission of Ardis Publishers.

Excerpt from a letter to Lili Brik by Vladimir Mayakovsky from *Love Is the Heart of Everything: Correspondence Between Vladimir Mayakovsky and Lili Brik, 1915–1930*, edited by Bengt Jangfeldt and translated by Julian Graffy, reprinted by permission.